Scottish Legal History

Volume One

D1388867

For Alan and for Pippa

Scottish Legal History

VOLUME ONE: 1000–1707

Andrew R. C. Simpson and Adelyn L. M. Wilson

EDINBURGH
University Press

Edinburgh University Press is one of the leading university presses in the UK. We publish academic books and journals in our selected subject areas across the humanities and social sciences, combining cutting-edge scholarship with high editorial and production values to produce academic works of lasting importance. For more information visit our website: edinburghuniversitypress.com

© Andrew R. C. Simpson and Adelyn L. M. Wilson, 2017

Edinburgh University Press Ltd
The Tun – Holyrood Road
12 (2f) Jackson's Entry
Edinburgh EH8 8PJ

Typeset in 11/13 Ehrhardt by
Servis Filmsetting Ltd, Stockport, Cheshire,
and printed and bound in Great Britain by
CPI Group (UK) Ltd, Croydon CR0 4YY

A CIP record for this book is available from the British Library

ISBN 978 0 7486 9739 7 (hardback)
ISBN 978 0 7486 9740 3 (paperback)
ISBN 978 0 7486 9742 7 (webready PDF)
ISBN 978 0 7486 9741 0 (epub)

Contents

PART FOUR: REGAL UNION WITH ENGLAND, c. 1580–1707

Preface

A. THE PURPOSE OF THIS BOOK

The aim of this book is to provide an introduction to the study of Scottish legal history prior to 1707. That year witnessed the union of the parliaments of Scotland and England, which was to have far-reaching consequences for the histories of both nations. Nonetheless, in 1707 Scots law was preserved as a separate legal system. Over 300 years later, significant distinctions between Scots law and English law remain.

It is hoped that this book may be useful to those who wish to go on to explore the historical reasons why those differences have persisted. But the major purpose of the present volume is to explain how a law commonly applicable among all Scots came into being in the first place and developed thereafter until 1707. In so doing, it explores the developing authority of that legal system within the Scottish kingdom during the medieval and early modern periods. It focuses on how that system was used in the resolution of legal disputes between Scots, and discusses the ways in which Scots lawyers conceptualised the authority of different sources of law. It also examines how the authority of the law was forged and transformed by political, religious, economic, social and also purely legal factors. Ultimately, of course, these developments made a significant contribution to the rise of the modern system of Scots law, which will be explored in more detail in the second volume of this history.

B. WHY PUBLISH A BOOK ON SCOTTISH LEGAL HISTORY NOW?

Writing an introductory work of this sort is challenging because the discipline of Scottish legal history is still at an early stage in its development. This perhaps raises the question of why the task has been attempted at all. The impetus to write the book arose from the expansion of teaching of Scottish legal history at the University of Aberdeen and its introduction at the University of Bergen between 2012 and 2016. Due to significant investment in the discipline at Aberdeen, followed by curriculum reform that created room in the Bachelor of Laws (LLB) for optional subjects, the authors of the present work found themselves in a position to develop a course of lectures and tutorials on the history of Scots law, targeted primarily at second-year students. This supplemented the successful Scottish Legal History (Honours) course previously run by the late Professor Angelo Forte. The course attracted over sixty students in its first year. Yet when teaching the discipline, the lack of a single, affordable book that was accessible to students presented something of a challenge to the effective communication of the subject. The *Introduction to Scottish Legal History* written by a team of authors and published by the Stair Society in 1958 remains extremely useful in some regards, but much of the work has been superseded by current scholarship.[1] It cannot now be used in teaching unless the lecturer is on hand to caveat much of what is said. In this regard it contrasts markedly with the excellent 'Historical Introduction' written by Professor John Cairns and published in 2000 in *A History of Private Law in Scotland* edited by Professors Kenneth Reid and Reinhard Zimmermann.[2] That work remains the most scholarly and detailed overview of the history of Scots law, even though a series of book-length studies published in the last fifteen years or so have augmented and to some extent challenged some of the arguments put forward therein.[3] This last point made it necessary to develop a work to supplement John Cairns's text as a reference point for

---

[1] G. C. H. Paton (ed.), *An Introduction to Scottish Legal History by Various Authors* (Edinburgh: Stair Society, 1958).

[2] John W. Cairns, 'Historical introduction', in Kenneth Reid and Reinhard Zimmermann (eds), *A History of Private Law in Scotland* (Oxford: Oxford University Press, 2000) I, 14–184.

[3] Among the most important contributions published during this time that are relevant to this volume are John Finlay, *Men of Law in Pre-Reformation Scotland* (East Linton: Tuckwell Press, 2000); J. D. Ford, *Law and Opinion in Scotland during the Seventeenth Century* (Oxford and Portland: Hart Publishing, 2007); A. M. Godfrey, *Civil Justice in Renaissance Scotland: The Origins of a Central Court* (Leiden: Brill, 2009); and Alice Taylor, *The Shape of the State in Medieval Scotland, 1124–1290* (Oxford: Oxford University Press, 2016). The reprint of Hector L. MacQueen, *Common Law and Feudal Society*, reprinted edn (Edinburgh: Edinburgh University Press, 2016) also makes this extremely important monograph available to a new generation of scholars. First published in 1993, it had been out of print for several years.

teaching. Nonetheless, his introduction remains indispensable reading for any serious student.

What was needed was an affordable and accessible introduction to the subject which took into account as much of the most recent literature as was possible. Several scholars within the field agreed that the lack of such a work was one of the things holding back the teaching of the discipline in other institutions. In addition, the initial success of the course at Aberdeen formed the basis of a discussion with Professor Jørn Øyrehagen Sunde of the Research Group for Legal Culture at the University of Bergen which led to a version of the course – with a more comparative focus – being taught at Bergen. All of this created further impetus to publish an introductory work on the subject, primarily with students in mind. The authors were also encouraged greatly by the enthusiastic reception that John Watson at Edinburgh University Press gave to their initial proposal to submit a work of this sort for publication. Once the book contract was signed, the additional generous support Jørn Sunde provided to allow Andrew Simpson the opportunity to attend Bergen Law Faculty as a visiting scholar in late October and November 2014 made it possible for him to write the initial drafts of the chapters on the medieval period. The support of colleagues at Aberdeen, and in particular the Head of School, Anne-Michelle Slater, also made this period away possible. In addition, the feedback provided by the Scottish Legal History (Ordinary) class at Aberdeen to early drafts of the book circulated in the first semester of 2015–16 was extremely useful. In this regard, the writers wish to thank Finn O'Neill in particular, whose comments were invaluable, and whose surprising penchant for brieves was most encouraging.

All of this generous help, and indeed other support which will be mentioned below, made the goal of producing this work possible, but no less daunting. As stated, the study of Scottish legal history is still at an early stage of development, even though several excellent monographs have been written on the subject and the Stair Society continues to publish extremely high-quality work which drives the discipline forward. Consequently, it must be emphasised that the result is the writers' perspective on the subject as it stands at present. It is quite possible that not all specialists will agree with everything that is said. However, efforts have been made to indicate which matters are being debated at present and to develop those topics, at times at the expense of others where consensus has emerged or where further research is needed. So, as regards the medieval period, current discussions concerning the extent to which there existed a truly 'common law' based on the brieves are given detailed attention, while older debates concerning the date of the important text *Regiam Majestatem* are treated more briefly, as scholarly consensus appears to be emerging in that regard – albeit that *Regiam* could, and should, be subjected to much more rigorous analysis in the future. The coverage is also necessarily selective, both to allow a coherent theme related to the development of legal authority to emerge and additionally because of the state of current research. Some topics receive very little treatment at all. The development of law in the burghs, for example, should be given greater attention, perhaps in a future edition. This will undoubtedly be facilitated by the work being undertaken by the *Law in the Aberdeen Council Registers 1398–1511* project, which is funded by the Leverhulme Trust and is led by Dr Jackson Armstrong.[4]

All that said, the writers believe that the current work will make a significant contribution to the development of the discipline. Ultimately, that must be the primary justification for publishing a work such as this. Its main goal is to introduce students to the subject as it stands, and to facilitate the teaching of the subject beyond Aberdeen. Equally the book has been written with the aim of engaging a wider audience of non-specialists who are interested in the legal past, which is an extremely rich element of Scottish heritage. No prior knowledge of the subject is assumed. Furthermore, the book provides specialists with an overview of the subject which makes an original contribution and should help to stimulate further debate. As stated, the book explores the authors' understanding of how a law commonly applicable to all Scots emerged and developed before 1707. In so doing, it considers in some depth how the authority of that legal system developed, and how it was conceptualised and re-conceptualised by generations of legal practitioners. Of course, this reflects the interests of several specialists in the field at present, and the arguments presented could not have been constructed without drawing on the detailed scholarship of others. Nonetheless, both of the authors have attempted to develop those themes, and in so doing have incorporated their original research into the book.

The present volume, it should be noted, traces the history of Scots law to 1707 and the union of the parliaments of Scotland and England. The decision to pause at 1707 relates to the fact that further original research needs to be undertaken in the next few years to construct a satisfactory picture of legal change in the eighteenth, nineteenth and twentieth centuries. Furthermore, the original plan of treatment would have made the resulting work rather unwieldy if it were to have been taken up to the modern era in a single volume. Thus the second volume of this work will

---

[4] See https://aberdeenregisters.org/.

bring the study begun here up to the present day. This will be a fascinating if challenging task, given that current generations are living through what is a period of remarkable legal and constitutional change, of which the British exit from the European Union and the possibility of a second referendum on Scottish independence are simply the most obvious effects.

C. THE TEXT AND ACKNOWLEDGEMENTS

It remains to say a few words about the structure of the book, and also to acknowledge with thanks the efforts of those who have helped the authors to write it. In the course of the work the history of Scots law prior to 1707 is divided into four broad sections. The first (Chapter 1) explores the foundations of the Scottish common law, to c. 1230; the second (Chapters 2–5) explores the consolidation of that common law, in the period c. 1230–c. 1450; and the third (Chapters 6–10) considers the transformation of the common law through the work of the session in the period c. 1450–c. 1580. These chapters – representing the first half of the book – were drafted by Andrew Simpson. The fourth and largest section of the book (Chapters 11–19) explores the monumental shifts that took place in the period between c. 1580–1707, making particular reference to the backdrop of regal union with England from 1603. These chapters – representing the second half of the work – were drafted by Adelyn Wilson. However, the resulting work should be taken to represent a joint effort and perspective on the issues discussed, and the writers have endeavoured to adopt a reasonably uniform style of writing. The periodisation chosen is, they believe, germane to the material studied.

A few further points should be noted. It was decided to limit the number of references provided in the footnotes to reflect the fact that this book is designed to be used to introduce students to the subject. Nonetheless, the sources cited, together with the further reading at the end of each chapter, should enable those who wish to take their studies further to do so. For the sake of convenience, the modern practice is followed of treating 1 January as the start of a new year, even though in the medieval period – and for some time thereafter – the new year was dated from 25 March.

The above explanation of their purposes in writing has enabled the authors to thank some, but not all, of the many people who have helped them in preparing the final version of the text. Professor John Ford at Aberdeen University kindly read the whole manuscript and provided incisive and intelligent insights into how the work could be improved. Indeed, the debt of gratitude to Professor Ford is deeper, in that in the past he has generously read and commented upon virtually all of the writers' original research that they have drawn upon in this book. Both are particularly grateful to him for his encouragement. Jørn Sunde has already been mentioned, but it should perhaps be made clear that without his support for the current project it is difficult to see how it could have been completed. In particular, his direct and very constructive criticism of the original plan of approach to the medieval material was invaluable. One feature of the book, which is that many chapters begin with an account of an actual dispute as a means of introducing students to a difficult legal topic, results from a suggestion he made. The invitation from the Research Group for Legal Culture at Bergen University Law Faculty to Andrew Simpson to be a visiting scholar at Bergen Law Faculty in late 2014 has already been acknowledged with thanks. The authors would also like to recognise with thanks the extensive help given by Dr Julian Goodare of Edinburgh University, whose guidance and insight have been invaluable with respect to aiding the authors to contextualise legal matters mentioned in the second and third parts of the book within the wider history of the relevant periods.

Other specialists in the field have generously given of their time in reading drafts of the text. Particular thanks in this regard must go to Professor John Finlay of Glasgow University, Professor Mark Godfrey of Glasgow University, Professor Søren Koch of Bergen University and Dr Alice Taylor of King's College, London. In addition, non-specialists and students have read the text and given valuable feedback, notably Professor Tina Hunter of Aberdeen University, Finn O'Neill, an undergraduate student at Aberdeen, Andrew Simpson's father Arthur Edmond Simpson and Adelyn Wilson's mother Fiona McKenzie. Other senior colleagues have provided great encouragement to the authors, both in this project and in their research more broadly, notably Professor John Cairns and Professor Hector MacQueen of Edinburgh University. Both have in the past given generously of their time to comment on much of the original research the writers have incorporated here. Among other colleagues and friends particular thanks are due to Professor Roderick Paisley and Dr Greg Gordon of Aberdeen University for their sound advice throughout. Any errors in the book remain our own.

Yet the greatest thanks must go to the writers' respective partners. Andrew's wife Pippa and Adelyn's partner Alan have provided unfailing support throughout, and their enthusiasm for the work has been an extremely important source of inspiration. It is entirely fitting that the book should be dedicated to them.

Old Aberdeen, 31 October 2016

PART ONE

The Origins of the Scottish Common Law to c. 1230

The origins of the Scottish common law can be traced to the twelfth century. The words 'common law' here refer to a law applicable – at least in principle – to all subjects of the Scottish king. The aim of the first part of this book is to explain how and why that common law came into being. In the early twelfth century, it seems that there was great diversity in the ways in which legal disputes were resolved. Rules governing the resolution of such conflicts varied from region to region and even from kinship group to kinship group. Yet during the second half of the twelfth century in particular this began to change. Monarchs such as William I (r. 1165–1214) developed procedures that they expected their great lords and their legal officials to use in order to address disputes over land, moveable property and what might today be called 'criminal' matters. In other words, the king sought to ensure that some of these procedures would be applied commonly to deal with cases arising across the kingdom.

In attempting to explain these developments, the current chapter will begin by considering one of the procedural mechanisms that may have been commonly applicable across the realm by c. 1200. In so doing, it will consider both an actual dispute that took place in 1197 and also the legal actors involved in the dispute. It will explain how they interacted with the emerging common law and contributed to its development. One of the actors involved in the case was the king himself, William I.

It will be suggested that one of the most important causes of the legal change identified lay in the king's own seemingly paradoxical policy of giving away land to consolidate his power. To explain, those gifts had to be articulated and protected in appropriate legal language. The need to realise that goal catalysed the development of new legal tools, which would, in turn, develop into the common law.[1]

---

[1] The work of the scholars who have formulated the theses presented here (and in the other introductory parts of this book) will be acknowledged in the chapters themselves.

The Origins of the Scottish
Common Law of Tort

CHAPTER I

From Legal Diversity to Some Legal Commonality

A. INTRODUCTION

Prior to the twelfth century, the area now known as Scotland seems to have been characterised by legal diversity. Disputes were resolved using a range of customs and rules that varied from region to region, and even from kinship-group to kinship-group. This changed during the 1100s and the early 1200s. Common mechanisms and broad rules governing conflict resolution began to be recognised across much of the Scottish realm. How and why did this happen?

This chapter will seek to answer that question. It will begin by examining a dispute of 1197, towards the end of the period under consideration here. This illustrates how one common mechanism for conflict resolution was used to address a particular legal problem. Yet it also serves to introduce the work of a series of important legal actors who shaped the Scottish legal system during the twelfth century. Among them were the Gaelic-speaking *judices*, the sheriffs, the justices and the kings themselves. What is known about those legal actors, and the historical development of their roles, will then be examined. This in turn sheds light on how the diverse laws and customs found in twelfth-century Scotland began to be replaced with a nascent Scottish common law. By a 'common law' here is meant a law applicable amongst all of the subjects of the king.

B. A TYPICAL DISPUTE

The dispute just mentioned was concerned with the lands of Balfeith in the rich agricultural region of the Mearns, in north-east Scotland.[1] In 1197

---

[1] The dispute is discussed in Geoffrey W. S. Barrow, *The Kingdom of the Scots*, 2nd edn (Edinburgh: Edinburgh University Press, 2003), 57–67 and in Dauvit Broun,

Humphey de Berkeley decided to give the lands of Balfeith to Arbroath Abbey. More specifically, he sought to give the lands 'to God and the church of the blessed Thomas, martyr, of Arbroath and to the monks who are serving, and will be serving God, there'. But there was a problem. One of Humphrey's neighbours, Walter, son of Sibbald, disputed the extent of the lands of Balfeith. The two men also disagreed about 'the rights pertaining to [those] lands'. Obviously, Humphrey wanted to resolve these disputes before he made the transfer. Otherwise, the nature and extent of his gift to God, St Thomas and the monks would remain uncertain.

At this stage the Scottish king intervened, probably at Humphrey's request. Why was he willing to do so? Perhaps, in part, this was because Humphrey had received the lands from the king in exchange for various services. Indeed, the king retained an interest in the land. If Humphrey failed to provide the services required, he would forfeit them. But the king had duties too. Suppose he had granted Humphrey more land than he had had to give. Suppose that, as a result, Humphrey then lost some of his lands he wanted to give Arbroath Abbey. In that scenario, the king would have been obliged to compensate Humphrey for his losses.[2] However, this may not fully explain the king's involvement in this case, as will be shown below.

In response to the conflict between Humphrey and Walter, the king ordered that a court should be convened at Balfeith itself. So it is necessary to imagine a court meeting in the open air, actually on the disputed fields. The aim of the court was 'to break off the dispute'. The court was to be made up of several individuals. The first and second, Matthew, Bishop of Aberdeen, and Gille Brigte, Earl of Strathearn, were referred to as the royal 'justices'.[3] Another man whose presence seems to have been required was named Mael Brigte.[4] He described his office as being

---

'The king's brithem (Gaelic for "judge") and the recording of dispute-resolutions', *Paradox of Medieval Scotland 1093–1286*, Feature of the month: no. 11, April 2010, http://paradox.poms.ac.uk/feature/april10.html. See also Alice Taylor, *The Shape of the State in Medieval Scotland* (Oxford: Oxford University Press, 2016), 312–13. The work of Barrow, Broun and Taylor forms the basis of the discussion here. The perambulation described may have taken place in 1197 or 1198; Broun favours the former date.

[2] Such a claim would have been based on the king's 'warrandice'; see Hector L. MacQueen, *Common Law and Feudal Society*, reprinted edn (Edinburgh: Edinburgh University Press, 2016), 45–7, 150–1.

[3] It is possible that only Gille Brigte was, in fact, a justice; see Taylor, *Shape of the State*, 130 n. 91.

[4] The Latin form of his name is given as 'Bricius' in the surviving sources.

that of '*Judex domini Regis*' – literally meaning 'judge of the lord king'. Finally, various 'good men who knew well the bounds of the lands' of Humphrey and Walter were ordered to attend. Note that Humphrey himself was a royal officer of the law known as a sheriff.

These men gathered at Balfeith; one can imagine them standing in the muddy rigs of the fields. Mael Brigte, the *judex*, then produced a shrine. This shrine was probably a casket of some sort, which might well have been richly decorated with jewels and precious metals. It was probably quite small; Mael Brigte later recalled that the men present had received it from his hand. Importantly, it would have contained 'relics'. Frequently relics were the earthly remains of Christians who had been marked in life as unusually favoured by God himself. This favour might have manifested itself through the performance of miracles or unusual piety.[5]

Mael Brigte then asked the 'good men who knew well the bounds of the lands' to swear an oath upon the relics. He asked them to declare truthfully where the boundaries of Humphrey's lands lay. To do this, they would perambulate – literally, walk around – the lands to point out their boundaries. In so doing, they would implement the command of the king. The men would have approached the task of swearing this oath with some trepidation. They firmly believed that the relics were those of a person who was now alive in heaven. In other words, he or she was a saint. This immortal figure continued to channel God's power in earthly matters through his or her remains. Those who swore falsely by those remains might bring down God's wrath upon them; they might even spend eternity in the fires of Hell.

Having sworn the oath, the 'good men' perambulated the lands according to their knowledge. In this way they declared where they knew the boundaries to lie. Humphrey then gave his lands at Balfeith to Arbroath Abbey. He would have given 'sasine', meaning he would have put the Abbey in possession of the lands. Usually this was done symbolically. Humphrey, or one of his men, would probably have scooped up stone and earth from the ground and then handed it to the Abbey's representative.[6] He then declared the grant in a charter. Yet there was

---

[5] On oaths in the medieval Scottish courts, see Philip J. Hamilton-Grierson, *Habakkuk Bisset's Rolment of Courtis* (Edinburgh and London: Scottish Text Society, 1919–26) III, 161; William Croft Dickinson, *The Sheriff Court Book of Fife 1515–1522* (Edinburgh: Scottish History Society, 1928), 289, 318; Cynthia Neville, *Land, Law and People in Medieval Scotland* (Edinburgh: Edinburgh University Press, 2010), 28–9.

[6] See George L. Gretton, 'The feudal system', in Kenneth G. C. Reid, *The Law of Property in Scotland* (Edinburgh: Butterworths, 1996), paras. 41–113 at para. 89.

a problem; it will be recalled that Humphrey actually held the lands from the king in exchange for services. Now he was granting the lands to Arbroath Abbey. Who would perform the services, which were possibly military in nature? Humphrey's grant made it clear that he and his heirs would still perform the services due for the lands. In return, the monks of Arbroath would offer prayers for Humphrey, his family and the royal family. In this way these worldly men might hope to receive divine salvation.

C. *HUMPHREY DE BERKELY* (1197): THE NASCENT SCOTTISH COMMON LAW

This case illustrates many points about Scots law in c. 1200. But for current purposes it is very useful because it introduces various central features of the early Scottish legal system. It reveals some of the Scottish courts that resolved disputes at the time, the royal legal officers who operated within them, and also the types of rules and procedures that they employed. Yet it also raises many questions. What was so valuable about land like Balfeith, and how was it used by the community? Put more broadly, what was the social and economic context of the dispute? Furthermore, what were the precise functions of the *judices*, the sheriffs and the justices? And why exactly did the king become involved in the resolution of this boundary dispute? These questions will be considered next. In the process, the possibility that a Scottish common law gradually began to emerge at this time will be considered.

(1) Land and Community: The Social and Economic Context of the Dispute

Like the case of *Humphrey de Berkeley* (1197), many legal disputes in medieval Scotland were in some way connected with the control of land or rights associated with land. Why was this so? The answer lies in the obvious fact that the land upon which medieval Scots lived was the fundamental source of their sustenance. Arable farming has been described as 'the subsistence element of the economy'. If the crop failed, the people might starve. But the land also provided opportunities to 'improve one's [social] situation', perhaps primarily through the 'pastoral farming' of animals.[7] In times of plenty, those who used the land to farm both crops

---

[7] See Fiona Watson, 'Landscape and people', in Edward J. Cowan and Lizanne

and herds of livestock could provide for their families. But they could also hope to do more. They could dispose of those animals that they did not need in a variety of ways. For example, they might make gifts to their neighbours, who were perhaps in need. Those who received such largesse might thereafter be under some sort of obligation to the donors. In this way, farming families might gradually acquire wealth and power over their neighbours. Obviously, excess wealth could also be used to acquire commodities.

The excess wealth produced through pastoral farming of cattle was clearly of great social and economic importance. For example, it made it possible for violent acts, such as spilling blood or killings, to be remedied through the payment of compensation. To give an example, the compensation for the violent death of a peasant, a payment known in Gaelic as '*cró*', was set at sixteen cows. The *cró* would be paid by the wrongdoer to the peasant's kinsmen.[8] This provided an alternative mechanism of dispute resolution to a feud – prolonged reactive violence – between the families of the victim and the wrongdoer, which might involve widespread destruction of resources essential to the community.

Thus land, and the wealth that it generated, underpinned social and legal developments in medieval Scotland. It is worth noting in passing that various 'rights' also became associated with the land over time, and had the effect of 'burdening' it. To explain with reference to a familiar example, when Humphrey de Berkeley granted the lands of Balfeith to Arbroath Abbey, he simultaneously 'burdened' his neighbouring lands of Conveth and Kinkell. He did this by giving the monks of Arbroath Abbey the rights to pasture their animals on Conveth and Kinkell, and to extract fuel and wood from those estates. Land was burdened like this in a variety of ways across Scotland. From some lands the obligation of '*cáin*' or tribute was owed; sometimes this tribute was measured in cattle. *Cáin* could be transmitted by the holder to a third party. Other lands were burdened with the obligation of '*coinnmed*', meaning the king or a local lord was entitled to hospitality when he arrived in the locality.[9] Yet there was

---

Henderson (eds), *A History of Everyday Life in Medieval Scotland, 1000 to 1600* (Edinburgh: Edinburgh University Press, 2011), 25–35 at 27. Of course, to some extent what follows in this paragraph is somewhat speculative.

[8] See Alice Taylor, '*Leges Scocie* and the lawcodes of David I, William the Lion and Alexander II', *Scottish Historical Review* 88 (2009), 207–88 at 286–8 (the text known as the *Leges Scocie* cap. 21).

[9] See, above all, Taylor, *Shape of the State*, 84–93, which argues convincingly that the burdens of *cáin* and *coinnmed* were *not* commonly owed from all lands to the king, as has been argued previously. For other helpful observations on the subject, see

variation in local practice, as can be seen from the Gospel-book known as the Book of Deer. This was kept by the monks of the Abbey of Deer, which was about thirty miles north of Aberdeen in a region known as Buchan. Historically the land had been burdened, meaning that the monks had to render services or dues to powerful local figures. Sometimes the rights of these figures in the monks' lands were labelled '*cuit*', a term unknown elsewhere in Scotland. '*Cuit*' probably meant a 'share' or 'portion'. The Book of Deer records the monks' attempts to secure freedom from these burdens. Eventually David I (r. 1124–53) confirmed that the monks were to be 'quit and immune from all lay service and improper exaction' as was 'written in their book'. The monks also received the king's special protection. David I declared that no-one was to 'dare to do any harm to [the monks] or to their goods'.[10] Such grants of royal protection were of great importance in the development of the later law.[11]

Much more could be said concerning the significance of the land to medieval Scots. Yet these comments do serve to illustrate the value of land and rights in land, and to explain why the extent of such rights was frequently contested in practice. The comments made also set in context the dispute in the case of *Humphrey de Berkeley* (1197) over the boundaries of Balfeith. It is now important to consider the officers who were called upon to assist in the resolution of that matter.

(2) The *Judices*, the Laws and the Customs of Gaelic-Speaking Scotland

Of the legal officers present in the court at Balfeith in 1197, least is known about the *judex* and his role. It is quite likely that the *judices* were a group of men who knew the laws applicable in various parts of Gaelic-speaking Scotland.[12] Note that, during the twelfth century, much of Scotland was

---

W. David H. Sellar, 'Celtic law and Scots law: survival and integration', *Scottish Studies* 29 (1989), 16–17; Alex Woolf, *From Pictland to Alba 789–1070* (Edinburgh: Edinburgh University Press, 2007) 25, 323–4.

[10] Dauvit Broun, 'The property records in the Book of Deer as a source for early Scottish society', in Katherine Forsyth (ed.), *Studies on the Book of Deer* (Dublin: Four Courts Press, 2008), 313–60; see also Katherine Forsyth, Dauvit Broun and Thomas Clancy, 'The property records: text and translation', in *idem*, 131–44; the passages quoted are at 133 and 143.

[11] See Alan Harding, 'The medieval brieves of protection and the development of the common law', *Juridical Review* (1966), 115–49; this must now be read in light of Taylor, *Shape of the State*, 164–9, which outlines an important challenge to Harding's arguments.

[12] The leading study of the *judices* is now Taylor, *Shape of the State*, 117–35.

dominated by Gaelic culture from Ireland and the Gaelic language. Different groups of *judices* operated in different parts of the kingdom. Most of the surviving evidence concerns those who operated north of the Forth, although there were also *judices* in Galloway, which had its own distinctive laws.[13]

Early Scottish sources make a few scattered references to *judices* who clearly knew the laws applicable in their own localities. Whether a reference to 'Lagmannaibh na n-Innsedh' (the lawmen of the isles) in a chronicle of 974 is to a Scandinavian or a native Gaelic institution is unclear.[14] Scandinavian lawmen might conceivably have been operating the western isles of Scotland, where Norsemen had settled during the previous century.[15] But the Scottish Gaelic-speaking *judices* were certainly active by the early twelfth century. In c. 1128 some Gaelic-speaking monks in Fife complained to the king, David I (r. 1124–53), about one of their neighbours. The monks claimed that Sir Robert the Burgundian, that 'fire and furnace of all iniquity', had seized from them the fourth part of the lands of Kirkness. David I intervened and ordered a great number of lords from Fife to gather to deal with the dispute. The matter was decided by three *judices*. One, the Earl of Fife, was described as *magnus judex in Scotia*, or great judge in Scotia (meaning Scotland between the rivers Forth and Spey). Another, Dufgal, was an old man who was said to have *juris peritia*, or expertise in the law. It was to him that the other *judices* deferred when they gave judgement in favour of the monks.[16]

The fact that Dufgal had legal expertise raises an important question. What was the basis of his expertise? Did the *judices* gain their learning through the study of written law? Or was their legal knowledge transmitted only through oral traditions? One historian of the period, Alice Taylor, has considered these questions.[17] She notes that in near-contemporary Wales, men of law who look similar to the *judices* were in operation. Their expertise seems to have been based at least in part on written legal texts, some of which survive virtually intact. By contrast, no complete Scottish tracts survive expounding the learning of the *judices*. Nonetheless, Taylor

---

[13] On the Laws of Galloway, see, for example, Hector L. MacQueen, 'The Laws of Galloway: A Preliminary Survey', in Richard D. Oram and Geoffrey P. Stell (eds), *Galloway: Land and Lordship* (Edinburgh: Scottish Society for Northern Studies, 1991), 131–43.

[14] See Woolf, *Pictland to Alba*, 212–13 and the source cited there, the *Annals of the Four Masters*, available at http://cett.ucc.ie/published/G100005B/index.html (the website also hosts a translation of the text).

[15] Thanks are due to Professor Jørn Øyrehagen Sunde for pointing this out.

[16] Barrow, *Kingdom*, 58.

[17] Taylor, *Shape of the State*, 117–23.

argues that such tracts may once have existed and suggests that fragments of those works still survive. In making this argument, she draws attention to a series of texts that are sometimes labelled the *Leges inter Brettos et Scotos* (hereafter *LBS*). *LBS* laid out the blood prices owed to the kindred of a man who had been wrongfully killed. The blood price or '*cró*' of a peasant was noted above; it was set at sixteen cows. By contrast, the blood price of the king was set at one thousand cows. Beyond this, *LBS* also required a smaller payment to be made to any lord whose peace had been broken by the killing. Additionally, *LBS* and associated texts laid out the compensation to be paid for the spilling of blood.

Taylor argues that the expertise of the *judices* may, at least in part, have rested on familiarity with *LBS* and other such texts. Alternatively, the *judices'* expertise may be represented by their later written content. Taylor's reasons for thinking along these lines can be summarised briefly. First, she notes that large numbers of variant versions of texts such as *LBS* survive today. This may indicate that many people read the text during the twelfth and thirteenth centuries and subsequently amended it to suit their own situations. If it is asked who the readers were, the *judices* seem to be potential candidates, given that they were literate men who clearly dealt with legal disputes in Scotland at this time. Second, while the earliest version of *LBS* survives in French, it preserves Gaelic legal terminology, such as the word '*cró*'. It seems plausible to argue that the first readers and transmitters of these texts understood such terminology. This strengthens the possibility that those readers were the *judices*, who were the only known 'caste' of expert lawyers in Gaelic-speaking Scotland north of the Forth.[18]

As a result, one can hypothesise that the expertise of the *judices* was at least partly based on texts such as *LBS*, of which only fragments now survive.[19] Nonetheless, it does not follow that all *judices* would have possessed exactly the same expertise across Gaelic-speaking Scotland. It is well known that the *judices* of Galloway, in the south-west of the country, presided over their own distinctive laws. Yet even north of the Forth, there must have been great regional variations in the expertise required of a *judex*. This is because the surviving evidence indicates that diverse local customs were in operation across this area. In Fife, there was a law that applied only to one kindred – *Clann Duib* – and it was designed to prevent trials by battle being fought to the death.[20] It was explained

---

[18]   Taylor, *Shape of the State*, 123–9.
[19]   Taylor, *Shape of the State*, 123–32.
[20]   See Angelo D. M. Forte, '"A strange archaic provision of mercy": the procedural

above that in Buchan in the north burdens known as *'cuit'* could be taken from lands, but these are unknown elsewhere. This probably helps to explain why *judices* are frequently described as *judices* of particular provinces. Consequently, all *judices* may have drawn on some core written learning as the basis of their expertise, at least in Scotland north of the Forth. Yet a *judex* must also have required additional learning that was specific to his own province.

Thus it is plausible to suggest the authority of the *judices* to resolve disputes rested upon their legal expertise, at least in part. Taylor argues that the same expertise underpinned the authority they possessed to reform and develop the law. For example, in 1221 they acted together with the king, Alexander II (r. 1214–49), to promulgate a new law. This concerned the common burden of army service, which affected lands throughout the Scottish kingdom.[21] The law provided that those who failed to answer a royal call to arms would face significant fines.

It is intriguing that the king and the *judices* had the power to act together to make law. This raises another important question. What was the relationship between the authority of the *judices* to decide legal disputes and to make law, on the one hand, and the authority of the king, on the other? It has been suggested thus far that the authority of the *judices* to decide disputes rested primarily on their legal expertise. Yet the law of 1221 presents law-making as something that could be done by the king acting with his *judices*. As will be seen shortly, at the same time kings started to present certain *judices* as *their own judices*. Royal authority was being linked closely with the work of these Gaelic-speaking legal experts. Can anything more be said about the nature of this link?

Taylor argues that the earliest evidence, dating from the 1120s, presents the *judices* as virtually autonomous law-makers. In other words, the laws they made were binding without any royal intervention.[22] The authority of their laws, like their own authority to decide disputes, presumably rested on their apparent expertise. Yet Taylor then suggests that the apparent autonomy of the *judices* began to be eroded during the second half of the twelfth century. Scottish kings began to attempt to associate the work of the *judices* more closely with their own

---

rules for the *Duellum* under the law of *Clann Duib*', *Edinburgh Law Review* 14 (2010), 418–50.

[21] For such common burdens (army, aid and labour service), see Taylor, *Shape of the State*, 84–113.

[22] Taylor, *Shape of the State*, 117–32.

authority. Obviously there had always been *some* association between the authority of the king and that of the *judices*: in the Kirkness case mentioned above of c. 1128, the *judices* gave judgement in response to royal intervention in the dispute. Yet this link between the king and the *judices* strengthened from the mid-twelfth century. One of the few laws that can undoubtedly be attributed to David I (r. 1124–53) was made at Montrose, in Angus (exactly when it was promulgated is uncertain). It declared that when the king arrived in a particular province, the *judices* of that province had to meet with him. If one of them failed to do so, he would be fined eight cows – a significant sum.[23] A similar attempt to link royal power with that of the *judices* can be found in a charter granted between 1150 and 1153. There David I conferred a privilege to the tenants of Dunfermline Abbey at Newburn in Fife. David declared that the tenants of Newburn were not to answer in respect of any 'lawsuits or charges' brought against them except in the court of Dunfermline Abbey. Yet he also commanded that *his judex* of Fife was to go with those engaged in disputations in the court of the Abbey. This was to ensure that lawsuits should be dealt with justly. Here a *judex* was still linked with a particular locality, but he was now regarded as the king's *judex* in that area.[24] From 1153 onwards, one can find frequent references to the *judices domini regis* – the *judices* of the lord king. These men were not only linked with the exercise of royal power; they were entrusted with that power in ensuring that justice was done in the courts. It might be thought that the association was somehow simply to the benefit of the *judices*, as it gave them prestige. But that would probably be not quite the whole story. By supporting the *judices* the kings associated themselves with the enforcement of the customary laws applied across the Gaelic-speaking parts of their kingdom. Why they may have been doing this will be considered shortly.

Further information concerning the work of the *judices* survives from the second half of the twelfth century. There is evidence to suggest they kept written records of disputes with which they were involved. Dauvit Broun has argued convincingly that Mael Brigte, the *judex domini regis*, probably did so in the case of *Humphrey de Berkeley*.[25] Furthermore it seems that the *judices* continued to be involved in law-making. Yet

---

[23] Taylor, *Shape of the State*, 130.

[24] Geoffrey W. S. Barrow (ed.), *The Written Acts of David I King of Scots, 1124–53, and of His Son Henry Earl of Northumberland, 1139–52* (Woodbridge: Boydell & Brewer, 1999), 147, charter no. 190.

[25] Broun, 'The king's brithem'.

now they did not appear as *autonomous* law-givers, but rather as men who assented to the making of *the king's* law – as in the case of the act of 1221.[26] Perhaps during the reign of William I (r. 1165–1214), a very curious law was enacted at Perth by the king acting with the earls, barons and *judices* of Scotia (Scotia was that part of William's kingdom between the rivers Forth and Spey). Again, the precise date of promulgation is uncertain. The law declared that 'the mid-stream [of a river] ought to be so free to the extent that one three-year-old well-fed pig is of length that neither the pig's snout nor his tail come near the bank'. Having made this proclamation, it then concluded that 'the mid-stream ought to be so free that no-one may catch fish there from Saturday after Vespers until Monday when the sun has risen'. The aim of this law was evidently to protect fishings – probably salmon fishings – in Scotia. Its authenticity has been questioned, but it has been defended by the leading expert on the manuscript traditions underpinning the texts of medieval Scots law.[27] Just possibly, the authority of the earls, barons and *judices* was being drawn upon by the king to promulgate laws that would be applicable throughout much of his realm.

(3) Feudal Courts, Sheriffs and Justiciars

In 1197 Mael Brigte the *judex* was not the only official whose presence was required in the court assembled at Balfeith. The king ordered his justices of Scotia to attend. It will be recalled that they were Matthew, Bishop of Aberdeen, and Gille Brigte, Earl of Menteith. In addition, Humphrey de Berkeley himself was the local sheriff. As will be explained, that meant that he too had various duties as regards the administration of justice.

Unlike the *judices*, whose ultimate origins are unknown, the offices of justice and sheriff were introduced into Scotland during the twelfth century, initially by David I (r. 1124–53). At first they were operative in the southern and eastern lands ruled by the Scottish kings. Those lands were largely English-speaking and had only recently been incorporated into the Scottish kingdom. But over time, sheriffs began to appear in the Gaelic-speaking areas of the country too. David I's grandsons, Malcolm IV (r. 1153–65) and William I (r. 1165–1214), appointed more sheriffs in the north and west of the country. These two kings also appointed officers known as justices (later known as justiciars). Note that the individuals appointed to hold these offices were often very powerful noblemen.

---

[26] See generally Taylor, *Shape of the State*, 114–35.
[27] Taylor, '*Leges Scocie*', 219–20, 282 (*Leges Scocie* cap. 5).

Some – but by no means all – had been brought to Scotland from Norman England. Also note that the offices had parallels in the administration of the law in England. It is widely acknowledged that the Scottish offices were modelled on the English equivalents.[28]

What did these officers do? The evidence suggests that their functions developed considerably during the second half of the twelfth century, particularly in Scotland north of the Forth.[29] One of their most important roles related to the supervision of the administration of justice by great territorial lords. To explain, William I in particular made many gifts of lands north of the Forth to established Scottish and to incoming Anglo-Norman noblemen. In the process, he often transferred significant powers over the lands in question to the grantees. This important phenomenon – which Taylor dubs the 'territorialisation' of power[30] – will be discussed further below. For now what matters is that many of William's gifts of lands came with fairly extensive jurisdictional rights. In other words, the recipients of William's largesse received the right to judge a wide range of disputes that arose within their territories. With those grants often came rights to the 'profits' of justice. For example, a lord who had the right to hear an accusation of theft in his court would have the right to seize the goods of the accused if he was subsequently found guilty.[31] An example of a court of a great territorial lord that has already been considered is that of the Abbot of Dunfermline.

The king retained an interest in the functioning of these courts, for a variety of reasons. It was here that the sheriffs and the justices had a role. As regards the justices, the point can be illustrated from a grant of lands William I executed in favour of a powerful Norman nobleman called Robert de Brus. This happened south of the Forth, at some point between 1165 and 1172. The gift was made '*in feudo et hereditate*' – meaning that the land was granted as a 'feu' and that feu was granted to

---

[28] On the early justices (and justiciars), see Barrow, *Kingdom*, 68–111; on the sheriffs, see Croft Dickinson, *Sheriff Court Book of Fife*, xi–cv, 309–407. These older works must now be read in light of Taylor, *Shape of the State*, 191–265. On the early English justiciars and sheriffs, see, for example, John H. Baker, *An Introduction to English Legal History*, 4th edn (London: Butterworths, 2002), 9, 14–16.

[29] The argument presented in the current section of this chapter draws heavily on Taylor, *Shape of the State*, 152–175, 191–265.

[30] See Taylor, *Shape of the State*, 177–87.

[31] On the development of lordly jurisdiction at this time, see Taylor, *Shape of the State*, 152–75.

Brus and his heirs – in return for the service of ten knights.[32] Of course, this grant is 'characteristically feudal', as MacQueen puts it.[33] This is because the service specified in the heritable grant is primarily military. The grant also conferred on Brus the right to hold a court. In other words, it gave him jurisdiction over those who lived on the lands that he received. This sort of court will be referred to hereafter as a feudal court, and the jurisdiction conferred as 'franchisal' jurisdiction.[34] But this court did not hold unfettered power to resolve disputes. Brus was allowed to hear all pleas except those known as the *regalia*. These were the pleas of fraudulent concealment of treasure trove, murder, premeditated assault, rape, arson and robbery. William I declared that he reserved these pleas to himself, and they had to be heard before his justices within a local administrative unit known as the sheriffdom.[35] Of course, the king's interest in these pleas was partly financial. It seems likely that the profits of justice arising from such serious cases would have gone to the king, as they did in a later period.

The king's interest in supervising the operation of the feudal courts extended to the protection of the rights of other powerful interests within the kingdom. For example, in a charter granted to the Bishop of Moray between 1185 and 1189, William I explained how he would enforce the payment of teinds. Teinds were payments due to the church from its parishioners. They might be made in cash or, perhaps more commonly, with the produce of lands. William I explained that if individual parishioners failed to hand over their teinds, the lords of the territories in which they lived would have primary responsibility for compelling them to pay. If the lords failed to do this, they would be fined by the local sheriff, acting as a royal officer. If the sheriff failed to act, then he would be fined by the justice. The important point to note is that primary responsibility for the implementation of the law was left with the territorial lords. Only where they failed to act would the royal officers intervene. In this way, royal law could be enforced through the threat of punishment of those

---

[32] Geoffrey W. S. Barrow and W. W. Scott (eds), *The Acts of William I King of Scots 1165–1214* (Edinburgh: Edinburgh University Press, 1971), 178–9 (charter no. 80).

[33] MacQueen, *Common Law*, 34.

[34] On franchsial jurisdication, see Alexander Grant, 'Franchises north of the border: baronies and regalities in medieval Scotland', in Michael Prestwich (ed.), *Liberties and Identities in the Medieval British Isles* (Woodbridge: Boydell & Brewer, 2008), 155–99. Properly the term 'franchisal jurisdiction' should be reserved to describe such jurisdictions in a later period; the term is used here for convenience.

[35] On the development of the sheriffdom, see in particular Taylor, *Shape of the State*, 195–205.

lords who failed to apply it. Those entrusted with *supervision* of the lords were the sheriffs and the justices.[36]

The role of the sheriffs and the justices as supervisors of the feudal courts was confirmed in a law promulgated by William I in 1180. The law was made 'with the assent of the earls and barons'. It declared that 'neither bishops nor abbots nor earls nor barons nor any other holding [lands] freely' would 'hold their court unless the king's sheriff or his sergeand was present or was summoned to be present to see that the court was conducted properly'. The court could then proceed even if the sheriff or his sergeand failed to appear; but they had to be given the opportunity to be present. If they were present, and the lord was negligent in the administration of justice, there is evidence that in some cases the king's officers could step in and do right to a claimant. Nonetheless, again the basic assumption was that jurisdiction over a wide range of matters would be exercised through the great territorial lords. Only certain matters were reserved to the king – and presumably his justices. So the law of 1180 stated that four pleas pertained 'to the king's business' in all courts – these being rape, robbery, arson and murder.[37]

By the 1180s, the sheriffs and the justices were not simply exercising supervisory jurisdiction north of the Forth. They were also holding their own courts in that region, as they probably had been doing for some time south of the Forth. This can be seen from a law promulgated by William I in 1184. It refers to the court of the sheriff, which was in theory to be held every forty days. Representatives of the Scottish nobility were bound to attend the sheriff's court when it sat. By contrast, the nobility themselves were bound to attend sittings of the justice's court.[38]

During the 1180s, it seems that each sheriff court presided over a small territory known as the sheriffdom. This was always focused on a royal trading town or 'burgh' and spread out to parts of the surrounding countryside.[39] Often the sheriffdoms would be bounded by the great territorial lordships, where the sheriffs had primarily supervisory roles. At about this time, the work of the justices also took on a new shape. By the 1220s, different justices – now referred to as 'justiciars' – came to operate north and south of the Forth. Within these large regions they went on

---

[36] Taylor, *Shape of the State*, 152–7.
[37] Taylor, '*Leges Scocie*', 282–3 (*Leges Scocie* cap. 7). The significance of the law is discussed in Taylor, *Shape of the State*, 206–10.
[38] Taylor, '*Leges Scocie*', 284 (*Leges Scocie* cap. 14). The significance of the law is discussed in Taylor, *Shape of the State*, 205–10.
[39] Taylor, *Shape of the State*, 202–5.

'ayre' through each sheriffdom, judging disputes that fell within their jurisdiction.[40] Note that the courts of the justiciars always had powers to deal with a wider range of matters than those of the sheriffs. For example, the criminal jurisdiction of the sheriffs within their sheriffdoms seems to have been limited to cases of theft and homicide that did not amount to murder. The justiciar could hear pleas concerning all criminal matters, including the serious matters covered by the pleas of the crown. More will be said concerning those pleas shortly.

It may be helpful to summarise the points just made. Thus far it has been seen that William I in particular gave away many lands north of the Forth to great lords. With those gifts came jurisdictional rights to determine the outcome of many disputes on the lands in question. This meant that, by the late twelfth century, the king expected most legal disputes to be dealt with by his lords. Nonetheless, various royal officers had the power to supervise the exercise of a lord's jurisdiction, at least in theory. Furthermore, these officers – the sheriffs and justiciars – held their own courts across Scotland from the mid-1180s. The courts of the sheriffs and the justiciars were modelled on those of their English counterparts who administered the English common law.

The fact that the feudal courts and the courts of the sheriffs and the justiciars were established by Scottish kings during the twelfth century is intriguing. It seems as though those kings were attempting to develop new mechanisms to ensure their laws were observed within their realm. They apparently tried to do so through the great territorial lords, but also through royal officers. Earlier it was said that at the same period Scottish kings also gave their support and authority to some individual *judices*. Those individuals evidently knew the customs of particular localities in Gaelic Scotland, a land that was legally diverse. This reinforces the impression that twelfth-century kings were increasingly laying down a range of procedural mechanisms according to which disputes could be resolved. This could allow those disputes to be resolved in broadly common ways across their realm.[41] Perhaps, importantly, the work of the *judices* as described above could be incorporated into the new courts. This is what is seen in the dispute over the lands of Balfeith. There the work of Mael Brigte the *judex* was incorporated into a sitting of the

---

[40]   Taylor, *Shape of the State*, 210–44.
[41]   This suggestion owes much to the argument developed in Alice Taylor, 'Crime without punishment: medieval Scotland in comparative perspective', in D. Bates (ed.), *Anglo-Norman Studies 35: Proceedings of the Battle Conference 2012* (Woodbridge: Boydell Press, 2013), 287–304 at 300.

justiciar's court. In the process, the customs that the *judices* knew best could be enforced through new mechanisms for the administration of justice – meaning the courts of the sheriffs and the justiciars, and also (presumably) the feudal courts.

Yet all this in turn raises other questions. Why were Scottish kings attempting to develop new ways of enforcing the law at this time? And why did they draw inspiration from English law in the process? To answer these questions something must now be said concerning the twelfth-century Scottish monarchs.

(4) The King and God

In 1197 William I demonstrated his firm resolve that his laws should be observed. He gathered together an assembly of all bishops, abbots, earls, barons and thanes. Together they swore an oath that they would bring wrongdoers to justice 'with all their might'. Furthermore, they promised that they would not protect murderers, robbers or thieves; rather, they would help the king to hunt them down. In addition, they accepted that anyone who failed to keep the oath would lose his court in perpetuity. It seems plausible to suggest that the oath was sworn on holy relics, like that sworn in the same year at Balfeith before Mael Brigte the *judex*. If so, the king was relying on divine power to compel his clerical and lay magnates to observe 'the justice of the land'.[42]

This reinforces the impression that William I wished to develop new ways of ensuring the maintenance of law and order within his realm. Now a lord who broke his oath to uphold the law would lose his court. The enactment of 1197 also underlines the point that he expected the law to be enforced by the great territorial lords who had received his gifts of jurisdiction.[43] First and foremost it was *they* who were entrusted with the pursuit of murderers, thieves and robbers. So why did the king try to develop yet another way of compelling his lords to uphold his laws? Equally importantly, why did he succeed? Why did the clergymen, nobility and *judices* acquiesce in, and indeed actively support, this process?

Part of the answer lies in the methods used by William I to cement his power. In this regard, he was influenced by the kingship of his grandfather, David I (r. 1124–53). It is necessary to outline the structures of royal authority that David I inherited in order to explain how he and his heirs departed from those structures.

---

[42] Taylor, '*Leges Scocie*, 285 (*Leges Scocie* cap. 15).
[43] See Taylor, *Shape of the State*, 170–2.

David I's father, Mael Coluim III (r. 1058–93), was the heir of a
Gaelic-speaking line of kings of central and northern Scotland. They had
maintained their kingship in the face of Scandinavian invasions throughout the ninth and tenth centuries. In the process they seem to have
forged an alliance with the Scottish church and promised to protect it.
For its part, the church seems to have allowed the kings and their noble
followers to make use of church lands. In this way, it was hoped they
would be able to support the armies required to defend the realm against
the Vikings. Often strange situations developed where small and very
poor austere groups of monks lived at the heart of church communities
whose resources were diverted to very secular ends. David's ancestors
were arguably among the warlords who drew upon such resources to
maintain their position.[44]

Within the kingdom which these Gaelic-speaking kings created,
power and legal obligations seem to have been conceptualised fundamentally in terms of kinship relations. That was at least the position
by the beginning of the twelfth century; evidence for the earlier period
is extremely limited. The peoples within each province were led by a
mormaer (plural *mormaír*), probably originally meaning a 'great steward'.
The *mormaír* seem to have been the heads of the dominant kindreds
within their provinces. As a result of this position, they were able to rule
the lesser kindreds of the same province. Each of these kinship-groups
was led by its own *toísech* (plural *toísig*). On the death of a *mormaer* his
successor might come from a different branch of the dominant kindred,
or indeed there might conceivably have been a power struggle between
kinship-groups. The king's capacity to interfere in this process would
have varied. His power to intervene would have depended in part on the
strength of his personal links with the great men – including the *toísig*
– of each province.[45] Likewise his power to interfere in the administration of justice would have depended on his links with the local *judices*, at
least to some extent. Certainly it was his summons to the notables and
judices of Fife that resolved the dispute between the monks of Lochleven
and Robert the Burgundian.

Yet David I was not just the heir to this Gaelic kingship. His mother
was an Anglo-Saxon princess (born and brought up in Hungary),
Margaret, later St Margaret. She was a senior member of the English

---

[44] On such aspects of David's Gaelic heritage, see Woolf, *Pictland to Alba*, particularly
313–50; see also Richard Oram, *Domination and Lordship. Scotland 1070–1230*
(Edinburgh: Edinburgh University Press, 2011), particularly 1–73, 197–232.

[45] On the *mormaír* and the *toísig*, see Taylor, *Shape of the State*, 25–83.

royal family from the period prior to the Norman Conquest of 1066. She was also a very pious woman who approved of contemporary reforms to the Roman Catholic Church. These were ultimately being driven by the papacy in Rome. The popes argued that God's wrath was directed against the lax morals of the clergy. Consequently they tried to regulate their lives and conduct to a much greater extent than had hitherto been thought possible, or indeed appropriate. This is an important point. Many rules of medieval canon law stemmed from these developments, and in time these came to shape Scots law. More will be said about this in the fourth chapter. But amongst the aims of the reformers was the goal of reforming monastic practices. Across Europe, they discovered arrangements whereby the wealth of the church had been seized by secular powers. It was forgotten that the reason for this had been to protect Christendom from heathen attacks. The reformers simply sought to recover religious property.[46]

Margaret and her descendants keenly promoted such reforms. They brought new monastic orders to Scotland from continental Europe. Throughout the twelfth century, the royal family eagerly gifted the lands of the Gaelic-speaking clergy to the incomers. The process was underway during the reign of Margaret's son, Alexander I (r. 1107–24).[47] It continued during the reigns of David I, his brother, and David's grandsons, Mael Coluim IV (r. 1153–65) and William I (r. 1165–1214).

At the same time, the last three kings adopted a similar policy to cement their secular power within different parts of the kingdom which they had each in turn inherited. Broadly, they sought to give away royal lands within different regions of the kingdom to ensure the support of powerful aristocrats. The pressure to secure such support may have been driven in part by the various dynastic challenges they faced. David I's gift-giving focused on lands at his disposal south of the Forth. Yet his grandson, William I, gave away extensive lands north of the Forth to maintain his position there. During William's reign, the grants of land were frequently feudal in nature, such as the charter mentioned above conferring lands on Robert de Brus. Like Robert, some of the recipients of the Scottish royal largesse were Anglo-Norman noblemen from England. Nonetheless, many were members of the more powerful Gaelic-speaking kindreds. Indeed, some of those kindreds received royal 'gifts' of lands which they may well have occupied for many decades. It is perhaps puzzling that

[46] See Woolf, *Pictland to Alba*, particularly 313–50.
[47] See Barrow, *Kingdom*, 151–230.

they evidently co-operated with this process. Taylor points out that they may have done so partly because a royal gift of land carried with it intensive power *over* that land and potentially lucrative rights to decide legal disputes. This certainly seems to have been the case with the *mormaír*. Their vague but extensive power over their provinces weakened during the twelfth century. Yet at the same time they gained much more direct and intensive control over particular lands within their provinces. These became the earldoms of later medieval Scotland and the *mormaír* became the earls.[48]

Twelfth-century kings also gave other important gifts to augment their power, this time to a third type of community. Many of the trading towns or burghs of Scotland were reconstituted as royal burghs. That meant they received various privileges, including control of trade in their hinterlands. The king backed up these gifts of trading privileges with a promise to protect them. In exchange, burghs paid the king a 'set amount … each year' known as the burgh 'ferm'.[49] This increased royal revenue and so augmented royal power. Burghs also received jurisdictional privileges. They were given the right to hold their own courts. They developed special laws and customs to resolve disputes between its burgesses – that is to say, its privileged traders and craftsmen. By the thirteenth century, the burgh courts were staffed by provosts and bailies. These royal officers were chosen by the burgesses in elections.[50] By the mid-thirteenth century, their work and their jurisdiction were supervised by another royal official, the chamberlain.[51]

The effects of all of the royal gifts of land, jurisdiction and trading privileges mentioned above were considerable. At the beginning of the twelfth century, much church land had been in the hands of quite secular men. Simultaneously, the power of the Gaelic-speaking noblemen north of the Forth had been based predominantly on kinship links. Trading towns north of the Forth seem to have been few and far between. By the end of the century, extensive and sometimes quite complex royal gifts of lands and trading privileges had been made to bishops, new religious monastic orders, great lords and burghs. With those gifts often came

[48] On these developments, see Taylor, *Shape of the State*, 25–83, 176–87.
[49] Taylor, *Shape of the State*, 254.
[50] On the burghs, see Hector L. MacQueen and William J. Windram, 'Laws and courts in the burghs', in Michael Lynch, Michael Spearman and Geoffrey Stell (eds), *The Scottish Medieval Town* (Edinburgh: John Donald, 1988), 208–27; see also William Croft Dickinson, *Early Records of the Burgh of Aberdeen 1317, 1398–1400* (Edinburgh: Scottish History Society, 1957), xvii–cli.
[51] On the chamberlain, see Taylor, *Shape of the State*, 244–62.

significant jurisdictional rights over the territories in question. As Taylor puts it, power became 'territorialised'.[52]

Nonetheless, Taylor argues that Scottish kings faced a difficulty in promoting this territorialisation of power. This was that they needed to frame their gifts of land in appropriate legal language. One might have expected them to turn to the expertise of the *judices* for guidance. Yet as Taylor points out, that would have been problematic. The tracts that were arguably used by the *judices* seem to have been designed to regulate power relations in a society structured primarily around relations between people, meaning people both as individuals and in groups, such as kinship groups. The tracts of the *judices* articulated the older social order in which kings ruled through their personal links with the *mormaír*, who in turn relied on the dominance of their kin over a province to rule the *toísig* of the lesser kindreds there. Within that order, the key legal problems arose when there was a killing or assault that might lead to a feud between kindreds. Thus one element of the work of the *judices* seems to have been focused on establishing the levels of compensation to be paid in relation to offences that could arise in the course of feuds. They may also have had some role in determining the obligations to the king owed by those living in particular lands (e.g. in relation to army service). Yet even those obligations were originally enforced through reliance on the *mormaír* and their powerful kin. Thus the laws of the *judices* were engaged with power structures that were based on kinship bonds. They were not designed to deal with the new power structures based on gifts of land and – importantly – jurisdiction. There is little or nothing in the surviving Gaelic legal terminology of the twelfth century that indicates that it possessed the technical vocabulary to describe such gifts. Given that those gifts became increasingly complex, the problem must rapidly have become quite obvious. What, then, was the solution?[53]

Scottish kings knew of one legal system that possessed the language and technical vocabulary that would allow them to articulate and describe their gifts as they wished. Of course, this was the law used in near-contemporary Anglo-Norman and Angevin England. In the last few decades of the twelfth century, increasingly large numbers of gifts of lands, privileges and jurisdictions came to be expressed in English terms. Put another way, formulae from English charters were borrowed and adapted to suit the Scottish situation. During the late twelfth century and the first four decades of the thirteenth century, royal laws also began

[52] See the summary in Taylor, *Shape of the State*, 176–87.
[53] Taylor, *Shape of the State*, 183–7.

to engage with the territorialisation of power. Again, English influence was present. To explain, these laws do not generally seem to have been made on the authority of expert *judices*, as they often had been in the past. Rather, they were made simply by the king acting with the assent of his great ecclesiastical and secular territorial lords. The new law-making process was clearly influenced by that used by contemporary English kings. The name given to the resulting Scottish laws – 'assizes' – was also borrowed from England. Some of those laws introduced forms of action for protecting the king's gifts of lands to his noblemen in his courts. These forms of actions were also often modelled on English equivalents usually referred to as the writs. In Scotland, they were known as the brieves. Even in the late twelfth century, at least one of these forms of action may already have been commonly available to all of the king's subjects. For example, one brieve commanded the justiciar to deal with a boundary dispute by holding a perambulation. This brieve of perambulation may well have been used in the case of *Humphrey de Berkeley* (1197), which was discussed above.[54]

Thus the king began to develop standardised forms of action for use in the royal courts. It seems quite possible that at least one of them was commonly available to all his subjects by the end of the twelfth century. If so, then this was the period that witnessed the birth of what would become the Scottish common law. It has been explained that the reason for this development lay largely in William I's desire to articulate and then protect extensive gifts of land, jurisdiction and trading privileges to churchmen, noblemen and burgesses alike. In secular terms, those gifts helped to cement his power in Scotland north of the Forth. Yet William I also believed that the ecclesiastical gifts would achieve more. This king, the founder of Arbroath Abbey and other religious houses, shared the beliefs of Humphrey de Berkeley about the value of giving gifts of land and jurisdiction to the saints and to God. Such piety would secure the powerful prayers and support of the immortal men and women who stood before the divine throne. Articulating royal gifts properly, and then protecting them, could secure both human and divine support for William's kingship.

---

[54] Taylor, *Shape of the State*, 132–5, 183–7, 312–15; on perambulation, see also MacQueen, *Common Law*, 108; Neville, *Land, Law and People*, 41–71.

D. CONCLUSION

William I sought to maintain his power through giving gifts of land and jurisdiction. Granting great lords territories and the right to hold their own courts was part of a broader strategy to cement his authority. Yet an equally important part of that strategy was making those same territorial lords *accountable* for the ways in which they exercised their jurisdictions. They were held accountable through the supervisory work of the sheriffs and the justiciars. They were also held accountable through the oath of 1197. If they failed to maintain certain basic standards of law and order, as laid down by William I himself, they would forfeit their courts. Thus these mechanisms that compelled the great lords to observe royal laws were of some importance. They left the king with some control over the new 'territorialised' power structures that he had created.

At the same time, the king needed to develop new ways of protecting those 'territorialised' power structures. At a very basic level, he needed to develop mechanisms to articulate royal gifts of lands clearly. He also needed to establish procedural mechanisms to protect his grants and to resolve any disputes that arose from them – such as boundary disputes. One such procedural mechanism – the brieve of perambulation – may have already been available in the late 1190s. As has been explained, the legal language used to articulate royal grants, and the forms of action that were eventually introduced to defend them, were largely adapted from English models.

Yet in adopting the English forms, kings like William I did not seek to suppress the older systems of law that had existed in Gaelic-speaking Scotland. Admittedly those laws were not equipped to engage with the territorialisation of power. Yet they were still valid laws, which were capable of resolving other types of disputes. So Scottish kings do not seem to have attempted to supplant this older legal system, which was based on obligations of kinship. Rather, they probably did something that was much more effective. They approved of some of the older laws and structures used within their realm to administer justice, and then sought to take them over.[55] Put another way, David I, William I and his successors did not try to challenge the work of the *judices* directly. Rather, they required the *judices* of a particular province to attend them when they entered that locality. They also appointed their own *judices*

---

[55]   The inspiration for this argument comes from Jenny Wormald, 'Bloodfeud, kindred and government in early modern Scotland', *Past and Present* 87 (1980), 54–97 at 90. Wormald's discussion concerns a different matter.

domini regis. Provincial *judices* like Mael Brigte were drawn into the work of the new courts of the justiciars and the sheriffs. Their important roles in the resolution of disputes in twelfth-century Scotland could now be made to serve the aims of the king. Like the justiciars, the sheriffs and the nobles introduced to Scotland, they would help to maintain the radical restructuring of power promoted by monarchs like William I. Even some of the laws of the *judices* were re-packaged as royal assizes. The *judices* may have acquiesced in this process in order to share in the growing power of the king and his lords to resolve disputes within the realm. However, this last point is speculative.

The effects of these developments on the law were significant. The somewhat diverse customs of Gaelic-speaking Scotland were increasingly presented as expressions of a single royal authority. Furthermore, William I's determination to find new ways to enforce his laws through the great territorial lords made the emergence of a more 'common' law possible. Additionally, his resolve to protect his gifts of land and jurisdiction probably resulted in the creation of a procedural device – a brieve – to resolve boundary disputes. This seems to have been commonly available to all subjects of the Scottish king. In such developments, one can trace the origins of the medieval Scottish common law. The next three chapters will explore how William I's successors consolidated that common law during the thirteenth, fourteenth and early fifteenth centuries.

E. SELECTED BIBLIOGRAPHY AND FURTHER READING

(1) Books

Baker, John H., *An Introduction to English Legal History*, 4th edn (London: Butterworths, 2002).

Barrow, Geoffrey W. S., *The Kingdom of the Scots*, 2nd edn (Edinburgh: Edinburgh University Press, 2003).

Barrow, Geoffrey W. S. (ed.), *The Written Acts of David I King of Scots, 1124–53, and of His Son Henry Earl of Northumberland, 1139–52* (Woodbridge: Boydell & Brewer, 1999).

Barrow, Geoffrey W. S., and W. W. Scott (eds), *The Acts of William I King of Scots 1165–1214* (Edinburgh: Edinburgh University Press, 1971).

Dickinson, William Croft, *The Sheriff Court Book of Fife 1515–1522* (Edinburgh: Scottish History Society, 1928).

Dickinson, William Croft, *Early Records of the Burgh of Aberdeen 1317, 1398–1400* (Edinburgh: Scottish History Society, 1957).

MacQueen, Hector L., *Common Law and Feudal Society*, reprinted edn (Edinburgh: Edinburgh University Press, 2016).

Neville, Cynthia, *Land, Law and People in Medieval Scotland* (Edinburgh: Edinburgh University Press, 2010).

Taylor, Alice, *The Shape of the State in Medieval Scotland* (Oxford: Oxford University Press, 2016).

(2) Chapters in Books

Broun, Dauvit, 'The property records in the Book of Deer as a source for early Scottish society', in Katherine Forsyth (ed.), *Studies on the Book of Deer* (Dublin: Four Courts Press, 2008), 313–60.

Cairns, J. W., 'Historical introduction', in Kenneth Reid and Reinhard Zimmermann (eds), *A History of Private Law in Scotland* (Oxford: Oxford University Press, 2000), 14–184 [this text constitutes further reading relevant to all chapters in this book].

Forsyth, Katherine, Dauvit Broun and Thomas Clancy, 'The property records: text and translation', in Katherine Forsyth (ed.), *Studies on the Book of Deer* (Dublin: Four Courts Press, 2008), 131–44.

Grant, Alexander, 'Franchises north of the border: baronies and regalities in medieval Scotland', in Michael Prestwich (ed.), *Liberties and Identities in the Medieval British Isles* (Woodbridge: Boydell & Brewer, 2008), 155–99.

MacQueen, Hector L., 'The Laws of Galloway: A Preliminary Survey', in Richard D. Oram and Geoffrey P. Stell (eds), *Galloway: Land and Lordship* (Edinburgh: Scottish Society for Northern Studies, 1991), 131–43.

MacQueen, Hector L., and William J. Windram, 'Laws and courts in the burghs', in Michael Lynch, Michael Spearman and Geoffrey Stell (eds), *The Scottish Medieval Town* (Edinburgh: John Donald, 1988).

Sellar, W. David H., 'The resilience of the Scottish common law', in David L. Carey Miller and Reinhard Zimmermann (eds), *The Civilian Tradition and Scots Law: Aberdeen Quincentenary Essays* (Berlin: Duncker and Humblot, 1997), 149–64.

Sellar, W. David H., 'Birlaw courts and Birleymen', in Hector L. MacQueen (ed.), *Stair Society Miscellany Seven* (Edinburgh: Stair Society, 2015), 163–77.

Taylor, Alice, 'Crime without punishment: medieval Scotland in comparative perspective', in D. Bates (ed.), *Anglo-Norman Studies 35:*

Proceedings of the Battle Conference 2012 (Woodbridge: Boydell Press, 2013), 287–304.

(3) Articles in Journals

Barrow, G. W. S., 'Popular courts in early medieval Scotland: some suggested place name evidence', *Scottish Studies* 25 (1981), 1–24.

Forte, Angelo D. M., '"A strange archaic provision of mercy": the procedural rules for the *Duellum* under the law of *Clann Duib*', *Edinburgh Law Review* 14 (2010), 418–50.

Harding, Alan, 'The medieval brieves of protection and the development of the common law', *Juridical Review* (1966), 115–49.

Sellar, W. David H., 'Celtic law and Scots law: survival and integration', *Scottish Studies* 29 (1989), 16.

Sellar, W. David H., 'Scots law: mixed from the very beginning? A tale of two receptions', *Edinburgh Law Review* 4 (2000), 3–18.

Taylor, Alice, '*Leges Scocie* and the lawcodes of David I, William the Lion and Alexander II', *Scottish Historical Review* 88 (2009), 286–8.

(4) Digital Sources

Broun, Dauvit, 'The king's brithem (Gaelic for "judge") and the recording of dispute-resolutions', in *Paradox of Medieval Scotland 1093–1286*, Feature of the month: no.11, April 2010, http://paradox.poms.ac.uk/feature/april10.html.

PART TWO

The Consolidation of the Scottish Common Law, c. 1230–c. 1450

The first part of this book explored the origins of the Scottish common law. By 1230, some procedural mechanisms had emerged that were, in principle, commonly available for the resolution of disputes arising amongst all subjects of the Scottish king. Some of those procedural mechanisms were forms of action known as the 'brieves'. Others dealt with matters that might today be termed 'criminal'.

The aim of the second section of this book will be to explore the consolidation and development of this emergent Scottish common law. Much of the surviving evidence of the operation and scope of that common law is expressed in the brieves, and so they will receive particular attention here. Chapter 2 will explore the structure of the common law that was articulated through brieves. Chapter 3 will then consider a debate that has developed recently concerning the extent to which some of these brieves were truly commonly available to *all* subjects of the Scottish king. In the process, reference will be made to the influence of the English common law on the development of the Scottish system.

Chapter 4 will then explore how Scottish kings developed common procedures to deal with criminal matters. Particular reference will be made to how those monarchs addressed the problem of robbery – that is to say, theft with violence. Increasingly, the procedures they used were designed to demonstrate that Scottish monarchs were able to deal with allegations of 'criminal' wrongdoing forcefully and swiftly. Arguably this resulted in the erosion of various protections that had been given to those accused of crimes in earlier periods. It will be suggested that much of the inspiration for this approach came from canon law, albeit that the canonist rules and principles were adapted to Scottish royal policies and purposes.

It will be argued that the Scottish common law was growing more powerful as a means of dispute resolution, thus tightening its grip during the period c. 1230–c. 1450. Yet the way in which it did this in the West

Highlands and the Western Isles calls for special attention. In those regions there may have been other systems of dispute resolution that had been established by various lords of the Isles. The interaction of the common law with the large area of the Scottish kingdom over which they presided will be discussed in the fifth chapter.

CHAPTER 2

The Brieves (Part One)

A. INTRODUCTION

During the course of the first chapter, it was shown that the Scottish realm of the eleventh and early twelfth centuries was characterised by some significant legal diversity. It was then explained that this began to change during the reigns of a series of kings, most notably William I (r. 1165–1214). He promoted a degree of 'commonality' in the application of the law across their kingdom. One mechanism through which he sought to achieve this was the royal writ or 'brieve'. Brief reference was made to the brieve of perambulation. An early version of this brieve may stand behind *Humphrey de Berkeley v Walter, son of Sibbald* (1197). But what exactly were the brieves? This question merits detailed consideration here, in part because much of the surviving evidence concerning the operation of the common law relates to the brieves.

Several of the brieves can be thought of as forms of action – that is, procedural devices to bring disputes before courts. They contained a set of royal instructions to remedy a range of particular wrongs. Suppose a man was in dispute with his neighbour. Suppose he then alleged that the neighbour had committed a wrong mentioned in one of the brieves. Subject to certain important caveats, that man would be able to approach the king for help. He could ask the king to send the relevant brieve – that is, the royal command to remedy the wrong – to one of his officers. The officers in question would have been the sheriffs or the justiciars. Those officers would then fulfil the commands in the brieve. They would ensure that the dispute was resolved according to the king's justice. Note that the brieves could not be used to deal with all disputes. Generally only those wrongs already dealt with in the brieves could be resolved by brieve. There was some flexibility in the system, allowing for new brieves to be developed to address new problems. Yet generally a litigant had to try to make his dispute 'fit' into one of the existing categories of wrong in order to litigate by brieve.[1]

It should be noted here that not all brieves were forms of action designed to remedy wrongs. Some were standardised commands to officers to investigate the truth of certain matters. For example, one of the brieves of inquest might be used to establish who had the right to inherit particular lands. Nonetheless, such brieves could still be useful in the course of litigation. This point will be discussed further below.[2]

This chapter and the next will explain these points further. In so doing, reference will be made to the story of the remarkable litigator James Douglas of Dalkeith (d. 1420). He used brieves to protect and augment his rights in various lands. The current chapter will examine, in turn, the brieves of novel dissasine, mortancestry and right. Reference will also be made to the brieves of perambulation and recognition. It should be emphasised at the outset that while the brieves were often of central importance to dispute resolution at the time, frequently they were not used in isolation. The threat of litigation by brieve was often used as a starting point for negotiation. It could even end with trial by battle. So the significance of the brieves must be explored in this context.

Having considered these matters, the next chapter will then consider the broader question of the extent to which the brieves truly gave effect to a Scottish 'common law'. One argument in favour of this position relates to the so-called brieves rule. The rule, which was recognised or established in statute in 1318, declared that a man could not be ejected from many forms of landholding that were based on feudal tenure except by means of a royal 'pleadable' brieve or another similar brieve. What this rule actually meant will be considered in detail below. Prima facie, it looks as though it meant that the brieves gave rise to a truly common law applicable in a very large number of disputes over land across the Scottish kingdom.[3] Nonetheless, the appearance may be deceptive. Some historians have pointed out that even after 1318 the royal brieves may not have had effect in various parts of the kingdom.[4] It was explained in the

---

[1] On the brieves, see generally Hector L. MacQueen, *Common Law and Feudal Society*, reprinted edn (Edinburgh: Edinburgh University Press, 2016). As regards the thirteenth-century position, this must now be read alongside Alice Taylor, *The Shape of the State in Medieval Scotland* (Oxford: Oxford University Press, 2016), 285–93, 297–334, 344–8.

[2] Taylor, *Shape of the State*, 318–19, 323–4.

[3] See MacQueen, *Common Law*, 105–13.

[4] See David Carpenter, 'Scottish royal government in the thirteenth century from an English perspective', in Matthew Hammond (ed.), *New Perspectives on Medieval*

first chapter that some of the great earls, bishops and abbots held grants of 'franchisal' jurisdiction from the king. This meant that they received delegated royal powers to administer justice within their territories in 'regality'. Regalities covered almost half of the country, and if the royal brieves did not operate there then an important question arises.[5] To what extent can the law administered through the brieves be described as a Scottish 'common' law? Put another way, if only half of the population could use the brieves system, was it truly a *common* law, available to all of the monarch's subjects? The question becomes even more pertinent when it is realised that only some of the brieves operated in the burghs.[6] Furthermore, the diverse Scottish 'men of law' who used brieves in practice may have approached these writs with widely different assumptions concerning how best to interpret them. The extent to which the brieves can be described as part of a Scottish 'common' law will be discussed further below.[7]

B. *JAMES DOUGLAS OF DALKEITH V THOMAS ERSKINE* (1368)

In 1353 William Douglas of Liddesdale, described as a man who 'had notoriously lived by the sword', was assassinated in Ettrick Forest in the south of Scotland.[8] His daughter, Mary Douglas, inherited some of his vast estates. Mary subsequently married Thomas Erskine, the son of a great Scottish nobleman. A few years later, Mary died in childbirth, and the child did not survive her. Mary's heir was her cousin, James Douglas of Dalkeith, a powerful landowner. He claimed his inheritance. But there was a problem. Mary's widower, Thomas Erskine, refused to

---

Scotland 1093–1286 (Woodbridge: Boydell Press, 2013), 117–59; Taylor, *Shape of the State*, 344–6.

5 See Alexander Grant, 'Franchises north of the border: baronics and regalities in medieval Scotland', in Michael Prestwich (ed.), *Liberties and Identities in the Medieval British Isles* (Woodbridge: Boydell & Brewer, 2008), 155–99.

6 See MacQueen, *Common Law*, 155–7.

7 The argument presented here draws to some extent on Andrew R. C. Simpson, 'Foreword: common law and feudal society in scholarship since 1993', in Hector L. MacQueen, *Common Law and Feudal Society* (Edinburgh: Edinburgh University Press, 2016), xxix–lxi. Like other works on the topic, this article must now be read in light of Taylor, *Shape of the State*.

8 The dispute is discussed in W. David H. Sellar, 'Courtesy, battle and the brieve of right, 1368 – a story continued', in W. David H. Sellar (ed.), *Stair Society Miscellany Two* (Edinburgh: Stair Society, 1984), 1–12. The quotation can be found at p. 1.

give up possession of Mary's lands. This was because he believed he had a claim to the lands based on the right known as 'courtesy'. To explain, in the situation where a woman died leaving a widower, that widower was entitled to possess and enjoy the fruits of her lands for life. In other words, the widower was entitled to a liferent of the lands once owned by his wife. This right was known as 'courtesy', and it was this that Thomas Erskine claimed in the estates of his dead wife. But there was a condition that had to be satisfied before courtesy could operate. A man could not claim courtesy in his wife's estates unless 'a child had been born of the marriage and that child had been heard to cry'.[9] The point was that the child had to have been born alive. It was undisputed that Mary Douglas had died giving birth to Thomas Erskine's child. But had the child been 'heard to cry' before it too died? Only if it had would Erskine's right to courtesy have been established. Erskine insisted that the child had been born alive. James Douglas of Dalkeith maintained the contrary. He refused to believe Erskine's claims. And it is easy to understand why. If Erskine were to succeed in his claim to courtesy – a right he would enjoy for life – Douglas would only be able to take possession of the lands on Erskine's death.

Douglas initiated litigation on this point. What was the nature of his claim? Put another way, which form of action did he use? Historians have argued that he may have used an action known as the brieve of right to make his claim. This brieve dealt with questions of ultimate feudal ownership of land. Part of this chapter will be concerned with explaining why historians think it was used in this case. As will be seen shortly, this is a useful way to introduce the system of actions relating to the protection of rights in land that the brieves expressed.

To continue with the account of the dispute, once Douglas had made his claim, Erskine responded by restating his position. This was that his child had been heard to cry. Consequently, Erskine demanded his courtesy. Thus the litigation was ultimately concerned with a matter of fact. Had the child been born alive? Both parties resolved to settle the issue by means of a judicial duel. That meant that the matter would be determined by means of a battle between them, to the death if necessary. In late 1367 and early 1368 they bought the necessary armour and weapons in London. It is recorded that Douglas bought 'a pair of plates, a haubergeon, gauntlets, a helmet, bracers and leg armour, long arms and coverings for two horses, two daggers and the head of a lance'.[10] Erskine purchased similar arms.

---

[9] Sellar, 'Courtesy, battle and the brieve', 4.
[10] Sellar, 'Courtesy, battle and the brieve', 1.

The fight itself was to take place in Edinburgh in a 'park' in front of the king, and presumably other spectators. Rather dramatically, the king, David II (r. 1329–71), intervened personally. He separated the combatants before either of them did any serious harm to the other. He led them both outside the park and organised a negotiated settlement. According to this, Erskine renounced his claim to the lands in exchange for a payment of a sum of money. Some of this came from Douglas and some of it was paid by the king himself. It may be asked why the king concerned himself with the dispute to this extent. The answer is that both Douglas and Erskine were closely related to very powerful men within the royal court. The dispute over Mary Douglas's lands might have turned into a factional political conflict and generated serious and violent disorder.

As was mentioned earlier, it is thought that James Douglas of Dalkeith may have initiated his claim on the basis of a brieve of right. The argument in favour of this view is complex and only one element of it need be considered here. Drawing on Sellar's work, MacQueen argues that two of the most important brieves used in disputes over lands – novel dissasine and mortancestry – would not have been available to Douglas. Arguably the only other brieve that he could have used in the circumstances would have been the brieve of right.[11] This brieve can be described as one that provided a remedy in many disputes over title to lands where the brieves of novel dissasine and mortancestry were not available.

These last points will be explored below. In the first place, the chapter will consider the nature of the brieves of novel dissasine and mortancestry. It will be explained that they were indeed unavailable to Douglas. It will also become clear that several other brieves – such as recognition and perambulation – do not seem to fit the surviving facts of the case. By contrast, it will be shown that the brieve of right was available to Douglas.

Some readers may wonder why all this matters. They might point out that even if the brieve of right set proceedings in motion, it achieved little more. After all, the ultimate settlement in the case was by an abortive battle and a negotiation. And yet the use of the brieve here *would* have achieved something important. It would have provided the legal mechanism through which Douglas advanced his claim against Erskine. Consequently, it would have served to force Erskine to answer Douglas's claim. Finally, it would have caused Erskine to raise the defence that his wife had given birth to a child which had been heard to cry. The rest

---

[11] See Sellar, 'Courtesy, battle and the brieve', 7–8; MacQueen, *Common Law*, 198–9.

of the story, while important, was evidently shaped by its legal context. Exploring the forms of action open to Douglas, and so the brieves, serves to illuminate that context.

C. INTRODUCING THE BRIEVES

(1) The Brieve of Novel Dissasine

In 1230 Alexander II (r. 1214–49) gathered an assembly of noblemen and clergymen at Stirling. Among them were the justiciars of the realm. There the king promulgated a series of statutes. One introduced the brieve of novel dissasine into Scots law. Note that this brieve was modelled on the English writ of novel disseisin.[12] As might be expected, it remedied the wrong of 'dissasine'. So what was a 'dissasine'?

As one historian has put it, to have 'sasine' was 'to have been put into possession of land by the grantor, typically although not invariably the lord of whom the lands were to be held'.[13] This comment must be understood in the context of the feudal relationship. Consider again the example of *Humphrey de Berkeley v Walter, son of Sibbald* (1197). In that case, it seems that Humphrey held his lands of Balfeith directly from the king. The king was the feudal lord and Humphrey his vassal. Ownership of the lands was divided between the king and Humphrey. Humphrey then granted sasine of the lands to Arbroath Abbey. Now Humphrey was the feudal lord in the relationship with Arbroath Abbey, his vassal. As a result, ownership of the lands was divided between the king, Humphrey and Arbroath Abbey. Furthermore, Arbroath Abbey held sasine of the lands from Humphrey.

Suppose that someone had then subsequently dispossessed Arbroath Abbey from the lands. This might have been some third party or Humphrey himself. In either case, the Abbey would have been *dissaised* – it would have lost sasine. The feudal relationship between lord and vassal would have been broken. As a result, the Abbey would have been able to seek justice for the wrong of *dissasine*. If the dispute had happened after

---

[12] See MacQueen, *Common Law*, 136–66; MacQueen's arguments must now be read alongside Taylor, *Shape of the State*, 285–93. For novel disseisin in England, see John H. Baker, *An Introduction to English Legal History*, 4th edn (London: Butterworths, 2002), 233–4. A version of the text of the Scottish brieve is reproduced at the end of this chapter.

[13] MacQueen, *Common Law*, 140.

1230, it could have asked the king to issue a brieve of dissasine, directing the justiciar to remedy the wrong. The remedy that the brieve of novel dissasine promised was the restoration of sasine between the dissaised and the land's lord.[14] That was exactly what the Abbey sought in a real case, *Arbroath Abbey v Sir Walter Mowbray* (1342). There the Abbey complained that Sir William 'had dissaised the abbot and convent of the abbey of Arbroath unjustly and without a judgement of various lands in the Mearns'.[15]

Note that arguments have recently been made to suggest that the brieve of novel dissasine might only have been used in practice by the very wealthy in the thirteenth century. The reason is simple. If a pursuer failed to sustain his claim in the brieve then he risked falling into the king's mercy. Arguably this meant that he would suffer the king's 'full forfeiture' of £10. This sum was about half of the annual income for an average Scottish knight in the late 1200s. Significantly, there survives the record of a case showing that one litigant who failed to sustain his claim of novel dissasine was forced to pay £10 in 1262.[16] Two other unofficial legal works compiled during the fourteenth century confirm that this was the case.[17] Against this view, it can be argued that the thirteenth-century evidence does not actually say that all litigants automatically suffered the king's 'full forfeiture'. There is other evidence to suggest that 'full forfeiture' may not have been the 'default' consequence of falling into the king's mercy. Nonetheless, the case that litigation on the brieve of novel dissasine presented great financial risk to the litigant is compelling. Here it is assumed that this argument is correct, in the absence of convincing evidence to the contrary.[18]

Regardless of this, shortly after the end of the thirteenth century, procedure on brieve was thought sufficiently significant to merit reform. To explain, the wrong of dissasine seems to have been rife during the Wars of Independence (1296–1328). During this period many of the political enemies of Robert I (r. 1306–29) had been dispossessed of their lands. Famously Robert I won the Battle of Bannockburn in 1314, resulting in the preservation of the Scottish kingship and a separate Scottish jurisdiction. By 1318, he had resolved to offer many of his former enemies the

---

[14] MacQueen, *Common Law*, 140.
[15] MacQueen, *Common Law*, 153.
[16] Carpenter, 'Scottish royal government', 148–50.
[17] Taylor, *Shape of the State*, 291–3.
[18] See also the argument pursued in Simpson, 'Foreword: common law and feudal society', xliii–xlvi.

opportunity to recover their lands. These individuals were known as the 'disinherited'. But Robert knew that that would result in some upheaval, particularly in the situation where his supporters had simply seized the lands of the disinherited. The problem was particularly acute because the king's supporters had then frequently given sasine of the lands to innocent third parties. As the law stood before 1318, only the current possessors of lands could be sued under the brieve of novel dissasine. So if a noblemen had dissaised one of the disinherited, and then had granted sasine of the lands to an innocent third party, the disinherited would not be able to sue the original dissaisor. Rather, he would be obliged to sue the innocent third party. The penalty for dissasine was £10 Scots; this was a serious fine, given that the average annual income of a knight at the time was £20 Scots, as was stated above.[19] Consequently there was a real risk that innocent third parties, and not the actual dissaisors, might suffer this penalty if the disinherited were to use the brieve of novel dissasine to recover their lands. Robert I's solution was to reform the law by statute in parliament in 1318.[20] Now a dissaised individual had to name and summon all of those involved in the original dissasine in the brieve *alongside* the current feudal vassal or 'tenant' holding the lands. As MacQueen puts it, '[a] crucial consequence was the spreading of the pains of losing the action.'[21]

Thus the brieve of novel dissasine provided a remedy for those who were dissaised of lands. In other words, it was only available to one who had once had sasine, and had then suffered wrongful loss of that sasine. Note that this explains why the use of this form of action would have been entirely inappropriate in the case of *James Douglas of Dalkeith v Thomas Erskine* (1368), mentioned above. This is because in that case Douglas had never had sasine of the lands of his cousin, Mary Douglas. Mary had inherited those lands from her father. After she died in childbirth, her widower, Thomas Erskine, retained possession of her estates. Consequently, James Douglas had neither been *saised* nor *dissaised* of the disputed lands. It followed that the brieve of novel dissasine would have been of no help to him.

---

[19]   See Carpenter, 'Scottish royal government', 148.
[20]   See Records of the Parliaments of Scotland (*RPS*) 1318/15.
[21]   MacQueen, *Common Law*, 146–53; quote is at 151. The use of novel dissasine to deal with the returning disinherited in the reign of Robert I is also discussed in Alice Taylor, 'The assizes of David I, king of Scots, 1124–53', *Scottish Historical Review* 91 (2012), 197–238 at 216–21.

(2) The Brieve of Mortancestry

The surviving evidence indicates that the brieve of mortancestry was introduced at roughly the same time as the brieve of novel dissasine. Again, it was modelled on the English writ of mort d'ancestor.[22] It was certainly available to litigants by the 1250s. So MacQueen notes that in 1253 Emma of Smeaton 'sued the abbey of Dunfermline by royal letters of mortancestry, claiming lands in the fee of Musselburgh which had been held by her father'. By the fourteenth century, the brieve enabled a litigant to make a 'claim to succeed to an immediate ancestor who had died vest and saised in lands which were now being unjustly withheld by some unentitled person'.[23]

A good example of these rules in action can be seen from another case involving James Douglas of Dalkeith, decided in 1368 (*James Douglas of Dalkeith v Roger Carruthers & Isabella Carruthers*). James claimed that his uncle, William Douglas of Liddesdale, had died with sasine ('saised') of certain lands in Peebleshire. James then stated that they were now wrongfully withheld from him by a certain Roger Carruthers and his wife, Isabella. Presumably Roger Carruthers and his wife had taken possession of the lands following William Douglas's death. James sought to remedy this by means of the brieve of mortancestry. Note that James could not use a brieve of novel dissasine in this case because he had never had sasine of the lands himself. To succeed using mortancestry, James had to show that his uncle had held sasine of the lands when he died. As a result he, as heir, should have been saised of the lands, and therefore Carruthers and his wife had no lawful basis for retaining possession.[24]

Thus the brieve was available to a litigant who was prepared to prove the following points. First, he had to show that he was the heir of a close relative – at first the relative in question had to be a parent, an uncle, an aunt or a sibling. Second, he then had to show that the relative had died saised of certain lands. Third, he had to show that those lands were now unjustly withheld by another. If the litigant could demonstrate all that, then he would be saised of the lands himself. These fundamental rules remained largely unchanged throughout the fourteenth and fifteenth

---

[22] See MacQueen, *Common Law*, 167–87; Taylor, *Shape of the State*, 308–9. For mort d'ancestor, see Baker, *Introduction*, 234.

[23] MacQueen, *Common Law*, 167. It must be emphasised that the language of the brieve may well have developed during the thirteenth century; see Taylor, *Shape of the State*, 285–93.

[24] MacQueen, *Common Law*, 175, 180.

centuries, with one major exception. From 1318 it was possible to sue on the basis of a brieve of mortancestry if one's *grandparent* had been saised of the lands in question.[25] Yet if one claimed to be the heir of a relative more distant than a parent, sibling, grandparent, uncle or aunt, then the brieve of mortancestry remained unavailable.

This in turn explains why James Douglas of Dalkeith was unable to use the brieve of mortancestry in the dispute with Thomas Erskine in 1368. He could not use this brieve because it did not allow him to lay claim to his *cousin's* lands. A cousin was a more distant relative than a parent, sibling, grandparent, uncle or aunt. Furthermore, as has already been explained, Douglas could not use the brieve of novel dissasine because he had never had sasine of those estates.

Before leaving the brieve of mortancestry, one final point should be noted. It seems that those who litigated by brieve of mortancestry did not risk being fined £10 if they failed to succeed in their action. That fine seems to have applied only to those who failed to sustain actions initiated by brieve of novel dissasine. As a result, in practice the brieve of mortancestry would presumably have been more widely available than that of novel dissasine.[26]

(3) The Brieve of Right

Sellar suggests that James Douglas may have initiated his dispute with Thomas Erskine by means of a brieve of right. Broadly speaking, the brieve of right came to provide a mechanism for laying claim to lands where the specific remedies of novel dissasine and mortancestry were not available. Yet it is possible to be more precise than this. To explain how, it is necessary to say a little more about the scope of those two brieves. It must be emphasised here that the focus of this section is on the four-teenth-century evidence. This evidence allows one to draw clear con-clusions about the relationships between the brieves of novel dissasine, mortancestry and right. However, those relationships evolved over time, and may have been understood differently in the thirteenth century.[27]

Thus far it has been said that the brieve of novel dissasine was avail-able to one who had been dissaised of lands. Yet it should now be added

---

[25] *RPS* 1318/25, read together with MacQueen, *Common Law*, 169 n. 11.

[26] See Taylor, *Shape of the State*, 309.

[27] For an important account of the thirteenth-century evidence, see Taylor, *Shape of the State*, 285–93, 297–334. Evidence concerning the scope of the thirteenth-century brieve of right is discussed in Taylor, *Shape of the State*, 315–18.

that – in its developed, fourteenth-century form – the brieve specified that it was available to one dissaised of lands where he held those lands on the basis of 'free holding'. What was a 'free holding'? MacQueen has argued that a free holding was 'in effect any life interest in land, whether or not that interest was heritable'. For example, a liferent was a free holding.[28] The liferenter saised of lands could not pass his interest to any heir. But he did have sasine of a free holding, and consequently his interest in the land could be protected by the brieve of novel dissasine. Similarly, if a man died, his widow was not entitled to courtesy, but rather terce, meaning a liferent of part of her husband's estate. Again, she would be saised of that liferent interest, meaning that she was a free holder with the protection of the brieve of novel dissasine.

Thus novel dissasine could be used to recover sasine of a free holding. But it could not, as has been seen, be used by a litigant to gain sasine of lands of which he had never been saised himself. If he sought sasine of lands as heir of a close relative, he might use the brieve of mortancestry. In that instance, his claim was clearly not simply for a 'free holding'. A free holding was not necessarily a heritable right – a right transmissible down the generations. But by definition one who used a brieve of mortancestry sought sasine of lands on the basis of a *heritable* right. That heritable interest in the lands was described as a holding 'in fee'.[29] Clearly only one who argued his ancestor was saised of lands 'as of fee' – that is to say, heritably – could hope to succeed in the brieve of mortancestry.

Thus far it has been said that novel dissasine could give a remedy to one who had been dissaised of a freehold right. Mortancestry could give a remedy to one whose ancestor had been saised of the fee in certain lands – a heritable right. Yet it has also been seen that in some cases neither novel dissasine nor mortancestry was available. In the case of *Douglas of Dalkeith v Erskine*, could Douglas have used the brieve of novel dissasine? No, he could not; he had never been saised in his cousin Mary's lands. Could he have used the brieve of mortancestry? No, he could not. He alleged he had a heritable right in the lands, but Mary was too distant a relative for his claim to operate under the terms of the brieve.

Consequently, in such cases another remedy was required. At issue was the need to establish ultimate *right* in the lands – in a feudal context – without necessarily making reference to a past sasine. The brieve of right made that possible. In short, it allowed parties to address deeper questions about rights in land. Regardless of who had last been saised of the

[28] MacQueen, *Common Law*, 157.
[29] MacQueen, *Common Law*, 157; Carpenter, 'Scottish royal government', 144.

land, who *should* have been saised? Given that the brieve of right involved such a final determination of 'just right', it might be asked why litigants bothered using novel dissasine and mortancestry at all. Presumably the answer is that it was often easier for litigants to make reference to past sasine to establish an interest in lands. Consequently novel dissasine and mortancestry were potentially useful remedies. But where they and other more appropriate remedies were unavailable, the brieve of right could be used to settle disputes over who had the ultimate right in land once and for all.[30] Note also that someone who *lost* an action based on a brieve of novel dissasine or mortancestry could still proceed to use a brieve of right to establish such an ultimate right. For this reason the Scottish medieval text *Regiam Majestatem*, probably composed during the reign of Robert I (r. 1306–29), treated the brieve of right as exceeding both novel dissasine and mortancestry in its scope. In summary, it explained that novel dissasine provided a remedy for loss of sasine of a freehold interest. Mortancestry provided a remedy for interference with lands of which the litigant's ancestor had been saised as of fee. The brieve of right enabled one to look deeper, to the underlying question of 'just right' in lands.[31] Put more simply, the brieves of novel dissasine and mortancestry dealt with claims relating to sasine, that is to say possession conferred by the feudal lord of the lands. By contrast, the brieve of right dealt with claims relating to the ultimate feudal right in the land, in modern parlance the right of 'ownership'.[32]

This is part of the reason why it is thought that James Douglas of

---

[30] See generally MacQueen, *Common Law*, 188–214. Sometimes litigants who could not use either a brieve of novel dissasine or a brieve of mortancestry might have another remedy than the brieve of right. Suppose a woman claimed a liferent interest of terce in lands but had never been saised. Could she use the brieve of novel dissasine? No, she could not; she alleged a free hold right, but no prior sasine. Could she use the brieve of mortancestry? No, she could not; she did not allege she had any heritable right 'in fee' in the lands. Her remedy lay in the brieve of terce, as discussed in MacQueen, *Common Law*, 123; Archibald A. M. Duncan, *Scottish Formularies* (Edinburgh: Stair Society, 2011), 66–8 (reference no. E37); Thomas M. Cooper, *Select Scottish Cases of the Thirteenth Century* (Edinburgh and London: William Hodge and Company, 1944), 52–3 (case no. 39).

[31] See MacQueen, *Common Law*, 205, discussing *Regiam Majestatem* (in *The Acts of the Parliaments of Scotland, 1124–1707 (APS)*, eds T. Thompson et al. (Edinburgh, 1814–75)), IV.40; Thomas M. Cooper (ed.), *Regiam Majestatem and Quoniam Attachiamenta* (Edinburgh: Stair Society, 1947), 295–7.

[32] MacQueen describes the right pursued under the brieve of right as follows; he states it was probably 'as full a right of ownership as was possible in a tenurial structure of land law.' See MacQueen, *Common Law*, 205.

Dalkeith relied upon a brieve of right in his action against Thomas Erskine.[33] Assuming he used a brieve to recover his lands, then it must have been a brieve of right. Only by means of the brieve of right could he recover the lands withheld from him by his cousin's widower. Only by showing his underlying right, as distinct from sasine, could he establish his claim. To reiterate this point once more, he could not have founded his claim on his own sasine. This was because he had never had sasine of the lands. Consequently, he could not have used novel dissasine. Nor could he have relied on his cousin's sasine as the basis of his claim. This was because she was too distant a relative for his claim to operate under the terms of the brieve of mortancestry. As a result, his claim must have been founded on his assertion that he had the ultimate right of 'ownership' in the lands.

Note that this outline reveals that the structure of the law – at least in its developed form in the fourteenth century – was sophisticated. It was also radically different from modern Scots land law.

D. CONCLUSION

The aim of this chapter has been to sketch some important elements of the structure of the law that was expressed in the royal brieves. It has not been possible to examine all of the brieves here. Nor has it been possible to consider all aspects of their historical development. Yet it is useful, by way of conclusion, to make reference to one final type of brieve – that of recognition. This is because examining it raises a problem to be considered in the next chapter.

On many levels, the brieve of recognition was quite similar to that of perambulation. One who faced a challenge to his sasine could seek a brieve of recognition. This would command 'the justiciar to "make recognition" of his or her lands, "by their right marches"'.[34] In other words, it would enable the claimant to establish the extent of his lands. The justiciar would then be obliged to ensure that the claimant would hold those lands 'firmly ... following the assize of the land'.[35] Unfortunately, that assize seems to be lost. Yet what matters here is that this brieve was

---

[33] Note that the arguments pursued in Sellar, 'Courtesy, battle and the brieve', 7–8 and MacQueen, *Common Law*, 198–9 are slightly more complex than those presented here.

[34] Taylor, *Shape of the State*, 315.

[35] Taylor, *Shape of the State*, 315.

only available to a small class of litigants. It was only available to those who held land 'in chief from the king' – that is, directly from the king.[36]

That the brieve of recognition was only available to those who held lands directly from the monarch is intriguing. Such people would generally have been high-status individuals, such as the great territorial lords mentioned in the first chapter. Likewise, while the brieve of novel dissasine was technically available to all who had been wrongfully dissaised, it seems that in practice it was only available to those who could risk a large fine of £10. Furthermore, Taylor argues during the thirteenth century the brieve of right may only have been available to those who held 'in chief' from the crown.[37]

Taken together, these points indicate that several royal brieves were primarily available to high-status, wealthy individuals. So why were they so limited in their scope? Taylor explains this phenomenon as an extension of the royal policy observed in Chapter 1. It will be recalled that William I sought to enforce his laws primarily *through* the work of great territorial lords. This policy seems to have continued into the thirteenth century. Its corollary was that kings did not seek to interfere extensively in the operation of aristocratic justice *within* the great territorial jurisdictions. Instead they preferred to exercise supervisory jurisdiction over them through the sheriffs and the justiciars, and to fine the lords if they failed to do right. Developing royal brieves to facilitate interference in the work of the franchisal courts would have been inconsistent with this policy. Obviously, where disputes arose *between* the great territorial lords, or others who held 'in chief' of the crown, then the king *would* step in. In such cases, the royal brieves of novel dissasine, recognition and right would undoubtedly have been available.

All this underlines a point made above in the introduction concerning the geographical scope of the royal brieves. Generally speaking, it seems that they could not be used in the great franchisal jurisdictions. If this is so, then to what extent did the brieves express a truly 'common' law that was available to all of the king's subjects? These questions, and several related matters, will be considered in more detail in the next chapter.

---

[36] Taylor, *Shape of the State*, 315.
[37] See Taylor, *Shape of the State*, 315–18, 326–32.

E. APPENDIX: THE BRIEVE OF NOVEL DISSASINE IN THE AYR MANUSCRIPT (1318×1329)

The king to the justiciar etc. A, by his grave complaint, has shown us that B unlawfully and without judgement dissaised him of the land of C with its appurtenances in the tenement of E within the sheriffdom of B, of which he was vest and saised for days and years as of feu or of dower or of farm for a term which has not yet past. Wherefore we command and order that, having taken safe and secure pledges from A for the prosecution of his claim, you cause a recognition to be done lawfully and following the assize of the land, by the worthy and sworn men of the locality [to decide] if it is as the said A has shown to us. If, through the said recognition, done lawfully and according to the assize of the land, you should decide it to be so, you shall cause the said A to have sasine of the said land of C with its appurtenances and, without delay, take for our need the amercement belonging to us from the above for the unlawful dissasine done by him. But if, by the same recognition, done lawfully and following the assize of the land, it appears otherwise to you, you should take for our use the amercement belonging to us from the above A for his unlawful suit.[38]

F. SELECTED BIBLIOGRAPHY AND FURTHER READING

(1) Records of the Parliaments of Scotland (*RPS*)

Act concerning the brieves rule: *RPS* 1318/15.

(2) Books

Baker, John H., *An Introduction to English Legal History*, 4th edn (London: Butterworths, 2002).

Cooper, Thomas M., *Select Scottish Cases of the Thirteenth Century* (Edinburgh and London: William Hodge and Company, 1944).

Cooper, Thomas M. (ed.), *Regiam Majestatem and Quoniam Attachiamenta* (Edinburgh: Stair Society, 1947).

---

[38] This text is taken from Taylor, *Shape of the State*, 288; the date of the Ayr Manuscript is given at 259.

Duncan, Archibald A. M., *Scottish Formularies* (Edinburgh: Stair Society, 2011).

MacQueen, Hector L., *Common Law and Feudal Society*, reprinted edn (Edinburgh: Edinburgh University Press, 2016).

Taylor, Alice, *The Shape of the State in Medieval Scotland* (Oxford: Oxford University Press, 2016).

(3) Chapters in Books

Carpenter, David, 'Scottish royal government in the thirteenth century from an English perspective', in Matthew Hammond (ed.), *New Perspectives on Medieval Scotland 1093–1286* (Woodbridge: Boydell Press, 2013), 117–59.

Grant, Alexander, 'Franchises north of the border: baronies and regalities in medieval Scotland', in Michael Prestwich (ed.), *Liberties and Identities in the Medieval British Isles* (Woodbridge: Boydell & Brewer, 2008), 155–99.

Sellar, W. David H., 'Courtesy, battle and the brieve of right, 1368 – a story continued', in W. David H. Sellar (ed.), *Stair Society Miscellany Two* (Edinburgh: Stair Society, 1984), 1–12.

Simpson, Andrew R. C., 'Foreword: Common Law and Feudal Society in scholarship since 1993', in Hector L. MacQueen, *Common Law and Feudal Society* (Edinburgh: Edinburgh University Press, 2016), xxix–lxi.

Taylor, Alice, 'Crime without punishment: medieval Scotland in comparative perspective', in D. Bates (ed.), *Anglo-Norman Studies 35: Proceedings of the Battle Conference 2012* (Woodbridge: Boydell Press, 2013), 287–304.

(4) Articles in Journals

Taylor, Alice, 'The assizes of David I, king of Scots, 1124–53', *Scottish Historical Review* 91 (2012), 197–238.

CHAPTER 3

The Brieves (Part Two)

A. INTRODUCTION

The last chapter explained how several brieves could be used to remedy a range of wrongs relating to land. It is now possible to turn to broader questions concerning the extent to which they were used in practice. Did they express a truly 'common' law, which was available to all of the Scottish king's subjects? Any attempt to answer this question in the affirmative would have to deal with a series of objections. For example, towards the end of the last chapter, it was mentioned that the authority of the royal brieves could be limited in the great franchisal jurisdictions, or even excluded altogether. Furthermore, the diverse Scottish 'men of law' who used brieves in practice may have approached these writs with widely different assumptions concerning how best to interpret them. As a result, it is difficult to be sure that the brieves would have been applied in broadly the same ways in different courts.

Consequently, some historians question the extent to which it is appropriate to speak of the brieves as expressions of a law that was truly 'common' to all of the king's subjects.[1] Their questions have generated debate, and this chapter will attempt to summarise and advance various elements of the discussion. It will begin by exploring some of the strongest evidence in favour of the view that the brieves were widely

---

[1] Contributions to the debate include Hector L. MacQueen, *Common Law and Feudal Society*, reprinted edn (Edinburgh: Edinburgh University Press, 2016); David Carpenter, 'Scottish royal government in the thirteenth century from an English perspective', in Matthew Hammond (ed.), *New Perspectives on Medieval Scotland 1093–1286* (Woodbridge: Boydell Press, 2013); Andrew R. C. Simpson, 'Foreword: common law and feudal society in scholarship since 1993', in Hector L. MacQueen, *Common Law and Feudal Society* (Edinburgh: Edinburgh University Press, 2016), xxxv–xlvi; Alice Taylor, *The Shape of the State in Medieval Scotland* (Oxford: Oxford University Press, 2016), 266–348.

used in practice and could, in principle, be used by all of the king's subjects.

B. THE BRIEVES RULE

Many arguments concerning the widespread use of brieves in practice focus on the brieves rule, which was mentioned briefly in the introduction of the last chapter. As has been explained, in 1318 Robert I gathered a parliament which reformed the rules governing novel dissasine and mortancestry. It also enacted a law in the following terms:

> no one is to be ejected from his free holding of which he claims to be vest and saised as of fee without the king's pleadable brieve or some similar brieve nor without being first reasonably summoned to a certain day and place for his free holding ...[2]

At first sight this looks like an affirmation not only of the significance and perceived utility of brieves in practice; it also looks like a rule requiring the use of the brieve in virtually all disputes over land. If no-one could be ejected from land without a brieve, surely all litigation over land – a large amount of the civil litigation of the day – depended upon procedure by brieve. That would indicate that the brieves did represent a truly common law which was not only *available* to all of the king's subjects; rather, it *had* to be used by the king's subjects. Yet, on closer inspection, that is not quite what the 1318 act just cited actually says. First, note that the brieves rule only applied where an individual had a free holding 'of which he claim[ed] to be vest and saised as of fee'. In other words, the rule only protected those who alleged they had a right *in fee* – that is, some sort of heritable right to the lands. It was not enough to allege that one simply had a free holding. So it would seem that the rule did not protect liferenters, for example.[3]

Second, note that the scope of the protection afforded by the 1318 legislation is not altogether clear. The statute states that a man could not be ejected from land without the king's 'pleadable' brieve or some similar brieve. Yet what was a pleadable brieve? Two views have emerged on the subject, one advanced by Hector MacQueen and the other by Alice Taylor. MacQueen argues that there were three broad categories

---

[2] MacQueen, *Common Law*, 106; see also *RPS* 1318/27.
[3] See the discussion in Carpenter, 'Scottish royal government', 144–5.

of brieves. These are as follows: first, there were 'pleadable' brieves; second, there were 'non-pleadable', 'non-retourable' brieves; and third, there were 'non-pleadable' but 'retourable' brieves. Examples of the pleadable brieves have already been encountered. They were the brieves of novel dissasine, mortancestry and right. Where pleadable brieves were used, 'the determination of the assize' – the word 'assize' here effectively meaning a group of men trusted to know the truth of the matter – 'was implemented by the court in which the case had been heard'. Furthermore, pleadable brieves were broad in their terms. They permitted the parties to engage in legal argument concerning what actually was in dispute in the case in question. By contrast, the non-pleadable, non-retourable brieves did not permit such legal argument. Among the non-pleadable, non-retourable brieves were those of perambulation and recognition. They could also be 'implemented by the court in which the case had been heard' – like the pleadable brieves. In this regard they were distinct from the third group of brieves – the non-pleadable yet retourable brieves. MacQueen argues that 'retourable' brieves 'commanded' a sheriff 'to hold an inquest to determine the answers to questions asked in the brieve itself, and then return, or "retour", the result taken to the king's chapel, where the next step of process would be taken'.[4] Such brieves can also be referred to as brieves 'of inquest'. Taylor has argued that their importance to the development of the law has been overlooked in the past. This important argument, together with an example of this type of brieve, will be discussed in more detail below.[5]

Taylor questions MacQueen's classification of the brieves. She argues that the category of pleadable brieves was not so clearly articulated in the late thirteenth and early fourteenth centuries as MacQueen suggests. Lists of 'pleadable' brieves dating from the reign of Robert I (r. 1306–29) vary significantly in terms of which brieves they include. Therefore, the distinctions drawn by MacQueen may have crystallised more clearly as the fourteenth century progressed. If they were not clearly understood in 1318, then it follows that the reference to the 'pleadable' brieves in the brieves rule might have been interpreted in various different ways. This, in turn, would show that the meaning of the brieves rule itself was perhaps more open to interpretation in the early fourteenth century than has previously been thought.[6] It is anticipated that the debate will continue.

---

[4] MacQueen, *Common Law*, 122–3.
[5] Taylor, *Shape of the State*, 323–48.
[6] Taylor, *Shape of the State*, 298–301.

Returning to the scope of the brieves rule, there was a third limitation on its operation. It evidently did not compel the use of *royal* pleadable brieves in all circumstances. It compelled the use of the king's pleadable brieve 'or some similar brieve'. What did the phrase 'some similar brieve' actually mean? This point will be discussed in more detail further below.

MacQueen points out that there was a fourth limitation on the brieves rule. Feudal lords did not have to use brieves when they exercised what was known as their 'disciplinary' jurisdiction. They did this by means of a procedure known as 'recognition', and it could result in the vassal temporarily losing his lands. Disciplinary jurisdiction was available where the tenant failed to render services owed to the lord, and on the basis of various particular causes of action. These included the vassal's unlicensed alienation of the lands to a third party, 'purpresture' – meaning encroachment on the lands of the lord – and 'showing the holding'.[7] 'Showing the holding' was

> an action by which, in its developed form, a lord compelled his tenant to display the charters on which he held his lands ... the aim of the process was not so much to challenge tenants' titles as to enable a lord to take stock of his tenants and the services which they owed him ... If the services had not been provided, the lord could recognosce [i.e. he could take the lands back, at least temporarily].[8]

Clearly this exception to the brieves rule could be open to abuse, a point recognised by a parliament in 1401 when it attempted to regulate recognitions further.[9] Nonetheless, the limitation of the brieves rule just mentioned *is* consistent with Taylor's general thesis that Scottish kings did not attempt to interfere extensively with the exercise of aristocratic jurisdiction.[10]

Even though all this is true, it remains the case that the brieves rule was a significant part of the medieval common law, from 1318 at the latest. Where disputes did 'touch' rights in fee – that is to say, heritable rights – then it was necessary to use a royal pleadable brieve or a similar brieve. In that sense at least, it can be argued that law-makers thought the brieves to be of sufficient utility to *compel* their use in practice in those circumstances. Yet before it can be concluded that the brieves expressed

---

[7] MacQueen, *Common Law*, 115–22.
[8] MacQueen, *Common Law*, 120–1.
[9] *RPS* 1401/2/5.
[10] Taylor, *Shape of the State*; the thesis is summarised at 438–46.

and enforced a Scottish common law, another problem must be considered. Were the brieves limited in their scope and their operation by the operation of the great franchisal jurisdictions – meaning the regalities? Some historians have advanced this argument.[11] It was also noted above that some of the brieves did not operate in the burghs. So to what extent did they express a law that was commonly available and applicable to all subjects of the Scottish kings, even after 1318?

C. THE BRIEVES AND THE COMMON LAW

This point can be debated as regards the thirteenth-century evidence with reference to the works of two historians, MacQueen and Carpenter. The debate is also relevant to the later period, as will become clear. One of Carpenter's basic arguments is that '[i]n terms of its geographical range ... the Scottish common law was not common at all' during the 1200s.[12] Part of his point is that sheriffs and justiciars were not active across the whole kingdom, and could not interfere in the great territorial regalities. Yet MacQueen's argument does anticipate such an objection. He emphasises the point that from the twelfth century onwards royal officers were given authority in principle to supervise the administration of justice in the provincial lordships. It will be recalled that the sheriff or his sergeand was to be present in such courts under the terms of the statute of 1180 discussed in the first chapter. It will also be recalled that the *judices domini regis* also had such supervisory functions in some instances. Consequently, while a royal officer might have had no authority to use his *own* court to interfere in the exercise of a lord's jurisdiction, he may have been able to do so by virtue of his supervisory jurisdiction in the *lord's* court.[13] Such a role was certainly recognised by the 1400s. By that stage parliaments permitted sheriffs to interfere in the administration of justice in regalities where their lords were thought to be failing in their duties. This will be discussed in more detail in the next chapter.

Yet this in itself does not address the extent to which the *brieves* were commonly used across the realm in administration of justice during the thirteenth century. Carpenter notes that the forms of brieves preserved in the early fourteenth century are 'quite specifically for land

---

[11] Consider, for example, Carpenter, 'Scottish royal government', 142–3; see also the more nuanced comments in Taylor, *Shape of the State*, 346–8.

[12] Carpenter, 'Scottish royal government', 143.

[13] MacQueen, *Common Law*, 42–50, 193–4.

within the sheriffdoms' – that is, outwith the great territorial lordships.[14] Nonetheless, it has been suggested in the past that royal brieves *could* be addressed to the courts of the great lords. This is so even though one might think that the terms of the grants of jurisdiction to those lords excluded the operation of royal justice. One of the most important pieces of evidence in this regard is a case of 1270–73, which will be referred to here as the Kilpatrick case. In this case, three women and their husbands disputed the right of Paisley Abbey to the lands of Kilpatrick, which were within the earldom of Menteith. As a result, the dispute was heard within the earl's court. In other words, it was held in a court of one of the great territorial jurisdictions. At one stage, towards the end of the dispute, the women and their husbands were said to have brought the case back into the earl's court following an earlier attempt at compromise. They did this '*per litteras regias*' – that is, 'by royal letters'. What exactly did that phrase mean? In 1993 MacQueen explored and then discounted the possibility that this was a reference to a brieve of novel dissasine or mortancestry. He then suggested that the challenge to the Abbey's underlying right in the lands could have been initiated by means of a brieve of right. It would then follow that a form of this brieve *could* have been addressed to the court of a major aristocratic jurisdiction.[15]

   Taylor disagrees.[16] In the process, she shows how other brieves – the brieves of inquest – may have been more widely used in practice than the better-known pleadable brieves of right, mortancestry and novel dissasine. Drawing on her detailed study of the surviving evidence, she notes that one royal brieve used in the Kilpatrick case does survive. This is not a brieve of right addressed to the earl, but rather a brieve of inquest that was addressed to the local sheriff.[17] It did what other brieves of inquest did. It instructed the local sheriff to ask local 'worthy and sworn men' a focused question. In a later period, such men came to be known as assizers. Assizers are sometimes compared to jurors, although the comparison is far from exact. Assizers were trusted to know the truth of a matter, as the 'worthy and sworn men' were in the Kilpatrick case. They were not simply trusted to consider evidence presented to them impartially. The finding of the assizers – the 'worthy and sworn men' – would be returned to the king, who *might* take further action if appropriate.

---

[14] Carpenter, 'Scottish royal government', 142.
[15] MacQueen, *Common Law*, 193–4.
[16] Taylor, *Shape of the State*, 326–32.
[17] The case is complicated by the fact that the local sheriff and the local earl were one and the same person, but it is important to distinguish the various 'hats' they wore.

In the Kilpatrick case, the question posed in the brieve of inquest was simple. Were the women who claimed the disputed lands the rightful heirs of the last man to hold them, or were they not? The 'worthy and sworn men' of the locality found that they were indeed the rightful heirs of the last holder of the disputed lands. That *could* have strengthened their claim in their dispute with Paisley Abbey. In the event, the findings of the inquest initiated by royal brieve were 'deemed sufficient', to use Taylor's words, to bring the women's case back into the court of the Earl of Menteith.[18]

Ideally historians would know more about exactly *why* the findings of the royal brieve were 'deemed sufficient' to re-open the women's case in the earl's court. Is it possible that *further* royal interference was needed to prompt this development? Further debate may emerge around this point. However, Taylor's argument that the brieve used in this case was a brieve of inquest, and not a brieve of right, is significant. If correct, it would undermine an important part of the case in favour of the view that the brieve of right could be addressed to a lord's court, at least in the thirteenth century. In making these arguments, Taylor seeks to strengthen her own broad thesis, that the royal brieves were not designed to allow kings to interfere with aristocratic jurisdictions at this time. Additionally, Taylor's analysis of the evidence reveals another potentially important point. Brieves of inquest *were* popular amongst litigants. While it seems they were not directed to the courts of the great lords, their findings could evidently have important consequences for litigation in those courts. The Kilpatrick case shows that *sometimes* they could even be used to reopen cases that had already been decided in the territorial jurisdictions. Thus establishing elements of a claim by means of a brieve of inquest – such as one's position as the heir of a deceased individual – could *influence* the exercise of aristocratic jurisdiction, even if it did not *interfere* with it directly.[19]

Nonetheless, Taylor's arguments indicate that *royal* brieves were not used extensively in the courts of the earls and the regality courts in the thirteenth century. One possible explanation of this can be found in the surviving evidence concerning the actual operation of those courts – which comes from the fifteenth and early sixteenth centuries. It seems that the earls and the lords of regality issued *their own pleadable brieves modelled on the royal equivalents*. The surviving evidence suggests that in fact the brieves issued by the lords of regality actually followed the royal

[18] For the passage in question, see Taylor, *Shape of the State*, 329.
[19] Taylor, *Shape of the State*, 323–34, 344–8.

brieves quite closely.[20] This may explain what the 1318 act meant when it said that a man could not be ejected from lands of which he claimed to be vested as of fee without the king's pleadable brieve *or some similar brieve*. Perhaps the act explicitly recognised that brieves similar to the royal brieves were commonly in use in the great regalities. If so, it was providing that the basic system of remedies outlined in the brieves was to be used across the kingdom, both within and outwith the great franchisal jurisdictions. If so, the objection that the great franchisal jurisdictions made it difficult for a truly common law to emerge across the kingdom becomes much less compelling. Taylor advances a similar argument when she emphasises that the '[l]ay aristocratic courts were supposed to operate "following the law of the land"'.[21] Seen in light of that, the rules compelling the use of brieves in cases concerned with lands held 'as of fee' can be seen as clear evidence of the emergence of a truly common law. Nonetheless it should be noted that, as in the earlier period, the monarchs did not seek to control all aspects of the administration of justice. Perhaps they did not particularly care if the definition of technical legal terms in Fife varied in its details from that used in Lennox. What did matter was that basic royal procedural standards for handling problems like novel dissasine were observed when reaching judgement.[22] That was the sort of common law the kings of Scotland fostered in the medieval period. Perhaps – and this is somewhat speculative – the supervisory roles of the sheriffs, their sergeands and, at an early period, the *judices domini regis* – were of central importance in making that sort of common law a reality.

One finds a similar, but not identical, picture in the burghs. There is evidence to show that some brieves could be addressed to the burgh courts, such as the brieve of right used in *John, son of Laurence and Marjory, daughter of Brice de Cragy, v Emma, daughter of Brice de Cragy* (1317).[23] But the burghs had their own mechanisms to remedy wrongs similar to novel dissasine, which were available in their own courts. For example, the action of 'fresh force' essentially replicated the remedy available through the brieve of novel dissasine in landward areas. Once again, there is some evidence to suggest that various

---

[20] MacQueen, *Common Law*, 112–13.

[21] Taylor, *Shape of the State*, 346–7, the passage quoted is at 347.

[22] As in the first chapter, this argument owes a considerable debt to that pursued in Alice Taylor, 'Crime without punishment: medieval Scotland in comparative perspective', in D. Bates (ed.), *Anglo-Norman Studies 35: Proceedings of the Battle Conference 2012* (Woodbridge: Boydell Press, 2013).

[23] MacQueen, *Common Law*, 189.

kings, including Robert I, sought to regulate these additional forms of action.[24]

This should hardly be surprising. In 1318 Robert I also reformed the law relating to another action frequently brought in the burghs and other local courts, known as the plea of 'wrang et unlaw'. This plea could be used to deal with a host of problems, 'including broken agreements, unpaid debts, seizure of one's goods by another, and the infliction of other injuries of various kinds'.[25] For example, in *Richard Leadbetter v John Lean* (1317), Richard Leadbetter summoned John Lean to appear in the burgh court of Aberdeen because his wife Beatrix had 'defamed and struck' him 'with wrang and unlaw' in the streets of Futty. Futty (or Fittie) was a fishing community on the edge of the city. Leadbetter assessed his damages at twenty shillings. Lean denied the wrang and unlaw, and both parties referred the matter to the testimony of their neighbours. The court held that the party who was found to be in the wrong would be in the court's mercy – this probably meaning that he or she would be liable to a fine or some appropriate punishment. MacQueen notes that '[p]resumably Beatrix' blow did not draw blood or break bone'. This is because in that case the burgh court would not have had jurisdiction over the matter. Rather, he suggests that 'we should perhaps envisage a noisy scuffle in the lanes of Futty, with Richard seeking to evade an angry woman's verbal and physical attack rather than return it'.[26]

Note that in this instance Lean's defence began with an outright denial of the case. It seems to have been a rule of pleading in such actions that such a simple denial was a necessary preliminary to any defence. But in landward areas – as opposed to the burghs – it was also then necessary to refute the claim word by word and line by line according to the very technical rules of pleading that were in force. In 1318 Robert I relaxed these rules and promulgated a statute to bring proceedings in the landward areas in line with the position in the burghs. Now a simple denial without a subsequent word-for-word refutation of the pursuer's case sufficed to make a defence valid. Again, Robert I sought to ensure that basic royal procedural standards for handling legal problems were observed when reaching judgement throughout the realm.[27]

---

[24] MacQueen, *Common Law*, 155–6.
[25] Hector L. MacQueen, 'Some notes on wrang and unlaw', in Hector L. MacQueen (ed.), *Stair Society Miscellany Five* (Edinburgh: Stair Society, 2006), 13–26 at 23.
[26] MacQueen, 'Some notes on wrang and unlaw', 20.
[27] MacQueen, 'Some notes on wrang and unlaw', particularly at 23–4; *RPS* 1318/19.

D. MEN OF LAW AND LEGAL LITERATURE

(1) The Men of Law

Let it be supposed the kings were promoting the use of a common law throughout the kingdom in this broad sense. It remains possible that the legal standards they promoted were more 'common' in their application across the realm than the above analysis suggests. Such 'commonality' in the application of the law could have been facilitated through the work of an active and relatively homogeneous legal profession. Such lawyers might have been expected to consider at least some matters concerning how best to interpret the laws as settled. They might have read technical terms in the brieves in similar ways regardless of whether they practised in the burgh of Aberdeen, the sheriff court of Fife or a regality in the highlands.

Nonetheless, it seems that there was no such organised legal profession in Scotland during the period with which this chapter is concerned. The *judices* of the twelfth and thirteenth centuries seem to have been associated with particular localities. Even if they all used the same core texts in some areas of their work, there must have been significant regional variations in their attitudes and training. It might be objected that the emergence of the *judices domini regis* indicates that monarchs were attempting to incorporate their work into the frameworks of emerging royal courts. But this does not prove that a *judex domini regis* in Angus would have interpreted rules of procedure laid down by the king in the same way as a *judex domini regis* in Fife or Buchan. Furthermore, even if the *judices* were a more homogeneous body than has been suggested here, their functions seem to have changed during the fourteenth century. At least some of them went on to become the doomsters of a later period. The doomsters were court officials whose original duties remain unclear. Eventually their role was simply to pronounce sentence of death.[28] One additional possibility is that the functions of the *judices* as repositories of legal knowledge concerning boundaries of lands and as those who administered oaths were taken over by the emerging class of notaries public. Note that Mael Brigte the *judex domini regis* was charged with the administration of an oath in *Humphrey de Berkeley v Walter, son of Sibbald* (1197), and that he also probably recorded the outcome in writing. These aspects of his work have parallels with that of the later notary public.

---

[28]   See W. David H. Sellar, 'Celtic law and Scots law: survival and integration', *Scottish Studies* 29 (1989), 3–4.

Perhaps further attention should be given to the possibility that some *judices* are absent from the later records because they acquired the training of notaries public and were then referred to as such.

Notaries public should be briefly mentioned here too.[29] Essentially they recorded legal acts and transactions in written documents. Once authenticated by notaries such documents were frequently termed 'instruments' in the records. Often it is possible to find statements that a party 'asked an instrument' or 'took an instrument' concerning a particular matter. This usually meant that he sought or received a document authenticated by a notary that recorded the transaction. Frequently notaries recorded acts of sasine, the creation of rights in security in land, such as wadsets and reversions, marriage contracts, oaths that had been sworn and last wills and testaments. Sometimes they also recorded 'procuratories', by which individuals would appoint 'procurators' to act and plead on their behalf in disputes in court.

Very few notaries have been traced in Scotland in the thirteenth-century records. Their numbers increased somewhat in the fourteenth century, and much more significantly in the fifteenth century. Nonetheless, even by the fifteenth century the extent to which they can be thought of as part of a homogeneous Scottish legal 'profession' is open to question. Various different parties came to have the right to create notaries. At first all had to be appointed on papal or imperial authority, but from 1469 James III (r. 1460–88) claimed this privilege on the basis that he was an emperor within his own realm – a claim that will be discussed in more detail below. From that point onwards, Scottish bishops had authority to appoint notaries with power to act within Scotland, and sometimes this power was delegated. This facilitated the great increase in the numbers of notaries active during the fifteenth century, but not necessarily consistency in the exercise of the power. As regards their qualifications, notaries were expected to have sufficient Latin to draft legal documents and also training in penmanship, but the legal styles that they used in practice might vary depending upon which senior notary trained them. Furthermore, while some were educated in Roman law and canon law in continental universities, others were simply educated

[29] For what follows concerning the work of notaries, see John Durkan, 'The early Scottish notary', in Ian B. Cowan and Duncan Shaw (eds), *The Renaissance and Reformation in Scotland. Essays in honour of Gordon Donaldson* (Edinburgh: Scottish Academic Press, 1983), 22–40. See also W. W. Scott, 'William Cranston, Notary Public *c* 1395–1425, and some contemporaries', in Hector L. MacQueen (ed.), *Stair Society Miscellany Seven* (Edinburgh: Stair Society, 2015), 125–32.

in local parish schools and apprenticed to senior notaries. Additionally, very little is known about the regulation of notaries in the period with which this chapter is concerned. Consequently, the extent to which notarial practice in the drafting and execution of legal documents was broadly uniform is open to question.

A similar point can be made about the men of law who pleaded the cases of clients in the courts.[30] Did they in any sense form a 'profession' which might have been expected to interpret at least some legal concepts in a broadly uniform manner? Undoubtedly there is considerable evidence to show that such '*procuratores*' were active. Yet there seems to have been great diversity in their educational backgrounds. While some were trained in Roman and canon law, exactly what legal learning the others possessed is unclear. Furthermore, additional research needs to be carried out to establish the extent to which procurators who were familiar with the work of one court – such as the burgh court in Aberdeen – might also have had the skills and knowledge required to plead in other courts – such as the local sheriff and ecclesiastical courts. Such a study might reveal the extent to which common assumptions concerning the interpretation of legal terms operated across jurisdictions.

Yet, given the state of historical research into such matters at present, it remains plausible to argue that the procurators were characterised by great diversity in the ways in which they handled legal questions. However, at least one king – James I (r. 1406–37) – did attempt to regulate the conduct of some who pleaded in the courts. So in 1426 a parliament promulgated legislation declaring that 'nane be admyttyt till be attournay in the justis ayre' – the justice ayre being a reference to the justiciar's court as it went on circuit around the country –

> bot geyff he be ane honest, sufficiande persoune of discretioune for that offyce, the quhilk sall be knawin throu the justis and the barouns than beand present geyff ony dout be tharoff.[31]

This can be rendered in modern English as follows:

> unless he may be an honest, sufficient person of discretion for that office, the which shall be determined by the justiciar and the barons then being present, if there shall be any doubt.

---

[30] Regarding such procurators, the discussion in MacQueen, *Common Law*, 75–84 is a useful starting point.

[31] *RPS* 1426/12.

In other words, the justiciar and the barons present in the justiciar's court in a locality were given charge of determining who was and who was not qualified to plead in that forum. Obviously that would have affected who was entitled to plead in cases begun by brieves of novel dissasine and mortancestry, which were heard before the justiciar.

(2) The Legal Literature

It would be unsafe to conclude from such evidence alone that there existed, even in the justiciar's court, a body of men with similar training and assumptions concerning how at least some elements of the law should be interpreted in practice. Yet it must be emphasised that many notaries and procurators *do* seem to have accepted that there was such a thing as a Scottish common law. Importantly, they also seem to have recognised that it found expression in sources other than the common forms of procedure promoted by the king. Those sources were certain authoritative legal texts. Their role within the legal system can be introduced with reference to a statute promulgated by James I in March 1426. This appointed six commissioners from each estate of the realm (i.e. the clergy, the nobility and the burgesses) to 'se and examyn the bukis of law of this realme, that is to say Regiam Majestatem, Quoniam Attachiamenta'. The aim of the commission was to ensure

> that all lauchefull exceptioune of law be admittit, and all frivolus and fraudfull exceptioune be repulsyt and put away be the jugeis, sa that the causis be nocht prolongit wrangwisly in scath and prejudice of the party and fraude of the law.[32]

This can be rendered in modern English as follows:

> that all lawful exceptions of law should be admitted, and all frivolous and fraudulent [i.e. illegitimate] exceptions should be repelled and put away by the judges, so that disputes should not be prolonged wrongfully, to the harm and prejudice of the party and in fraud of the law.

Thus the commissioners were expected to study the texts and to determine authoritatively what 'lauchefull exceptioune[s]' of law they permitted. What did that mean? 'Exceptions' are defences to actions. An example can

[32] *RPS* 1426/13.

be seen from *James Douglas of Dalkeith v Thomas Erskine* (1368), discussed above. Arguably, Douglas sued Erskine by means of the brieve of right for the lands once owned by Erksine's widow. Erskine responded with a defence or exception that Douglas should not be given sasine of the lands. This was *because* Erskine was entitled to the liferent right of courtesy in his dead wife's estates. This exception to Douglas's claim was of a very simple nature. Yet over time men of law seem to have developed increasingly numerous and complex exceptions to the brieve of right and other such forms of action. Of course, that would have caused the legal system to become more sophisticated. Yet it would also have had the potential to cause procedural delay as more and more exceptions came to be recognised in the practices of various courts. One aim of the commission, then, was to distinguish which exceptions were 'lauchefull' and which were 'frivolus and fraudfull'. To achieve this end, the commissioners were to 'se and examyn' the texts *Regiam Majestatem* and *Quoniam Attachiamenta*. Those texts had authority as 'bukis of law of this realme' and so could be trusted to reveal which exceptions were lawful, and which were not.

Thus, in 1426 parliament thought the texts known as *Regiam* and *Quoniam* enjoyed a special place within the legal system. They provided authoritative guidance concerning which defences could – and could not – be raised against actions in court. In other words, they enabled courts to interpret the extent to which those actions might be limited by exceptions. Put another way, the texts facilitated the interpretation of the *scope* of the actions. It should be admitted here that one group of manuscript witnesses of the 1426 act also indicate that the commissioners were empowered to 'mend' the texts of *Regiam* and *Quoniam*. What that meant is unclear, and it is possible the instruction did not actually form part of the original statute. Even if it did, it remains clear that *Regiam* and *Quoniam* were treated as generally authoritative guides to lawful exceptions – albeit that the texts were in need of 'mending'.

So what were *Regiam* and *Quoniam*? *Regiam* was written as a guide to pleading in the courts; at least at the outset, its focus was on the royal courts.[33] By contrast, *Quoniam* 'in its essentials' focused on procedure in the feudal courts of the barons; its alternative name was the *Leges Baronum*.[34] Based on internal evidence, both were probably composed in the first half of the fourteenth century. More precisely, it is widely thought that *Regiam* may have been written towards the end of the reign

---

[33] Consider *Regiam Majestatem* in *The Acts of the Parliaments of Scotland, 1124–1707* (*APS*), eds T. Thompson *et al.* (Edinburgh, 1814–75), I.4–28.

[34] T. David Fergus, *Quoniam Attachiamenta* (Edinburgh: Stair Society, 1996), 60–1.

of Robert I, during the 1320s.[35] The identity of the author of the work is unknown. Yet the inclusion of ideas drawn from canon law in one section of the treatise may indicate that he was a canonist by training.[36] Nonetheless, the major source relied upon by the compiler of *Regiam* was not canon law, but rather an English treatise. This is known as *Glanvill*, and it was probably composed in the late 1180s. The work was written to aid those pleading in the courts of Henry II of England (r. 1153–89).[37] The extent to which this was seen as an effective guide to pleading in the Scottish royal courts in the thirteenth century is unclear. In the Berne Manuscript of c. 1270, a copy of *Glanvill* is bound together with two other Scottish legal compilations. These are the *Leges Burgorum*, or laws of the burghs, and the *Leges Scocie*, or the laws of Scotland.[38] The latter text contains materials largely dateable to the reign of William I (r. 1165–1214). Yet the extent to which thirteenth-century Scottish men of law saw *Glanvill* as relevant to their practice is unclear. What is certain is that whoever compiled *Regiam* saw *Glanvill* as an excellent starting point for a discussion of the common law of Scotland. It should also be emphasised that the compiler of *Regiam* did not follow *Glanvill* slavishly. Rather, he adapted *Glanvill* in light of sources similar to the *Leges Scocie* to take distinctively Scottish practices and rules into account. About the first third of *Regiam* is heavily edited in this way. There then follows a section that is *Glanvill* lightly edited. Some believe that this indicates the work of the compiler was interrupted, and perhaps that the completion of the work was rushed. Finally, towards the end of the work, there can be found a series of Scottish rules concerned primarily with what today would be called criminal matters.[39]

---

[35] Fergus, *Quonium*, 106–7; Archibald A. M. Duncan, '"Regiam Majestatem": a reconsideration', *Juridical Review* (1961), 199–217; but note that the general view that the text was written after 1318 is open to challenge. See Alice Taylor, 'The assizes of David I, king of Scots, 1124–53', *Scottish Historical Review* 91 (2012), 234–5, 236–7. Taylor does not seem to dispute an early fourteenth-century date for *Regiam*; see Taylor, 'Crime without punishment', 296.

[36] See Peter Stein, 'The source of the Romano-canonical part of *Regiam Majestatem*', *Scottish Historical Review* 48 (1969), 107–23.

[37] See John H. Baker, *An Introduction to English Legal History*, 4th edn (London: Butterworths, 2002), 175–6.

[38] See Alice Taylor, '*Leges Scocie* and the lawcodes of David I, William the Lion and Alexander II', *Scottish Historical Review* 88 (2009), 207–88; the *Leges Burgorum* are considered in Hector L. MacQueen and William J. Windram, 'Laws and courts in the burghs', in Michael Lynch, Michael Spearman and Geoffrey Stell (eds), *The Scottish Medieval Town* (Edinburgh: John Donald, 1988), 208–27.

[39] See Thomas M. Cooper (ed.), *Regiam Majestatem and Quoniam Attachiamenta* (Edinburgh: Stair Society, 1947), 20–2, 32–40.

It is worth noting in passing that *Quoniam* is not based on any English or canonist text.

Earlier it was said that in 1426 *parliament* treated *Regiam* and *Quoniam* as forming an authoritative guide to the Scottish common law. Can the same be said of fourteenth-century and fifteenth-century Scottish notaries and procurators? As regards the fourteenth century, the evidence is very thin. Nonetheless, the reputation of the works as statements of the Scottish common law by 1426 was presumably based on their use in practice, at least to some extent. It is not unreasonable to suggest that this reputation – and so the texts themselves – may have had fourteenth-century origins. In the case of *Quoniam* there is also more concrete evidence that the text enjoyed the respect of men of law prior to 1426. This can be found in a work named *Omne Gaderum*. *Omne Gaderum* was written in 1425 by one William Kinnaird, clerk of the St Andrews diocese and notary public by imperial authority. Rather curiously, he chose to note that he began to write following a good breakfast, with his dog 'Flowry' and his cat 'Wery-ratoune' (Worry-rat) with him as witnesses. In introducing the work, he said that he had written to collect together older legal materials both ecclesiastical and civil that were not to be found in the *Leges Baronum* and the *Leges Burgorum*. The implication may be that he saw the *Leges Baronum* and the *Leges Burgorum* as authoritative yet incomplete guides to the law; and it seems plausible to suggest that Kinnaird meant to refer to *Quoniam* when he spoke of the *Leges Baronum*, given that that was *Quoniam*'s alternative title.[40]

If so, William Kinnaird was not alone among fifteenth-century men of law in treating *Quoniam* in this way. MacQueen cites a series of cases that show that *Regiam* and *Quoniam* were used in practice. Examples include *Montrose v Dundee* (1448) and *Gilbert Lord Kennedy v Robert Lord Fleming* (1466). The latter case was initiated by a brieve of mortancestry by Lord Kennedy. He sought various lands in which his brother John had been saised. In response, Lord Fleming, the feudal lord of the lands, argued that John, his vassal, had committed treason against the king. Relevant to this was a passage in *Regiam*, which provided that the lands of *convicted* traitors were to pass to the king for a year and a day. After that they were to revert to the traitor's feudal lord – in this case, Lord Fleming. The problem for Lord Fleming was that he could not prove John Kennedy had actually been *convicted* of treason. All that he could show was that he had been imprisoned in Stirling for the crime in 1430. Subsequently he

---

40 On *Omne Gaderum*, see Athol L. Murray, 'The town clerk of Perth's *Liber Omne Gaderum*, 1425', *Scottish Archives* 5 (1999), 63–6.

had mysteriously disappeared. Interestingly – in a sign of things to come – Lord Fleming's man of law argued that the lack of a conviction was potentially no obstacle in this case. This was because a constitution of the Roman Emperor Marcus Aurelius, found in the *Codex* of Justinian, permitted the conviction of traitors after their deaths. Here historians witness the use of *Regiam* to establish the scope of the brieve of mortancestry, and the use of Roman law to augment and so interpret provisions in *Regiam*. Lord Fleming expressly stated that Lord Kennedy's claim could not succeed 'be any law of Scotland or be law canon or civile'. The increasing role of Roman law and canon law in late medieval and early modern Scotland will be discussed in subsequent chapters.[41]

E. CONCLUSION

It was argued above that thirteenth- and fourteenth-century Scottish kings promoted the use of broadly common procedural standards in the administration of justice. In this sense they encouraged the development of a Scottish common law. Yet the final sections of this chapter have advanced the view that at least some men of law thought the common law was something more than that. Together with parliament, they took the view that the forms of action recognised at common law could be interpreted and developed in light of authoritative legal literature. That literature included the texts *Regiam Majestatem*, *Quoniam Attachiamenta* and the *Leges Burgorum*. Other treatises came to be commonly used by men of law in practice too. They included collections of statutes and short works on subjects such as obligations and 'tailzies'. (Tailzies were feudal devices that altered the normal order of feudal succession to heritage, normally in favour of heirs male.)[42]

Nonetheless, there may well have remained great diversity in the approaches of the men of law to the interpretation of the brieves and these authoritative texts. This can be assumed due to a variety of factors, including their widely divergent educational backgrounds and professional activities. But it can also be assumed due to the fact that texts such as *Regiam* and *Quoniam* were transmitted in 'relatively uncritical

---

[41] MacQueen, *Common Law*, 95–8, 182–3.
[42] See, for example, National Library of Scotland (NLS) MS Advocates 7.1.9 f.48ʳ; British Library (BL) MS Harley 4700 f.256ᵛ-257ʳ; Gretton, 'Feudal system', para. III.

and private' manuscript traditions.[43] Scribal errors and interpolations caused multiple versions of *Regiam* and *Quoniam* to circulate in practice. Consequently it became unclear which versions of the texts were actually authoritative. This was such a significant problem that in 1469 parliament considered 'the reductione of the kingis lawis, *Regiam Majestatem*, actis, statutis and uthir bukis' into 'a volum and tobe autoriyit [authorised]'. In other words, there would be one, single authoritative text of *Regiam*. The 'laif' – the remaining manuscripts – were 'to be distroyit'.[44] The project – if it got off the ground at all – did not achieve these aims. Yet confusion as regards the content of the Scottish common law came to be a significant problem. For these and other reasons the brieves, together with the medieval Scottish common law structured around them, were increasingly found inadequate to meet the needs of litigants in practice. The precise nature of the problems, and how Scottish kings and men of law reacted to them, will be traced in subsequent chapters. It will be shown that, in the process, the common law heritage came to be transformed in light of the learning of Roman law and canon law.

F. SELECTED BIBLIOGRAPHY AND FURTHER READING

(1) Records of the Parliaments of Scotland (*RPS*)

Act concerning the brieves rule: *RPS* 1318/15.
Act concerning those admitted to plead in the Justice Ayre: *RPS* 1426/12.
Act concerning *Regiam Majestatem* and *Quoniam Attachiamenta*: *RPS* 1426/13.
Act concerning *Regiam Majestatem* and law books: *RPS* 1469/34.

(2) Books

Baker, John H., *An Introduction to English Legal History*, 4th edn (London: Butterworths, 2002).
Cooper, Thomas M., *Select Scottish Cases of the Thirteenth Century* (Edinburgh and London: William Hodge and Company, 1944).
Cooper, Thomas M. (ed.), *Regiam Majestatem and Quoniam Attachiamenta*

---

[43]   Hector L. MacQueen, '*Regiam Majestatem*, Scots law, and national identity', *Scottish Historical Review* 74 (1995), 1–25 at 15.
[44]   *RPS* 1469/34.

(Edinburgh: Stair Society, 1947).

Duncan, Archibald A. M., *Scottish Formularies* (Edinburgh: Stair Society, 2011).

Fergus, T. David, *Quoniam Attachiamenta* (Edinburgh: Stair Society, 1996).

Frankot, Edda, *'Of Laws of Ships and Shipmen': Medieval Maritime Law and its Practice in Urban Northern Europe* (Edinburgh: Edinburgh University Press, 2012).

MacQueen, Hector L., *Common Law and Feudal Society*, reprinted edn (Edinburgh: Edinburgh University Press, 2016).

Taylor, Alice, *The Shape of the State in Medieval Scotland* (Oxford: Oxford University Press, 2016).

(3) Chapters in Books

Carpenter, David, 'Scottish royal government in the thirteenth century from an English perspective', in Matthew Hammond (ed.), *New Perspectives on Medieval Scotland 1093–1286* (Woodbridge: Boydell Press, 2013), 117–59.

Durkan, John, 'The early Scottish notary', in Ian B. Cowan and Duncan Shaw (eds), *The Renaissance and Reformation in Scotland. Essays in honour of Gordon Donaldson* (Edinburgh: Scottish Academic Press, 1983), 22–40.

Grant, Alexander, 'Franchises north of the border: baronies and regalities in medieval Scotland', in Michael Prestwich (ed.), *Liberties and Identities in the Medieval British Isles* (Woodbridge: Boydell & Brewer, 2008), 155–99.

MacQueen, Hector L., 'Some notes on wrang and unlaw', in Hector L. MacQueen (ed.), *Stair Society Miscellany Five* (Edinburgh: Stair Society, 2006), 13–26.

Scott, W. W., 'William Cranston, Notary Public *c* 1395–1425, and some contemporaries', in Hector L. MacQueen (ed.), *Stair Society Miscellany Seven* (Edinburgh: Stair Society, 2015), 125–32.

Simpson, Andrew R. C., 'Foreword: common law and feudal society in scholarship since 1993', in Hector L. MacQueen, *Common Law and Feudal Society* (Edinburgh: Edinburgh University Press, 2016), xxix–lxi.

Taylor, Alice, 'Crime without punishment: medieval Scotland in comparative perspective', in D. Bates (ed.), *Anglo-Norman Studies 35: Proceedings of the Battle Conference 2012* (Woodbridge: Boydell Press, 2013), 287–304.

(4) Articles in Journals

Duncan, Archibald A. M., '"Regiam Majestatem": a reconsideration', *Juridical Review* (1961), 199–217.

MacQueen, Hector L., '*Regiam Majestatem*, Scots law, and national identity', *Scottish Historical Review* 74 (1995), 1–25.

Murray, Athol L., 'The town clerk of Perth's *Liber Omne Gaderum*, 1425', *Scottish Archives* 5 (1999), 63–6.

Stein, Peter, 'The source of the Romano-canonical part of *Regiam Majestatem*', *Scottish Historical Review* 48 (1969), 107–23.

Taylor, Alice, 'The assizes of David I, king of Scots, 1124–53', *Scottish Historical Review* 91 (2012), 197–238.

CHAPTER 4

'Crimes'

A. INTRODUCTION

During the course of the previous chapter, it was explained that the Scottish monarchs of the thirteenth, fourteenth and fifteenth centuries fostered the development of a 'common' law within their realm. They sought to ensure that basic royal procedural standards for handling problems like novel dissasine were observed when reaching judgement. Some of the procedural mechanisms that they used to achieve this goal were considered. Particular reference was made to the brieves of novel dissasine, mortancestry and right. Of course, the kings promoted the use of many other such brieves. Among them were the brieves of recognition and perambulation, which have already been mentioned, and the brieves of compulsion and distress. These last two brieves could be used to deal with debts. All this serves to underline the point that the brieves were designed to deal primarily with what modern lawyers would call 'civil' disputes. Yet what can be said about 'criminal' prosecutions? Did the Scottish kings seek to enforce broadly common procedural standards for use in relation to such matters too?

On one level, the question is badly formulated. This is because medieval law-makers and men of law did not always draw sharp distinctions between civil and criminal pleas. Nonetheless, the distinction can be found in *Regiam Majestatem*.[1] This text distinguished civil from criminal pleas by making reference to the *penalty* for criminal pleas. A criminal penalty *could* involve the shedding of blood, death or mutilation. It will become clear in this chapter that the threat of such punishments did

---

[1] *Regiam Majestatem* in *The Acts of the Parliaments of Scotland, 1124–1707 (APS)*, eds T. Thompson *et al.* (Edinburgh, 1814–75), I.1; see also the useful discussion of the point in Alice Taylor, *The Shape of the State in Medieval Scotland* (Oxford: Oxford University Press, 2016), 135–52.

indeed hover over the heads of those convicted of crimes. Yet convicts could frequently obtain remissions or pardons in exchange for the payment of money.[2] This chapter will follow *Regiam* in treating 'criminal' pleas as a particular category of pleas, meriting attention in their own right. Nonetheless, it must be emphasised again that such an approach risks anachronism. This would arise if it were to be assumed that the distinction adopted in *Regiam* between the civil and the criminal was universally – or even widely – followed in practice.

Regiam went on to state that some criminal pleas pertained to the king or to the justiciar. Among them were the pleas of murder, rape, robbery and arson. Of course, kings could – and often did – transfer the right to hear such pleas to the great lords of regality. By contrast pleas of theft and homicide could, in certain circumstances, be heard by the sheriffs. Alternatively they might be heard by bishops, abbots, provosts of burghs or barons, if their original feudal grants permitted this.[3] So it was quite common for the barons to receive grants carrying the right to administer justice '*cum furca et fossa*' – with pit and gallows. In other words, they had the right to mete out capital punishment.[4] This applied in cases of theft and homicide, where the homicide did not constitute murder. The definition of 'murder' will be considered further below. For now it suffices to say it was a homicide committed in secret.

From the thirteenth century onwards, criminal pleas were dealt with within this complex jurisdictional framework. But did monarchs promote the idea that common procedural standards were to be used throughout the realm in the prosecution of such matters? And to what extent did they tolerate diversity in the definition, prosecution and punishment of crime? These questions can be considered through the lens of one important case: the case of the sons of the Wolf of Badenoch and their accomplices (1392).[5]

---

[2] See Christopher H. W. Gane, 'The effect of a pardon in Scots law', *Juridical Review* (1980), 18–46 at 18–21 (which admittedly focuses on evidence drawn from a later period).

[3] *Regiam Majestatem (APS)*, I.2.

[4] John W. Cairns, 'Historical introduction', in Kenneth Reid and Reinhard Zimmermann (eds), *A History of Private Law in Scotland* (Oxford: Oxford University Press, 2000) I, 14–184 at 25.

[5] The argument presented in this chapter draws heavily upon Andrew R. C. Simpson, 'Procedures for dealing with robbery in Scotland before 1400', in Andrew R. C. Simpson, Scott Crichton Styles, Euan West and Adelyn L. M. Wilson (eds), *Continuity, Change and Pragmatism in the Law. Essays in Memory of Professor Angelo Forte* (Aberdeen: Aberdeen University Press, 2016), 95–149.

B. THE SONS OF THE WOLF OF BADENOCH AND THEIR ACCOMPLICES (1392)

In 1392 a host of highland raiders from Perthshire descended upon lowland Angus. The attackers plundered and burned the fertile farmlands.[6] They then made for the hills, carrying off with them a great deal of cattle. The local sheriff, Sir Walter Ogilvy, together with the crusading knight Sir David Lindsay of Glenesk, pursued them with a small force. Lindsay and the sheriff caught up with the highlanders, but they were defeated in battle. The sheriff was killed, and Lindsay had to be removed from the field when he tried to fight on after being impaled on a highlander's sword.

The raid could not go unanswered. Robert Stewart, the Earl of Fife and governor of the realm in the stead of his brother, Robert III (r. 1391–1406), summoned a parliament to respond. The matter was particularly serious, because among the ring-leaders of the raid were members of the royal family. They were the sons of Alexander Stewart, Earl of Buchan and Lord of Badenoch, brother of the king and the Earl of Fife. This betrays the fact that the raid was not simply motivated by a desire for plunder. Its roots lay in a complex power struggle between three brothers – the king, Fife and Buchan.[7] These men had inherited and wrestled with a power vacuum in the central highlands. Theoretically the area was in the hands of great earls and lords of regality, but earlier in the century those houses had run into dynastic difficulties that weakened their position. As a result, numerous warring kindreds had risen to prominence across the region. They sought to augment their power through violence and through cattle-raiding. One of Buchan's achievements during his father's reign had been to bring some order to this chaotic situation. But his methods had been unorthodox, to say the least. He maintained an army of 'caterans' – a term derived from a Gaelic word meaning a troop of soldiers – to establish control of the region. And the caterans had to be fed. Buchan's solution was, in part, to allow them to raid the lands of his enemies to sustain themselves. Sometimes those enemies included vassals of the powerful bishops of Moray and Aberdeen. In 1384 they complained to Buchan's eldest brother, the Earl of Carrick and future king Robert III. Subsequently, Carrick's failure to curb Buchan's power

---

[6]   See *RPS* 1392/3/1; see also David Laing (ed.), *The Orygynale Cronykil of Scotland by Androw of Wynton Vol. III* (Edinburgh: William Paterson, 1879), 58–60.

[7]   For the discussion of the politics of the period that follows, see Stephen Boardman, *The Early Stewart Kings. Robert II and Robert III* (Edinburgh: John Donald, 1996).

effectively cost him his position of power within the government. This was seized by his brother, the Earl of Fife. From 1388, Fife sought to undermine Buchan's position in the north, with the support of the Bishop of Moray. For example, he stripped Buchan of his office of justiciar north of the Forth. In 1390 Buchan's response was to burn down the bishop's cathedral at Elgin, and a period of conflict followed. For such deeds Buchan came to be remembered as the 'Wolf of Badenoch' among lowland Scots.

After their father's death in 1391, Carrick, Fife and Buchan were briefly reconciled. Carrick became king, but Fife retained his role as governor of the kingdom. Yet Buchan still felt threatened. Tensions escalated, and, as mentioned above, in early 1392 his sons allied themselves with *Clann Donnachaidh* (from which the later Clan Robertson emerged) and raided lowland Angus. Having burned and looted the countryside, they killed the sheriff of Angus in battle and retreated into the mountains.

Under Fife's leadership parliament did not take long to react. It promulgated an act in March 1392 that strongly condemned the raid.[8] The raiders were accused of robberies, acts of arson, homicides and destruction of the country. Yet parliament did not summon the ring-leaders and their long list of alleged accomplices to answer for their crimes. Parliament simply ordered the northern sheriffs to declare the wrongdoers to be outlaws, and to condemn them to death. In so doing, the act stated that the crimes of the wrongdoers were 'notorious'. The significance of this – if any – will be discussed further below.

All this may seem rather startling. One might think that the alleged accomplices of the ring-leaders of the raid, if not the ring-leaders themselves, would have been entitled to some sort of trial in person. Yet would this normally have been the case? How were crimes like robbery and homicide actually dealt with? Were there common procedural rules and protections that applied to all subjects of the Scottish king when accused of such wrongs? And if there were such protections, why were they apparently waived in the case of the sons of the Wolf of Badenoch? Is it possible that the Stewart government saw the highlands as a particularly lawless region where normal rules of law might be suspended in order to secure basic levels of order? These questions will be considered below in turn.

---

[8] *RPS* 1392/3/1.

C. COMMON PROCEDURES FOR DEALING WITH CRIMES?

(1) Accusatorial Procedure

Some of the best surviving evidence concerning how crimes were dealt with around about 1200 relates to the wrongs of theft and robbery. Robbery was probably understood as theft with violence. Some evidence suggests that even at this early period, robbery had to be tried in the court of the justiciar (or justice), at least in theory. However, it would also seem that there was a procedure for establishing who should be accused of robbery – or theft – that did not have to be dealt with before the justiciar's court. This was outlined in *Leges Scocie* capitulum 1, which was probably produced in the reign of William I (r. 1165–1214).[9] There is some evidence to suggest that the basic procedures it employed had roots in the reign of David I (r. 1124–53). *Leges Scocie* cap. 1 explained that if someone was robbed he could seek redress by tracking down his cattle. He would then formally accuse the possessor of robbery. It is not clear which official he had to approach to do this. This probably reflects a period in which the jurisdictional frameworks of a later period were only beginning to take shape.[10] The initial accusation could probably be made before the sheriff or a feudal lord. The cattle would then be impounded, and carried to a place of protection. But the accusation would not proceed straight to proof. The accused was entitled to respond that he had not robbed or stolen the cattle, but bought or received them from someone else. Obviously that third party might have been the real robber. In any event, he might be able to attest to the innocence of the accused. The third party was described in *Leges Scocie* cap. 1 as the accused's 'warrantor'. *Leges Scocie* cap. 1 then outlined a series of rules concerning how the warrantor was to be compelled to attend.

If the accused could not produce a warrantor, then the matter was to proceed to trial. How was guilt or innocence established? Modern readers might expect that a judge or a jury would determine this. But at this period among the available methods of proof were those made by fire, water and battle. Such trials can be termed 'trials by ordeal'. Sometimes other forms of proof were possible – such as proof of one's

---

[9] See Alice Taylor, '*Leges Scocie* and the lawcodes of David I, William the Lion and Alexander II', *Scottish Historical Review* 88 (2009), 223–6, 280–1; the law is also discussed in Taylor, *Shape of the State*, 144–7.

[10] See Taylor, *Shape of the State*, 152–64.

innocence through the oaths of good men, or (probably) through the tes-timony of two eye-witnesses. Some burgesses jealously guarded the priv-ilege of having their guilt or innocence determined by the oaths of their neighbours.[11] But outside these communities of burgesses the ordeal was also possible, and could sometimes be demanded by the accused. It could take various forms. For example, in trial by fire, red-hot metal might be applied to the accused's flesh. His guilt or innocence would be established with reference to whether or not his wound had festered after a few days. As Baker puts it, 'if the burn had festered, God was taken to have decided against the party'. In the ordeal of cold water, the accused would be 'trussed and lowered into a pond; if he sank, the water was deemed to have "received him" with God's blessing, and so he was quickly fished out.'[12]

Trial by combat was somewhat different. There the litigants would literally fight to determine who was in the right. The rationale for using such methods of proof was again based on the assumption that God's judgement was active at all times in this world. Clerics would ask God to intervene to declare his will through the ordeal. They might bless the instruments to be used in the trial. The parties might also commend themselves to God's judgement, perhaps swearing on relics like those produced by Mael Brigte at Balfeith in the case of the perambulation. Then the ordeal would proceed. Those declared guilty might face pun-ishment or death. All this may seem very strange to modern readers. Yet contemporaries would have thought it made some sense. Assuming that God's judgements could be divined through ordeals, it was surely far better to refer the whole matter to Him.[13]

After the ordeal, those who were cleared of wrongdoing got the cattle back. The accuser who maintained his accusation of robbery was still allowed to proceed against any warrantor who had refused to turn up in court. He was presumably the real wrongdoer and the actual robber. These points highlight the difficulty of thinking of this procedure as

---

[11] See Cairns, 'Historical introduction', 27.

[12] John H. Baker, *An Introduction to English Legal History*, 4th edn (London: Butterworths, 2002), 5.

[13] For the methods of proof discussed in this paragraph, see Cairns, 'Historical introduction', 27; Angelo D. M. Forte, '"A strange archaic provision of mercy": the procedural rules for the *Duellum* under the law of *Clann Duib*', *Edinburgh Law Review* 14 (2010), 418–50; George Neilson, *Trial by Combat Before the Middle Ages to 1819 A.D.* (Boston: G. A. Jackson, 1909); see also Baker, *Introduction*, 5, 72–3; S. F. C. Milson, *A Natural History of the Common Law* (New York: Columbia University Press, 2003), 6–7.

purely 'criminal', as *Regiam* defined a criminal plea. Evidently there were 'civil' as well as 'criminal' consequences that could follow when it was used. In any event, from here onwards this procedure will be labelled the 'accusatorial' procedure of *Leges Scocie* cap. 1.[14] Note that while the origins of these Scottish rules are unknown, contemporary English law was virtually identical in its essentials. But that does not prove the direct influence of English law here.[15] Similar rules could be found in Welsh law, for example.[16] Furthermore, at one time the ordeal was found across Europe.

Perhaps the central feature of the accusatorial procedure was the need for prosecutions to be brought by a 'private' individual. Usually this 'private' individual would have been the man or woman who had been the victim of robbery or theft. Yet what relevance do these rules have in relation to crimes more generally? There is evidence from *Regiam* that homicides and rapes *could* also be dealt with by means of accusatorial procedure. So the family of a slaughtered individual might accuse a man of the homicide. The result might be a trial by ordeal, as in the case of theft or robbery. Similarly a raped woman or her family might have accused a particular individual of the crime.[17]

Obviously this system was open to abuse. Powerful wrongdoers might have escaped punishment if their victims feared coming forward. Yet there was probably another problem inherent in its operation. A statute promulgated in 1230, during the reign of Alexander II (r. 1214–49), indicates that those who made criminal accusations took a significant risk, at least from that point in time onwards.[18] If they could not prove their accusations, they would fall into the king's mercy. The consequence would have been a heavy fine, or worse (*Statuti Alexandri* cap. 6).[19] In this context, the odds were stacked in favour of the powerful accused – and in particular the powerful accused with the physical strength to deny his guilt in battle. Yet prior to 1230 the accusatorial procedure seems to

---

[14] The label 'accusatorial' is not found in the Scottish sources.
[15] Baker, *Introduction*, 503–5.
[16] Daffyd Jenkins, 'Crime and tort and the three columns of law', in T. M. Charles-Edwards and Paul Russell (eds), Tair Colofn Cyfraith *The Three Columns of Law in Medieval Wales: Homicide, Theft and Fire*, (Bangor: Welsh Legal History Society, 2007), 1–25 at 3–12.
[17] *Regiam Majestatem* (*APS*), I.1, IV 7
[18] See Taylor, *Shape of the State*, 162–3.
[19] The authors are grateful to Dr Alice Taylor for allowing us to consult a draft version of her reconstruction of *Statuti Alexandri* cap. 6; for this law, see Taylor, *Shape of the State*, 280–4.

have been the primary mechanism used to prosecute crimes. That does not mean to say that it did not operate alongside other procedures, which were perhaps older. For example, a victim of theft who acted quickly might call his neighbours to help him. They would then pursue the wrongdoer with the 'hue and cry' of the neighbourhood. If they caught the thief in possession of the stolen goods, then they could hang him on the spot.[20] Nonetheless, the accusatorial procedure seems to have been of significant importance by 1200. This can be discerned from the surviving literature on the procedure and the subsequent attempts to reform it.

Before turning to those reforms, it should be noted that there is no evidence in the record that accusatorial procedure was used in the case of the sons of the Wolf of Badenoch and their accomplices (1392). No-one was identified as the accuser of those who had slaughtered, robbed and burned in Angus. Evidently no-one ran any risk of failing to prove the accusations. Furthermore, there was no indication that the accused were actually summoned to answer a definite accuser. Finally, there is no indication that the ordeal or anything like it was used to prove the alleged crimes. Perhaps the normal rules governing criminal proceedings were simply ignored when dealing with the violence of the Wolf's associates. Alternatively, it is known that an 'inquisitorial' procedure based on indictment was being used long before the end of the fourteenth century.[21] Perhaps this was employed to establish the guilt of the raiders in 1392. Considering the process and its origins may shed further light on this question.

(2) Inquisitorial Procedure

In October 1230, Alexander II gathered leading representatives of the clergy and the nobility of Scotland together at Stirling. Among those who gathered were William Malveisin, Bishop of St Andrews and Scotland's most senior clergyman. Also present were the justiciars, William Comyn, Earl of Buchan, and Walter Olifard.[22] Perhaps they met at the medieval castle on the volcanic rock within the town. Regardless, these senior clergymen and noblemen agreed to enact a series of reforms that would have

---

[20] Taylor, '*Leges Scocie*', 281 (*Leges Scocie* cap. 4).

[21] Again, the label 'inquisitorial' is not found in the contemporary sources.

[22] For law-making in Alexander II's reign, see Hector L. MacQueen, 'Canon law, custom and legislation: law in the reign of Alexander II', in Richard Oram (ed.), *The Reign of Alexander II, 1214–49*, (Boston and Leiden: Brill, 2005), 223–50. MacQueen's conclusions must now be read alongside Taylor, *Shape of the State*, in particular at 135–64, 323–4.

wide-ranging consequences. Reference has already been made to their decision to introduce the brieve of novel dissasine. But in two further acts they began to reform the rules relating to prosecution of crimes. These will be considered here.

First, the lords assembled at Stirling declared that trials by fire and water were no longer to be permitted, in *Statuti Alexandri* cap. 6. Instead, the accused was to be entitled to be judged by his peers among the men of the locality who knew best the truth of the matter. In this one can see something like the later jury trial – albeit that the comparison is not exact, as was explained above. Rather than referring questions to the all-powerful and just God, these men now had to decide them for themselves. The reform was supposed to apply across Scotland. So what had led to such a significant change, and why had the lords agreed to it?

(a) The canonist background

The answer can be found in developments in contemporary canon law. This was in itself influenced by changing scholarly assumptions about proof. It is likely that the source of the reform was Bishop Malveisin of St Andrews, who was present at Stirling in 1230. More importantly, he had also been present in Rome at a great Council of the Church in 1215. This was known as the Fourth Lateran Council.[23] At the Fourth Lateran Council, Malveisin would have witnessed Pope Innocent III's ruling that no clergyman was to participate in an ordeal thereafter. The reasons for this reform were very complex, and need not detain us here. Canonists and theologians objected to the ordeal on various grounds. Almost no warrant could be found for it in the Bible, save for an obscure passage in the book of Numbers. But in reality more important than this were the practical problems that arose from the ordeal. As explained in the first chapter, ever since the mid-eleventh century, the papacy had been trying to exercise greater control over the lives and discipline of the clergy. It was particularly interested in dealing with problems such as clerical concubinage. Put another way, it wanted clergy to be celibate, and to stop living with women as if they were married to them. The problem of clerical concubinage was rife across Europe at this time. But it was difficult to prove. Normal canon law required proof of crimes to be made on the evidence of two eye-witnesses, failing which the ordeal might be used. This frustrated the papacy. In cases where there was widespread public knowledge that a priest was almost certainly guilty

[23] MacQueen, 'Canon law, custom and legislation', 238–41.

of clerical concubinage, the church had very little control of the matter because of its own rules of proof. It was thought that ordeals were too easily manipulated and controlled locally. Also, those who made accusations of wrongdoing risked facing punishment if they failed to sustain their claims, as in Scotland. This last point was important. It also served to discourage litigants from coming forward to make criminal accusations, particularly where there were difficulties of proof. Innocent III was determined to remedy these problems.

Innocent III's solution was to use the theological and scriptural arguments against the ordeal to ban it. In its place he introduced a new method of procedure to establish guilt. This was procedure *per inquisitionem*. There the judge effectively acted as prosecutor. Importantly, no one had to initiate proceedings by making a formal accusation. Thus no one risked punishment for making allegations he could not sustain. The judge would decide whether to proceed against an accused. He could do so simply on the basis that an individual was widely reputed to be guilty of some crime within his community. Furthermore, a series of partial or circumstantial proofs could be relied upon in the place of the evidence of two eye-witnesses.[24]

(b) The Scottish response

Alexander II's decision to follow Innocent III in the abolition of the ordeal by iron (i.e. fire) and water – but not battle – came at a time when the Scottish king wished to secure papal favour. This was in part because he wanted the pope to recognise his independence from the English monarch.[25] Yet in the process Bishop Malveisin seems to have persuaded Alexander to go further in following the papal lead than was perhaps nec-

---

24 On the canon law background, see James A. Brundage, *Medieval Canon Law* (London and New York: Longman, 1995), 120–53; Richard M Fraher, 'The theoretical justification for the new criminal law of the High Middle Ages: *"Rei Publicae Interest, Ne Criminia Remaneant Impunita"*', *University of Illinois Law Review* (1984), 577–95; Richard M. Fraher, 'According to conscience: the medieval jurists' debate concerning judicial discretion and the law of proof', *Law and History Review* 7 (1989), 23–88; Richard M. Fraher, 'Preventing crime in the High Middle Ages: the medieval lawyers' search for deterrence', in James R Sweeney and Stanley Chodorow (eds), *Popes, Teachers and Canon Law in the Middle Ages* (Ithaca and London: Cornell University Press, 1989), 212–33.

25 Consider, for example, the discussion in Dauvit Broun, *Scottish Independence and the Idea of Britain from the Picts to Alexander III* (Edinburgh: Edinburgh University Press, 2007), 161–212.

essary. The decision to develop the idea of trial by the inquiry of an assize resembled the new canonical procedure to some extent. More will be said about this shortly, but note that the influence of the *English* trial by assize was also probably present here.[26] And yet in 1230 the king clearly did not follow the papal policy in its entirety. In most criminal cases it remained necessary to initiate proceedings by means of an accusation. This was expressly preserved in relation to cases of robbery. Furthermore, the accuser risked punishment if he failed to sustain his claim *in most cases*. However, an exception was made to this rule in another act of 1230 (*Statuti Alexandri* cap. 5).[27] This was to prove of significance in shaping future developments, and once again the influence of canon law seems quite clear.

Statuti Alexandri cap. 5 declared what was to happen where monks, clerics, widows, or those 'unable to fight' were victims of theft. It seems that *they* did not have to make a formal accusation against anyone to initiate proceedings. Rather, they were to bring their case before a local official. He and the good men of the neighbourhood then had the duty of investigating the crime. They had to act as both accusers and judges, as did the canonical judge in Innocent III's reforms. The litigants mentioned here – widows and clergymen, and those 'unable to fight' – were therefore privileged. They did not have to make a criminal accusation to gain redress. Unlike all other litigants, they were also excused from having to participate in a trial by battle even if the accused desired it. The terms of the privilege leaves little doubt that Alexander II was following papal policy to defend those who were most vulnerable in society for whom, as king, he had a special responsibility.[28] Simultaneously, his grant of a very special protection to the clergy might have resulted in greater papal favour.

Fourteen years later these rules were developed significantly. In 1244 the king declared that *anyone* could be accused of *any* crime on the basis of his ill-repute within the community.[29] No one had to make

---

[26] As suggested in MacQueen, 'Canon law, custom and legislation', 242; Geoffrey W. S. Barrow, *The Kingdom of the Scots*, 2nd edn (Edinburgh: Edinburgh University Press, 2003), 90.

[27] Again, the authors are very grateful to Alice Taylor for sharing with them her draft transcript of *Statuti Alexandri* cap. 5.

[28] On this special responsibility, see Hector L. MacQueen, *Common Law and Feudal Society*, reprinted edn (Edinburgh: Edinburgh University Press, 2016), 220. For a slightly different perspective on *Statuti Alexandri* cap. 5 (that is not necessarily inconsistent with what is said here), see Taylor, *Shape of the State*, 277–80.

[29] *Statuti Alexandri* cap. 2. Again, the authors are very grateful to Dr Taylor for

a formal accusation of wrongdoing. Thereafter the accused would be summoned to answer before a trial of his peers. There he would enjoy the normal procedural protections of the common law. However, if the victim wanted some form of restitution of the goods taken from him in cases of robbery or theft, or compensation in other situations, he probably still had to use accusatorial procedure.[30] Thus the old 'accusatorial' procedure and the new 'inquisitiorial' procedure of 1244 continued to operate side-by-side. It should also be noted that the 'inquisitorial' procedure of 1244 is frequently referred to in the literature as 'procedure on dittay' ('dittay' comes from the word 'indictment'). The 1244 act also evinces the separation of the crown pleas – such as murder and robbery – from pleas that could be heard before the barons – such as theft and homicide. In the case of the former pleas, it was provided that the forfeited or 'escheated' goods of a criminal were to pass to the king. In the case of the latter pleas, the forfeited goods of the criminal were to pass to the baron on whose lands they were found. The administration of justice was a lucrative business, as attested by the early accounts of the justiciar's 'ayre' from the 1260s (the reference to the justiciar's 'ayre' is a reference to his progress around the sheriffdoms).[31] This point is of significance, especially when it is recalled that it was also possible to buy remissions (pardons) for crimes.

By way of conclusion, once again it is clear that the inquisitorial form of process was not employed in the case of the sons of the Wolf of Badenoch and their accomplices (1392). The wrongdoers were not summoned to answer prior to conviction for their homicides, robberies and acts of arson in the raid upon Angus. Perhaps some other procedure was at work. Alternatively, the normal protections available at common law for those accused of crimes may simply have been waived due to the fury of the government led by the Earl of Fife.

(3) Procedure *Per Notorium?*

The accusatorial and inquisitorial forms of procedure survived the thirteenth century and into the fourteenth. As has been explained, accusato-

---

sharing with them her draft transcript of *Statuti Alexandri* cap. 2. It is discussed in more detail in Taylor, *Shape of the State*, 293–4. Originally the enactment of 1244 was limited to Lothian, but soon afterwards it was extended to Scotia; see Taylor, *Shape of the State*, 240–3, 294.

30   This point is argued in Simpson, 'Procedures for dealing with robbery'.

31   For the early justiciar's ayre, see now Taylor, *Shape of the State*, 233–44.

rial procedure features in *Regiam*. It is also known that it was reformed in a statute of 1384,[32] and used in the burgh court of Aberdeen in the case of *Buchan v Baxter* (1398).[33] There the dispute – which was based on a plea of wrang and unlaw – concerned the stolen carcass of a cow. Likewise there is evidence for the use of 'inquisitorial' procedure on dittay in the north-east of Scotland by the mid-thirteenth century. Again, the case – which was brought before the justiciar – was concerned with the theft of cattle.[34] There is abundant evidence that procedure on dittay flourished in medieval Scotland, and that it was commonly used in the fourteenth and fifteenth centuries.[35]

Yet, as has been seen, neither accusatorial nor inquisitorial procedure was used in the case of the sons of the Wolf of Badenoch. How is this to be explained? It may be thought that the decision of the Earl of Fife and parliament simply represented a draconian and arbitrary rejection of the common law rules of procedure. Arguably that would be quite wrong. In order to consider this further it is necessary to look closely at the wording of the act of 1392 that condemned the raiders. For one thing, the act declared that the wrong-doing was 'notorious' and so worthy of condemnation. What did that mean? For another, the act emphasised that the deeds had been 'premeditated'. Again, was that of any relevance, and if so, why?

This wording implies that those who promulgated the act of 1392 may have had in mind the rules of an earlier statute of 1372.[36] This was concerned specifically with homicide, and the different types of homicide recognised in the Scottish common law. The act had declared that where a man's guilt of homicide was so widely known within his community as

---

[32] *RPS* 1384/11/7.

[33] William Croft Dickinson, *Early Records of the Burgh of Aberdeen 1317, 1398–1400* (Edinburgh: Scottish History Society, 1957), 25; Hector L. MacQueen, 'Some notes on wrang and unlaw', in Hector L. MacQueen (ed.), *Stair Society Miscellany Five* (Edinburgh: Stair Society, 2006), 21.

[34] Barrow, *Kingdom*, 90.

[35] See, for example, Jackson Armstrong, 'The justice ayre in the border sheriffdoms, 1493–1498', *Scottish Historical Review* 92 (2013), 1–37.

[36] *RPS* 1372/3/6–12, discussed in W. David H. Sellar, 'Forethocht felony, malice aforethought and classification of homicide', in William M. Gordon and T. David Fergus (eds), *Legal History in the Making. Proceedings of the Ninth British Legal History Conference Glasgow 1989* (London and Rio Grande: Hambledon Press, 1991), 42–59; Alexander Grant, 'Murder will out: kingship, kinship and killing in medieval Scotland', in Stephen Boardman and Julian Goodare (eds), *Kings, Lords and Men in Scotland and Britain, 1300–1625* (Edinburgh: Edinburgh University Press, 2014), 193–226.

to be beyond doubt, then it could be presumed. Such an individual was then to be brought before an assize with all haste to discover whether he committed homicide in the heat of the moment, or in secret, or with premeditation. If he had acted in the heat of the moment, or *chaudmella*, then he was to be allowed a trial according to the normal procedures of law. If convicted, he would then probably have been able to buy a remission – a pardon from the crown. But if the accused had acted in secrecy, or with premeditation, then he was to be executed immediately. His guilt was presumed on the basis that his crime was well-known within his community, and not merely suspected, as was required for the initiation of 'inquisitorial' procedure. Depending on the nature of his act he would face a trial or immediate execution.

Again, elements of this procedure were drawn from both English law and canon law. The special rules applying to those who acted *chaudmella* seem to have been drawn from England.[37] Yet the influence from canon law seems to be visible in the statement that a killer's guilt had to be '*notorius*' or notorious before it could be presumed. In Innocent III's time, another procedure had been devised in canon law to deal with particularly manifest crimes.[38] If an individual was not merely suspected of criminal conduct, but generally believed within his community to be guilty so as to admit of almost no doubt, a judge could proceed to convict him. This highly controversial procedure was known as procedure *per notorium*. Innocent III justified it on the grounds that it was in the public interest that crimes should not remain unpunished. Again, this rule was designed to make it possible to convict clerics of secret crimes. But in Scotland it was appropriated to deal with a wider range of crimes, including homicide. Why was this so? The act of 1372 makes it clear that the Scottish kings were not simply concerned to punish 'secret' crimes. Its scope extended beyond murder, or secret killing, to other types of homicide. Rather, the aim of the kings was to make punishment speedier, and to prevent delays in the administration of justice. That policy perhaps seemed to make sense in a time of serious disorder, like that which was created by Buchan and his sons. But it had the potential to lead to gross injustice for those accused of crimes. Consider just how far the law had gone in eroding the accused's position. Accusatorial procedure had placed the accused in a strong position, requiring someone else to take the risk of punishment prior to making a criminal accusation.

---

[37]   See Sellar, 'Forethocht felony'.
[38]   For the canonist background, see the sources cited in footnote 24 above.

Inquisitorial procedure had removed that protection, but had still left the accused with a normal summons and subsequent trial. Procedure *per notorium* removed even those protections. And this was all because parliament wished to show it could be tough on crime, and deal with it very quickly.

This form of procedure was probably used to justify the act of parliament condemning the associates of the sons of Buchan in 1392. As has already been explained, the act expressly stated that their deeds were *notorius* and that they had acted with premeditation. Both points were uncontroversial. The deeds were notorious, and there could be no doubt that such notorious deeds could only have been premeditated. One could hardly invade Angus from Perthshire *chaudmella*. Thus, on the basis of the principles laid down in the 1372 act, no further proceedings were required to convict. However, perhaps someone in parliament had some qualms about what was done. It was provided that those convicted in this way would have fifteen days *following* the proclamation of their conviction to come before the sheriff and agree to undergo trial. During that period they remained under sentence, and anyone could lawfully kill them as outlaws. Indeed, anyone who saw them was obliged to apprehend or kill them, or face being treated as their associate.

(4) Continued Experimentation and Reform

Note that this form of radical procedure *per notorium* originally only supplemented accusatorial and inquisitorial procedures in times of extreme necessity. The 1392 act was designed to deal with a particular problem. The same seems to have been the case with the 1372 act, and it was promulgated with a 'sunset' clause. After three years, it was no longer to have effect unless re-enacted. And the government of the 1390s does seem to have thought that the form of procedure *per notorium* was to be used sparingly. In 1398 other problems arose, again in relation to the administration of law and order in the highlands. A general council, a law-making body which had most of the powers of a parliament, was convened in that year to address the disorder. Yet it did not decide to employ procedures *per notorium* to deal with the situation. Rather, in so far as it did address the issues, it focused on reforming the older, inquisitorial procedures. To explain, the general council of 1398 probably witnessed sustained complaints about the treatment of the clerical establishment in Moray. This time the alleged malefactor was not the Wolf of Badenoch, or his sons. Rather, it was Alexander, Lord of Lochaber, the brother of Donald,

Lord of the Isles.[39] At this time the Lord of the Isles was one of the most powerful magnates in the realm, and he dominated the western seaboard. The general council lamented the robberies, burnings and homicides that were apparently commonplace at the time. It then revisited and reformed a statute promulgated a year earlier. That act (of 1397) had required sheriffs to lead inquests to establish the identity of the 'common destroyouris of the countre'. The sheriffs were then required to arrest those men. They would subsequently be released if they provided surety that they would appear before the next justice ayre. If they failed to provide such surety then they would be tried immediately by the sheriff and an assize, and condemned to death if found guilty. On the other hand, those who were able to provide surety that they would appear before the justiciar were to be released until their trial. If they subsequently failed to appear in court, then they were to be outlawed. Those who had stood surety for them would then be commanded to compensate or 'assyth' the 'party pleygnand' – presumably this was one who had made a complaint of wrongdoing to the sheriff prior to the inquest.[40]

Evidently the 1397 act gave the sheriff powers to punish murderers, arsonists and robbers, amongst others. Formerly this power had been reserved to the justiciar alone. Furthermore, it held out the prospect of compensation for those who made complaints through the 'inquisitorial' procedure. Now it would seem that it was no longer necessary to make a criminal complaint through 'accusatorial' procedure in order to secure some form of compensation for a wrong sustained. One of the reasons for this development may have been to increase the speed with which justice could be administered in criminal matters. Theoretically, justiciar courts were supposed to appear in each locality twice a year. By contrast, sheriff courts were supposed to sit every forty days.

In 1398 these provisions were augmented by a general council at Perth, which declared that after the sheriff had identified the 'common destroyouris of the countre' by means of an inquest, he was then to declare publicly who they were.[41] Having been denounced in this way, the accused were then required to present themselves before the sheriff so that they could be assigned a day to stand trial. If they failed to do this within forty days, then they were to be outlawed or 'put to the horn'. This meant that the sheriff or his officials would read their names publicly and then blow a horn. This was a formal ceremony through

[39] Boardman, *Early Stewart Kings*, 209–11.
[40] *RPS* 1397/1–2.
[41] *RPS* 1398/9–10.

which an individual was placed beyond the normal protections of the law.[42]

The 1398 act was clearly more draconian than the 1397 act. It made it clear that those who did not comply within forty days with the summons to appear before the sheriff would be put to the horn. It was also clear that such individuals lost any right to a trial before the justiciar. Yet these rules were not as forceful as the 1392 act. It will be recalled that this had denied the sons of the Wolf of Badenoch and their associates any opportunity to be summoned for trial or tried before they were put to the horn. Ultimately, the acts of 1397 and 1398 reformed existing inquisitorial proceedings. But they retained more protections for those accused of crimes than were available in procedure *per notorium*. Yet it would be wrong to think that the procedures of the acts of 1372 and 1392 were abandoned as failed experiments. They were to influence the law in later periods. This was particularly so from 1438. In that year a new procedure to deal with robbery and a wrong called 'spoliation' was developed by the king's council.[43] That procedure was probably influenced both by procedure *per notorium* and by the reforms of 1397–8. The development of this procedure to remedy spoliation ultimately led to the recognition of the action of 'spuilzie'. This action was to prove extremely popular with litigants, and came to be used to remedy a range of acts of wrongful dispossession.

D. CONCLUSION

Scottish monarchs of the thirteenth, fourteenth and early fifteenth centuries did promote the use of broadly common procedural standards in the prosecution of crimes. Yet this point is subject to important caveats. There is little evidence to suggest that they sought to control the precise definition of crimes. Robbery was almost certainly theft with violence. Yet the earliest Scottish definition of the crime comes from the late sixteenth century. The same point can be made about murder and theft. Furthermore, it has been seen that the punishment of many crimes was largely left to feudal barons. Nonetheless, as was seen in relation to the brieves, the Scottish kings were interested in promoting the use of common procedures to deal with criminal problems. Reference has been

[42] See Philip J. Hamilton-Grierson, *Habakkuk Bisset's Rolment of Courtis* (Edinburgh and London: Scottish Text Society, 1919–26) III, 136–7.
[43] *RPS* A1438/12/1.

made to the old accusatorial procedures, which were developed through
a series of laws promulgated between the late twelfth century and the
late fourteenth century. Similarly, inquisitorial procedure on dittay was
probably originally introduced in part to deal with the short-comings of
accusatorial procedure. It then flourished for centuries, albeit that it was
reformed in the 1390s. Furthermore, towards the end of the period considered here, Scottish monarchs continued to develop procedural tools
to deal with crime quickly and forcefully. This is illustrated in the case of
the sons of the Wolf of Badenoch and their accomplices. In their case, the
parliament summoned by the Earl of Fife seems to have chosen to utilise
a third form of procedure. This had previously been used to deal with
particularly notorious homicides, and potentially permitted conviction
without summons or trial. Once the procedure found its way into the
common law, it proved influential.

It should be noted again that many objections can be advanced against
the claim that the brieves expressed a Scottish common law. Similar
objections can be raised against the claim that procedures to remedy
murders, robberies, acts of arson and thefts were applied commonly
across the realm. Such objections can also be met with similar responses.
So in the regalities it is true that some of the greatest lords of regality
had relative freedom from the justiciar in the administration of justice.
However, from the late fourteenth century at the latest this freedom
was curbed. In 1398 parliament commanded the justiciars to investigate the extent to which the sheriffs and the bailies of the regalities had
implemented the 1397 act mentioned above. The bailies of regality were
the representatives of the lords of regality in judicial matters. In other
words, they actually dealt with the cases and disputes that their lords
were empowered to decide. The justiciar was also empowered to declare
that negligent bailies of regality were at the mercy of their lords. And if
the lords of regality failed to punish their negligent bailies appropriately
then they would 'undergo a challenge' in the presence of the king. If a
lord was found somehow culpable – the act was vague on this point – he
would lose his regality, at least in theory.[44] This was a sign of things to
come. In 1404 a general council commanded that procedural reforms
in the administration of justice in the courts of the justiciars and the
sheriffs should be observed in the regality courts.[45] In an act of 1438 on
robbery and spoliation, the king's council went a step further. It directly
empowered the sheriff to interfere in the administration of justice in the

[44]   *RPS* 1398/10.
[45]   *RPS* 1404/9.

regalities where the lords of regality failed to implement the terms of the act.[46] The common law was tightening its grip. The process accelerated as the fifteenth century progressed. This was true even in regions of the kingdom where the power of the Scottish monarchs had traditionally been weak, such as the highlands and islands. The next chapter will explore this last point in more detail.

E. SELECTED BIBLIOGRAPHY AND FURTHER READING

(1) Records of the Parliaments of Scotland (*RPS*)

Acts concerning the classification of homicides: *RPS* 1372/3/6–12.
Act condemning the sons of the Earl of Buchan: *RPS* 1392/3/1.
Act concerning the prosecution of crimes: *RPS* 1397/1–2.
Act concerning the prosecution of crimes: *RPS* 1398/9–10.
Act concerning the loss of regalities for negligence: *RPS* 1404/9.
Act concerning robbery and spuilzie: *RPS* A1438/12/1.

(2) Books

Baker, John H., *An Introduction to English Legal History*, 4th edn (London: Butterworths, 2002).
Brundage, James A., *Medieval Canon Law* (London and New York: Longman, 1995).
Cooper, Thomas M (ed.), *Regiam Majestatem and Quoniam Attachiamenta* (Edinburgh: Stair Society, 1947).
Duncan, Archibald A. M., *Scottish Formularies* (Edinburgh: Stair Society, 2011).
Fergus, T. David, *Quoniam Attachiamenta* (Edinburgh: Stair Society, 1996).
MacQueen, Hector L., *Common Law and Feudal Society*, reprinted edn (Edinburgh: Edinburgh University Press, 2016).
Neilson, George, *Trial by Combat before the Middle Ages to 1819 A.D.* (Boston: G. A. Jackson, 1909).
Taylor, Alice, *The Shape of the State in Medieval Scotland* (Oxford: Oxford University Press, 2016).

---

[46] *RPS* A1438/12/1.

(3) Chapters in Books

Fraher, Richard M., 'Preventing crime in the High Middle Ages: the medieval lawyers' search for deterrence', in James R. Sweeney and Stanley Chodorow (eds), *Popes, Teachers and Canon Law in the Middle Ages* (Ithaca and London: Cornell University Press, 1989), 212–33.

Grant, Alexander, 'Franchises north of the border: baronies and regalities in medieval Scotland', in Michael Prestwich (ed.), *Liberties and Identities in the Medieval British Isles* (Woodbridge: Boydell & Brewer, 2008), 155–99.

Grant, Alexander, 'Murder will out: kingship, kinship and killing in medieval Scotland', in Stephen Boardman and Julian Goodare (eds), *Kings, Lords and Men in Scotland and Britain, 1300–1625* (Edinburgh: Edinburgh University Press, 2014), 193–226.

Jenkins, Dafydd, 'Crime and tort and the three columns of law', in T. M. Charles-Edwards and Paul Russell (eds), Tair Colofn Cyfraith *The Three Columns of Law in Medieval Wales: Homicide, Theft and Fire* (Bangor: Welsh Legal History Society, 2007), 1–25.

MacQueen, Hector L., 'Canon law, custom and legislation: law in the reign of Alexander II', in Richard Oram (ed.), *The Reign of Alexander II, 1214–49* (Boston and Leiden: Brill, 2005), 223–50.

Sellar, W. David H., 'Forethocht felony, malice aforethought and classification of homicide', in William M. Gordon and T. David Fergus (eds), *Legal History in the Making. Proceedings of the Ninth British Legal History Conference Glasgow 1989* (London and Rio Grande: Hambledon Press, 1991), 42–59.

Simpson, Andrew R. C., 'Foreword: common law and feudal society in scholarship since 1993', in Hector L. MacQueen, *Common Law and Feudal Society* (Edinburgh: Edinburgh University Press, 2016), xxix–lxi.

Simpson, Andrew R. C., 'Procedures for dealing with robbery in Scotland before 1400', in Andrew R. C. Simpson, Scott Crichton Styles, Euan West and Adelyn L. M. Wilson (eds), *Continuity, Change and Pragmatism in the Law. Essays in Memory of Professor Angelo Forte* (Aberdeen: Aberdeen University Press, 2016), 95–149.

Taylor, Alice, 'Crime without punishment: medieval Scotland in comparative perspective', in D. Bates (ed.), *Anglo-Norman Studies 35: Proceedings of the Battle Conference 2012* (Woodbridge: Boydell Press, 2013), 287–304.

(4) Articles in Journals

Armstrong, Jackson, 'The justice ayre in the border sheriffdoms, 1493–1498', *Scottish Historical Review* 92 (2013), 1–37.

Gane, Christopher H. W., 'The effect of a pardon in Scots law', *Juridical Review* (1980), 18–46.

Fraher, Richard M., 'The theoretical justification for the new criminal law of the High Middle Ages: "*Rei Publicae Interest, Ne Criminia Remaneant Impunita*"', *University of Illinois Law Review* (1984), 577–95.

Fraher, Richard M., 'According to conscience: the medieval jurists' debate concerning judicial discretion and the law of proof', *Law and History Review* 7 (1989), 23–88.

CHAPTER 5

Law and Order in the Highlands and Islands

A. INTRODUCTION

The previous chapter opened by making reference to the prosecution of the sons of the Wolf of Badenoch following their raid on the lands of Angus. The story was used to introduce various different mechanisms or procedures that existed at common law for the prosecution of crimes. Considering those procedures made it possible to explore the extent to which Scottish monarchs were developing a truly 'common' law in criminal matters.

The determination of parliament to punish the sons of the Wolf of Badenoch and their accomplices illustrates another point concerning the development of the common law. Such raids were seen by parliaments and general councils in straightforward terms. They were indicative of the lawless state of the highlands and islands. The response of the Stewart heirs of Robert II was simple. They attempted to bring their order – their common law – to bear on the northern and western regions of the kingdom. Scottish kings pursued this policy consistently and aggressively throughout the late fourteenth and fifteenth centuries. Frequently they did so in alliance with great Gaelic kindreds, such as the Campbells, with varying degrees of success.[1] In the more general process of bringing their order to the region they seem to have destroyed a system of dispute resolution that was known in the Hebrides. For reasons that will become clear, this is highly relevant to a study of how the Scottish common law emerged.

---

[1] The history of the relationship between the Stewart monarchs and the Campbells is complex. See Stephen Boardman, *The Campbells 1250–1513* (Edinburgh: John Donald, 2006).

B. MAINTAINING LAW AND ORDER IN THE HIGHLANDS AND ISLANDS

(1) *Lagmannaibh*, Breves and Lords

Most of the legal history of the highlands and islands before the six-teenth century is very obscure. Hebridean '*lagmannaibh na n-Innsedh*', or lawmen of the Isles, appear in an Irish chronicle in 974, and also, it seems, in 962. In 962 they were taking part in a raid with a local warlord on County Louth and County Dublin. The *lagmannaibh* then proceeded to avenge the death of one of their number in Munster, and plundered Cork. Ultimately they in turn were attacked and 365 of them were killed, 'so that none escaped but the crews of three ships'. Yet the lawmen of the Isles, even at this period, were presumably more than just warlords. Having pointed out that much of the western seaboard was under the rule of Scandinavians at this time, one historian has attempted to explain the functions of the lawmen. He suggests that they may have been like their Swedish equivalents. Provinces in the Swedish interior 'were ruled by assemblies of freeholders who regularly elected lawmen to preside over their public affairs'. He goes on to suggest that each island 'or island group' in the Hebrides may have had its own assembly.[2]

Note that it should not be assumed that such *lagamannaibh* were simply Hebridean versions of the Scottish *judices*. Whether or not the twelfth-century *judices* ever had a military role similar to that of the tenth-century *lagamannaibh* is unclear. Furthermore, the *judices* all seem to have operated within political structures where lordship was held by others, and not by themselves. By contrast, the lawmen of the Hebrides appear in the record as autonomous warlords (at least in the late 900s). Perhaps this point is worth emphasising. Some historical writing implies that the systems of dispute resolution in the highlands and islands largely preserved what had existed in the rest of the Scottish mainland before the reign of David I. There may be a great deal of truth in that. Nonetheless, the apparent differences in functions between the *lagamannaibh* and the *judices* should encourage historians to exercise caution in making such assumptions.

Aside from the scattered references to the lawmen of the Isles, very little is known generally about dispute resolution in the Hebrides during the eleventh and twelfth centuries. At this time the kings of Norway

---

[2] See Alex Woolf, *From Pictland to Alba 789–1070* (Edinburgh: Edinburgh University Press, 2007), 213 and the source cited there.

came to assert ultimate authority over the region, but that does not necessarily reveal much about dispute resolution there. Much has been written about the political careers of great lords like Somerled, who had united much of the western seaboard under his rule by the time of his death in 1164. Exactly how the lawmen interacted with his authority – if at all – is unclear.[3] From Somerled were descended the powerful MacDougalls and MacDonalds. The chiefs of the latter were the lords of the Isles during the fourteenth and fifteenth centuries. Nonetheless, while more can be said about politics and warfare in the Hebrides than the administration of justice, considering the political situation does at times shed light on dispute resolution there. For example, following a period of conflict between Alexander III of Scotland (r. 1249–86) and Magnus VI of Norway (r. 1263–80), the latter ceded all rights the king of Norway had in the Hebrides to the king of Scots. The agreement between the two kings was embodied in the Treaty of Perth (1266). Of particular importance for present purposes was the provision in this treaty that thereafter the inhabitants of the Isles were to be subjected to the laws and customs of the kingdom of Scotland ('*subiaceant legibus et consuetudinibus regni Scocie*'). Thus through the treaty Alexander had established the *idea* that the Hebrides were subject to the laws and customs of his realm, and not those of Norway.[4] Yet the extent to which the idea bore very much relation to reality at this time is unclear. It must be remembered that it was Alexander MacDonald of Islay who informed Edward I that 'many people' believed that the brieves rule was recognised in the Scottish common law in 1296. At the time he was discussing the situation in Kintyre, which, while not part of the Hebrides, is on the western seaboard. It must also be remembered that feudal tenure had gradually been becoming more common in the central highlands during the thirteenth century. During this period, Scottish monarchs seem to have granted some larger lordships in exchange for military service in highland regions.[5] Furthermore, one early reference to Assynt, which

---

[3] See Richard Oram, *Domination and Lordship. Scotland 1070–1230* (Edinburgh: Edinburgh University Press, 2011), 119–29.

[4] Cynthia J. Neville and Grant G. Simpson (eds), *The Acts of Alexander III King of Scots 1249–1286* (Edinburgh: Edinburgh University Press, 2013), 100–5 (charter no. 61); for the conflict between the Scottish and Norwegian kings, see, for example, A. A. M. Duncan, *Scotland: The Making of the Kingdom* (Edinburgh: Mercat Press, 1975), 577–83.

[5] See Geoffrey W. S. Barrow, *Feudal Britain* (London: E. Arnold, 1956), 253. Note that the existence of feudal grants can distract the historian from 'the range of forms and changing processes by which power was exercised' in the late twelfth and thirteenth centuries. In Moray, for example, '[t]he new lords' relationship with the

is located in the far north-west highlands, can be found in a charter of David II granted in 1343. David II granted lands in Assynt, together with a fortified island in Loch Assynt, to Torquhil MacLeod of Lewis. The grant was made '*in feodo et hereditate*' in exchange for the military service of one twenty-oared galley.[6]

Nonetheless, it is important not to make too much of this evidence. The infrastructure for administering royal justice in the highlands and islands beyond the Great Glen was simply lacking in the thirteenth century. It was largely focused around Inverness prior to the 1290s. *Leges Scocie* cap. 1 makes reference to a sheriff of Inverness with jurisdiction in parts of Moray, Ross, Caithness and Argyll – a huge territory. Royal authority really made itself felt in the region through the loyal service of great families, such as the Comyn lords of Lochaber. During the reign of John Balliol (r. 1292–6) attempts were made to create new sheriffdoms of Skye, Lorne and Kintyre, but the plans faltered shortly thereafter, during the Wars of Independence.[7] As has been seen, Robert I (r. 1306–29) largely relied upon the great earls and lords of regality to keep order in the highlands. So if the evidence that disputes in the region were resolved using the Scottish common law is thin, how were they addressed?

It is difficult to answer this question with any certainty. The surviving evidence on the point was largely committed to writing during the sixteenth and the seventeenth centuries. It describes some judicial structures that had already vanished. Nonetheless, it is worth considering here. It was noted a moment ago that Torqhuil MacLeod of Lewis had a feudal grant of lands in Assynt from David II. Yet he was not granted the lands '*cum fossa et furca*' – with pit and gallows – as were some major lowland and highland lords. Whether this is of any significance is unclear. But other evidence indicates that justice in his territories in Lewis was in fact administered by lawmen known as 'breves'. Obviously they must not be confused with the 'brieves'. The breves of Lewis were drawn from the Morrison family, and they held office by hereditary right. The surviving evidence concerning the activities of these breves indicates that they were both lawmen and warlords. Conceivably this may suggest some link between the later breves and the earlier *lagamannaibh*. As regards

crown was perhaps defined in "feudal" terms, but the lordship which they exercised rested on pre-feudal structures'. See Oram, *Domination and Lordship*, 232, and more generally at 197–232.

[6] Bruce Webster (ed.), *The Acts of David II King of Scots 1329–1371* (Edinburgh: Edinburgh University Press, 1982), 507 (charter no. 487).

[7] See William Croft Dickinson, *The Sheriff Court Book of Fife 1515–1522* (Edinburgh: Scottish History Society, 1928), 362–3.

their role as men of law, the evidence is fragmentary, but one breve of Lewis is said to have written 'succinct and pithy verses which define the boundaries of lands on the West Side of Lewis'.[8] The work of the breves of Lewis was discussed in more detail by Sir Robert Gordon, who wrote in the mid-seventeenth century. He described the breve as '[a] kind of Judge among the Islanders who hath an absolute Judicatory, and unto whose authority and censure they willingly submit themselves'.[9] Nonetheless, in earlier times the judicial authority of the breves may not have been quite so absolute. Hugh MacDonald, also writing in the seventeenth century, claimed that

> there was a judge in every isle for the discussion of all controversies, who had land from MacDonald (*i.e.* of the Isles) for their trouble, and likewise the eleventh part of every action decided. But there might still be an appeal to the Council of the Isles ...[10]

A full discussion of the 'council of the Isles' is beyond the scope of this chapter. It suffices to note that it seems to have functioned to some extent, under the presidency of the lords of the Isles. Charters were occasionally issued by the lords 'with the consent, assent, and mature deliberation of all our council'. Nicholson identifies this 'council' with the Council of the Isles that sat at Finlagan on Islay.[11] In 1549 the body was described by Donald Monro, Archdeacon of the Isles. He began by outlining its composition. Apparently it consisted of '14 of the Iles best Barons' drawn from the noble families of the isles (including the MacLeods of Lewis). Monro continued:

> Thir 14 persons sat down in the Counsell-Ile, and decernit, decreitit and gave suits furth upon all debaitable matters according to the Laws made be Renald McSomharkle callit in his time King of the Occident Iles, and albeit thair Lord were at his hunting or at ony uther games, zit thai sate every ane at thair Counsell ministring justice. In thair time thair was great peace and welth in the Iles throw the ministration of justice.[12]

---

[8] Derick S. Thomson, 'Gaelic learned orders and literati in medieval Scotland', *Scottish Studies* 12 (1968), 57–78 at 58–61; the passage quoted is at 60.

[9] Quoted in Thomson, 'Gaelic learned orders', 59.

[10] Quoted in Thomson, 'Gaelic learned orders', 59.

[11] Ranald Nicholson, *Scotland: The Later Middle Ages* (Edinburgh: Mercat Press, 1974), 208–9.

[12] *A Description of the Western Islands of Scotland Circa 1695; A Late Voyage to St*

This can be rendered in modern English as follows:

> These fourteen persons sat down in the council Isle, and deter-
> mined, decreed and gave suits forth upon all debatable matters
> according to the laws made by Ranald, son of Somerled, called in
> his time the King of the Western Isles. And although their lord was
> at his hunting or at any games [past-times], nonetheless they all sat
> at their council ministering justice. In their time there was great
> peace and wealth in the Isles through the administration of justice.

The evidence assembled indicates that the lords of the Isles, whose
territories at one time stretched from Lewis in the north to Islay in the
south, may have presided over some sort of judicial system that operated within the Hebrides.[13] Breves acting on the lords' authority served
as judges over individual islands, and their decisions could be revisited
by the council of the Isles. Additionally, there may well have been a
senior breve who presided over the others. One charter issued by the
council in 1485 was witnessed by William '*archiiudex*'; Bannerman suggests he was the breve of the Lord of the Isles himself.[14] Bannerman also
cites evidence to suggest that the lordship had considerable machinery
for the administration of government at its disposal. For example, a
seventeenth-century historian makes reference to a keeper of the records
of the Isles. That such written records did exist is attested by the survival
of a charter granted by Donald, Lord of the Isles, to Brian Vicar MacKay
in 1408.[15] It should be noted that the extent to which this charter was in
any sense 'feudal' in nature is unclear. Certainly lords of the Isles did
make feudal grants of lands. An example can be found in the charter of
the lands of Lochbroom, Lochcarron, Torridon and Kishorn made by
John, Earl of Ross and Lord of the Isles, in 1463 in favour of his brother

---

Kilda [by] *Martin Martin; with A Description of the Occidental i.e. Western Islands
of Scotland* [by] *Donald Monro*, introduced by Charles Withers and R. W. Munro
(Edinburgh: Birlinn, 1999), 309–10.

[13] Lamont warns that it is difficult to be sure of the nature and extent of the operation
of that system; see W. D. Lamont, 'The Islay Charter of 1408', *Proceedings of the
Royal Irish Academy. Section C: Archaeology, Celtic Studies, History, Linguistics,
Literature* 60 (1959/1960), 163–87 at 171–2.

[14] See John Bannerman, 'The Lordship of the Isles', in Jenny M. Brown, *Scottish
Society in the Fifteenth Century* (London: Edward Arnold, 1977), 209–40 at 227,
233–4.

[15] Lamont, 'Islay Charter'.

Celestine.[16] By contrast, the charter of 1408 did not make a grant in heritable fee. Rather, it gave lands to Brian 'and to his heirs after him for ever and ever, for his services' to the lords of the Isles. The grant was 'on convenant and on condition' that Brian and his heirs should render to Donald, Lord of the Isles, and his heirs 'four cows fit for killing' every year. If such cows could 'not be found', then forty-two marks were to be paid instead. Donald's grant continued:

> And for the same causes [Brian's services] I am binding myself and binding my heirs after me, to the end of the world, these lands, together with their fruits of sea and land, to defend and maintain to the above Brian Vicar MacKay and to his heirs for ever after him in like manner.[17]

The charter was witnessed by John MacDonald, probably the nephew of the granter, and also by Patrick 'M'a Briuin' and Fergus MacBeth. Patrick's surname is probably a variant of a Gaelic word meaning 'son of the brehon', brehon being another word for 'breve'. Perhaps he was the breve of Islay at this time. If so, he was illiterate; he did not sign the charter, but simply made a mark. By contrast, Fergus MacBeth, a man learned in medical matters, did sign the charter. The handwriting in his signature, when compared with the handwriting in which the charter is preserved, reveals that he probably composed it. The charter reveals that the breves were probably active in witnessing grants of land, as one might expect.[18] Other evidence implies that many grants of lands made at the time were verbal.[19]

This discussion outlines the surviving evidence concerning the work of the breves and dispute resolution in the lordship of the Isles. Yet it must be emphasised again that much of the surviving evidence is late. The extent to which the system it described actually operated during the fifteenth century or earlier is unclear. Furthermore, if the Isles did use their own particular laws, as Dean Monro indicated, these are now lost. The same can be said for the official records of the Isles, if they existed. Nonetheless, it is worth noting that modern historians have compiled

---

[16] See Jean Munro and R. W. Munro, *Acts of the Lords of the Isles 1336–1493* (Edinburgh: Scottish History Society, 1986), 117–19 (charter no. 76).

[17] A translation of the grant can be found in Lamont, 'Islay Charter', 165–6.

[18] Lamont, 'Islay Charter', 170–2.

[19] See Jean Munro, 'The Lordship of the Isles', in Loraine MacLean (ed.), *The Middle Ages in the Highlands* (Inverness: Inverness Field Club, 1981), 23–37 at 26.

the acts of the lords from the surviving records. Most are preserved in Latin.[20]

(2) The Lordship of the Isles and the Scottish Common Law

Insofar as Monro's system of dispute resolution did operate, its fate and its fortunes were tied up with those of the lordship of the Isles. This is not the place to discuss the history of the lordship in any detail. It suffices to note the following points.[21] Angus Og of Islay, a descendent of Somerled and the head of the MacDonald kindred, had been rewarded for his services to Robert I (r. 1306–29) with the important lordship of Lochaber. This had once been held by Robert's enemies, the Comyns. Angus also received Morvern and Ardnamurchan, making him one of the most powerful men in the west of Scotland. This marked the beginning of a process whereby he and his son, John of Islay, acquired control of most of the Hebrides. By 1354 John of Islay had taken the title 'Lord of the Isles'. Yet his relationship with the Bruce dynasty was not entirely straightforward. This was particularly the case during the closing years of the reign of Robert I's son, David II (r. 1329–71). Following a period of imprisonment in England, David II and the three estates of Scotland – the clergy, the nobility and the burgesses – had to pay a huge ransom for his release. This was resented by the estates, and in trying to identify untapped sources of income they turned their eyes on the western lords. In 1366 an act of parliament was passed stating

> that those rebels, namely of Atholl, Argyll, Badenoch, Lochaber and Ross, and others if there are any, in the northern regions or elsewhere, should be arrested by the king and his armed force to undergo common justice and particularly for paying off the contribution, and otherwise they may be corrected as shall be more opportune for the peace and utility of the community and the kingdom.[22]

Financial constraint had prompted parliament to demand that the lords of the west should share one particular financial burden with others in

---

[20] Munro and Munro, *Acts of the Lords of the Isles*.
[21] For the political history of the Lordship given here, see Bannermann, 'The Lordship of the Isles'; Munro, 'The Lordship of the Isles'; Nicholson, *Scotland: The Later Middle Ages*, 74, 89, 112, 142–3, 154–6, 174–9, 207–10, 232–7, 315–16, 374, 376, 396, 401–3, 406–7, 480–2, 542, 544–6.
[22] *RPS* 1366/7/10.

the kingdom. Part of the problem was the lack of infrastructure and sheriffdoms to enforce the king's will in the highlands and islands. As one historian puts it, 'the lack of responsiveness to financial demands became entwined with the issue of non-adherence to the common law'.[23] Two years later, David II promulgated a statute declaring that no disputes were to be dealt with other than by the course of common justice. Obviously he meant that they were not to be resolved by violent conflict between nobles. At the same time he followed this statute with another, stating that the 'Islesmen' should be 'constrained ... not to bring harm to others'.[24] Other highland lords present in parliament were required to 'preserve the communities of the realm unharmed from all those living within the bounds of their lordships; and that they will not let any malefactors wishing to harm others to cross those bounds or be received within them'.[25] Boardman speculates that the real problem underlying this was cattle-raiding.[26] Those lords who failed to administer justice properly would face punishment. David II backed these statutes with the force of arms. In 1369 he led a force to Inverness where he received the submission of John, Lord of the Isles. John acknowledged David II as his lord, agreed to obey royal officials and promised to pay contributions when required.[27]

The power of the lords of the Isles only increased in the decades that followed. John, Lord of the Isles, had married Margaret, daughter of Robert II (r. 1371–91). Their son, Donald, in turn married the heiress of the Earl of Ross, ultimately bringing another vast territory within the MacDonald patrimony. Donald, Lord of the Isles, was even able to threaten the city of Aberdeen before he was forced to withdraw after the bloody Battle of Harlaw (1411). At the same time, the determination of the governments of Robert III (r. 1391–1406) and James I (r. 1406–37) to enforce basic levels of royal order in the highlands was undiminished. This is at least part of the context of the legislation of 1398 that reformed inquisitorial procedure following the raids of Alexander, Lord of Lochaber, and brother of Donald, Lord of the Isles. Donald's son Alexander, Earl of Ross and Lord of the Isles, was also later named as justiciar of the north. This involved him directly in the administration of the common law within the territories through which the justiciar pro-

23 Boardman, *The Campbells*, 78.
24 *RPS* 1368/6/10–11.
25 *RPS* 1368/6/12.
26 Boardman, *The Campbells*, 78–9.
27 Nicholson, *Scotland: The Later Middle Ages*, 178–9.

gressed on 'ayre'. Nonetheless, the extent to which he administered the common law in the Hebrides and his other territories remains unclear.

The fall of the lordship of the Isles came in the time of Alexander's son, John. To oversimplify, John was forfeited in 1474 following the revelation that he had entered into a treasonable bond with the king of England twelve years earlier. Broadly he agreed to become the king of England's liegeman. In exchange, after an invasion of Scotland – which never came – John would receive authority over much of the realm north of the Forth. In 1474 the English king revealed this treason to his Scottish counterpart, James III (r. 1460–88), in part to distract James from other activities. The Lord of the Isles did not fight when parliament forfeited his life, lands and goods. Rather, he accepted the loss of Ross and other territories, and then submitted to the king and was allowed to retain the rest of his inheritance. Yet this divided his kindred, and the unity of the Isles was broken in conflict over how to react to this humiliation. Finally, in 1493, James IV (r. 1488–1513) finished the work his father had begun. He forfeited John, last Lord of the Isles, who subsequently died in obscurity. John's grandson, Donald Dubh, attempted to reclaim his grandfather's power, and rose in rebellion. In 1504 parliament sought to suppress this rising. But it also reacted strongly against the apparent power vacuum that had arisen in the north-west highlands and islands following the destruction of the lordship.[28] Parliament complained that the people were 'almaist gane wilde'.[29] It blamed the problem on the lack of sheriffdoms and justice ayres in the region. At last some attempt was made to remedy the problem. New sheriffs were established at Ross and Caithness, and the north-west islands were to be served by a sheriff and a justice-depute based at Inverness. A further sheriff and a further justice-depute were to administer justice in the southern islands.[30] Thus the administrative machinery required to enforce the Scottish common law in the west began to emerge. Note that the breves, such as the Morrison breves of Lewis, did not disappear in the face of this challenge. But evidently the Scottish monarchy had put in place judicial structures that might give them competition.

[28] Nicholson, *Scotland: The Later Middle Ages*, 544–6.
[29] *RPS* 1504/3/103.
[30] *RPS* 1504/3/103–5.

C. CONCLUSION

The parliament of 1504 that panicked about the 'wilde' people of the west, and decided to give them justice-deputes and sheriffs in the hope of dealing with the problem, also promulgated the following statute:

> Item, it is statute and ordanit that all oure soverane lord liegis beande under his obeysance, and in speciale the Ilis, be reulit be oure soverane lordis aune lawis and the commoune lawis of the realme ande be nain uther lawis.[31]

This can be rendered in modern English as follows:

> Likewise, it is enacted and ordained that all our sovereign lord's subjects, being under his obedience, and especially the [inhabitants of the] Isles, are to be governed by our sovereign lord's own laws and the common laws of the realm, and by no other laws.

If the council of the Isles and the breves had used the laws of Ranald, son of Somerled – whatever they were – then this was no longer to be tolerated. Like his predecessors, James IV (r. 1488–1513) ambitiously sought to establish one law commonly applicable among all of his subjects. The origins of those ambitions can be traced to the reign of William I (r. 1165–1214) and his acts outlining basic procedures to be followed in relation to certain pleas, such as theft and robbery. His insistence that certain pleas – later called 'criminal' pleas – were reserved to the king and his justiciars was also to prove to be of great importance. Ambitions to create a common law began to crystallise in the time of Alexander II (r. 1214–49), who introduced the brieves of novel dissasine and mortancestry, and procedure on dittay. Undoubtedly his heirs achieved considerable success in creating a legal system commonly applicable among their subjects. In relation to the protection of feudal rights in land in particular, the recognition of the brieves rule evidently marked a great step forward in this regard. As stated above, it was established in statute in 1318. But on the evidence of Alexander MacDonald of Islay it may have operated prior to 1296. Regardless, once it formed part of the common law, none of the king's subjects could be ejected from lands of which they were vest and saised as of fee without the king's pleadable brieve or some similar brieve. In theory at least, broad procedural standards were

---

[31] *RPS* A1504/3/124; see also *RPS* 1504/3/45.

now enforceable in important disputes throughout the realm of the king of Scots. Ultimately this enabled James IV to develop his own much more ambitious goal, that a single Scottish common law would govern all matters throughout the realm.

Of course, legal diversity remained, particularly in the north-west highlands and the islands. There the operation of procedural mechanisms such as brieves may well have been hampered by the lack of administrative machinery to enforce them. Furthermore, in the islands the people may have used their own laws, regardless of royal views on the subject. In Orkney and Shetland even greater diversity persisted. Those islands had passed to the Scottish crown as a dowry from the king of Denmark in 1468 and 1469. Their laws and customs were expressly preserved. It was to be a long time before they were incorporated within the ambit of the Scottish common law.[32] Furthermore, even where the brieves were applied, there was probably diversity as regards the manner in which they and other forms of action were interpreted by men of law and courts in practice. The lack of a relatively homogeneous legal profession was perhaps a stumbling-block in the path of the development of a truly 'common' law in Scotland. Even the legal literature that might have guided practitioners concerning the meaning of technical terms in the brieves was confused, and increasingly out of date.

It is worth emphasising that these matters were not necessarily at the forefront of the minds of contemporaries. Many Scots were more concerned about other matters relating to the administration of the common law. Fifteenth-century parliaments received repeated complaints about the *quality* of justice administered by the common law courts of the sheriffs and the justiciars. The royal response to this would ultimately lead to radical, if perhaps unintended, reforms of the common law itself. By the 1540s the brieves of right, mortancestry and novel dissasine had all fallen out of use. The rights available at common law were enforced by other

---

[32] See Nicholson, *Scotland: The Later Middle Ages*, 414–18; John W. Cairns, 'Historical introduction', in Kenneth Reid and Reinhard Zimmermann (eds), *A History of Private Law in Scotland* (Oxford: Oxford University Press, 2000) I, 56–67, 93–4; Katherine Anderson, 'The influence of Scots and Norse law on law and governance in Orkney and Shetland 1450–1650' (unpublished PhD thesis, University of Aberdeen, 2015); Jørn Øyrehagen Sunde, 'A dubious tale of misfortune revealing the true nature of Udal Law on Shetland and the Schound Bill – Shetland law at the beginning of the seventeenth century', in Andrew R. C. Simpson, Scott Crichton Styles, Euan West and Adelyn L. M. Wilson (eds), *Continuity, Change and Pragmatism in the Law. Essays in Memory of Professor Angelo Forte* (Aberdeen: Aberdeen University Press, 2016), 150–74.

means, and before a new court. This was the session. The next chapter will discuss its origins and the decline of procedure on brieve.

D. SELECTED BIBLIOGRAPHY AND FURTHER READING

(1) Records of the Parliaments of Scotland (*RPS*)

Act requiring the highland lords to make payments: *RPS* 1366/7/10.

Acts concerning the duties of highland lords to prevent crimes: *RPS* 1368/6/10–11.

Acts concerning the duties of highland lords to prevent crimes: *RPS* 1368/6/12.

Acts concerning the administration of justice in the highlands: *RPS* 1504/3/103–5.

Act concerning the observation of law in the highlands: *RPS* 1504/3/45.

Act concerning the observation of law in the highlands: *RPS* A1504/3/124.

(2) Books

A Description of the Western Islands of Scotland Circa 1695; A Late Voyage to St Kilda [by] *Martin Martin; with A Description of the Occidental i.e. Western Islands of Scotland* [by] *Donald Monro*, introduced by Charles Withers and R. W. Munro (Edinburgh: Birlinn, 1999).

Bannerman, John W. M., *Kingship, Church and Culture: Collected Studies and Essays* (Edinburgh: John Donald, 2016).

[MacInnes, John] Newton, Michael (ed.), *Dùthchas Nan Gàidheal: Selected Essays of John MacInnes* (Edinburgh: Birlin, 2006).

MacQueen, Hector L., *Common Law and Feudal Society*, reprinted edn (Edinburgh: Edinburgh University Press, 2016).

Munro, Jean, and R. W. Munro, *Acts of the Lords of the Isles 1336–1493* (Edinburgh: Scottish History Society, 1986).

Neville, Cynthia J., and Grant G. Simpson (eds), *The Acts of Alexander III King of Scots 1249–1286* (Edinburgh: Edinburgh University Press, 2013).

Webster, Bruce (ed.), *The Acts of David II King of Scots 1329–1371* (Edinburgh: Edinburgh University Press, 1982).

(3) Chapters in Books

Bannerman, John, 'The Lordship of the Isles', in Jenny M. Brown, *Scottish Society in the Fifteenth Century* (London: Edward Arnold, 1977), 209–40.

Grant, Alexander, 'Franchises north of the border: baronies and regalities in medieval Scotland', in Michael Prestwich (ed.), *Liberties and Identities in the Medieval British Isles* (Woodbridge: Boydell & Brewer, 2008), 155–99.

Munro, Jean, 'The Lordship of the Isles', in Loraine MacLean (ed.), *The Middle Ages in the Highlands* (Inverness: Inverness Field Club, 1981), 23–37.

Sunde, Jørn Øyrehagen, 'A dubious tale of misfortune revealing the true nature of Udal Law on Shetland and the Schound Bill – Shetland law at the beginning of the seventeenth century', in Andrew R. C. Simpson, Scott Crichton Styles, Euan West and Adelyn L. M. Wilson (eds), *Continuity, Change and Pragmatism in the Law. Essays in Memory of Professor Angelo Forte* (Aberdeen: Aberdeen University Press, 2016), 150–74.

(4) Articles in Journals

Lamont, W. D., 'The Islay charter of 1408', *Proceedings of the Royal Irish Academy. Section C: Archaeology, Celtic Studies, History, Linguistics, Literature* 60 (1959/1960), 163–87.

Thomson, Derick S., 'Gaelic learned orders and literati in medieval Scotland', *Scottish Studies* 12 (1968), 57–78.

(5) Unpublished PhD Theses

Anderson, Katherine, 'The influence of Scots and Norse law on law and governance in Orkney and Shetland 1450–1650' (University of Aberdeen, 2015).

PART THREE

The Transformation of the Scottish Common Law and the Session, c. 1450–c. 1580

If in one sense the Scottish common law was tightening its grip in the medieval period, in another sense it faced various problems. The system of brieves, and the courts that administered them, began to run into difficulties. Procedure on brieve began to be associated by some with significant delays in the administration of justice. The judges to whom the brieves were addressed were also sometimes accused of partiality and ignorance of the law. As a result, litigants increasingly took their complaints directly to the king and his closest advisers. Those advisers sat as judges and exercised the jurisdiction of a body known as the king's council to provide litigants with remedies so as to supplement – but not supplant – the work of the older courts. The judges sat in judicial 'sessions' of the king's council. The session was frequently staffed by judges who possessed expertise in the learned laws (i.e. the learning that had built up around the texts of Roman law and canon law). They used this learning to interpret and augment the old medieval common law.

By the 1520s it would seem that the judges on the session – the 'lords of session' – had acquired de facto supreme jurisdiction in Scottish civil matters. In 1532 the old session was reconstituted as the College of Justice. As will be seen, this placed the session on a new institutional footing, and made it easier to regulate who could and who could not sit as a judge within the court. The idea that a lord of session should have expertise in the learned laws began to crystallise at this time. Increasing numbers of legal practitioners also began to appear before the new court, and they too generally possessed expertise in Roman law and canon law. As will be explained, the judges and practitioners accepted the idea that that which they recognised as consistent with justice and legal 'truth' could possess the binding force of law. They treated Roman law as a repository of learning concerning such truth. By contrast, many were less confident about the status of the texts of the old Scottish common law as repositories of such learning. Where conflict arose between the latter texts and the learned laws, lawyers and the lords of session tended to construe the Scottish materials narrowly. That ensured that the scope for the application of the learned laws, and the intrinsic justice that lawyers discerned therein, was very wide. Evidence from the 1540s demonstrates the importance of this approach.

The points already mentioned will be considered in Chapters 6 and 7. Chapter 8 will explore the impact of the Reformation (traditionally dated to 1560) on the development of the Scottish legal system. The political and spiritual turbulence that resulted encouraged some Scots to point to the older common law as a source of authority around which the whole realm could unite. This may, in part, have inspired some lawyers and lords of session to reconceptualise the laws of the realm as a body of learning, akin to Roman law. This development will be considered in Chapter 9. Some further ramifications of this change will be considered in Chapter 10, along with the ways in which legal learning came to be used to discuss the limits – or the lack thereof – of the power of parliament to make law. Throughout, it will be shown that the lawyers and judges who operated within the College of Justice transformed the old medieval Scottish common law in light of their expertise in the learned laws.

CHAPTER 6

The Jurisdiction of the Session

A. INTRODUCTION

The last few chapters have explored questions relating to the emergence of the Scottish common law. Kings of the twelfth and thirteenth centuries increasingly promoted the use of common procedures for the resolution of certain types of disputes. By the fourteenth and fifteenth centuries, parliaments and men of law began to assert that the common law was not simply expressed in those forms of action. Those forms of action were to be interpreted in light of authoritative legal literature, including texts such as *Regiam Majestatem* and *Quoniam Attachiamenta*. Those texts in turn were beginning to be handled and interpreted in light of the learned literature of Roman law and canon law.

Nonetheless, the extent to which the forms of actions known as brieves, and the literature that interpreted them, constituted a common law should not be overstated. Considerable diversity remained. The reasons for this have already been explored, but it is worth reiterating a few points. First, the texts of *Regiam* and *Quoniam* were not static. They were probably read in different ways in different courts. Second, the training and learning of judges and men of law also varied enormously across the realm. Complaints about corrupt or simply ignorant common law judges can frequently be traced in fifteenth-century records. For these and other reasons, the common law structured around the brieves, and the courts that administered it, were increasingly found inadequate to meet the needs of litigants in practice.

The next five chapters will explore how such problems were addressed between the mid fifteenth and the late sixteenth centuries. The current chapter will begin by considering a dispute drawn from the end of the period, *Wemyss v Forbes* (1543).[1] This serves to introduce three radical changes in the Scottish legal system that took place between c. 1450 and c. 1550. First, the period witnessed the development of a new court,

known as the session. By 1532 the session had acquired supreme jurisdiction in Scottish civil matters, and so over much of the old common
law.[2] In the process, it effectively left the old pleadable brieves 'with no
useful application'.[3] Second, the century under consideration here also
witnessed the reconstitution of the session as a College of Justice, in
1532. That catalysed the emergence of what would ultimately become
the Scottish legal profession.[4] From this time onwards, the judges and
men of law who staffed the College of Justice were generally expected
to possess expertise in the learned laws. Third, in tandem with this last
development, Roman and canonical legal learning began to transform the
Scottish common law itself, and Scottish legal literature.[5] The first point
will be considered in this chapter, while the second and third points will
be considered in Chapters 7–10.

---

[1]　See Athol L. Murray and Gero Dolezalek (eds), *Sinclair's Practicks*, http://home.
uni-leipzig.de/jurarom/scotland/dat/sinclair.html, case note 308; Hector L.
MacQueen, 'Jurisdiction in heritage and the Lords of Council and Session after
1532', in W. David H. Sellar (ed.), *Stair Society Miscellany Two* (Edinburgh: Stair
Society, 1984), 61–85; Hector L. MacQueen, *Common Law and Feudal Society*,
reprinted edn (Edinburgh: Edinburgh University Press, 2016), 241–2. Note
that MacQueen's comments should now be read in light of A. Mark Godfrey,
'Jurisdiction in heritage and the foundation of the College of Justice in 1532', in
Hector L. MacQueen (ed.), *Stair Society Miscellany Four* (Edinburgh: Stair Society,
2002), 9–36 and A. Mark Godfrey, *Civil Justice in Renaissance Scotland* (Leiden:
Brill, 2009), 308, 315, 319.

[2]　While it is true to say that the session enjoyed supremacy in civil matters, its
jurisdictional relationships with some courts (such as the exchequer) were complex;
even there, the session seems to have enjoyed a supervisory role. A full discussion of
this point is beyond the scope of the present work.

[3]　See Godfrey, *Civil Justice*, 452. Much of the argument presented below is deeply
indebted to Godfrey's work, and to MacQueen's earlier study of the medieval
common law.

[4]　See generally John Finlay, *Men of Law in Pre-Reformation Scotland* (East Linton:
Tuckwell Press, 2000).

[5]　The literature on this last point is vast, and will be discussed in the next chapter.
One important contribution is J. D. Ford, *Law and Opinion in Scotland during the
Seventeenth Century* (Oxford and Portland: Hart, 2007), which engages extensively
with the sixteenth-century legal context, for example at 181–246; see also John W.
Cairns, *Law, Lawyers and Humanism. Selected Essays on the History of Scots Law,
Volume 1* (Edinburgh: Edinburgh University Press, 2015).

B. 'NOCHT ... USIT IN THIS REALME': THE STRANGE FATE OF THE BRIEVE OF RIGHT

In February 1543 Patrick Wemyss of Pittencrieff raised an action against Arthur Forbes of Reres as part of a dispute over lands in Fife. Wemyss sought to achieve the reduction of Forbes's 'infeftment' in the lands. In other words, he sought the nullification of Forbes's feudal title to the lands. Wemyss brought his action before judges styled the 'lords of council' who sat in a court known as the 'session'. At this time, the session generally met in the old Tolbooth in Edinburgh.[6] This was located at the north-west corner of what is today St Giles' Cathedral.

It may be helpful to visualise what Wemyss and Forbes would have seen there in 1543, assuming they attended court in person. Approaching the large medieval Tolbooth, with its crow-step gables and its walls inlaid with niches containing statues of the saints, the litigants would have witnessed a hive of activity, both legal and commercial. The lords of session jostled with the courts of the justiciar, of sheriffs and the burgh for the use of the building, which also lay at the heart of the city's bustling marketplace. Traders, merchants, notaries and men of law had offices or 'booths' to the east of the Tolbooth. A great throng of people would have been transacting business in and around these predominantly wattle and timber structures, under the shadow of the great kirk of St Giles. Goods would have been bought and sold, legal transactions would have been concluded and notaries would have produced their all-important instruments. It seems that mercantile activities regularly interfered with the business of the courts themselves. Complaints had been made in the past about the 'multitud of pcplc' who passed through the Tolbooth and who made 'gret noys and misreule'. Most were probably more interested in using the Tolbooth as a place to transact commerce than as a legal forum. A constant frenzy of activity would have been accompanied by the conflicting shouts of traders and pleadings of

---

[6] Sometimes they met in other locations, such as the house just off the Lawnmarket owned by Alexander Myln, Abbot of Cambuskenneth, who was lord president of the session from 1532 until his death in 1548. Yet in the apparent absence of evidence to the contrary, it will be assumed here that they met in the Tolbooth on the occasion described here. For the slightly peripatetic nature of the early court, see Finlay, *Men of Law*, 91–2. C. A. Malcolm, 'The parliament house and its antecedents', in G. C. H. Paton (ed.), *An Introduction to Scottish Legal History* (Edinburgh: Stair Society, 1958), 448–58, can be read as suggesting that the lords sat exclusively in the Abbot of Cambuskenneth's house between February 1539 and 1552. The evidence cited by Malcolm would not support such a reading.

men of law. The resulting confusion would only have been exacerbated by the tendency of powerful clients to bring large retinues of armed men with them to court, to underline the force of their case.[7]

Against this setting one can imagine the laird of Reres, Arthur Forbes, walking through the throng to seek out his man of law, so as to consult him about the action Wemyss had raised. The man of law in question had a booth on the north side of the Tolbooth; his name was Master Thomas Marjoribanks. As his title of 'Master' indicates, Marjoribanks had university training. Specifically, he had studied the learned law at Orléans in France. At this time, most senior men of law studied the learned laws abroad, even though a handful of law graduates from the fifteenth-century Scottish universities were active in public life.[8]

On hearing that Wemyss had raised an action for the reduction or nullification of his client's title, Marjoribanks formulated a series of defences or 'exceptions' to the claim. Wemyss's action would have been 'tabled', that is to say listed on a table fixed to the door of the Tolbooth. The table would have indicated the date on which the dispute was to be heard. Actions that were called without having first been tabled would generally be treated as null.[9] On 28 February the day came, and a macer called the litigants in *Wemyss v Forbes* to appear before the lords of session. Marjoribanks would have appeared before them, probably on the first floor of the Tolbooth. There was a bar in the court where the men of law pleaded, and behind this bar sat the lords of session, around a table. In total there were fifteen lords, although not all of them necessarily sat at once. Both their table and their chairs were covered with green cloth. Those who appeared before the lords were expected to be dressed appropriately, perhaps in gowns. The judges themselves may have worn purple gowns, faced with red velvet, as they did a century later. Those studying to become men of law were generally permitted to sit nearby.[10]

Within this setting, the first defence Marjoribanks advanced against the action for the reduction of his client's infeftment was fairly stark. He alleged that the lords of session 'wer na judges competent' in this case,

> becaus thairthrow vald cum in disputatioun of the rycht of his landis, quhilk ground rycht of auld aucht be act of parliament be

---

[7]   Much of this description is taken from Finlay, *Men of Law*, 90–6, 104.

[8]   Marjoribanks's career is discussed alongside the careers of other contemporary lawyers in Finlay, *Men of Law*, 53–71.

[9]   See Finlay, *Men of Law*, 98–102.

[10]   See Finlay, *Men of Law*, 92–3.

decydit be ane breif of rycht befoir the justice, and nocht befoir the lordis of sessioun.[11]

The sense of this can be rendered in modern English as follows. Marjoribanks argued that the lords did not have authority to decide the dispute:

> because as a result the right of his lands would come into disputation. That ground right of old ought to be decided by a brieve of right before the justiciar, and not before the lords of session, according to a rule laid down by act of parliament.

Marjoribanks's argument was that the case brought into 'disputatioun' the underlying right, or title to the lands. He then seems to have argued that such a challenge to underlying title had to be initiated by means of a brieve of right. He justified this by making reference to an 'act of parliament'. This was presumably the statute of 1318 by which Robert I had declared that no one was 'to be ejected from his free holding of which he claims to be vest and saised as of fee without the king's pleadable brieve or some similar brieve'.[12] It will be recalled that the brieve of right could indeed be used to consider underlying questions of title or rights in land, particularly where the brieves of novel dissasine and mortancestry were unavailable.

Based on what was said in Chapters 2 and 3, it might be thought that Marjoribanks's argument would have been compelling. Nonetheless, it was rejected. The lords of session:

> decernit thame competent judges in this mater, sic as thai wer thir divers yeiris in use of calling sic materis befoir thame and divers sic interlocutoris gevin, *ut in causa domini de Sanquhair et in causa cuiusdam Pringill de Torsounis et aliis diversis*, and als becaus the breif of rycht is (nor hes) nocht yit bene mony yeiris usit in this realme.[13]

The sense of this can be rendered into modern English as follows:

> The lords of [session] notwithstanding found themselves to be competent judges in this matter. For they had been in the habit of

---

[11] The quotation is from Murray and Dolezalek (eds), *Sinclair's Practicks*, cn. 308.
[12] See Chapter 3 above; the quotation is from MacQueen, *Common Law*, 106.
[13] The quotation is from Murray and Dolezalek (eds), *Sinclair's Practicks*, cn. 308.

calling such matters before them over many years, and of giving many interlocutors on the point – as in the cause of the *Lord of Sanquhar* and in the cause of a certain *Pringle of Torsonce* and of diverse others. Also the lords made this decision because the brieve of right has not been used in this realm for many years.

In other words, the lords found themselves to have authority to judge the dispute. Contrary to what Marjoribanks argued, the lords had the power to reduce his client's infeftment – his feudal title. The lords justified the exercise of their authority in this case on two grounds. First, they made reference to past decisions of the session, in which they had already asserted jurisdiction in actions to reduce infeftments. Second, the lords also asserted that the brieve of right had fallen out of use. By implication the same could be said about the statutory rule enjoining its use in practice. Note that both elements of the lords' reasoning were evidently shaped by assumptions about how law could be made, and how it could lose its force and effect. Law could be shaped through decisions of the lords. Conversely, even statutory rules could lose their force and effect when they fell out of use. As will be explained in the next chapter, these assumptions were deeply indebted to arguments advanced by expert Roman lawyers concerning how laws could emerge.

Wemyss v Forbes highlights just how radically Scots law had been transformed since the early fifteenth century. Perhaps the most surprising change relates to the role of the brieve of right. One hundred years prior to the decision in *Wemyss*, the brieve lay at the heart of the medieval Scottish forms of action. Other brieves enabled litigants to seek redress for very particular types of interference with rights in land. So it will be recalled that the brieve of novel dissasine allowed one who had lost sasine of a freehold interest to seek recovery thereof. The brieve of mortancestry allowed one to recover lands of which a close relative had been saised as of fee. Yet the brieve of right allowed a court to look deeper, to the underlying question of just right in the lands. This brieve, and this brieve alone, enabled a court to make a final determination of 'right' in lands – in modern parlance, to determine ultimate ownership. Without this form of action, the brieves could not deal with the most fundamental questions of feudal title to lands. And yet the brieve of right had, apparently, fallen out of use by 1543. What had caused this radical development? And had Scots law provided an alternative form of action for litigants who sought to determine the ownership of lands?

As will be explained, the fate of the brieve of right is intimately bound up with another change illustrated by *Wemyss v Forbes*. By 1543 the court that declared the brieves rule to have no useful application, the session, had come to enjoy supreme jurisdiction in Scottish civil matters. A century earlier its ultimate antecedent, the king's council, had exercised a much less extensive jurisdiction. At that time, the power of the council to decide disputes had been significantly curtailed by the jurisdictions of the common law courts of the justiciars and the sheriffs. The radical development of the session calls for explanation, and this will be discussed in the current chapter alongside the decline of the brieves. Consequently the focus of this chapter will be on the developing *jurisdiction* of the session. Nonetheless, it should be noted here that the court also underwent another major change during the period under consideration here. It was reconstituted and placed on a new institutional footing as the College of Justice in 1532. That in turn resulted in the emergence of a community of legal experts. This would, in time, develop into the Scottish legal profession. One of the first members of this community of learned lawyers was Thomas Marjoribanks, who appeared in the case of *Wemyss*. Those judges and men of law were steeped in the learning of Roman law and canon law. It will be shown that they used this to transform the common law that they had inherited from their medieval predecessors. These last points will be considered below in Chapters 7–9.

C. THE BRIEVES, THE COMMON LAW COURTS AND THE SESSIONS

(1) Fifteenth-century Problems in the Administration of Justice

In *Wemyss*, the lords of session linked their authority to hear actions concerning the reduction of infeftments with the decline of the brieves system. This underlines the fact that, in order to explain the development of the session, it may first be helpful to consider some of the problems that had emerged in relation to procedure on brieve by the mid-fifteenth century. Four types of problems merit particular consideration here.[14] First, difficulties arose as a result of the basic assumption that underpinned the whole brieves system. This was that local problems should be dealt with in each locality. As has been explained, when a dispute emerged in a particular region one of the disputants

---

[14] The following discussion of the problems that emerged regarding the administration of justice in the common law courts is largely drawn from MacQueen, *Common Law*, 257–9.

could approach the king – or a lord of regality – for a brieve to remedy the problem. This would then be addressed to a sheriff or justiciar or bailie who operated in the locality where the dispute had arisen. The judge would then convene a local assize to determine the true facts of the matter at hand. Not unreasonably, it was assumed that only such local assizers could have the knowledge required to establish the truth. For example, only they could be expected to know the true locations of local territorial boundaries. Furthermore, only they could be expected to know whether or not the claimant truly was the heir of a deceased individual. While intelligible, this approach to dispute resolution began to run into problems as local knowledge came to be only one source of information required to render a just decision. For example, in 1455 an assize operating on the basis of a brieve of mortancestry considered the case of Margaret Mundell. She wished to claim that she was entitled to some land in Dumfriesshire, which was then in the possession of her sisters. The assize decided that Margaret's sisters were illegitimate, and so determined that she had a rightful claim to the land. What seems to have been unknown to the assize in 1455 was that Mundell's sisters had in fact been declared legitimate by the pope eighteen years earlier. Thus they should not have been barred from the succession. This illustrates the problems that could arise where courts simply depended on local knowledge to resolve a dispute.

A second, and related, problem was that increasingly the collective memory of assizers was not the only basis on which they made their decisions. As MacQueen states, 'by the fifteenth century, cases turned not on what the assizers had seen and heard themselves but on the interpretation of complicated technical documents (which might be forged)'.[15] Put another way, an assize faced with a brieve of right commanding them to establish who held title to particular lands might have had to consider a bewildering range of documents. Among them could have been old charters, tailzies and instruments of sasine. The potential range of documentation that assizers might have to consider increased as land came to be used in complex commercial transactions, for example as security for debt. A statute of 1469 regulated a process whereby a debtor might transfer his lands to a creditor subject to a deed known as a reversion.[16] The reversion could subsequently be used by the debtor to force the creditor to return the lands on repayment of the debt. The use of land as a commercial asset underlined the need to record in writing the various rights of different

15 MacQueen, *Common Law*, 257.
16 *RPS* 1469/17.

parties therein. Furthermore, as explained above, a host of other rights in land could exist, such as terce and courtesy. All might be expressed through some form of documentary evidence. Where the legal training required to interpret such evidence correctly was lacking, injustices could easily result.

A third problem was associated with the local judges who presided over disputes initiated by brieve. From the mid-fifteenth century, litigants frequently complained that the royal judicial officers, like their counterparts in the regalities, lacked the understanding of the law required to discharge their duties. Such understanding might have assisted with ensuring the observance of due process, or indeed with the resolution of more substantial legal difficulties. The problem was probably exacerbated by the fact that the primary qualification for holding many judicial offices was not knowledge of the law, but rather hereditary right. The regality courts were obviously held on a hereditary basis, and by the fifteenth century the same could be said for many sheriffdoms. Scottish monarchs did recognise the problem and attempted to improve the education of their judicial officers. For example, the Education Act 1496 commanded the sons of nobles to go to 'the sculis of art and jure [i.e. law]'.[17] The aim of the statute was to ensure that:

> thai that ar schireffis or jugeis ordinaris under the kingis hienes may have knawlege to do justice, that the pure pepill sulde have na need to seik oure soverane lordis principale auditouris for ilk small iniure.[18]

This can be rendered in modern English as follows:

> they that are sheriffs or ordinary judges may have knowledge to do justice that the poor people should have no need to seek our sovereign lord's principal auditors [judges] for each small injury.

This statute was passed a year after the University of Aberdeen was founded; historians have argued that there was some link between the two initiatives.[19]

---

[17] *RPS* A1496/6/4.

[18] *RPS* A1496/6/4.

[19] See, for example, Leslie J. Macfarlane, *William Elphinstone and the Kingdom of Scotland 1431–1514. The Struggle for Order* (Aberdeen: Aberdeen University Press, 1985), 312–13.

A fourth problem arose from the fact that procedure on brieve had become highly cumbersome and complex by the late fifteenth century. Delay in the administration of justice was a persistent problem. The brieve of right could only be initiated 'at the thrice-yearly head courts of the sheriff and the burgh'.[20] Actions begun by brieves of novel dissasine and mortancestry could only be heard when the justiciar arrived on his progress – which was twice a year at most. Furthermore, the procedure associated with the brieve of right allowed a defender four separate excuses in response to a summons before he had to appear in court. Parliament sought to regulate the large numbers of defences or exceptions that the diverse men of law devised to delay procedure on brieve. Many such exceptions seem to have existed, and not all were particularly sophisticated. A statute of 1430 seems to reflect a situation in which brieves were often challenged on the basis that they were 'raisit' or 'blobit' (meaning 'erased' or 'blotted') in 'suspect placis'.[21] Challenges also seem to have been advanced when innovations were made in the wording and form of brieves. Determining the question of ultimate feudal right in lands through brieve, then, could be a long process. In *Bisset v Dishington of Ardross*, for example, litigation on brieve commenced in 1471, and it was still on-going in 1478.[22]

Thus, broadly speaking, process on brieve was hindered both by deficiencies in the courts that heard this type of action and also by the delays that had come to be inherent in the procedure itself. The deficiencies in the courts were primarily associated with the ignorance of assizers and judges. Such ignorance increasingly resulted in problems as the law grew more sophisticated. The deficiencies with the brieves were connected with the willingness and apparent ability of men of law to develop procedural delaying tactics. It seems that the common law judges (who were themselves typically laymen) were unwilling, or unable, to respond effectively to those tactics.

When faced with such problems, fifteenth-century litigants increasingly turned directly to the king and his close advisers for remedies. Successive Stewart monarchs responded with the aid of two institutions. The first was parliament, and the second was the king's council. The ways in which the monarchs used those institutions to address problems in the administration of justice will be discussed next. As will be explained, the session ultimately emerged from the exercise of the

---

[20] MacQueen, *Common Law*, 258.
[21] MacQueen, *Common Law*, 258; *RPS* 1430/5.
[22] MacQueen, *Common Law*, 179, 258.

jurisdiction of the king's council (hereafter this may be referred to as 'conciliar jurisdiction').

(2) The Initial Royal Response

It was mentioned above that James I (r. 1406–37) held a parliament in 1426 which promoted the study of the older laws of the realm. Part of the aim was to distinguish 'lauchefull' from 'frivolus' defences to forms of actions such as the brieves.[23] However, this parliament also heard calls for more rigorous reform in the administration of royal justice. Litigants did not simply complain about the procedural delays in their actions that had been caused by 'fraudfull' exceptions. It would appear that they also brought the actions in question before the king sitting in parliament. In other words, the king and parliament were not only asked to remedy procedural delays by reforming the law; it seems that they were also asked to address the problem much more directly, by deciding cases that may well have dragged on for some time.

The decision of litigants to bring their complaints directly before the king and parliament was not as strange in the early fifteenth century as it may appear today. The medieval king was ultimately personally responsible for the administration of justice. This is illustrated by a story told by the historian Walter Bower, Abbot of Inchcolm, about James I. Bower praised the king's administration of justice and the 'firm peace' he brought to the realm. In so doing, he did not discuss *institutional* reform, but rather the king's *personal* willingness to intervene in disputes.[24] This he illustrated with a narrative of a dispute – which may not be wholly historically true – in which a poor woman had been robbed by a notorious brigand from Ross, in the far north of the kingdom. She swore in his presence that she would not wear shoes until she had brought her complaint before the king. The brigand said she was swearing falsely. To prove his point, in a particularly gruesome attack, he nailed horseshoes to her feet. Undeterred, the remarkable woman recovered from her injuries and brought her complaint before the king. Enraged, James I wrote to the sheriff of Ross and demanded that he arrest the wrongdoer and bring him to trial before his monarch. Having been brought before the king, the brigand was convicted. He was humiliated by being walked through

---

[23] *RPS* 1426/13.
[24] See D. E. R. Watt *et al.* (eds), *Scotichronicon by Walter Bower in Latin and English* (Aberdeen: Aberdeen University Press, 1987–98) VIII, 318–21. For the date of the work, see Watt *et al.* (eds), *Bower's Scotichronicon* XI, 207–8.

the streets of Perth for two days wearing a linen surcoat depicting a man nailing horse's shoes to a woman's feet. Assuming at least this element of Bower's story is true, one must not imagine the good burgesses of Perth standing by and watching in disapproving, judgemental silence. More likely they would have been jeering at him, and pelting him with whatever unpleasant things came to hand. Finally, the brigand was dragged through the streets by a horse, and then hung on a gibbet.

The fact that Bower chose this as one of two stories to illustrate James I's excellent qualities as one who maintained law and order is intriguing. This applies regardless of whether or not the events narrated actually happened as Bower suggested. He could have focused on James's experimentation with procedural and institutional reforms, of which more will be said shortly. Yet he did not. Bower instead chose to emphasise that James I fulfilled contemporaries' expectations of a medieval Scottish monarch in the administration of justice. Where necessary, he was expected to intervene personally to protect his subjects from unlawful violence and from the loss of their property. He was expected to ensure that local sheriffs discharged their duties effectively. It was also his duty to mete out harsh punishments on those who broke his laws. Bower held up this model of the monarch prepared to administer justice personally and forcibly as being worthy of imitation. Undoubtedly contemporaries would have recognised that model, and approved of it.

Thus a litigant's decision to bring a complaint before James I himself was perfectly intelligible in this context. Similarly, it made sense to bring disputes directly before parliament. While parliaments made laws through the promulgation of statutes, they also acted as law courts, as judicial fora for the resolution of disputes.[25] For example, parliaments had authority to hear treason trials in Scotland. Furthermore, as the highest secular courts in the land, parliaments could hear suits concerning less serious matters. They could 'false' the 'dooms' or judgements of lower courts, including sheriff courts, burgh courts and courts of the justiciar. During the fifteenth century they also attempted to interfere in the exercise of jurisdiction in the regalities. Various acts of parliament threatened those who held regality courts with the intervention of royal

---

[25] For parliament's judicial functions, as outlined here, see Godfrey, *Civil Justice*, 7–39; A. Mark Godfrey, 'Parliament and the law', in Keith M. Brown and Alan R. MacDonald (eds), *Parliament in Context, 1235–1707* (Edinburgh: Edinburgh University Press, 2010), 157–85 at 161–8. This is the third of the three volumes in Keith M. Brown (ed.), *The History of the Scottish Parliament* (Edinburgh: Edinburgh University Press, 2004–10). This is currently the best general history of the Scottish parliaments in the period prior to 1707.

officers if their own subordinates failed to do justice according to the standards of the common law.[26] Serious failures on the part of lords of regality could result in punishment and even in the forfeiture of their judicial rights, at least in theory.[27] The extent to which such statutes were effective is unclear. Nonetheless, their promulgation signalled parliament's assertion of a supreme jurisdiction in temporal, non-spiritual matters.

By 1426, significant demands on parliament as a judicial forum would appear to have been interfering with other aspects of its business.[28] James I wished to free his highest court from the burden of hearing large numbers of minor disputes. Consequently, he inaugurated what became known as the 'sessions'. In each session, a royal officer was to sit with 'certane dyscreyt persouns of the thre estatis' for fourteen days in each quarter of the year, wherever the king commanded. The reference to the 'thre estatis' here is a reference to the three sections or 'estates' of the Scottish populace who were represented in parliament. They were the clergy, the nobility and the burgesses. The 'dyscreyt persouns' chosen from those estates were to determine in their sessions all matters that could be heard before the king's council.[29] The expedient was clearly designed to relieve some of the pressure of judicial business in parliament and in council. Nonetheless, the fact that the sessions were only empowered to resolve disputes that could be heard in *council* did constitute an important limitation on their authority. To explain, the king's council was a smaller, more flexible body than parliament. Its members were selected by the king from among senior members of the clergy and the nobility.[30] By the mid-fifteenth century it also included increasing numbers of university-educated administrators and diplomats. Like parliament, council had important judicial functions. Yet in the early fifteenth century its jurisdiction was technically quite limited. It had authority to hear cases concerning certain privileged litigants to whom the king was thought to owe a special duty of protection. They included members of the clergy, widows, orphans, the poor and foreigners who were in Scotland. The council could also hear cases concerning complaints that the king's officers had been negligent in the administration

---

[26] Consider, for example, *RPS* 1450/1/9–10.

[27] See, to name some examples, *RPS* 1434/5; *RPS* 1436/10/2; *RPS* 1458/3/17; *RPS* 1487/10/7

[28] The rest of the discussion in this section of the chapter is substantially based upon Godfrey, *Civil Justice*, 40–66.

[29] *RPS* 1426/25.

[30] See Godfrey, *Civil Justice*, 11–12.

of their duties.[31] However, for reasons that will become clear shortly, the council did *not* have authority to hear disputes initiated by brieve. So while the early sessions would undoubtedly have relieved some of the pressure of judicial business from parliament, this should not be overstated. It seems clear that this new institution – if it can be called that – was not intended to replace the roles of parliament or the king's council. Over the next forty years, James I and his son, James II, continued to experiment with the administration of royal justice. Yet very little is known about the functions and operation of these early sessions, although the session of 1458 had jurisdiction over a relatively new form of action, known as spuilzie. This will be discussed in more detail later in the current chapter.

The judicial business before the king's council increased as the fifteenth century progressed. However, in 1487, a highly controversial experiment was attempted by a parliament of James III, son of James II. It reveals something about contemporary attitudes to the problems in the administration of justice at this time. Parliament sought to refuse litigants any access to the council in the first instance. All cases had to be brought first in the local courts.[32] Godfrey notes that the aim may have been to relieve the council of its judicial duties, or simply to 'galvanise'[33] the courts in the localities. Macdougall has also suggested that various magnates who held jurisdictional privileges, such as regality courts, may have forced the king to promulgate the act. He suggests that they may have sought to put an end to what they saw as the encroachment of conciliar jurisdiction within their territories.[34] Regardless, the experiment failed. In 1488 it was accepted that this policy 'wer deferring of justice to mony partiis that couthe nocht gett law ministrit to thame before thare ordinaris' (i.e. it 'was hindering justice for many parties, who could not get law administered to them before their ordinary judges').[35] Again, local justice was seen as defective; litigants wanted to turn to the king himself to resolve disputes.

Yet this episode is revealing. In general, Scottish parliaments of the fifteenth century did not wish to supplant the framework of courts that existed in the regions. Instead, they sought to remedy the problems that existed in those courts. According to this approach, the function of

[31] See MacQueen, *Common Law*, 220.
[32] *RPS* 1487/10/14.
[33] Godfrey, *Civil Justice*, 66.
[34] Norman Macdougall, *James III* (Edinburgh: John Donald, 2009), 310.
[35] *RPS* 1488/1/25.

the ideal king remained that outlined by Bower. He would be a strong monarch, who would work tirelessly through the traditional structures of the common law to ensure his sheriffs and other officers would do justice to the satisfaction of the lieges. That was what James I had done in the case of the poor woman mentioned above. In other words, it was still thought credible to argue that justice ought to be administered locally by local courts – albeit under the watchful eye of a forceful monarch. Royal councils and parliaments were only to interfere directly if absolutely necessary. Their primary function was to make sure the local courts operated effectively; it was not to replace them. Hence the statute in 1487 declared that litigants were to initiate all actions before their local judges. Indeed, to some extent the Education Act 1496 dovetailed with this approach in that it required the education of the sons of noblemen who were likely to hold judicial office. This was one way of responding to the problem, but it was ultimately ineffective in itself. A more complex response seemed necessary in order to remedy the matter.[36]

(3) The Conciliar Sessions

Macdougall argues that James III himself did not share the assumptions just outlined concerning the administration of justice. On the contrary, he suggests that the king supported the augmentation of council's juris-diction. According to this view, James was hindered in realising his goal by magnates who were keen to preserve their highly lucrative jurisdic-tional privileges. Macdougall goes so far as to suggest that James's han-dling of this conflict may have been one of the causes of the breakdown in relations between the king and some of his leading nobles in 1488.[37] Some of them rebelled, having found a leader in the king's eldest son. On 11 June 1488 the rebels met the king in battle near Stirling, and he was killed shortly afterwards. To this day no one knows who struck the fatal blow. A parliament that met later in 1488 famously commented that the

---

[36] This would undoubtedly have been recognised by the framer of the Education Act 1496, assuming he was, as Macfarlane suggests, Bishop William Elphinstone of Aberdeen (see Macfarlane, *Elphinstone*, 312–13). The terms of the statute indicate that Elphinstone was still keen to improve the quality of local justice, while at the same time it is well-known that he personally participated in the development of conciliar jurisdiction (see Macfarlane, *Elphinstone*, 422–4). In other words, he valued the older approach of making the local courts work properly, but felt that this was only a partial solution to the problem.

[37] Macdougall, *James III*, 310, 321–51.

king 'happinnit to be slane' ('happened to be slain') following the battle.[38] That parliament was, of course, attended by the rebel lords, and by their leader, James IV (r. 1488–1513).

James IV's magnatial supporters may well have had some doubts about the growing competence of the king's council to deal with civil litigation. Yet it would seem that ordinary litigants did not share those doubts. Increasingly the king showed that he agreed with them, and he distanced himself from the more conservative approach manifested in 1487. He developed more regular 'sessions', which were quite different from the old parliamentary sessions. The sessions of James IV (the origins of which may be traced to the reign of James III) were sittings of the king's council that were dedicated to the resolution of legal disputes. From this time onwards, the judges who sat in these judicial sessions of council – sometimes called the 'conciliar' sessions – were often referred to as 'lords of session'.[39] Nonetheless, they also retained their older title of 'lords of council'. Frequently they were clergymen, who had studied Roman law and canon law in continental Europe. For example, Bishop William Elphinstone of Aberdeen sat as a lord of session for many years. Indeed, he exercised a leading role within the council as chancellor of the realm. He had studied canon law at Paris and civil law at Orléans in the 1460s and the 1470s before returning to Scotland.[40] In the past such learning had equipped men like Elphinstone for a variety of important tasks in the service of the king. These included diplomacy and the representation of Scottish interests before the papal courts. Yet increasingly it was found useful in the administration of internal affairs and of justice. The reasons for this will be discussed in subsequent chapters. For now it suffices to state that this sort of legal learning helped the lords of session to resolve the complex disputes that were emerging in Scotland at this time. In this regard, they were quite unlike most of the sheriffs who administered justice under the old common law.

Nonetheless, while James IV and Elphinstone promoted the development of the conciliar session, its jurisdiction remained limited. Whether or not this was influenced by the concerns of the great magnates to preserve their jurisdictional privileges is unclear. As was stated earlier, one significant limitation on the jurisdiction of the session at this point

---

38 *RPS* 1488/10/51.
39 The discussion of the conciliar sessions in the current section of this chapter draws heavily on Godfrey, *Civil Justice*, 67–79.
40 Regarding Elphinstone's career, see Macfarlane, *Elphinstone*; his early career is discussed at 16–47.

in time was that it could not hear actions initiated by brieve. Brieves were addressed by the king to his officers, such as his justiciars and his sheriffs. As a result, they could not be addressed to the lords of session, and so the king's council, because the king was a member of his council. After all, the king could not issue an instruction to himself to do justice.[41] Furthermore, it would not necessarily have been straightforward to change this by reforming procedure on brieve. Brieves were, of course, well-established mechanisms for regulating disputes over rights in land. Such rights were jealously guarded. Consequently, direct attempts to change radically the ways in which they could be enforced might well have been met with stiff resistance from powerful members of the land-holding classes. Some at least might have preferred to see such matters dealt with within their own local spheres of influence.

Additionally, another rule limited the power of the lords of session to hear civil disputes concerning rights in land. This was known as the fee and heritage rule.[42] Its operation can be illustrated by a dispute of 1479 between John and Thomas Wemyss, on the one part, and Arthur Forbes in Reres, on the other.[43] The claimant, Forbes, sued the brothers John and Thomas Wemyss before the council. The claim was for the spuilzie of oxen and corns. The action of spuilzie could arise where a man had been in possession of a thing, and was then violently dispossessed of it. The remedy was restitution. That the council had jurisdiction over spuilzies had been confirmed by parliament in 1458.[44] However, as MacQueen notes, sometimes 'the defender's justification for seizing the goods [in a spuilzie] was his assertion of some right in land'.[45] In the action of spuilzie brought in *Forbes v Wemyss* (1479), the lords declined to exercise jurisdiction 'because the landis that the said gudis was takin of is clamyt fee and heretage be baith the said parties and the questioun of the richt dependis apoun heritage' (i.e. 'because the said lands from which the said goods were taken is claimed as of fee and heritage by both the said parties, and the question of right depends upon heritage').[46] In other words, the dispute over possession of the oxen and corns was underpinned by a deeper dispute concerning underlying 'ownership'

---

[41] See Godfrey, *Civil Justice*, 21.

[42] For the fee and heritage rule, see MacQueen, *Common Law*, 215–42; elements of MacQueen's thesis are challenged effectively in Godfrey, *Civil Justice*, 268–312.

[43] See MacQueen, *Common Law*, 227

[44] *RPS* 1458/3/3. Note that this statute indicates the lords were originally only to exercise this jurisdiction for a fixed period of time.

[45] MacQueen, *Common Law*, 224–5.

[46] MacQueen, *Common Law*, 227.

of the lands. Two competing titles were alleged to those lands. It was the deeper question relating to the final determination of right that the council refused to decide. Indeed, the lords felt *barred* from deciding such matters. This jurisdictional bar is known as the 'fee and heritage rule'.

It might be thought that the fee and heritage rule was nothing other than the brieves rule in operation. Perhaps the lords declined jurisdiction because they thought that this dispute over lands had to be initiated by brieve. And yet MacQueen's analysis of the case demonstrates that this cannot have been so. The two rules were distinct. It will be recalled that the brieves rule, as laid down by statute in 1318, provided that no one was to be ejected from a free holding of which he claimed to be vest and saised as of fee without the king's pleadable brieve or some similar brieve. Yet MacQueen has demonstrated that in this case the Wemyss brothers could not have claimed that they had been 'vest and saised as of fee' of the disputed lands. Consequently, they could not have used the brieves rule as a defence against Forbes's action. The fact that they *did* success-fully invoke the fee and heritage rule to defend the action before the lords demonstrates that it was something different.[47] So what was it?

The successful invocation of the fee and heritage rule in this case resulted in it being sent back to an ordinary judge in Fife. That does provide a clue concerning the nature of the rule itself. MacQueen has argued that the 'true origin' of the rule lay in an older principle, that the jurisdiction of council and parliament was excluded where there was an ordinary remedy at common law.[48] Undoubtedly the scope of this exclusion was eroded during the fifteenth century. Yet it continued to operate, alongside the brieves rule, to limit the jurisdiction of council in disputes over land. Here it should be mentioned that Godfrey has shown the fee and heritage rule was narrower in scope than previous writers had thought. It only limited conciliar jurisdiction where there was 'more than one competing claim to a disputed title'. Even then, the authority of the lords was only limited if the decision would 'involve a final deter-mination of right'.[49] Nonetheless, the rule still limited the jurisdiction of the lords of session quite significantly. Furthermore, Godfrey's con-clusion does not undermine the basic arguments advanced here. First, the fee and heritage rule was distinct from the brieves rule. Second, *both*

---

[47] MacQueen, *Common Law*, 227.
[48] MacQueen, *Common Law*, 218–42 (which must now be read in conjunction with Godfrey, *Civil Justice*).
[49] Godfrey, *Civil Justice*, 310–12 (summarising the arguments advanced at 268–312).

rules operated to restrict the authority of the lords of session to decide cases.

The case of *Forbes v Wemyss and Wemyss* (1479) makes curious reading when compared with *Wemyss v Forbes* (1543), which was discussed above. Both cases in fact represented different stages in a long saga of litigation over the lands of Reres and Leuchars in Fife.[50] Several generations of the families involved fought out the dispute in the courts. Both cases dealt with broadly similar questions, concerning the underlying rights to the lands. In the first case, the fee and heritage rule was held to bar the jurisdiction of the lords of council, the forebears of the later lords of session. Yet in the second case, no such jurisdictional bar was recognised. Indeed, the lords expressly rejected the possibility that the old brieves rule might operate to prevent them from deciding the dispute. This shows that the jurisdiction of the lords over disputes concerning title to land had developed significantly between 1479 and 1543. How did this happen?

(4) The Developing Jurisdiction of the Lords of Session: Reduction of Infeftments

Both the brieves rule and also the fee and heritage rule had the effect of restricting the jurisdiction of the lords in disputes over feudal title. Nonetheless, the lords *did* have authority to decide *some* actions concerning such matters.[51] These were actions for reduction of infeftment, which began to emerge as actions in their own right in the late fifteenth century. Broadly speaking, these actions enabled litigants to petition the lords to seek the reduction or nullification of individual feudal titles. In other words, the lords could assess the intrinsic validity of such rights. The lords' acquisition of the power to decide such matters can be explained in various ways. Yet an important element of the explanation can be found from their power to decide actions of error.[52] Such actions were commonly used to deal with inheritance disputes before the lords during the second half of the fifteenth century. Their function can be explained as follows. Suppose one claiming to be the heir of a deceased landowner brought his claim before the sheriff. Normally the sheriff would have then summoned an assize, a group of local men chosen to

---

[50] See MacQueen, 'Jurisdiction in heritage'.
[51] For what follows in the current section of this chapter, see Godfrey, *Civil Justice*, 268–354.
[52] For actions of error, see Godfrey, *Civil Justice*, 231–5.

examine the claim. Assuming they upheld the claim, they would have served him heir, meaning that they would have put him into his lands. In the process, he would have been 'infeft' in the lands – meaning he would have received feudal title. Suppose then another individual appeared and claimed that he was in fact the rightful heir. Suppose he had been defrauded of his heritage by collusion between the claimant, the sheriff and the assize. He would have then been able to appear before the lords to raise an action of 'error' against the claimant, the sheriff and the assize. If successful, his remedy would have been reduction (nullification) of the wrongful infeftment in favour of the claimant. Godfrey outlines one reason that the lords may have acquired the power to decide such cases quite early on. This is that the lords *always* seem to have had jurisdiction to hear complaints against 'royal officers such as sheriffs for "wranguis and inordinat proceding"'.[53] The necessary corollary of this power to undo the actions of such sheriffs was the power to reduce or nullify the infeftments that proceeded from their judgements.

By the late fifteenth century, the power to reduce infeftments had facilitated the development of an action for reduction of infeftment that was distinct from the action of error. Litigants came to rely on this power in order to circumvent the limitations on the power of the lords to decide certain feudal disputes. This can be illustrated with reference to the case of *Spittal v Spittal* (1531).[54] Both Archibald Spittal, the pursuer, and Finlay Spittal, the defender, alleged some title to disputed heritable property. In other words, there were two competing allegations of feudal title to the same property. It might be thought that the fee and heritage rule would have operated to bar the jurisdiction of the lords of session. Alternatively, it might be thought that the dispute could only have been resolved by procedure on brieve. But in this case, Archibald did not argue that his title to heritable property was better than that of Finlay, who was in possession. Rather, Archibald raised an action for reduction of Finlay's infeftment. This allowed him to claim that Finlay's title was intrinsically invalid. In this action, he was successful. Archibald was now the only person with any sort of valid title to the property. He then raised another action in 1532 against Finlay for wrongous occupation of the property. Because Finlay now had no valid title to the lands, Archibald was able to eject him.

It is worth spelling out *exactly* what had happened in this case. Archibald's use of the action for reduction of infeftment here had pre-

---

[53] Godfrey, *Civil Justice*, 232–3.
[54] See Godfrey, *Civil Justice*, 338–9.

vented *both* the fee and heritage rule and *also* the brieves rule from limiting the jurisdiction of the lords of session. First, the fee and heritage rule had been circumvented, because the dispute was not about two competing claims to title in land. It was simply about the intrinsic validity of one of those claims. Second, the brieves rule had also been circumvented. That rule could have protected Finlay from process before the lords of session if he could have claimed that he was vest and saised of his lands as of fee. If he could have advanced such a claim he could have demanded that he be pursued by means of a pleadable brieve. But he was unable to do this. Any feudal title he might once have had to the lands had been already reduced by the lords.

(5) Explaining *Wemyss v Forbes* (1543)

Thus the action for reduction of infeftment, in its developed form, effectively removed the last limitations on the jurisdiction of the lords of session. Yet the old pleadable brieves remained available to litigants, at least in theory. In principle, a litigant could choose to rely on the brieve of right in a sheriff court to resolve a dispute over feudal title. Alternatively, he now also had the option of using an action for reduction of infeftment (alongside an action for wrongous occupation) to achieve effectively the same result. Importantly, he could do all this before the lords of session. In effect, by the early sixteenth century there existed within Scots law two procedural frameworks – that is to say, two 'sets' of mechanisms for dealing with legal problems. The first was the old common law framework, which relied upon procedure on brieve. Its origins lay in English law. Secondly, there was the new procedural framework that had been created by the lords of session. This utilised new actions and procedures to enforce legal rights to land. It included actions like spuilzie, error, reduction of infeftment and wrongous occupation.[55]

While the two frameworks co-existed for a time, there was no doubt that the old common law system of brieves was in decline. So it seems that the last known dispute in which the lords felt the need to decline jurisdiction due to the fee and heritage rule occurred in 1513.[56] Never again did the lords refuse to hear a dispute on this basis, or on the basis of the brieves rule. The ultimate effect was that they had the capacity to deal with *all* such civil disputes. Put another way, they were left with de facto

---

[55] Godfrey advanced the argument that there existed two competing frameworks of remedies at this time; the point is summarised in Godfrey, *Civil Justice*, 449–53.
[56] Godfrey, *Civil Justice*, 304.

supreme jurisdiction in Scottish civil matters. Note that this extended to matters that arose within the territories of the old regality courts, which still continued to function. Procedurally, cases begun within those courts could be brought before the lords through a process called 'advocation'. Godfrey cites an example of the advocation of an action from the regality court of St Andrews.[57]

The points just discussed make it possible to go some way towards explaining the approach of the court in the case of *Wemyss v Forbes*. That case also reveals what finally happened to the old framework of actions initiated by pleadable brieve. It will be recalled that Wemyss sued Forbes, represented by Thomas Marjoribanks, for reduction of Forbes's infeftment. As an experienced practitioner, Marjoribanks would have been well aware that the lords of session had long exercised jurisdiction to reduce infeftments in actions like that brought against his client. Yet he knew that the older framework of common law actions, expressed in the brieves, could be read so as to challenge this practice. Perhaps he hoped to exploit this potential reading of the law to gain his client an advantage. Perhaps he aimed to use the brieves rule to have the case transferred to the ordinary judge, the sheriff. That would probably have had the effect of delaying the pursuer's ability to evict Majoribanks's client from the disputed lands, given the complexity of procedure on brieve. The request to relocate to the court of the sheriff could in itself have been a delaying tactic. The lords of session were having none of it. By 1543, their jurisdiction in reductions of infeftments, and indeed all civil matters, had been established for decades. They did not even feel any need to respond in terms that respected, and yet circumvented, the brieves rule and the fee and heritage rule. They simply informed him that 'the breif of rycht is (nor hes) nocht yit bene mony yeiris usit in this realme'. It had fallen out of use. It followed that rules compelling its use, such as the brieves rule of 1318, were no longer part of the law. They were in what lawyers called 'desuetude'. This term will be discussed in more detail in the next chapter. Marjoribanks 'protestit for remeid' against this decision, but this was to no avail.[58] He probably knew this was what the lords would decide. Immediately he proceeded to advance other defences against Wemyss's action. The pleadable brieves were dead.

---

[57] Godfrey, *Civil Justice*, 195 (for advocation generally, see 192–6).
[58] See MacQueen, 'Jurisdiction in heritage', 64.

(6) The Role of Litigants in Causing Legal Change

The changes discussed above were largely discovered by Godfrey in his ground-breaking study of the development of the session. Godfrey also emphasised an important point about those changes. They were driven by litigants.[59] The jurisdiction of the lords developed in response to the demands of litigants that they should hear their disputes. Many did not want to bring their claims before the sheriffs, or the other ordinary judges. They preferred the justice administered by the lords of session. It has been suggested that part of the reason for this may have been that many of those lords possessed legal training and expertise.[60] This meant that they were better placed to deal with the increasingly complex disputes that came before them than many sheriffs and other judicial officers.

D. CONCLUSION

The 150 years between 1450 and 1600 witnessed remarkable developments in the history of Scots law. This chapter has considered one of those changes by exploring the developing jurisdiction of the session. It opened by considering the case of *Weymss v Forbes* (1543), and posed two related questions. Was there a link between the development of the session's jurisdiction and the decline of procedure on brieve, as indicated in *Weymss*? If so, what was it? It was then explained that the old system of brieves, and the courts that administered them, began to run into difficulties in the first half of the fifteenth century. Royal attempts to make the administration of justice function properly in the older courts were ultimately insufficient to solve the problem. In the process, various other courts began to emerge. These exercised the jurisdiction of council and parliament to supplement – but not supplant – the jurisdiction of the older royal and franchisal courts. One of the courts that emerged was the judicial session of the king's council. This was generally staffed by at least some judges who were experts in canon law and Roman law. The session gradually developed its initially limited jurisdiction to provide litigants with the justice they increasingly demanded. The lords could

---

[59] The point is summarised in Godfrey, *Civil Justice*, 444–6.
[60] See MacQueen, *Common Law*, 257–9; MacQueen does, of course, point out that the full explanation for the growth of the session's jurisdiction was probably more complex. See MacQueen, *Common Law*, 259–67.

not hear actions initiated by brieve, but they developed new forms of action that could be used to achieve similar legal results. By the beginning of the sixteenth century, the only remaining limitations on the jurisdiction of the lords of session in civil matters arose from the brieves rule and the fee and heritage rule. In *Spittal v Spittal* (1531–2), both rules were circumvented by the lords through the use of the action to reduce infeftments together with the action for wrongous occupation. By this point in time, and probably for some years before that, the lack of limitations on the lords' jurisdiction had left them with de facto supreme jurisdiction in Scottish civil matters. This was so extensive that it was possible to use a procedure known as 'advocation' to bring disputes initiated in lower courts within the purview of the session. Taken together, these points demonstrate and explain the existence of a link between the decline of procedure on brieve, on the one hand, and the development of the session on the other.

At the beginning of this chapter the decision in *Wemyss v Forbes* (1543) was used to introduce two further matters for consideration. First, it was noted that the session did not simply experience an expansion in its jurisdiction. In 1532 it was also reconstituted as a College of Justice. That served as a catalyst for the emergence of a community of legal experts who judged and pleaded cases in that court. Second, these expert lawyers had a great impact on the development of the Scottish common law. The men of law who staffed the College of Justice reinterpreted and transformed the medieval Scottish legal system in light of their Romano-canonical learning. They also drew upon that learning to produce new types of legal literature. This in turn helped to lay the foundations of the modern legal system. The next four chapters will explore these developments.

E. SELECTED BIBLIOGRAPHY AND FURTHER READING

(1) Records of the Parliaments of Scotland (*RPS*)

Act concerning the parliamentary sessions: *RPS* 1426/25.

Act concerning reversions: *RPS* 1469/17.

Act concerning the need to bring disputes before ordinary judges: *RPS* 1487/10/14.

Act permitting litigants to bring disputes before the king's council: *RPS* 1488/1/25.

Act concerning the education of the sons of noblemen: *RPS* A1496/6/4.

(2) Books

Brown, Keith M. (ed.), *The History of the Scottish Parliament* (Edinburgh: Edinburgh University Press, 2004–10).

Cairns, John W., *Law, Lawyers and Humanism. Selected Essays on the History of Scots Law, Vol. 1* (Edinburgh: Edinburgh University Press, 2015).

Finlay, John, *Men of Law in Pre-Reformation Scotland* (East Linton: Tuckwell Press, 2000).

Godfrey, A. Mark, *Civil Justice in Renaissance Scotland* (Leiden: Brill, 2009).

[Hannay, R. K.], MacQueen, Hector L. (ed.), *The College of Justice. Essays by R. K. Hannay* (Edinburgh: Stair Society, 1990).

Macfarlane, Leslie J., *William Elphinstone and the Kingdom of Scotland 1431–1514. The Struggle for Order* (Aberdeen: Aberdeen University Press, 1985).

MacQueen, Hector L., *Common Law and Feudal Society*, reprinted edn (Edinburgh: Edinburgh University Press, 2016).

(3) Chapters in Books

Godfrey, A. Mark, 'Jurisdiction in heritage and the foundation of the College of Justice in 1532', in Hector L. MacQueen (ed.), *Stair Society Miscellany Four* (Edinburgh: Stair Society, 2002), 9–36.

Godfrey, A. Mark, 'Parliament and the law', in Keith M. Brown and Alan R. MacDonald (eds), *Parliament in Context, 1235–1707* (Edinburgh: Edinburgh University Press, 2010), 157–85.

MacQueen, Hector L., 'Jurisdiction in heritage and the Lords of Council and Session after 1532', in W. David H. Sellar (ed.), *Stair Society Miscellany Two* (Edinburgh: Stair Society, 1984), 61–85.

Malcolm, C. A., 'The parliament house and its antecedents', in G. C. H. Paton (ed.), *An Introduction to Scottish Legal History* (Edinburgh: Stair Society, 1958), 448–58.

(4) Electronic Resources

Murray, Athol L., and Gero Dolezalek (eds), *Sinclair's Practicks*, http:// home.uni-leipzig.de/jurarom/scotland/dat/sinclair.html.

CHAPTER 7

Legal Learning and Legal Authority in the College of Justice

A. INTRODUCTION

The last chapter opened by considering the decision in *Wemyss v Forbes* (1543). It was used to introduce a discussion of the session's acquisition of supreme jurisdiction in civil matters. It was explained that the session had possessed such jurisdiction for some time before the early 1530s. Towards the end of the chapter, it was also stated that the session underwent an important transformation in 1532. In that year it was placed on a new institutional footing, and reconstituted as the College of Justice.[1] This development helped to catalyse the emergence of a small yet recognisable community of expert judges and men of law.[2] Their primary focus was on the practice of Scots law within the court. It would perhaps be going too far to describe this community as a nascent legal profession. Nonetheless, it did in many ways prefigure and foreshadow elements of the profession that would emerge later, such as the Faculty of Advocates.

The aim of this chapter is to explore the ways in which the community of the College of Justice resolved disputes during the first years of its existence. The chapter will begin by examining the developments that led to the reconstitution of the session as a college in 1532. In the process it will outline evidence that shows the members of that college were expected to possess legal learning. Next, the chapter will examine the ways in which that community used its learning in Roman and canon law to resolve disputes from the outset. Reference will be made here to

[1] The most authoritative study of this development is to be found in A. Mark Godfrey, *Civil Justice in Renaissance Scotland* (Leiden: Brill, 2009). See also Hector L. MacQueen (ed.), *The College of Justice. Essays by R. K. Hannay* (Edinburgh: Stair Society, 1990).

[2] The most authoritative studies of that community are those of John Finlay; see, above all, John Finlay, *Men of Law in Pre-Reformation Scotland* (East Linton: Tuckwell Press, 2000).

the decisions or 'practicks' of the court reported by one of the lords of session, John Sinclair (c. 1510–66).

B. RECONSTITUTING THE SESSION AS A COLLEGE OF JUSTICE

In the last chapter it was explained that one of the probable reasons for the success of the session was that its judges possessed legal learning and expertise. This helps to explain why the lords of session were already exercising de facto supreme jurisdiction in Scottish civil matters by 1531. Yet at this point in time it remained the case that legal learning or expertise was not required as a *qualification* for service as a judge in this court. Indeed, the sessions were, formally speaking, still nothing more than judicial sittings of the king's council. This meant that any member of the king's council could in principle adjudicate in a case, and act as a judge – regardless of whether or not he had any real knowledge of the law. Thus the system was open to abuse. A powerful nobleman with no legal learning might favour one party in a dispute due to kinship ties or some other reason not related to the merits of the case itself. If he was a member of the king's council, he could sit on the session in order to influence the outcome of the dispute. Such a situation was clearly unsatisfactory in the long term.[3]

During the 1520s, Archbishop Gavin Dunbar of Glasgow seems to have sought to resolve the problem in his role of chancellor of the realm.[4] Both Godfrey and Cairns have come to the conclusion that, throughout the 1520s, Dunbar sought to ensure that the lords of session would all be 'litturate men of knawledge and experience'.[5] The requirement of 'literacy' here did not simply mean that all judges should be able to read and write. It meant that they would be required to be able to read and write Latin. This was the language in which the texts of Roman law and canon law were written. Cairns and Godfrey agree that the requirement of literacy here included the expectation that the lords of session would have a 'sophisticated education' in Roman law and canon law, as did Archbishop Dunbar himself.[6]

---

[3] See Godfrey, *Civil Justice*, 106–18 (which deals with attempts to address the problem between the mid-1520s and 1531).

[4] See Godfrey, *Civil Justice*, 106–26; John W. Cairns, 'Revisiting the foundation of the College of Justice', in Hector L. MacQueen (ed.), *Stair Society Miscellany Five* (Edinburgh: Stair Society, 2006), 27–50.

[5] The passage quoted can be found in Cairns, 'Revisiting the foundation', 33.

[6] The words quoted can be found in Cairns, 'Revisiting the foundation', 32.

In order to realise his goal, Dunbar seems to have suggested that the session should be placed on a new institutional footing. He promoted the idea that it should be reconstituted as a college of justice.[7] A 'college' was simply a society 'instituted for certain common purposes and possessing special rights and privileges'.[8] The members of the new college would inherit the jurisdiction of the old conciliar session. However, they would be selected for office only on the basis of their learning and experience as judges. The proposal met with the approval of James V (r. 1513–42), and it was put to Pope Clement VII. The support of the papacy was required in part because James V needed funding for the new court, and he hoped to secure this from the Roman Catholic Church. Clement VII gave his blessing to the scheme. As a result, on 17 May 1532, a Scottish parliament legislated to implement these changes. It also empowered the new court to make its own statutes to regulate its procedure. These came to be known as the 'acts of sederunt'. More will be said concerning some of the early acts of sederunt shortly.[9]

In this way, the session was reconstituted as the College of Justice. On 27 May 1532, it met on this new institutional footing for the first time.[10] Fourteen experienced lords of session, together with a presiding judge, known as the president, were appointed to serve in the College. It was decided that eight of them, including the lord president, would be 'spiritual' lords. In other words, they would be clergymen who possessed legal training, like Dunbar himself. The remaining seven judges would be 'temporal' lords, drawn from outwith the clerical estate. All of them continued to be known by their old titles of 'lords of session' and 'lords of council'. Yet from this time onwards they were also formally referred to as 'Senators of the College of Justice'. Eight men of law were given special licence to plead in all cases before them as the 'general procurators' of the court. Dunbar's ideal court staffed exclusively by learned judges and men of law looked like it might become a reality.

It is difficult to overstate the significance of these developments for the subsequent history of Scots law. From 1532 onwards, a considerable amount of legal change in Scotland would be driven by the community of the College of Justice. The members of that community brought their

---

[7] Godfrey, *Civil Justice*, 123–6.

[8] See Godfrey, *Civil Justice*, 124, quoting William Croft Dickinson, *Scotland from the Earliest Times to 1603* (Edinburgh: T. Nelson, 1961), 307 n. 3.

[9] For these developments, see Godfrey, *Civil Justice*, 113–26.

[10] For the events of 1532, and their immediate consequences, see Godfrey, *Civil Justice*, 126–60.

sophisticated learning in Roman and canon law to bear on the interpretation and augmentation of the old common law. Strong evidence in support of this statement can be found in the earliest surviving collection of notes of decisions or 'practicks' compiled by one of the lords of session. These are better known as the *Practicks* of John Sinclair, Dean of Restalrig (c. 1510–66). As will be seen, those notes reveal that at least some judges had developed arguments to justify their extensive use of Roman law and canon law in practice. Those arguments in turn reveal much of their thinking about what gave law its 'authority' or binding force.[11]

C. TRANSFORMING THE COMMON LAW: LEGAL LEARNING IN SINCLAIR'S *PRACTICKS*

Between 1540 and 1549, Sinclair noted over 500 decisions of the lords of session. Aside from being a lord of session, he was a clergyman who had formerly been professor of canon law at Aberdeen. In his *Practicks*, he displayed various ways in which the community of the College of Justice used the learning of Roman and canon law to develop – and ultimately transform – the old common law. This can be demonstrated with reference to his accounts of several cases. The first is that of *James Douglas, third Earl of Morton v Queen's Advocate* (1543). The second is *Seaton v Cockburns* (1549). The third is *Commendator of St Andrew's Priory v Bishop of Dunkeld* (1542).

(1) *James Douglas, third Earl of Morton v Queen's Advocate* (1543)

It is helpful to introduce Sinclair's account of the first case with a reasonably detailed outline of its facts. In April 1543, the aged James Douglas,

---

[11] The literature on this topic is growing. See, above all, J. D. Ford, *Law and Opinion in Scotland during the Seventeenth Century* (Oxford and Portland: Hart, 2007); for a different view (which is discussed by Ford at 222–33), see John W. Cairns, T. David Fergus and Hector L. MacQueen, 'Legal humanism and the history of Scots law: John Skene and Thomas Craig', in John MacQueen (ed.), *Humanism in Renaissance Scotland* (Edinburgh: Edinburgh University Press, 1990), 48–74. See also now Andrew R. C. Simpson, 'Legislation and authority in early-modern Scotland', in Mark Godfrey (ed.), *Law and Authority in British Legal History, 1200–1900* (Cambridge: Cambridge University Press, 2016), 85–119. Much of the argument presented below is drawn from the last-mentioned article at 91–100.

third Earl of Morton, raised an action before the lords of session.[12] He
sought recovery of lands that he had transferred or 'resigned' into the
hands of the late king, James V, in 1540. The reference to 'resignation'
perhaps requires some explanation. Those who held lands from the king
as feudal vassals were said to 'resign' those lands when they returned
direct control of them to the monarch. Perhaps surprisingly, this was a
relatively common procedure, in part because the king did not usually
retain the lands. Rather, he usually changed the terms of the original
grant and then re-granted the lands to the original resignor. Generally
the changes had actually been sought by the resignor, and they would
usually have been negotiated in advance.[13] Thus Morton's decision to
resign the lands into the hands of the king was not inherently suspicious.
However, Morton then explained that this had not been a pre-negotiated
resignation of lands so that they could be re-granted to him under new
terms. Rather, he stated that the king had in fact bullied him into resign-
ing the lands. In other words, his claim was that James V had used force
and fear to compel him to hand over his earldom.

This was a serious allegation, and it was backed up by a fairly hor-
rendous story. Morton explained to the lords of session that the late king
had required him to 'ward' in Inverness. In other words, the king had
required him to confine himself to a city in the far north of the kingdom.
Normally such a command would have been reserved for someone who
had incurred royal displeasure. Yet Morton claimed there had been no
just cause for the command. Furthermore, Morton lived in Dalkeith, in
the southern part of the realm, and it was winter. Even though he was
worried that he 'mycht nocht gudelie sustene the said trawell and waird

---

[12] Athol L. Murray and Gero Dolezalek (eds), *Sinclair's Practicks*, http://home.uni-
leipzig.de/jurarom/scotland/dat/sinclair.html, cns 315–16, 541.

[13] For example, landholders often sought to vary one particular term that was included
in most feudal grants. This declared that the feus in question would be inherited
by a form of primogeniture. In other words, when a man died, his eldest son would
inherit the lands; if he had no surviving sons, then the lands would be divided
between his surviving daughters. Some noblemen did not like this standard term
governing the succession to their lands. They wanted to make sure that their lands
could never pass down a female line. So they quite commonly resigned their lands to
the king in order to have them re-granted subject to a tailzie. 'Tailzies' were defined
in Chapter 3. They altered the normal order of succession to a feu, usually in favour
of a particular male line. So in this example, the nobleman's resignation of the lands
would have been designed to alter the original line of succession to his feu so as to
exclude female heirs. That would have been achieved through the royal re-grant of
the lands subject to an appropriately drafted tailize. See Gretton, 'Feudal system',
paras 97 111.

but danger of his lyf',[14] Morton set out for the north. He did this even
though he was well-known to suffer from 'diverse seiknes and infirmiteis'
and 'ane sare leg'. Morton was prepared, as he put it, to 'chaunge the
halsoum and warme air [of Dalkeith] with cauld and tempestuous air'.[15]
Ultimately the 'cauld and tempestuous air' got the better of him. About
mid-way between his home and Inverness he gave up, at the town of
Brechin. There he found the king. As Morton knelt before James V on
his 'sare leg', the king gave him a stark choice. He was required either to
proceed to Inverness or to resign his earldom. Fearing he would die if he
proceeded to Inverness, Morton resigned his lands. The king then withdrew his order that Morton should ward himself in the north.[16]

Whether or not it was representative of the whole truth, the story that
Morton's man of law told the lords of session portrayed the king, James
V, in an extremely negative light.[17] That such accusations could be made
so publicly was perhaps only possible because James himself had died a
few months earlier, in December 1542. He had then been succeeded by
his infant daughter, Mary, Queen of Scots (r. 1542–67). Since that time,
the lords of session had taken note of the fact that many noblemen were
claiming the late king had oppressed them. Consequently, they made an
act which was described in the following terms:

> it is provydit be ane act of the lordis of Counsall laitlie maid sen the
> deceis of the king that quhatsumevir complenis that thai war hurt
> in thair possessioun, landis, heretage, guidis or geir be the king and
> his servandis in and to his grace profeitt *mediat vel immediat* that it
> suld be lesum to thame to call the kingis advocat … to heir thame
> restorit agane to thair possessioun. And that becaus it wes havelie
> murmurit that the king oppressit sum of his liegis in sic sortis and
> in his lyfetyme and thai nocht complenit thairupone. And the lordis
> now for releve of thair conscience and saull devysit the same.[18]

This can be rendered into modern English as follows:

> it is provided by a recent act of the lords of council, made after the
> death of the king, that anyone who complains they were harmed

---

[14] Murray and Dolezalek (eds), *Sinclair's Practicks*, cn. 316.
[15] J. Cameron, *James V* (Edinburgh: John Donald, 1998), 143, 275.
[16] Most of the details of this story are outlined in Cameron, *James V*, 274–7.
[17] See Cameron, *James V*, 274–7, 331.
[18] Murray and Dolezalek (eds), *Sinclair's Practicks*, cn. 315.

in their possessions, lands, heritage, goods or gear by the king and his servants should be permitted to summon the king's advocate to seek restitution of their possessions. And that should be the case regardless of whether the harm they suffered resulted in direct or indirect profit to the king. And the lords made this act because it was widely complained that the king in his lifetime oppressed some of his lieges in such ways, even though they did not object. And so now the lords have devised the same act for the relief of their conscience and soul.

This act is fairly self-explanatory, save for the reference to the 'kingis advocat'. By 1543, he was of course the 'quenis advocat', the king having died several months earlier. Broadly the role of the queen's advocate was to ensure that 'the [monarch's] interests in all spheres of legal activity were protected'.[19] He oversaw the collection of rents due from those who held lands from the crown, and litigated against those who failed to pay. He could also pursue criminals; the crown had a direct financial interest in such pursuits, both because those convicted might forfeit their goods and also because they might buy pardons known as 'remissions'. The modern office of lord advocate is descended from that of the queen's advocate. In 1543, the queen's advocate was Master Henry Lauder of Saint Germains.[20]

Lauder did not react well to Morton's claim that he should recover lands from the crown because he had been compelled to resign them by unlawful force and fear. It would also seem he did not approve of the lords' act of sederunt condemning his late royal master for 'oppressioun'. Lauder attempted to advance an argument in defence of his young monarch. If successful, it would have effectively nullified the act of sederunt enacted by the lords. Lauder's exception to Morton's action rested on a passage in *Regiam Majestatem*. This gave rise to the maxim *minor non tenetur placitare super hereditatem*.[21] This meant that a minor, a person under the age of full legal capacity, was not required to plead in cases concerning a right of heritage in land. Only on reaching majority would he or she be required to answer. Mary, Queen of Scots, was undoubtedly a minor, at less than a year of age. Consequently, Lauder

---

[19] Finlay, *Men of Law*, 205.
[20] For the office of king's advocate, see generally Finlay, *Men of Law*, 170–205.
[21] A version of the text can be found in Thomas M. Cooper (ed.), *Regiam Majestatem and Quoniam Attachiamenta Based on the Text of Sir John Skene* (Edinburgh: Stair Society, 1947), III.32.15; see also Cooper's notes following this text.

argued '*de iure municipali regni Scotie*' – 'by the municipal law of the kingdom of Scotland' – the queen did not have to answer Morton's action until she entered her majority. While that would take over twenty years, the law was clear.

The lords were not prepared to accept this argument. This is hardly surprising. If upheld, it would have completely undermined their attempt to deal with what they perceived to be royal oppression. Yet the lords' reasoning for rejecting Lauder's exception is instructive. They explained that the 'municipall law', meaning the *minor non tenetur* rule found in *Regiam*, was

> ovirrigorous just or unjust, gif the erle of Mortoun and his airis suld vant his heretage wranguslie, as wes allegit, tane fra him *utpote per metum cadentem in constantem virum*.[22]

In modern English, this conclusion can be rendered:

> The municipal law [found in *Regiam*] was overly just, or unjust, if it meant that the earl of Morton and heirs should want their heritage wrongfully, as was alleged, it having been taken from him namely by force falling on a steadfast man.

In other words, the lords found that the application of the rule found in *Regiam* would be unjust *in this case*. In defending their argument, they drew attention to the alleged injustice suffered by the Earl of Morton. Interestingly, they described this injustice in terms that indicated they had the learning of Roman law and canon law in mind. According to the *Digest*, anything done as a result of force or fear ('*metus*') was to have no legal effect. However, the texts made it clear that the force or fear in question had to be such that it would have overcome the 'steadfast man' (the '*vir constans*'). If the 'steadfast man' would not have been daunted by the alleged force or fear, then legal acts that resulted from it would retain their validity.[23] Thus the lords maintained that Morton's actions resulted from *metus*. Furthermore, they held that this was the sort of *metus* mentioned in the texts of Roman law. It constituted *metus* that would have overcome the will of the *vir constans*. Morton had feared for his life, and so had resigned his lands in favour of the king, as even the

---

[22] Murray and Dolezalek (eds), *Sinclair's Practicks*, cn. 315.
[23] See Alan Watson (ed.), *The Digest of Justinian* (Philadelphia: University of Pennsylvania Press, 1985), 4.2.1 (Ulpian), 4.2.6 (Gaius).

vir constans would have done. Note the Roman principles were reiterated in the canon law.[24]

Thus the lords refused to apply the *minor non tenetur* rule drawn from the Scottish text of *Regiam*. They said that that would be 'ovirrigorous just or unjust', at least in this case. They then drew attention to the injustice suffered by Morton, and explained this using the principles and terminology of Roman law. In other words, they chose to ignore the rule in *Regiam*, and to uphold the Roman principles. Put another way, they recognised a conflict between the Scottish maxim and the learning expressed in the Roman texts. If they were to follow the Scottish maxim, Morton would have to wait to recover his lands until Queen Mary reached her majority. If the Scottish maxim were to be interpreted so that it would not apply in this case, then Morton would be able to proceed with his action to recover his lands. The lords then explained that following the Scottish rule would be unjust in this case. The clear implication was that following the Roman learning would be *just*. Indeed, this in turn implies that they thought that the Roman texts constituted a more reliable guide to 'justice' than the Scottish rule expressed in *Regiam*. This seems to have meant that the scope of the Scottish rule could and should be interpreted narrowly to have no effect in this case. Apparently that was because its application in this instance would have conflicted with the standards of justice laid out in Roman law. Of course, this left open the *possibility* that the Scottish rule might justly be applied in another case.

These conclusions raise a range of questions. Why were the lords so concerned to apply what they considered to be 'just' law in this case? Why did they think an understanding of 'justice' grounded in the texts of Roman law was more trustworthy than that suggested by a broad reading of the ancient laws of the Scottish realm? These questions are surely particularly pertinent when it is borne in mind that all this was being discussed in a *Scottish* court – the College of Justice. Furthermore, this decision is not an isolated example. Elsewhere the lords interpreted the Scottish *minor non tenetur* maxim very narrowly in light of the Romano-canonical principles. In *Seaton v Cockburns* (1549), Sinclair noted that Alexander Cockburn had allegedly defrauded Lady Seaton of certain lands.[25] Cockburn then transferred the lands to his son, who was a minor.

---

[24] See Professor Dolezalek's note 252 to Murray and Dolezalek (eds), *Sinclair's Practicks*, cn. 315.

[25] Murray and Dolezalek (eds), *Sinclair's Practicks*, cn. 459–61. The analysis presented here is again indebted in part to Professor Dolezalek's notes to the case (in particular note 453, citing earlier notes).

When Lady Seaton tried to recover the lands, *minor non tenetur* was pled on behalf of Cockburn's son. The lords refused to allow the exception in this case. In support of this decision, they cited the principle of Roman law and canon law that no one should be enriched at the expense and harm of another. This was especially relevant here, where it was alleged that the fraud had arisen as a result of the fault of the child's father. It would have been a great injustice if the Scottish *minor non tenetur* rule were to permit men to defraud others successfully simply by transferring their fraudulent gains to their infant children. As a result, the lords concluded 'the judge may lawfully depart from the strict severity of that municipal law of Scotland'.[26] Again, the Scottish rule in *Regiam* was set aside in individual cases at least partly on the basis that it was inconsistent with ideas of equity and justice drawn from Roman law and canon law. The scope of the old common law was being transformed through reliance on those learned laws.

(2) *Commendator of St Andrews Priory v Bishop of Dunkeld*

Before attempting to explain this phenomenon, it will be helpful to consider one further decision noted by Sinclair – *Commendator of St Andrews Priory v Bishop of Dunkeld* (1542).[27] It is worth emphasising that James V was still alive when this matter came before the lords. In this case, the pursuer was a child named James Stewart (the action would have been brought by his representatives). He was the illegitimate son of James V and Margaret Erskine, the wife of one of the king's nobles. He was made the 'commendator' of St Andrews Priory, a wealthy ecclesiastical foundation. This meant that he had the right to the revenues of St Andrews Priory – such as the rents or mails of its lands. It was also provided that any revenues he did not need were to go straight back to his father, the king.[28] The papacy tolerated such flagrant abuses of church property in order to maintain the loyalty of James V at a time when the Protestant Reformation was gathering strength across northern Europe.[29] This phenomenon threatened the spiritual and political authority of the Roman

---

[26] For this translation, see Athol L. Murray, 'Sinclair's Practicks', in Alan Harding (ed.), *Law-Making and Law-Makers in British History: Papers Presented to the Edinburgh Legal History Conference, 1977* (London: Royal Historical Society, 1980), 90–104 at 100.

[27] Murray and Dolezalek (eds), *Sinclair's Practicks*, cns 284–5.

[28] On the rights of the commendator, see Gordon Donaldson, *The Scottish Reformation* (Cambridge: Cambridge University Press, 1960), 37–40.

[29] See Donaldson, *Scottish Reformation*, 37.

Catholic Church; it will be discussed in more detail in the next chapter.

If the pursuer in this action could probably secure the best legal advice money could buy, then the defender was not in a very much weaker position. Bishop George Crichton of Dunkeld was actually a lord of session. Yet, if he was a prominent judge, he does not seem to have taken the study of the Bible quite as seriously. One later report stated that on one occasion Crichton 'thanked God that he knew neither the Old or the New Testaments, and yet had prospered well enough in his day'.[30] This particular report may be untrue. And yet, rightly or wrongly, the perception that some senior members of the Scottish clergy were unconcerned with spiritual matters was widespread at the time. That, coupled with the greedy appropriation of church property by the monarchy and the nobility, ultimately weakened the authority of the Roman Catholic Church. Again, this will be discussed in the next chapter.

The dispute between the young prior of St Andrews and the Bishop of Dunkeld concerned a nineteen-year lease. The pursuer sought reduction of the lease made in favour of the defender. Note that the background of the case, sketched above, gives an insight into the politics of the situation. The young James Stewart had been appointed as prior in 1538 (probably aged about seven). His representatives were now getting to grips with his assets, and seeking to nullify leases of valuable assets associated with the priory. In this way, those assets could be re-granted to someone else, and so generate more income. In other words, James Stewart's representatives were trying to maximise the revenues available to the priory. Ostensibly, they would have gone to the young commendator. In reality, as has been explained, they would have gone almost directly to James V.

In response to the action for reduction of the lease, the defender's man of law, James Macgill of Nether Rankeillor, raised an exception. Macgill argued that, as a clergyman, his client, the Bishop of Dunkeld, did not have to answer in a secular court. Rather, he had the right to state his case before an ecclesiastical court. This calls for some explanation. Thus far this book has focused on the secular courts that operated in medieval Scotland. These included the courts of the justiciars, the sheriffs, the burghs, the lords of regality, the barons, and so on and so forth. Sometimes senior churchmen too had the right to hold secular courts as feudal lords of regalities or baronies. Yet in addition to this they had

---

30   See George Brunton and David Haig, *An Historical Account of the Senators of the College of Justice of Scotland, From its Institution in 1532* (Edinburgh: T. Clark, 1832), 44–5.

their own jurisdiction – a spiritual jurisdiction.[31] Each bishop exercised such a jurisdiction in his spiritual court through a judge known as his 'official'. The courts of the officials – which were known as 'consistory' courts – had the right to deal with a range of matters. Their jurisdiction extended to all disputes concerning the validity of marriages, executry, the appointment of legal guardians and defamation, to name a few examples. The consistory courts also had jurisdiction over teinds.[32] Teinds were payments due to the church from its parishioners. They might be made in cash or, perhaps more commonly, with the produce of lands. Some churches had great difficulty in collecting teinds, which were very valuable assets. The solution many clergymen adopted was to lease the right to uplift the teinds to others – often secular lords and noblemen – in exchange for payments of lump sums. These leases were known as 'tacks of teinds'.[33] It is quite possible that the lease that had been made in favour of the Bishop of Dunkeld in this case was in fact a tack of teinds. The bishop's request to be heard in an ecclesiastical court may have proceeded from a belief that he would receive a more favourable judgement there.

This explains one element of what James Macgill meant when he said that his client had the right to be heard before a church court. Yet it does not explain the *basis* of that right. By which law was a bishop entitled to decline the jurisdiction of the lords of session? The answer was to be found in the canon law. This provided that priests – including bishops – had what was known as the *privilegium fori*. In other words, they were entitled to have their disputes heard in ecclesiastical courts, and not in civil courts. Note that Macgill was not suggesting that the lords did not possess supreme jurisdiction in civil matters. Rather, he was suggesting *that this was not a civil matter*. And in order to establish that point, he made reference to the *privilegium fori* of canon law. Thus Romano-canonical law could be used in argument to interpret the scope of the jurisdiction of the lords of session itself.[34]

---

[31] The leading study of the pre-Reformation courts of the officials is Simon Ollivant, *The Court of the Official in Pre-Reformation Scotland* (Edinburgh: Stair Society, 1982).

[32] See Ollivant, *Court of the Official*, 65–93.

[33] See Ollivant, *Court of the Official*, 77–80; Donaldson, *Scottish Reformation*, 40–2; Jane E. A. Dawson, *Scotland Re-formed 1488–1587* (Edinburgh: Edinburgh University Press, 2007), 17.

[34] For the *privilegium fori*, see Walter Ullmann, *Law and Politics in the Middle Ages* (Cambridge: Cambridge University Press, 1975), 183; for a helpful treatment of the point, see Gero Dolezalek, 'The Court of Session as a Ius Commune Court

In response to Macgill's exception, the representatives of the prior of St Andrews produced a past decision or 'practick' of the lords of session. They did this to 'verafie' the claim that the lords alone had exclusive jurisdiction in the reduction of nineteen-year leases. In other words, the practick was being used as evidence of what the law might be. This practice of citing past decisions of the lords to guide future decisions has already been observed. It was seen above in the case of *Weymss v Forbes* (1543), and will be discussed further in Chapter 9.[35] Yet on inspecting the past practick, the lords were not convinced that it did actually support the young prior's case. Even if it did, they were not prepared to follow it. Sinclair reports their conclusion in the following terms:

> thairfoir, conforme to the commoun law, thai by thair decrete and sentence remittit the said bischope to his ordinar juge ecclesiasti-call, becaus thai culd nocht understand the consuetude allegit in the contrair to be trew in the selff, nor yit thair wes ony sic practik or consuetude in sic caussis aganes kirkmen.[36]

This can be rendered into modern English as follows:

> therefore, in accordance with the *ius commune*, the lords by their decreet and sentence sent the bishop back to his ordinary eccle-siastical judge. This was because they could not understand the consuetude [custom] alleged on the contrary to be true in itself, nor yet that there was any such practick or consuetude in such matters against kirkmen.

It will be noted here that the old Scots words 'commoun law' have been rendered in the translation with the term '*ius commune*'. The term '*ius commune*' was frequently employed by contemporaries to refer to the

---

– witnessed by "Sinclair's Practicks", 1540–1549', in Hector L. MacQueen (ed.), *Stair Society Miscellany Four* (Edinburgh: Stair Society, 2002), 51–84 at 71–2.
On the role of the session in determining the scope of the spiritual jurisdiction, see Hector MacQueen, 'The king's council and church courts in later medieval Scotland', in Harry Dondorp, Jan Hallebeek, Tammo Wallinga and Laurens Winkel (eds), Ius Romanum – Ius Commune – Ius Hodiernum: *Studies in Honour of Eltjo Schrage on the Occasion of his 65th Birthday* (Amsterdam: Scientia Verlag, 2010), 277–87.

35 Murray and Dolezalek (eds), *Sinclair's Practicks*, cn. 308.
36 Murray and Dolezalek (eds), *Sinclair's Practicks*, cn. 285.

learned laws. Broadly it meant the laws commonly applied in all church courts across Christendom. In the *ius commune*, Roman law was usually applied where canon law was silent.[37] The phrase 'commoun law' in Sinclair's account was clearly a reference to the *ius commune*, and not the medieval Scottish common law. This is because the law that enabled clergyman to have their disputes heard before ecclesiastical judges formed part of the canon law, itself part of the *ius commune*. The rule did not arise from the medieval Scottish common law. This conclusion, that the reference to the 'commoun law' was a reference to the *ius commune*, seems to be confirmed by other near-contemporary manuscripts of Sinclair's work. These state that the judges proceeded according to the 'commoun cannon lawis'.[38]

Thus the Bishop of Dunkeld won. The lords of session declined jurisdiction on the grounds that the *ius commune* provided the matter should be dealt with before an ecclesiastical judge. James V would hardly have been pleased. His supreme court in civil matters had refused jurisdiction over a dispute which could have resulted in the augmentation of his own revenue. Worse still, the lords had remitted the matter to a court of clergymen. That court might well have been expected to give a very favourable hearing to the defender, the Bishop of Dunkeld. Note that the session itself was probably acting in part out of concern that the king's actions could further undermine the revenues of the clerical estate. It will be recalled that the majority of the permanent lords of session were clergymen. They certainly had at least an indirect interest in the outcome of the dispute.

Yet, rather more revealing than the complex politics of the early 1540s is the legal reasoning used by the lords of session to decline jurisdiction. The lords decided to apply the canon law *privilegium fori* in preference to any past practick of theirs to the contrary, even if it did support the pursuer's case. In an illuminating comment, Sinclair stated that this was because 'they could not understand the consuetude [custom] alleged on the contrary to be true in the self'. These comments require some unpacking. The lords had a choice between applying two inconsistent rules. One arose from the *ius commune*. It was alleged that the other arose from the local practick or custom of the realm. The lords applied the rule found in the *ius commune* as opposed to the rule that was arguably found

---

See Dolezalek, 'Court of Session as a Ius Commune Court', 52.
See National Library of Scotland (NLS) MS Advocates 24.1.11 f.23ʳ; Edinburgh University Library (EUL) Laing MS III.429 f.28ᵛ. The spelling of the three words varies in each manuscript; the EUL manuscript is quoted here.

in the local Scottish custom. This was because the Scottish rule was not 'true in the self'. What did they mean when they concluded that the practick was not 'true in the self'?

Whatever it meant, one thing seems clear. If the lords held that an ostensible rule was not legally 'true' in the case at hand, then that constituted good grounds for treating it as inapplicable in that case. Presumably, then, if the lords recognised that a rule *was* legally 'true', then that would be a good reason to apply it. This shows that the 'truth' of a rule could be an essential element of its authority. Furthermore, in the context of this case, a past practick of the lords was seen as a less reliable guide to such legal 'truth' than the learned laws – the *ius commune*.

This last observation is important. It reveals that the approach of the lords in *Commendator of St Andrews Priory v Bishop of Dunkeld* (1542) is similar to that found in *James Douglas, third Earl of Morton v Queen's Advocate* (1543) and *Seaton v Cockburns* (1549). In the last two cases, the Scottish *minor non tenetur* rule was construed very narrowly when it was seen as inconsistent with the inherent justice of Roman and canon law. In *Commendator of St Andrews Priory*, a putative past practick of the lords of session was treated as inapplicable on the grounds that it was not 'true in the self'. By contrast, the learned laws were apparently trusted as a more reliable guide to such 'truth'. In all three cases, Scottish rules were seen as less trustworthy repositories of learning concerning justice, equity and 'truth' than Roman and canon law. In a context where the consistency of a rule with legal 'truth' or justice could determine whether or not it would be applied in a particular case, this was clearly of great significance. If the inherent 'truth' or justice of a rule gave it authority, and if the learned laws were seen as better guides to truth than the old Scottish common law, then the learned laws could be very influential in practice. They could be used to reinterpret and reshape the medieval common law. Conceivably they could even be used to render its scope very narrow indeed. According to its own terms, the *minor non tenetur* rule could easily have been applied in *James Douglas, third Earl of Morton v Queen's Advocate* (1543) and in *Seaton v Cockburns* (1549). But it was not. In both cases, the lords preferred to rely on the authoritative and apparently inherent justice of the learned laws. In this way, they discerned the rule that possessed the binding force of law in the case at hand.

(3) Explaining the Approach found in Sinclair's *Practicks*

How are modern readers to explain the attitudes of the lords to legal authority, and to the authority of the learned laws in particular? The answer lies in the assumptions held by an influential group of medieval jurists.[39] Their attitudes were shaped by the *mos Italicus*.[40] The *mos Italicus* was a method designed to help lawyers study the learned laws in the universities and elsewhere. It was developed by various scholars and in particular by the Italian jurists Bartolus de Sassoferrato (c. 1314–57) and Baldus de Ubaldis (1327–1400). Among other things, the method was designed to help students to reconcile the learning of Roman law and canon law with the laws practised in jurisdictions across Europe. To explain, across the continent kings and their courts increasingly turned to men with expertise in the learned laws to help them develop their legal systems.[41] Frequently they realised, and sometimes even expected, that those experts would use their legal learning to resolve actual disputes that came before them. Yet that raised an obvious question. What would happen where the legal learning of Roman and canon law was inconsistent with the laws of the local jurisdiction? Which would be applied to resolve the disputes in question? As has been seen from the Scottish experience, such conflicts did arise quite frequently, as in the cases where the application of the *minor non tenetur* rule would have been inconsistent with the application of Roman law.

The response of Bartolus and Baldus to such questions was rooted in their attitudes to the authority of the texts of Roman and canon law. They saw those texts as reliable repositories of learning concerning legal 'truth'. They equated this 'truth' with justice and equity. They also believed that the force of law depended ultimately upon its consistency with this standard of legal truth.[42] What, then, of laws of individual jurisdictions that departed from this standard of justice as it was expressed in Roman and canon law? An example would be a local 'law' that nullified the *privilegium fori* of canon law. Were such rules not really laws at all? Were judges simply free to ignore them in practice, and to continue to apply the learned laws?

---

[39] Again, the comments made here summarise the more detailed arguments advanced in Simpson, 'Legislation and authority', 94–8.

[40] For the *mos Italicus*, see the sources cited in Simpson, 'Legislation and authority', 94 n. 36, including, for example, Peter Stein, *Roman Law in European History* (Cambridge: Cambridge University Press, 1999), 38–74, in particular at 71–4.

[41] Randall Lesaffer, *European Legal History. A Cultural and Political Perspective* (Cambridge: Cambridge University Press, 2009), 259–60.

[42] Again, see the sources cited in Simpson, 'Legislation and authority', 95 n. 40 and n. 41, including Walter Ullmann, *The Medieval Idea of Law* (London: Methuen and Co. Ltd., 1946), 74–6; Joseph Canning, *The Political Thought of Baldus de Ubaldis* (Cambridge: Cambridge University Press, 1987), 154–8; Ford, *Law and Opinion*, 18, 125 and (importantly) at 310–12.

Bartolus's response to these questions was complex. Furthermore, at first it will seem a little surprising, given his basic assumptions. First, he acknowledged that the local laws, that is to say the laws promulgated in individual European jurisdictions, could enjoy binding force. Indeed, they could, in some circumstances, enjoy even greater force than the learned laws. This meant that any lawyer looking at a legal problem should consider the local laws first before turning to the learned laws. Yet Bartolus was careful to hedge this last statement in with several caveats.[43]

First, he explained that the *reason* that local laws could enjoy greater force than the learning of Roman law and canon law was to be found in the texts of Roman law themselves. According to the *Digest*, Roman law did indeed permit its rules to be superseded by contrary custom. The basic idea was that, just as law could be constituted by the consent of the populace, so its force could also be lost when the populace as a whole ceased to obey it. Put another way, law could be established by 'consuetude' – which could be expressed in custom. It could lose its force if it fell into what was called 'desuetude' – when the people ceased to observe it and acted as if it were not law at all. So the local laws of European jurisdictions could be seen as new 'customs' that had caused the old Roman rules to fall into 'desuetude'. Incidentally, this explains how the lords of session were able to hold that the statutory brieves rule had ceased to have any force in *Wemyss v Forbes* (1543), as discussed in the previous chapter.

Second, Bartolus said that the older rules could *only* be permitted to fall wholly into desuetude in certain circumstances. Broadly, they could only be allowed to fall completely into desuetude if the new laws that replaced them somehow remained consistent with legal 'truth'. Famously he explained this with reference to a rule that the Venetians had developed concerning the formal validity of wills. In order to be executed validly in Roman law, a will had to have a minimum of five witnesses. The idea was to prevent fraud; the requirement of a high number

---

[43] The discussion that follows concerning Bartolus's assumptions is based on J. A. Clarence Smith, 'Bartolo on the conflict of laws', *American Journal of Legal History* 14 (1970), 157–183, 247–75, particularly at 163–74; Stein, *Roman Law in European History*, 71–2; Peter Stein, 'Bartolus, the conflict of laws and the Roman law', in Peter Feuerstein and Clive Parry (eds), *Multum non Multa. Festschrift für Kurt Lipstein Aus Anlass Seines 70 Geburtstages* (Heidelberg: C. F. Muller, 1980), 251–8; Peter Stein, 'Civil law reports and the case of San Marino', in Okko Behrends, Malte Diesselhorst and Wulf Echkart Voss (eds), *Römisches Recht in der europäischen Tradition. Symposium aus Anlaß des 75 Geburtstages von Franz Wieacker* (Ebelsbach: Verlag Rolf Gremer, 1985), 323–38 at 331–2.

of witnesses would make it more difficult to forge a will. The Venetians had dropped the required number of witnesses to three in their own laws. Bartolus commented that this could be presumed to be a 'bad' custom. It departed from the standards of legal truth found in the learned laws. Consequently, it might potentially be construed as narrowly as possible in practice. However, Bartolus then noted that Roman law had permitted departure from its own rules of formal validity in certain circumstances. For example, soldiers on campaign were not required to adhere to all of the formalities of the law because that would have presented practical difficulties. Those practical difficulties would have been so severe that they might not have been able to make wills at all. That would have infringed a basic principle of the Roman law – to allow men to regulate succession to their property after their deaths. Consequently, there was precedent in Roman law to permit the relaxation of its own rules concerning the form wills had to have in order to be valid. Bartolus then considered the situation in Venice. It was argued – perhaps rather implausibly – that the situation in Venice created practical problems in observing the rule requiring five witnesses. Apparently gathering together five adult male citizens of Venice to witness a will would have been difficult because of the great pressure of business. So to uphold the rule requiring five witnesses might have resulted in fewer wills actually being made. That would have breached the more fundamental Roman principle that men should be allowed to regulate the succession to their property after their deaths. Consequently, the Venetian rule concerning formal validity, while different from its Roman equivalent, remained consistent with an underlying principle of Roman law. It could therefore be said to be consistent with legal truth. *For this reason* it could be said to be valid.

Third, Bartolus was careful to insist that even such valid departures from the learning of Roman and canon law should be interpreted narrowly. In this way, the effect of the new rules in developing the underlying legal truth of the learned laws would be limited. Evidently there was a concern that the broad application of new rules might be unjust. The last point is readily intelligible, given Bartolus's other assumptions as outlined above. If it was assumed that the learned laws were the most reliable repositories of learning concerning legal truth, then it followed that departures from their teachings should be limited to very specific circumstances.

These Bartolist assumptions were clearly at work in the reasoning of the lords of session. In the cases mentioned above, they accepted the basic idea that the authority or binding force of law could be attributed to that which they recognised as consistent with legal truth or justice. Like the Bartolists, they seem to have effectively equated the two concepts, thinking of justice as legal truth. They also accepted that the learned laws constituted the most reliable guide to such legal truth. Nonetheless, like the Bartolists, they recognised the need to engage with the local laws. They did not doubt that those laws could possess binding force in individual disputes. However, the lords of session were generally only prepared to apply those laws in cases where they were 'true in the self' or where it would be just to do so. As has been explained, when determining which laws were true, and the circumstances in which they could justly be applied, the lords relied first and foremost on the learned laws. If applying the local laws in the dispute at hand would have been inconsistent with such learning, then the lords could avoid doing this. They could quite simply interpret the local laws narrowly in light of the learned laws so as to have no effect in the case in question.

(4) Texts as Repositories of Truth

One fairly obvious question remains. Why did the Bartolists and the lords of session treat the texts of Roman law and canon law as repositories of learning concerning truth? Part of the answer lay in the fact that they had been promulgated by figures possessed of apparently universal authority, such as Roman emperors and popes.[44] Yet it was also assumed that the texts were authoritative because they expressed the opinions of generations of legal experts. To explain, experts were trusted to uncover truth in all medieval disciplines. Where new students absorbed the learning of the old texts, they too became experts. When new questions arose, such experts were trusted to resolve them through the fresh application of the old textual learning. In the discipline of law, the relevant textual learning was primarily located in Roman law and canon law. Where a consensus emerged among legal experts concerning the resolution of a particular legal question, that consensus could acquire binding force. In Scotland, the legal experts whose views mattered in this regard were the members of the community of the College of Justice. Their consensus concerning legal truth possessed the authority of law.[45] As Ford has put

---

[44] See, for example, the comments in Franz Wieacker, *A History of Private Law in Europe with Particular Reference to Germany*, trans. Tony Weir (Oxford: Clarendon Press, 1995), 31.

[45] For this attitude to legal authority, see Ford, *Law and Opinion*, particularly at 181–246 (the discussion at 201–15 is relevant to the study of Sinclair); see also Simpson, 'Legislation and authority, 97–8, and the sources cited at 98 n. 54.

it, at this time law could still be conceptualised 'as a body of learning fashioned through expert debate'.[46]

D. CONCLUSION

This chapter began by exploring how the old session was reconstituted as the College of Justice in 1532. From the outset it was hoped that membership of the new community would be limited to those who had expertise in the learned laws. It was thought that this expertise would help the judges and men of law to deal effectively and justly with the disputes before them.

The chapter then demonstrated that this legal learning was used in practice, for example in the cases of *James Douglas, third Earl of Morton v Queen's Advocate* (1543) and *Seaton v Cockburns* (1549). It was shown that expertise in Roman and canon law could be used to interpret and indeed transform the application of the medieval Scottish common law. The older Scottish sources, such as *Regiam Majestatem*, could be construed narrowly where they conflicted with the legal truth that was thought to exist in the learned laws.

Underpinning this approach were two assumptions. First, learning which concerned justice or legal 'truth' could possess the binding force of law. Second, the learning expressed in the texts of Roman and canon law constituted the most reliable guides to such legal truth. The next three chapters will explain how both assumptions came under attack during the second half of the sixteenth century. The debates that resulted would continue to transform the medieval legal heritage during the sixteenth and seventeenth centuries. They would also lay some of the conceptual foundations of the modern Scottish legal system.

E. SELECTED BIBLIOGRAPHY AND FURTHER READING

(1) Books

Brown, Keith M. (ed.), *The History of the Scottish Parliament* (Edinburgh: Edinburgh University Press, 2004–10).
Brunton, George, and David Haig, *An Historical Account of the Senators

---

[46] Ford, *Law and Opinion*, 5.

of the College of Justice of Scotland, From its Institution in 1532 (Edinburgh: T. Clark, 1832).

Cairns, John W., *Law, Lawyers and Humanism. Selected Essays on the History of Scots Law, Vol. 1* (Edinburgh: Edinburgh University Press, 2015).

Canning, Joseph, *The Political Thought of Baldus de Ubaldis* (Cambridge: Cambridge University Press, 1987).

Finlay, John, *Men of Law in Pre-Reformation Scotland* (East Linton: Tuckwell Press, 2000).

Ford, J. D., *Law and Opinion in Scotland during the Seventeenth Century* (Oxford and Portland: Hart, 2007).

Godfrey, A. Mark, *Civil Justice in Renaissance Scotland* (Leiden: Brill, 2009).

[Hannay, R. K.], MacQueen, Hector L. (ed.), *The College of Justice. Essays by R. K. Hannay* (Edinburgh: Stair Society, 1990).

Lesaffer, Randall, *European Legal History. A Cultural and Political Perspective* (Cambridge: Cambridge University Press, 2009).

Macfarlane, Leslie J., *William Elphinstone and the Kingdom of Scotland 1431–1514. The Struggle for Order* (Aberdeen: Aberdeen University Press, 1985).

MacQueen, Hector L., *Common Law and Feudal Society*, reprinted edn (Edinburgh: Edinburgh University Press, 2016).

Ollivant, Simon, *The Court of the Official in Pre-Reformation Scotland* (Edinburgh: Stair Society, 1982).

Stein, Peter, *Roman Law in European History* (Cambridge: Cambridge University Press, 1999).

Ullmann, Walter, *The Medieval Idea of Law* (London: Methuen & Co. Ltd., 1946).

Wieacker, Franz, *A History of Private Law in Europe with Particular Reference to Germany*, trans. Tony Weir (Oxford: Clarendon Press, 1995).

(2) Chapters in Books

Cairns, John W., T. David Fergus and Hector L. MacQueen, 'Legal humanism and the history of Scots law: John Skene and Thomas Craig', in John MacQueen (ed.), *Humanism in Renaissance Scotland* (Edinburgh: Edinburgh University Press, 1990), 48–74.

Cairns, John W., 'Revisiting the foundation of the College of Justice', in Hector L. MacQueen (ed.), *Stair Society Miscellany Five* (Edinburgh: Stair Society, 2006), 27–50.

Dolezalek, Gero, 'The Court of Session as a Ius Commune Court – witnessed by "Sinclair's Practicks", 1540–1549', in Hector L. MacQueen (ed.), *Stair Society Miscellany Four* (Edinburgh: Stair Society, 2002), 51–84.

Godfrey, A. Mark, 'Parliament and the law', in Keith M. Brown and Alan R. MacDonald (eds), *Parliament in Context, 1235–1707* (Edinburgh: Edinburgh University Press, 2010), 157–85.

MacQueen, Hector, 'The king's council and church courts in later medieval Scotland', in Harry Dondorp, Jan Hallebeek, Tammo Wallinga and Laurens Winkel (eds), Ius Romanum – Ius Commune – Ius Hodiernum: *Studies in Honour of Eltjo Schrage on the Occasion of his 65th Birthday* (Amsterdam: Scientia Verlag, 2010), 277–87.

Malcolm, C. A., 'The Parliament House and its antecedents', in G. C. H. Paton (ed.), *An Introduction to Scottish Legal History* (Edinburgh: Stair Society, 1958), 448–58.

Murray, Athol L., 'Sinclair's Practicks', in Alan Harding (ed.), *Law-Making and Law-Makers in British History: Papers Presented to the Edinburgh Legal History Conference, 1977* (London: Royal Historical Society, 1980), 90–104.

Simpson, Andrew R. C., 'Legislation and authority in early-modern Scotland', in Mark Godfrey (ed.), *Law and Authority in British Legal History, 1200–1900* (Cambridge: Cambridge University Press, 2016), 85–119.

Stein, Peter, 'Bartolus, the conflict of laws and the Roman law', in Peter Feuerstein and Clive Parry (eds), *Multum non Multa. Festschrift für Kurt Lipstein Aus Anlass Seines 70 Geburtstages* (Heidelberg: C. F. Muller, 1980), 251–8.

Stein, Peter, 'Civil law reports and the case of San Marino', in Okko Behrends, Malte Diesselhorst and Wulf Echkart Voss (eds), *Römisches Recht in der europäischen Tradition. Symposium aus Anlaß des 75 Geburtstages von Franz Wieacker* (Ebelsbach: Verlag Rolf Gremer, 1985), 323–38.

(3) Articles in Journals

Clarence Smith, J. A., 'Bartolo on the conflict of laws', *American Journal of Legal History* 14 (1870), 157–83, 247–75.

(4) Electronic Resources

Murray, Athol L., and Gero Dolezalek (eds), *Sinclair's Practicks*, http://home.uni-leipzig.de/jurarom/scotland/dat/sinclair.html.

CHAPTER 8

Reformation, Revolution and the Legal System

A. INTRODUCTION

In 1564 the lords of session moved into new accommodation. During the 1550s they had made repeated complaints concerning the ruinous state of the medieval Tolbooth. The complaints were directed to the burgh council of Edinburgh, which was responsible for the Tolbooth's maintenance. The situation had deteriorated by February 1555. The lords had taken 'ane effray' (fright) at the condition of the building; one might imagine crumbling masonry coming down among them. Alarmed, they chose to withdraw completely, protesting to the burgh council as they left. They started holding their court in other locations in the city, including the Magdalen Chapel which still stands in Edinburgh's Cowgate. The burgh council eventually effected some repairs upon the Tolbooth, but the lords were still not satisfied. Eventually, the burgh council realised that the building was not even safe for its own meetings. In June 1560 it resolved to provide alternative accommodation for itself in a large adjacent building, much of which had just become vacant. However, the council was content to leave the ruinous Tolbooth for the use of the lords. The lords themselves had had enough of the town council of Edinburgh. They threatened to relocate the College of Justice to St Andrews, taking with them all the valuable business that thrived around the supreme civil court. At this point, the burgh council suddenly changed tack. Its members partitioned the half-vacant building that was being redesigned for the council's own use. New walls and floors were added. In the process, the council created new courtrooms for the lords of session, the burgh court, a new tribunal called the commissary court and the justiciar and his deputes. The courtrooms opened in 1564.[1]

---

[1] For these points, see Hector L. MacQueen (ed.), *The College of Justice. Essays by R. K. Hannay* (Edinburgh: Stair Society, 1990), 95–6; C. A. Malcolm, 'The parliament

What is perhaps surprising is that the half-vacant building chosen to host the new courtrooms was none other than the great collegiate church of St Giles (now St Giles' Cathedral). Ten years earlier, in the mid-1550s, the idea that the burgesses of Edinburgh would have sanctioned the architectural mutilation of their burgh kirk would have been unthinkable. For generations, merchants and tradesmen had lavished wealth and artistic patronage on the building at the heart of their city. They acted in pious devotion to God and his saints, and also in proud affirmation of their corporate civic identity. But now a great wall had been built, effectively splitting the kirk into two. While the east end was still devoted to religious purposes, the west end housed the secular courts. Entering from the High Street of Edinburgh through an ancient Normanesque arch, litigants would now pass up a flight of stairs to an upper floor constructed within the west end of the church. There they would probably have seen large numbers of pursuers and defenders waiting on the services of a still quite small number of men of law. Some of them would have been heard in a room known as the Outer House of the session, where three of the fifteen lords were appointed to sit to deal with routine matters and hear evidence from witnesses. Others would have been heard in the Inner House, where the remaining judges heard disputations concerning weightier matters.[2]

The stairs, the upper floor and even the arch are all gone now, following a series of subsequent efforts to reconceptualise the sanctity of St Giles' Cathedral in burgh life. Yet this story points to a fairly radical shift in the attitudes of the burgesses of Edinburgh. What could possibly have induced them to abandon their ancestors' assumptions concerning the sacredness of the building that lay at the heart of their town? Furthermore, what could have caused the Roman Catholic clergy who sat on the session to tolerate what they would surely have seen as an act of desecration? It must have proceeded from a revolution in religious attitudes.

This chapter will begin by exploring that revolution, which is of course better known as the Protestant Reformation. The Reformation, together

house and its antecedents', in G. C. H. Paton (ed.), *An Introduction to Scottish Legal History* (Edinburgh: Stair Society, 1958), 451–3; John Finlay, *Men of Law in Pre-Reformation Scotland* (East Linton: Tuckwell Press, 2000), 90–6; Hector L. MacQueen, 'Two visitors in the session, 1629 and 1636', in Hector L. MacQueen (ed.), *Stair Society Miscellany Four* (Edinburgh: Stair Society, 2002), 155–68; James D. Marwick (ed.), *Extracts from the Records of the Burgh of Edinburgh* (Edinburgh: Scottish Burgh Records Society, 1869–92), ii, 296 (discussing the 'effray' of 1555).

2   On the Outer House and the Inner House, see, for example, John W. Cairns, 'Historical introduction', in Kenneth Reid and Reinhard Zimmermann (eds), *A History of Private Law in Scotland* (Oxford: Oxford University Press, 2000) I, 85–6.

with various closely associated movements of the time, had an enormous impact on the development of Scottish politics and the Scottish legal system.[3] This was partly because it was deeply bound up with a series of political rebellions. Over time these targeted, to a lesser or greater extent, virtually all forms of established authority. The current chapter will explore the Reformation and the troubles of the 1540s and 1550s, together with their immediate impacts on the legal system. The next two chapters will then explore the longer-term effects of these developments. There it will be explained that they caused lawyers to articulate, defend and sometimes challenge fundamental assumptions concerning the authority of law that their predecessors had held in the 1540s. It will be recalled from the last chapter that these fundamental assumptions were twofold. First, Roman law and canon law were more reliable repositories of learning concerning justice and legal 'truth' than the medieval Scottish common law. Second, consensus amongst learned Scottish lawyers concerning the nature of legal 'truth' could enjoy the binding force of law. Both claims had been challenged by the mid-1570s. Yet, as stated, these developments can only be explained in light of the contexts of both the political and religious revolutions of the Reformation, and also their immediate effects on the legal system.

B. ASPECTS OF EARLY PROTESTANTISM

On 14 December 1542, James V lay dying in his royal palace at Falkland in Fife. A severe bout of vomiting and diarrhoea following a disastrous military campaign against England had fatally weakened the thirty-year-old king. At James's side was Cardinal David Beaton, an expert canon lawyer and the leading Roman Catholic prelate in the realm. Beaton implored the monarch to make arrangements for the governance of the kingdom following his death. At least the identity of the heir to the throne was certain. A few days earlier James's wife, Mary of Guise, had given birth to a daughter. She was Mary, Queen of Scots (r. 1542–67). Yet she would not be able to rule personally for decades. Who would be her regent? Beaton, determined to seize power, composed a notarial instrument purporting to contain the king's last wishes. This nominated

---

[3] On the Scottish Reformation, its context and its effects, see, for example Gordon Donaldson, *The Scottish Reformation* (Cambridge: Cambridge University Press, 1960); Jane E. A. Dawson, *Scotland Re-formed 1488–1587* (Edinburgh: Edinburgh University Press, 2007); consider also the additional sources cited by Dawson at 358.

Beaton and three Scottish earls – the earls of Moray, Huntly and Argyll – to rule on the infant Mary's behalf after the king's demise. James V, delirious and past any real capacity to act, may or may not have approved of the document, but Beaton claimed he did. Within hours, the king was dead.[4]

Beaton's actions were evidently designed to undermine the claims to the regency of another man, James Hamilton, second Earl of Arran. Arran was heir presumptive to the throne. What was perhaps troubling for Beaton was the fact that Arran was known to entertain heretical opinions.[5] 'Heretical' opinions were those that deviated from the official teachings of the Roman Catholic Church concerning God, man's salvation, and the role of the Catholic Church in mediating that salvation. Such heretical views increasingly became associated with a new series of new Christian movements collectively known as Protestantism. This is not the place to outline Protestant thinking in detail, but a few salient points should be noted. Catholics and Protestants alike tended to treat the Bible as a source of unquestionable truth. Nonetheless, the text had to be interpreted, and it was over this issue that divergences of opinion emerged. Did any particular institution possess ultimate authority to say what was, and what was not, an accurate reading of the Bible? Or could any believer find scriptural truth for himself through reading scripture directly?

The Roman Catholic Church claimed that it possessed ultimate authority to expound scripture. On this basis it had established what it presented as the authoritative interpretations and doctrines of the Bible. These were expressed through copious commentaries. Yet in the early sixteenth century, some scholars, such as Desiderius Erasmus, questioned excessive reliance on those commentaries. They felt that Christians should be able to read the words of Christ in the New Testament to find truth for themselves. Authoritative Catholic commentaries on those words might be helpful guides to truth. However, they were no more than that. Other writers, like Martin Luther, went much further. They maintained that the Roman Catholic interpreters of scripture had 'erred repeatedly and

---

[4]   See Margaret H. B. Sanderson, *Cardinal of Scotland: David Beaton c. 1494–1546*, revised edn (Edinburgh: John Donald, 2001), 148–58; Gordon Donaldson, *Scotland. James V – James VII*, revised edn (Edinburgh: Oliver and Boyd, 1971), 60–4; Dawson, *Scotland Re-formed*, 148–58. On this regency, and on regency generally in sixteenth-century Scotland, see too now Amy Blakeway, *Regency in Sixteenth-Century Scotland* (Woodbridge: Boydell Press, 2015).

[5]   See Dawson, *Scotland Re-formed*, 158–60.

contradicted themselves'.[6] For Luther, and for Protestants generally, the Bible alone revealed truth and the way to salvation. Luther believed that the conscience of any human being that was captive to scripture could discern the truth expressed therein.[7]

Drawing on this assumption, many Protestants went further still. They used scriptural arguments to attack the idea that the priesthood of the Catholic Church constituted the authoritative mediator of God's grace to man. Obviously this seriously threatened the power of that priesthood. To explain, the claim that the rites of the Catholic Church mediated salvation presented the Church with an obvious sanction for those who failed to obey it. The disobedient could be 'excommunicated', meaning that they would be refused access to its rites. In sixteenth-century Scotland, excommunication was known as 'cursing'. If the rites of the Catholic Church did indeed mediate salvation, then it followed that an excommunicate was not saved, but damned. He would spend eternity in the fires of Hell, body and soul. The threat of the curse was often taken very seriously. Certainly the Scottish clergy used it widely to compel obedience in a range of matters. So those who failed to pay teinds or obey judgements of the consistory courts might have sentences of cursing pronounced upon them.[8]

By contrast, the Protestants argued that man was justified before God by faith alone, which manifested the working of God's grace within him. If the Protestants were correct in this, it followed that the rites of the Catholic Church did not mediate salvation. Thus the Protestants could conclude that excommunication from those rites was nothing to be feared. At least, it was nothing to be feared on a spiritual level. It could give rise to other problems. By an act of parliament passed in 1450, cursed individuals were technically barred from raising actions in the secular courts. Indeed, those who remained under 'cursing' might

---

[6] Quoted in Peter Harrison, 'Philosophy and the crisis of religion', in James Hankins (ed.), *The Cambridge Companion to Renaissance Philosophy* (Cambridge: Cambridge University Press, 2007), 234–49 at 234.

[7] For these points, see, for example, Robert M. Adams (ed.), *Desiderius Erasmus: The Praise of Folly and Other Writings* (New York and London: W. W. Norton, 1989), 126; Harrison, 'Philosophy and the crisis of religion'; Quentin Skinner, *The Foundations of Modern Political Thought* (Cambridge: Cambridge University Press, 1978) II, 3–109.

[8] See, for example, Donaldson, *Scottish Reformation*, 41; Simon Ollivant, *The Court of the Official in Pre-Reformation Scotland* (Edinburgh: Stair Society, 1982), 149–55; Dawson, *Scotland Re-formed*, 112.

ultimately be 'put to the horn', or outlawed.[9] What is clear is that questioning the consequences of excommunication from the Catholic Church directly undermined its power.

C. POWER STRUGGLES: ENGLISH AND FRENCH INTERFERENCE

Thus Protestant sympathisers like Arran represented a serious threat to the authority of prelates like Beaton, and indeed the whole Catholic Church in Scotland. Furthermore, Arran was not alone. A number of prominent men at James V's court had developed Protestant beliefs towards the end of the reign. Among them was Master Henry Balnaves, one of the lords of session.[10] A struggle for the governorship of the realm broke out, with Arran apparently drawing his sword on Beaton during one meeting. Arran ultimately secured control of the situation and had Beaton imprisoned at Dalkeith.[11]

A factor that had helped Arran on the road to power had been the return of powerful Scottish noblemen to the realm. They had been imprisoned in England since James V's disastrous invasion of the country a few months earlier. Those noblemen had been freed by the English king, Henry VIII, on the condition that they should further his interests in Scotland. It should be noted here that Henry VIII had broken with the Roman Catholic Church a few years earlier, and now England was increasingly open to Protestant influence. Thus Arran's government now included individuals who had some loyalty to Henry VIII and also men committed to furthering the Protestant Reformation in Scotland.[12] The result was that Protestants generally became associated with a pro-English political stance. The supporters of the imprisoned Roman Catholic prelate Beaton, by contrast, became associated with a pro-French policy. The aid of Catholic France might help to repel English interference, and to preserve the interests of the Catholic Church in the realm.[13]

---

[9] Ollivant, *Court of the Official*, 154–5; *RPS* 1450/1/11.

[10] For Balnaves, see, for example, Jane Dawson, *John Knox* (New Haven and London: Yale University Press, 2015), 41–2, 44–5, 58, 186, 276.

[11] See Donaldson, *James V – James VII*, 63–5; Sanderson, *Cardinal of Scotland*, 155; Dawson, *Scotland Re-formed*, 156–7.

[12] The two groups should not be confused, although of course there were overlaps between them.

[13] Of course, this is an oversimplification of the extremely complex politics of the mid-1540s. Students who wish to understand those politics fully should consult Marcus

At the centre of the diplomatic manoeuvring between the two parties over the next few years would be the infant Queen Mary. Henry VIII saw her as a suitable bride for his son and heir Edward. Their marriage would ultimately unite the two kingdoms and neutralise any Scottish threat to Henry's northern borders. Those who favoured the preservation of Roman Catholicism in Scotland were obviously bitterly opposed to the match.[14]

Yet for now Arran had the upper hand. He summoned a parliament in March 1543. As was usual by this time, one of the first things parliament did was to appoint a committee known as the lords of the articles.[15] Representatives from each of the three parliamentary estates – the clergy, the nobility and the burgesses – would be chosen to sit on this committee. Its role was 'to draft legislation from the articles presented by the king, or more rarely a particular Estate or individual, which was then presented to the full parliamentary sederunt for final approval'.[16] In other words, the king or the members of an individual estate would present a proposal to introduce legislation on a particular matter – that is, an 'article' – to the chosen lords. The lords would then consider the article. If they approved it, they might rework it into legislation which could then be approved or rejected by parliament as a whole. Importantly, the lords had been known to reject articles presented to them by the king in the past. The older view, that they were wholly subservient to royal interests, no longer seems tenable.[17]

In March 1543, the debate amongst the lords of the articles was

Merriman, *The Rough Wooings. Mary Queen of Scots, 1542–1551* (East Linton: Tuckwell Press, 2000); Sanderson, *Cardinal of Scotland*, is also extremely helpful in this regard. For another authoritative and helpful study, see Dawson, *Scotland Re-formed*, 155–75.

14 See Dawson, *Scotland Re-formed*, 155–75.

15 Concerning the Lords of the Articles, and their ability to interfere with royal legislative agenda, see Roland J. Tanner, 'The Lords of the Articles before 1540: a reassessment', *Scottish Historical Review* 79 (2000), 189–212. Concerning the history of Scottish parliaments generally, see Keith M. Brown and Roland J. Tanner (eds), *The History of the Scottish Parliament, I: Parliament and Politics, 1235–1560* (Edinburgh: Edinburgh University Press, 2004); Keith M. Brown and Alistair J. Mann (eds), *The History of the Scottish Parliament, II: Parliament and Politics, 1567–1707* (Edinburgh: Edinburgh University Press, 2005); Keith M. Brown and Alan R. MacDonald (eds), *The History of the Scottish Parliament, III. Parliament in Context, 1235–1707* (Edinburgh: Edinburgh University Press, 2010).

16 Tanner, 'Lords of the Articles', 189.

17 See Tanner, 'Lords of the Articles', discussing views expressed in Robert S. Rait, *The Parliaments of Scotland* (Glasgow: Maclehose, Jackson and Co., 1924).

probably particularly acrimonious. Two proposals in particular would have excited animosity from the clerical estate. First, it was suggested that negotiations should begin with Henry VIII of England for the marriage of Queen Mary to his son Edward. Second, it was proposed that all Scots should be permitted to read the Bible for themselves in their own language without fear of punishment. It is known that two lords of session were at loggerheads over this last point. Henry Balnaves supplied arguments to Protestant sympathisers among the lords of the articles. Meanwhile, the elderly Gavin Dunbar, archbishop of Glasgow, led the clerical opposition to the proposal. Ultimately the representatives of the nobility and the burgesses forced through the committee the article permitting Scots to read the Bible in the vernacular.[18] It was subsequently passed in parliament, in the teeth of continued opposition from Dunbar and the first estate. They protested that they 'dissassentit' to the act '*simpliciter*'.[19] In other words, they were wholly opposed to it. The only consolation was that the lords of the articles had expressly prohibited public disputations concerning the meaning of scripture. It was well known that such disputations could lead to breaches of public order and damage to property. This was because Protestants tended to regard much of the apparatus of Catholic worship as idolatrous. Mobs who heard Protestant ministers had been known to react to their preaching by breaking statues of saints and ransacking church buildings. The Reformation challenged the sanctity of the old sacred spaces.

Meanwhile parliament also approved the opening of negotiations with Henry VIII for the marriage of Queen Mary to his son.[20] It looked like Scotland might be on the verge of embracing a Protestant Reformation and a firm alliance with England. Yet this did not come to pass in 1543. The reasons were complex, but one major factor was the return to Scotland of Arran's brother John Hamilton, abbot of Paisley. The latter was firmly in the clerical 'camp'. He persuaded his brother that his programme of ecclesiastical reform was wrong, and, remarkably, that Beaton should be released. Now with Arran's backing, Beaton's faction quickly regained the upper hand, and parliament promulgated acts to suppress heresy. Arran formally renounced Protestantism in September 1543. The marriage treaty with England was also broken. Henry VIII vented his wrath on the Scottish borders, ordering a series of destructive

---

[18]   See Donaldson, *James V – James VII*, 63–5; Sanderson, *Cardinal of Scotland*, 188; Dawson, *Scotland Re-formed*, 158–60.

[19]   *RPS* 1543/3/25–6.

[20]   *RPS* 1543/3/2.

campaigns to try to compel the Scots to keep their word. These are now commonly referred to as the 'Rough Wooings'. During this time Arran's government sought to develop an alliance with France, which was also at war with England, in order to resist English invasion.[21] Meanwhile Henry VIII identified Beaton as one of his chief opponents, and publicly encouraged an attempt on his life. Beaton had many enemies. A group of them chose to strike in 1546, perhaps driven by outrage at his recent decision to execute by burning at the stake a leading Protestant preacher, or by pro-English sympathy, or simply by personal feuds with the cardinal. Breaking into his castle at St Andrews by force, they discovered the cardinal had barricaded himself into his chamber. They set fires outside his door, eventually smoking him out. Bursting into his room, one of them delivered a sermon exhorting him to repent, before running him through with a sword. His body was hung from the window of his own fortress. Soon the assassins were joined in the castle by Henry Balnaves, and also two young men with legal training who would exercise great influence in the future. They were John Knox, a radical Protestant, and James Balfour, the latter a future lord president of the College of Justice.[22]

Eventually, in 1548, a treaty was signed with France to marry the young Queen Mary to the heir to the French throne. This had the backing of Mary's French mother, Mary of Guise. French military aid was dispatched to Scotland and English invading forces were repelled. By this point the French had already defeated the Protestants who held St Andrews. Men of substance like Balnaves were imprisoned. Others, like Knox and Balfour, were condemned to serve in French galleys, but a few years later they were released. Meanwhile, the French, who were unwilling to trust Arran to maintain a pro-French stance, pushed for the appointment of a new regent in his place. Arran acquiesced in this, having first been handsomely rewarded for his compliance. His successor was Mary of Guise, who was the mother of the queen, the widow of the last Stewart king and a powerful French noblewoman in her own right. She was officially invested as regent of the country in 1554. Her ambitions were primarily dynastic. Her daughter Mary was Queen of Scots and betrothed to the heir to the French throne. She also had a prominent place within the line of succession to the English throne. In 1554, the young Scottish queen could have been seen as second-in-line to inherit

---

[21] On these developments, see Merriman, *Rough Wooings*, 111–63; Dawson, *Scotland Re-formed*, 155–75.
[22] Sanderson, *Cardinal of Scotland*, 223–30; Dawson, *Knox*, 56–7.

that throne, after the English queen's sister Elizabeth. In attempting to realise dynastic ambitions for her daughter, it looked like Mary of Guise would ensure Scotland would remain a Catholic country, and closely allied with France.[23]

D. REVOLUTION AND REFORMATION

(1) A French Threat to the Laws and Liberties of the Realm?

As regent, Mary of Guise did not simply seek to promote her daughter's dynastic interests. She also attempted to effect various reforms to the exercise of power and the administration of justice in Scotland. Ultimately these reforms came to be perceived – rightly or wrongly – as constituting a fundamental threat to the survival of the traditional laws and liberties of the Scots. This contributed to her downfall, and the collapse of the pro-French, Catholic Scottish government. Some explanation is required of this here.[24]

Mary of Guise professed that she aimed to bring what she saw as 'a young nation' – Scotland – 'to a state of perfection'.[25] She sought to reform the ways in which power was exercised, government was conducted and justice was administered. One reform she attempted to introduce in this regard does, prima facie, seem very radical. Indeed, when set in its proper context, it seems so startling that historians still debate exactly what she hoped to achieve. The reform appears to have targeted the very widespread practice of 'bonding'.[26] This underpinned both the exercise of power in every part of the realm and also important systems of 'private' dispute resolution and justice. To explain, most members of Scottish society were bound together through private agreements known as bonds of manrent and maintenance. Minor landowners or 'lairds', burgesses and others made promises through bonds of manrent to serve great lords in all their quarrels and disputes. 'Service' might involve good counsel and legal advice; yet it might also involve armed support in a great lord's feuds with his neighbours. In return for a bond of manrent, the lord

---

[23] See Donaldson, *James V – James VII*, 80–4; Dawson, *Scotland Re-formed*, 167–9, 172–5, 176–99; Dawson, *Knox*, 53–8.

[24] On Mary of Guise and her government, see, above all, Pamela E. Ritchie, *Mary of Guise in Scotland, 1548–1560: a Political Career* (East Linton: Tuckwell Press, 2002).

[25] Ritchie, *Mary of Guise*, 141–2.

[26] See Ritchie, *Mary of Guise*, 132–3; see also Jenny Wormald, *Lords and Men in Scotland: Bonds of Manrent, 1442–1603* (Edinburgh: John Donald, 1985), 154–5.

would give a bond of maintenance. Through this he would promise to protect those in his service, together with their lands and possessions, by whatever means necessary. Technically the reciprocal duties owed by lord and man were absolute, save for one exception. The bond of manrent did not require a man to support his lord in rebellion against the monarch.[27]

As Wormald has shown, the practice of bonding did provide a remarkably effective system of dispute resolution in Scotland during the 1400s and 1500s. Disputes over lands and possessions might be settled through physical force in fulfilment of duties owed under the bonds. Undoubtedly this was a violent system, in that it drew large numbers of ordinary Scots into very bloody feuds. Yet bonding could also be a potent force for peacemaking. It came to be accepted that the great lords, while prepared to feud on behalf of their followers, could also act as arbiters on their behalf. The threat of feud lying behind this could compel men to agree. Furthermore, by and large Stewart monarchs engaged constructively with this system. Those who killed others in feuds within this complex system of dispute resolution could avoid royal wrath and punishment. Yet this would only follow if they paid compensation or 'assythement' to their victims' families. Paying such compensation could trigger a royal 'remission' or pardon. Wormald suggested that even the men of law who staffed the session quite happily engaged with systems of 'private' dispute resolution. They did this while simultaneously developing the more 'public' mechanisms of dispute resolution with which this book is primarily concerned. Those 'public' mechanisms were, of course, the forms of action at common law, many of which were superseded by the forms of action used before the lords of session.[28] Godfrey agrees with Wormald's assessment. He shows that those who settled their disputes through systems of 'private' dispute resolution often brought their agreements before the lords for registration in their records. Sometimes they even asked the lords to help them interpret their settlements. 'Private' mechanisms of dispute resolution thus operated in tandem with the 'public'.[29]

---

[27] The leading study of bonding is Wormald, *Lords and Men*. For a summary of some important points relating to bonding, see Jenny Wormald, *Court, Kirk and Community* (Edinburgh: Edinburgh University Press, 1981), 29–40.

[28] See Wormald, *Lords and Men*; Wormald, *Court, Kirk and Community*, 29–40. The point that 'private' mechanisms of dispute resolution were approved and taken over by increasingly professional lawyers is argued in Jenny Wormald, 'Bloodfeud, kindred and government in early modern Scotland', *Past and Present* 87 (1980), 54–97.

[29] See A. Mark Godfrey, *Civil Justice in Renaissance Scotland* (Leiden: Brill, 2009), 355–440, 446–8.

Virtually the whole of Scottish society operated in the context of bonding, and thus of the system of private dispute resolution outlined by Wormald and Godfrey. It must therefore have seemed quite a radical move when, in 1555, Mary of Guise promulgated an act nullifying all existing bonds and forbidding the creation of new bonds.[30] While the language of the act was general, Wormald was surely correct to argue that an attempt to neutralise Arran lay behind it. He could still draw significant power from his own web of bonds and so continue to threaten the position of Mary of Guise.[31] Nonetheless, the broad language of the act does make one wonder if Mary of Guise was seeking to undermine private mechanisms for dispute resolution more generally. The statute gave her officers sweeping authority to arrest and imprison those who entered into bonds. While it would have been impossible in practice to enforce the act against *all* offenders, perhaps the *ability* to act was all that the regent wanted. The act gave her the *power* to bring to account particularly troublesome lords and their followers. Against this backdrop, 'private' justice might well be left to operate much as before. Yet Mary of Guise wanted to make it clear that the 'public' justice of royal officers and courts was to remain more potent, as it had done in the past. On this reading all she did was to increase that potency by providing a new tool for the enforcement of royal order.

That the regent was prepared to send such a warning to the Scottish political elites might have given some cause for concern. Furthermore, there is no question that Mary of Guise wished to reform the 'public' mechanisms for the administration of justice just mentioned. Writing to her brother in 1557, she complained that her efforts were meeting with opposition:

> now that it is a question of my determination to see justice take a straightforward course, and they find me a little severe, they will not endure it, and say that these are laws of the French, and that their old laws are good, which for the most part are the greatest injustices in the world, not in themselves, but from the way in which they are administered. This is the cause of all our discord ...

In particular, she complained that 'the great lords' were 'so little desirous of justice' that they were always ready to 'find some complication which

---

[30] *RPS* A1555/6/18.
[31] Wormald, *Lords and Men*, 154.

may impede it'.[32] In 1554, she had sent for two French legal experts to come to advise on how best to remedy perceived defects in the administration of justice. Furthermore, she also introduced Frenchmen into the council, giving them senior offices of state. One became vice-chancellor, and exercised many of the functions of the chancellor himself. Another became comptroller, whose duties included in-gathering rents due from the royal estates and the burghs.[33] These moves infuriated some of the great Scottish noblemen. They came to believe that the regent's acts were calculated to undermine what they saw as their birth-right to serve as the royal counsellors. Meanwhile, the French troops who had helped to liberate the country from the English from 1548 onwards remained in possession of many Scottish castles. Fears began to emerge that it was now the French alliance that threatened traditional Scottish laws and liberties. At the same time, Protestant feeling began to grow again. The possibility emerged that there might be some alliance between the Protestants, on the one hand, and noblemen who were suspicious of the regent's reforms, on the other.[34]

(2) Patriotism, Rebellion and Reformation

In November 1558, the Catholic Queen Mary of England died. She was succeeded by her Protestant half-sister, Elizabeth I. This reopened the possibility that the Scottish Protestants might ally with the English and expel the French. They invited the radical Protestant preacher John Knox to return to Scotland. He preached an inflammatory sermon at Perth in May 1559. This provoked a riot.[35] The regent's attempts to restore order failed, and by June 1559 Protestant noblemen were in open rebellion. The leaders of the rebellion had entered into a political 'bond' to establish Protestantism within the realm. This foreshadowed the covenants that were later to be of such importance in Scottish religious and

---

[32] See the discussions in Ritchie, *Mary of Guise*, 140–3 and Dawson, *Scotland Re-formed*, 189–90; see also John Hungerford Pollen (ed.), *Papal Negotiations with Mary Queen of Scots During Her Reign in Scotland, 1561–1567* (Edinburgh: Scottish History Society, 1901), 427–30 (the passages quoted are at 428 and 430). On the general concern of the Scots to maintain their laws and liberties in the early modern period, see J. D. Ford, 'Four models of union', in Hector L. MacQueen (ed.), *Stair Society Miscellany Seven* (Edinburgh: Stair Society, 2015), 179–215.

[33] Ritchie, *Mary of Guise*, 124–30, 141.

[34] See Donaldson, *James V – James VII*, 100–1; Ritchie, *Mary of Guise*, 124–30, 141; Dawson, *Scotland Re-formed*, 176–212 (particularly at 208–12).

[35] See Dawson, *Scotland Re-formed*, 200–12; Dawson, *Knox*, 177–91.

political thought. Among the leaders of the rebellion was James Stewart, the prior of St Andrews and illegitimate son of James V who was mentioned in the last chapter. At first the Protestants did not have the upper hand. Yet they managed to gain more support by allying themselves with lords who were disaffected by what they saw as the regent's threats to the traditional laws and liberties of the realm. In October 1559, for example, it was stated that the French vice-chancellor was introducing 'a new ... styill and forme of ... pardonis and remissionis'. It was feared this might result in the 'haill subversioun and alteratioun' of the remaining laws of the realm.[36]

Ultimately the rebel lords secured English support and inflicted defeats on the French. Domestic troubles made it difficult for the French to offer further support. The regent's death in June 1560 resulted in the cessation of hostilites. French and English soldiers alike withdrew from Scotland. Now the Reformation might be established. The Protestant lords were in control of the situation. Many burghs like Edinburgh also had substantial Protestant populations by this point.[37] That explains the decision of the burgh council to partition St Giles' kirk in 1560, which was mentioned at the beginning of this chapter. Protestants did not regard the buildings of the Catholic Church as sacred. Indeed, they had to be purged of what were now seen as idolatrous relics, images and statues. Once purged, the buildings might be re-used for Protestant worship or for secular purposes. That was what happened to St Giles'. Other buildings were less fortunate. If they no longer served a practical purpose, they were simply left to fall into ruins.[38]

In August 1560 a parliament gathered in the old Tolbooth next to St Giles'.[39] It was packed with Protestant sympathisers, and the choice of Lords of the Articles reflected this. It promulgated a series of statutes prohibiting the saying of mass. The parliament also introduced a new confession of faith – that is to say, a statement of religious beliefs. All statutes that were inconsistent with it were abolished. In addition, parliament abolished papal jurisdiction in Scotland.[40] This resulted in the

---

[36] See David Laing (ed.), *The Works of John Knox* (Edinburgh: Wodrow Society, 1846–64) I, 446.

[37] See Dawson, *Scotland Re-formed*, 208–15.

[38] Donaldson, *Scottish Reformation*, 97–9.

[39] For this parliament, see, for example, Keith M. Brown, 'The Reformation parliament', in Keith M. Brown and Roland J. Tanner (eds), *The History of the Scottish Parliament, I: Parliament and Politics, 1235–1560* (Edinburgh: Edinburgh University Press, 2004), 203–31.

[40] *RPS* A1560/8/3–6.

suppression of the consistorial courts of the bishops' officials. That in turn created four years of chaos, as Green has shown. Who now had the right to decide the wide range of disputes formerly heard by the consistorial courts? In 1564 the consistorial courts were replaced by the commissary courts, which succeeded to the old consistorial jurisdiction. The first commissaries of Edinburgh sat in the same accommodation that had been prepared for the lords of session in the west end of the kirk of St Giles. Among them was James Balfour, who, like John Knox, had been released from the galleys of the French king years earlier.[41] Also a lord of session, he was to play an important role in the events that followed.

E. CONCLUSION

It might be thought that Protestantism had been firmly established in Scotland. With hindsight that was true, although at the time this was far from clear. A significant proportion of the population retained Catholic sympathies. Perhaps more significantly, so did the monarch. After the death of her husband, Queen Mary finally returned to her realm of Scotland to begin her personal rule in 1561. The rebel lords recognised her undoubted right to govern, and at first Mary herself made no attempt to undermine the Protestant settlement. Nonetheless, she also refused to ratify the legislation of 1560. This gave some people cause to question the legality of the Reformation.[42] Among them was John Sinclair, who was mentioned in the previous chapter. He was one of the lords of session who remained Catholic. John Knox memorably described him as 'blind of one eye in the body but of both in his soul'.[43]

The current chapter opened by implying that the Reformation caused great changes in the development of Scots law. Of course, this should not be overstated. There was continuity in legal development after

---

[41] See Thomas M. Green (ed.), *The Consistorial Decisions of the Commissaries of Edinburgh, 1564 to 1576/7* (Edinburgh: Stair Society, 2014), xvii–lxxvi. See too the important contribution in Thomas Green, 'The sources of early Scots consistorial law: reflections on law, authority and jurisdiction during the Scottish Reformation', in Mark Godfrey, *Law and Authority in British Legal History, 1200–1900* (Cambridge: Cambridge University Press, 2016), 120–39.

[42] See, for example, Julian Goodare, *The Government of Scotland 1560–1625* (Oxford: Oxford University Press, 2004), 75.

[43] See Athol L. Murray, 'Sinclair, John (c. 1510–1566)', *Oxford Dictionary of National Biography* (Oxford: Oxford University Press, 2004), http://www.oxforddnb.com/view/article/25624.

1560. Most 'public' systems of dispute resolution continued to function much as they had done before. The same could be said for the 'private' systems of dispute resolution structured around bonding and feuding. Nonetheless, it is important to emphasise the ways in which the conflicts, rebellions and religious changes of the 1540s and the 1550s had affected the Scottish legal system. Most ordinary Scots would have seen the effects primarily in the suppression of the consistorial courts. Yet the revolutions discussed here also provoked two further developments, the effects of which will be considered in the next two chapters.

First, the preservation of the ancient common laws and liberties of the realm had become associated with Scottish patriotism. Although the link was nothing new, it was clearly felt particularly strongly in the late 1550s and early 1560s. Lawyers were soon to reckon with such sentiments in reappraising the authority of the local laws of the realm. As will be explained, this probably helped to provoke a reconceptualisation of the local laws as a body of learning, like Roman law, that revealed justice and legal 'truth'. Obviously that represented a departure from the position of many lords of session in the 1540s, as seen in Sinclair's *Practicks*.

Second, parliament had taken upon itself increasingly powers to interfere in religious matters. In 1543 it had permitted reading of the Bible in the vernacular, in the teeth of clerical opposition. In 1560 it felt it had the power to abolish papal jurisdiction itself.[44] Such law-making was still couched in terms of the recognition of truth – the scriptural truth that was held to reveal the ungodliness of papal jurisdiction. Of course, Scottish parliaments had always been powerful – in the past they had forced royal retirements, restrained royal ambitions of military glory and refused to grant taxes desired by monarchs.[45] Yet it may be the case that parliament's decision in 1560 to alter so radically the existing legal order underpinned a growing sense of its own authority in the years to come. Ultimately, perhaps, this helped Protestant clergyman to formulate some very remarkable claims about parliamentary competence later in the century. At one point of crisis in the 1570s, those claims came close to threatening one basic assumption of Scots lawyers. This was the idea that expert consensus amongst Scottish lawyers concerning the nature of legal 'truth' could enjoy the binding force of law. How these two changes came about will be considered in the next two chapters.

[44] The importance of this is developed in Goodare, *Government of Scotland*, 75.
[45] These points are developed in the leading study of late medieval Scottish parliaments, this being Roland Tanner, *The Late Medieval Scottish Parliament* (East Linton: Tuckwell Press, 2001).

F. SELECTED BIBLIOGRAPHY AND FURTHER READING

(1) Records of the Parliaments of Scotland (*RPS*)

Acts relating to the Reformation in 1560: *RPS* A1560/8/3–6.

(2) Books

Blakeway, Amy, *Regency in Sixteenth-Century Scotland* (Woodbridge: Boydell Press, 2015).

Brown, Keith M. (ed.), *The History of the Scottish Parliament* (Edinburgh: Edinburgh University Press, 2004–10).

Cairns, John W., *Law, Lawyers and Humanism. Selected Essays on the History of Scots Law, Volume 1* (Edinburgh: Edinburgh University Press, 2015).

Dawson, Jane E. A., *Scotland Re-formed 1488–1587* (Edinburgh: Edinburgh University Press, 2007).

Dawson, Jane, *John Knox* (New Haven and London: Yale University Press, 2015).

Donaldson, Gordon, *The Scottish Reformation* (Cambridge: Cambridge University Press, 1960).

Finlay, John, *Men of Law in Pre-Reformation Scotland* (East Linton: Tuckwell Press, 2000).

Ford, J. D., *Law and Opinion in Scotland during the Seventeenth Century* (Oxford and Portland: Hart, 2007).

Goodare, Julian, *The Government of Scotland 1560–1625* (Oxford: Oxford University Press, 2004).

Green, Thomas M. (ed.), *The Consistorial Decisions of the Commissaries of Edinburgh, 1564 to 1576/7* (Edinburgh: Stair Society, 2014).

[Hannay, R. K.], MacQueen, Hector L. (ed.), *The College of Justice. Essays by R. K. Hannay* (Edinburgh: Stair Society, 1990).

Laing, David (ed.), *The Works of John Knox* (Edinburgh: Wodrow Society, 1846–64).

Ollivant, Simon, *The Court of the Official in Pre-Reformation Scotland* (Edinburgh: Stair Society, 1982).

Rait, Robert S., *The Parliaments of Scotland* (Glasgow: Maclehose, Jackson and Co., 1924).

Ritchie, Pamela E., *Mary of Guise in Scotland, 1548–1560: a Political Career* (East Linton: Tuckwell Press, 2002).

Skinner, Quentin, *The Foundations of Modern Political Thought* (Cambridge: Cambridge University Press, 1978).

Tanner, Roland, *The Late Medieval Scottish Parliaments* (East Linton: Tuckwell Press, 2001).

Wormald, Jenny, *Lords and Men in Scotland: Bonds of Manrent, 1442–1603* (Edinburgh: John Donald, 1985).

(3) Chapters in Books

Brown, Keith M., 'The Reformation parliament', in Keith M. Brown and Roland J. Tanner (eds), *The History of the Scottish Parliament, I: Parliament and Politics, 1235–1560* (Edinburgh: Edinburgh University Press, 2004), 203–31.

Ford, J. D., 'Four models of union', in Hector L. MacQueen (ed.), *Stair Society Miscellany Seven* (Edinburgh: Stair Society, 2015), 179–215.

Godfrey, A. Mark, 'Parliament and the law', in Keith M. Brown and Alan R. MacDonald (eds), *Parliament in Context, 1235–1707* (Edinburgh: Edinburgh University Press, 2010), 157–85.

Green, Thomas, 'The sources of early Scots consistorial law: reflections on law, authority and jurisdiction during the Scottish Reformation', in Mark Godfrey, *Law and Authority in British Legal History, 1200–1900* (Cambridge: Cambridge University Press, 2016), 120–39.

MacQueen, Hector L., 'Two visitors in the session, 1629 and 1636', in Hector L. MacQueen (ed.), *Stair Society Miscellany Four* (Edinburgh: Stair Society, 2002), 155–68.

Malcolm, C. A., 'The Parliament House and its antecedents', in G. C. H. Paton (ed.), *An Introduction to Scottish Legal History* (Edinburgh: Stair Society, 1958), 448–58.

Murray, Athol L., 'Sinclair's Practicks', in Alan Harding (ed.), *Law-Making and Law-Makers in British History: Papers Presented to the Edinburgh Legal History Conference, 1977* (London: Royal Historical Society, 1980), 90–104.

Simpson, Andrew R. C., 'Legislation and authority in early-modern Scotland', in Mark Godfrey (ed.), *Law and Authority in British Legal History, 1200–1900* (Cambridge: Cambridge University Press, 2016), 85–119.

(4) Articles in Journals

Tanner, Roland J., 'The Lords of the Articles before 1540: a reassessment', *Scottish Historical Review* 79 (2000), 189–212.

Wormald, Jenny, 'Bloodfeud, kindred and government in early modern Scotland', *Past and Present* 87 (1980), 54–97.

(5) Electronic Resources

Murray, Athol L., and Gero Dolezalek (eds), *Sinclair's Practicks*, http://home.uni-leipzig.de/jurarom/scotland/dat/sinclair.html.
Murray, Athol L., 'Sinclair, John (c. 1510–1566)', *Oxford Dictionary of National Biography* (Oxford: Oxford University Press, 2004), http://www.oxforddnb.com/view/article/25624.

CHAPTER 9

The Learned Authority of Scots Law

A. INTRODUCTION

Chapter 7 explained that many lords of session held two basic assumptions concerning the authority of law during the 1540s. First, they believed that the learning of Roman law and canon law constituted a more reliable guide to justice and legal 'truth' than the local laws of the Scottish realm. Second, they believed that what they and the members of the College of Justice collectively recognised to be just or legally 'true' could possess the binding force of law. At the beginning of the last chapter, it was stated that these assumptions began to be challenged during the mid-sixteenth century. However, it was also noted that these changes should be understood in light of the Protestant Reformation and the political rebellions associated with it. Consequently, the Reformation and its immediate effects on the Scottish legal system were discussed in Chapter 8.

In light of this context, it is now possible to begin to explain how the lords' assumptions concerning the authority of law began to be challenged during the 1560s and the 1570s. First, the assumption that the Roman law and canon law constituted a more reliable guide to justice and legal truth than the ancient laws of Scotland seems to have become problematic. It could not have sat easily with the patriotic call to defend those same Scottish laws and liberties against the foreign innovations and apparent machinations of Mary of Guise in 1559. Some lords were indeed sympathetic to such concerns. This chapter will show that this helps to explain *in part* the decision of some leading lords of session to reconceptualise the authority of the local laws of Scotland. In so doing, the lords did not challenge the status of Roman law or canon law as reliable repositories of legal learning. Rather, they argued that the Scottish laws expressed exactly the same sort of learning concerning justice as was found in Roman law and canon law. That claim meant that there was no need to work out whether the local laws were just or not by judging them against the standards of the learned laws. The laws of Scotland could be trusted as a reliable guide to justice and legal truth *in and of themselves*. Consequently they could be used confidently in practice to discern the legal truth that possessed the binding force of law.

Yet this line of argument still depended on the validity of the second assumption mentioned above. This was that what the experts in the College of Justice collectively recognised to be legally 'true' could possess the binding force of law. This assumption began to run into some difficulties in the early 1570s. The problem arose as some Scots reflected on the competence of parliament following the Reformation. If parliament could do things as radical as altering the religion of the realm, what else could it do? Were its actions in any way constrained by learning concerning legal truth? And even if the answer was that parliament could do 'practically anything', then another question remained. What conditions were required to establish a valid parliament? Could at least the validity of a parliamentary meeting be judged with reference to standards found in legal learning? As will be seen, the responses various Protestant preachers gave to these questions in one debate in the early 1570s were radical. Indeed, they challenged the extent to which it was correct to equate legal 'truth', on the one hand, with the binding force of law, on the other. The implications of the challenge were not to filter fully into the consciousness of Scottish lawyers for several decades. This will be discussed in a later chapter.

The current chapter will first consider the reconceptualisation of the local laws of the realm as a body of learning.[1] In order to do this, it will be necessary to say a little more about the political context of the 1560s. Subsequently, reference will be made to a project in 1566 to promote the study of the medieval laws of the realm. The next chapter will consider ways in which contemporaries explored the relationship between parliamentary competence and legal truth. In the process, reference will

---

[1] The argument presented here draws very heavily upon Andrew R. C. Simpson, 'Legislation and authority in early-modern Scotland', in Mark Godfrey (ed.), *Law and Authority in British Legal History, 1200–1900* (Cambridge: Cambridge University Press, 2016), 85–119, and ultimately upon Andrew R. C. Simpson, 'Early Modern Studies of the Scottish Legal Past: Tradition and Authority in Sixteenth Century Scots Law' (unpublished PhD dissertation, University of Cambridge, 2010). Note that an important challenge to some of the views expressed here has recently been published in Thomas Green, 'The sources of early Scots consistorial law: reflections on law, authority and jurisdiction during the Scottish Reformation', in Mark Godfrey, *Law and Authority in British Legal History, 1200–1900* (Cambridge: Cambridge University Press, 2016), particularly at 128–9 and 138–9.

be made to parliamentary commissions of 1567, 1575 and 1578. These are sometimes presented as attempts by parliament to 'codify' the existing law. Reference will also be made here to some late sixteenth-century literature produced by Scottish men of law.

B. RECONCEPTUALISING THE AUTHORITY OF THE LAWS OF THE REALM: THE COMMISSION OF 1566

(1) The Political Context

During the mid-1560s, rebellions continued to be justified as attempts to uphold the traditional laws and liberties of the realm. For example, in August 1565, James Stewart, Earl of Moray, led a revolt against the government of his half-sister Mary, Queen of Scots. One of the accusations he levelled against her was that she had left 'the wholesome advice and counsel' of her nobility. In place of this, she had chosen to follow the counsel of 'such men, strangers, as have neither judgment nor experience of the ancient laws and governance of [Scotland]'.[2] The allegation perhaps brought back unpleasant memories for Mary's supporters. They might have remembered that the Protestant lords had defended their rebellion against Mary's mother in 1559 on the grounds that she was ignoring the laws of the realm. Moray had been one of those lords, although at that stage he was known as the prior of St Andrews.

Of course, on both occasions the reasons for rebellion were more complex. The background to the rebellion of 1559 was discussed in the previous chapter. In 1565 Moray was alarmed by indications that Mary was changing her policy. Up until then, she had acquiesced in the face of the Protestant ascendancy. Now he suggested – without much basis – that she might seek the gradual restoration of Catholicism. More important for Moray was the queen's decision to marry her close relative, Henry Stewart, Lord Darnley, which resulted in Moray losing influence as one of Mary's closest political advisers. Indeed, factionalism and power struggles among the nobility were amongst the important causes of rebellion against Mary in the closing years of her personal reign. Yet it remained the case that, once again, rebellion had been *justified* on the grounds that the ruler was taking counsel from those who were ignorant of the laws of the realm.[3]

---

[2] Gordon Donaldson, *Scotland. James V – James VII*, revised edn (Edinburgh: Oliver and Boyd, 1971), 118–20; the passages quoted are to be found at 120.

[3] Donaldson, *James V – James VII*, 118–20; Jenny Wormald, *Mary Queen of Scots:*

Furthermore, it was all too easy for the rebels to argue there was substance to these fears. Mary had indeed appointed foreigners to sit within her government, albeit not to particularly senior posts. One, the Italian David Riccio, seems to have been particularly hated, in part because he treated Scottish noblemen with contempt. While Moray's rebellion failed, concern grew among the nobility that his fears were well-founded. In particular, they were concerned that Mary was weakening the traditional political power of the nobility within the realm. Riccio was a convenient target for their anger. On 1 March 1566, some of the lords agreed to strike, with the broader aim of using an attack on Riccio to effect a *coup d'état*. Determined to recover control of the government, they broke into a small, private dinner party at which Riccio was eating with the queen and her ladies. Riccio was dragged from the queen's side and stabbed to death. Mary – who was heavily pregnant – tried to defend him. She was prevented from doing so, in part because one of the attackers pointed a cocked pistol directly at her.[4]

This represented a curious way of going about upholding the laws and liberties of the realm.[5] Nonetheless, it certainly showed how dangerous Mary's position was. Remarkably Mary managed to regain control of the situation. Yet she must have realised how dangerous it was to allow herself to be presented as one whose government ignored the traditional laws of the kingdom.

(2) Appointing a Commission to Print the Laws (1566)

This context may help to explain why Mary was receptive to a proposal which was made at about this time by one of her closest advisers. John Leslie, Bishop of Ross (1527–96), suggested that the queen should set

---

A Study in Failure (London: George Philip, 1988), 150–8; see also the different analysis in Julian Goodare, 'Queen Mary's Catholic interlude', in Michael Lynch (ed.), *Mary Stewart: Queen in Three Kingdoms* (Oxford: Oxford University Press, 1988), 154–70. The argument presented there regarding the motivations of the nobles in the Riccio murder is accepted here.

[4] For these points, and the Riccio affair, see Goodare, 'Queen Mary's Catholic interlude'; see also Donaldson, *James V – James VII*, 117–22; Wormald, *Mary Queen of Scots*, 150–60; John Guy, *My Heart is My Own: The Life of Mary Queen of Scots* (London: Fourth Estate, 2004), 248–62.

[5] While curious, it should be noted that it was not unintelligible. See Andrew R. C. Simpson, 'Counsel and the Crown', *Journal of Legal History* 36 (2015), 3–42, particularly at 22–39.

up a commission to publish in print the laws of the realm.[6] That would create a reliable version of the texts of Scots law that had hitherto languished in confused manuscript traditions. That was something that several of Mary's predecessors had attempted, but none had achieved. If Mary were to follow Leslie's suggestion, she would be able to present herself as one of the great *defenders* of the ancient laws and liberties of the realm. She would be able to claim that she had done more than anyone before her to make those laws accessible to her judges and her people. That would, in turn, undermine the arguments of those who said that she *ignored* those laws.

Admittedly, there is no known direct evidence to demonstrate that this was why Mary decided to promote the publication of the laws of the kingdom in print. Yet it seems likely. On 1 May 1566, she set up a commission to publish in print the 'Lawis of this our Realme maid be us, and our maist Nobill progenitouris, be the auise of the thre Estatis in Parliament haldin be thame'. In modern English, the instruction was to print the 'laws of this our realm made by us, and by our most noble progenitors, by the advice of the three estates in parliaments held by them'. The commissioners were to begin 'at the buikis of the Law callit Regiam Maiestatem and Quoniam Attachiamenta' and to carry on up to the present day.[7]

The team assembled to carry out this task was quite impressive. Leslie himself was a former professor of canon law at Aberdeen University, a lord of session and a member of the queen's inner council of advisers, the privy council.[8] Also appointed to the commission was Edward Henryson. He was doctor of Roman law and canon law and a former professor of Roman law at Bourges in France. Bourges was one of the pre-eminent centres for the study of Roman law at this time; Henryson was, admittedly, quite a junior professor there. He had been recalled to Edinburgh

---

[6] Edward Henryson, 'Preface', in *The Actis and Constitutiounis of the Realme of Scotland … Anno. Do. 1566* (Edinburgh: Robert Lekprevik, 1566), sig. A.3ʳ–A.3ᵛ. Reference is made here to the version of the statutes published in October 1566; another version was published in November that year, omitting certain anti-Protestant legislation. On this project, see also Klaus Luig, *The Acts and Constitutions of the Realm of Scotland Edinburgh 1566: 'Black Acts'* (Glashütten/Taunus: Auvermann, 1971).

[7] *The Actis and Constitutiounis of the Realme of Scotland … Anno. Do. 1566* (Edinburgh: Robert Lekprevik, 1566), sig. A.2ʳ–A.2ᵛ.

[8] Rosalind K. Marshall, 'Lesley [Leslie], John (1527–1596)', *Oxford Dictionary of National Biography* (Oxford: Oxford University Press, 2004); online edn May 2007, http://www.oxforddnb.com/view/article/16492.

in the mid-1550s to teach Latin, Greek and law. Since then he had held office as advocate appointed to represent the causes of the poor, then as a judge in the commissary court, and then as a lord of session.[9] A third commissioner was Sir Richard Maitland of Lethington. Almost universally respected by contemporaries, Maitland was in his mid-seventies, blind and still very active as a lord of session. At this time he was collecting decisions of the session.[10] A fourth commissioner was David Chalmers of Ormond, a lord of session and a senior clergyman within the diocese of Ross.[11] A fifth was Sir James Balfour of Pittendreich. The former rebel and prisoner of the French had witnessed a remarkable transformation in his fortunes. Drawing on his undoubted legal abilities and on favour he found at court, he had become one of the first commissaries of Edinburgh and a lord of session. Recently he had also become the clerk register, one of the great offices of state. He acquired the role after his predecessor, James Macgill of Nether Rankeillor, had been implicated in the murder of Riccio. Among other things, Balfour's new role meant that he was now the keeper of the official records of the country. In that capacity he would, of course, play a role in facilitating the printing of the laws.[12]

Others were involved in the project, yet they need not be considered here. The commissioners got to work in the summer of 1566. While they did not manage to publish all of the laws of the realm, they did produce a printed edition of all statutes promulgated by Scottish parliaments since 1424. That in itself was a significant achievement. It would have enabled the queen to present herself as one who promoted the study of the laws of her ancestors.

Nonetheless, there was more to the project than a public relations

9 Marie-Claude Tucker, 'Henryson, Edward [Henry Éduoard] (1522–c. 1590)', *Oxford Dictionary of National Biography* (Oxford: Oxford University Press, 2004), http://www.oxforddnb.com/view/article/12982. On the advocate for the poor, see Finlay, *Men of Law*, 82–6.

10 Michael R. G. Spiller, 'Maitland, Sir Richard of Lethington (1496–1586)', *Oxford Dictionary of National Biography* (Oxford: Oxford University Press, 2004), http://www.oxforddnb.com/view/article/17831.

11 Julian Goodare, 'Chalmers [Chambers], David, of Ormond (c. 1533–1592)', *Oxford Dictionary of National Biography* (Oxford: Oxford University Press, 2004), http://www.oxforddnb.com/view/article/5069.

12 Peter G. B. McNeill, 'Balfour, Sir James, of Pittendreich (c. 1525–1583)', *Oxford Dictionary of National Biography* (Oxford: Oxford University Press, 2004), http://www.oxforddnb.com/view/article/1188; see also Peter G. B. McNeill, 'Introduction', in Peter G. B. McNeill (ed.), *The Practicks of Sir James Balfour of Pittendreich* (Edinburgh: Stair Society, 1962–63), xi–xxxii.

exercise in favour of the queen. As will be explained below, this can be seen in Edward Henryson's *Preface* to the statutes printed in 1566. It can also be seen in other works written by Leslie and Chalmers. Some of these works were also written to promote the use of the older laws of the realm at this time. The evidence indicates that these lords of session treated the local laws of the kingdom as a wholly reliable body of learning concerning justice and legal truth. Advancing this last argument was hardly necessary to demonstrate that Mary was the defender of the laws and liberties established by her ancestors. Something more was at work. Whatever it was, it was enough to persuade these leading lords of session to depart from the assumption that the learning of Scots law was inferior in its substance when compared with that of Roman law. These points will be discussed next. Reference will be made to Henryson's *Preface* and the works of Leslie and Chalmers.

(3) Henryson's *Preface*

Henryson's *Preface* introduced the statutes printed in October 1566.[13] It opened with the following words:

> It is maist certane, that na thing is swa eirnistlie to be socht and straitlie keipit, as the knawlege of the Lawis and thair authoritie. Because the Lawis rychtlie disponis, and ordouris to the best baith godlie, and manlie effairis, and banisis thairout all iniquitie.

This can be rendered into modern English as follows:

> It is most certain, that nothing is so earnestly to be sought and keenly observed, as the knowledge of the laws and their authority. This is because the laws put things in order correctly, and orders for the best both divine and human affairs, and banishes out of those affairs all iniquity.

This was a translation of a passage that introduced the *Digest* of Roman law:

> Whereas, therefore, nothing amongst all matters is learnt so eagerly as the authority of laws, which sets in good order affairs both divine and human, and casts out all injustice ...[14]

---

[13] Henryson, 'Preface', sig. A.3ʳ.

[14] *Constitutio Deo Auctore*, 1, in Alan Watson (ed.), *The Digest of Justinian* (Philadelphia: University of Pennsylvania Press, 1985) (translation slightly altered).

The translation was not word for word, and Henryson did not acknowledge its source. Yet it gives rise to a question. Why did Henryson choose to introduce a discussion of the authority of the Scottish statutes printed in 1566 by quoting a passage that declared the authority of Roman law? Furthermore, why did he choose to quote *this* passage, which introduced the authority of the *Digest*, one of the most important texts of Roman law?

The question becomes more pertinent when it is realised Henryson quoted from the *Digest* twice more in his *Preface*. Following the passage just quoted from his *Preface*, he said:

> Thay [the laws] ar the gift of God, the statute and decreit of wyse men, the amending and rychting of forthoct, and suddane faultis, the commoun promeis, band, and obligatioun of the Realme, and of ilk member thairof to uther, efter the quhilk it apportenis all the saidis members to leid thair lyfe, gif thay will not onlie leif, bot als manerlie, weill, and godlie leif.[15]

This passage can be rendered into modern English as follows:

> They [the laws] are the gift of God, the statute and decree of wise men, the amending and correcting of forethought, and sudden faults, the common promise, band, and obligation of the realm, and of each member thereof to the other, in accordance with which it behoves all the said members to lead their lives, if they will not only live, but also mannerly,[16] well and godly live.

This translated and augmented the following passage in the *Digest*, which again was written to describe the authority of Roman law:

> For Demosthenes the orator also defines it thus: 'Law is that which all men ought to obey for many reasons, and chiefly because all law is a discovery and gift of God, and yet at the same time is a resolution of wise men, a correction of misdeeds both voluntary and involuntary, and the common agreement of the *polis* according to whose terms all who live in the *polis* ought to live.'[17]

---

[15] Henryson, 'Preface', sig. A.3ʳ.
[16] To live 'mannerly' was to live politely, in accordance with good manners.
[17] *Digest*, 1.3.2.

By quoting this passage, Henryson explained his earlier exhortation to his readers to the effect that they should acquire knowledge of 'the Lawis and thair authoritie'. The laws were God-given, infused with divine and human wisdom, and upheld through the 'commoun promeis, band, and obligatioun' of the realm. Yet because Henryson did not acknowledge he was quoting Roman law here, only his learned readers could have been aware that he was making an additional claim. He was borrowing a quotation used to describe the authority of Roman law in the *Digest* and reapplying it to describe the authority of the laws of Scotland that were printed in 1566. Again, a link was made between the authority of Roman law, on the one hand, and the old Scottish common law, on the other.

The link he had in mind became clearer at the end of the *Preface*. There he encouraged the whole literate populace to study and then manifest in their lives their duty as expressed in the printed 'Law buke'. He told them to search therein for:

> doctrine of treuth and obedience to the Princeis, thair Magistratis, and Officiaris of Justice: Off honest lyfe, of abstinence fra iniuring and hurting ane a uther: Off geuing to ilk persoun his awin ...[18]

Rendered in modern English, Henryson's exhortation was that his readers should search in the printed statutes for:

> doctrine of truth and obedience to princes, to their magistrates and officers of justice; of honest life, of abstinence from injuring and hurting one another; of giving to every person his own ...

Again, Henryson was alluding to Roman law, and the three famous principles of justice attributed to Ulpian:

> Justice is a steady and enduring will to render unto everyone his right. 1. The basic principles of right are: to live honourably [*honeste vivere*], not to harm any other person, to render to each his own.[19]

Henryson's explicit claim was that Scots law – the law printed in 1566 – constituted a body of learning concerning 'doctrine of treuth'. That by 'treuth' he meant justice is very clear. He immediately explained what he

[18] Henryson, 'Preface', sig. A.3ᵛ.
[19] *Digest*, 1.1.10.1.

meant by 'doctrine of treuth' by quoting the three fundamental principles of justice found in Roman law.

It is easy to miss just how radical Henryson's claim actually was. The
basic principles of Roman law to which he referred could only be given
meaning through the study of a wider body of law. For example, the
principle that one should not 'harm any other person' was fairly mean-
ingless without some definition of 'harm'. Furthermore, the principle
that one should give each man his own, his due, was extremely vague.
To be of any practical use it would have to be developed through more
concrete rules, for example relating to property rights and obligations.

In order to expound the true meaning of such basic principles of
justice, many contemporary lawyers would have turned to the texts of
Roman law and canon law. For them, it was those texts which constituted the reliable guides to justice. They would reveal the extent to which
other laws, like the texts of Scots law, were consistent with such legal
truth. That was the assumption which had guided many lords of session
in the 1540s. They were prepared to interpret the Scottish common law
narrowly where it departed from the learned laws. This was because they
thought it was a less reliable guide to justice than Roman law and canon
law. By construing it narrowly, they hoped to minimise any resulting
injustice that might arise from its application.

Henryson evidently disagreed with such assessments of the Scottish
common law. He thought that the laws of the realm constituted a body
of learning that taught 'doctrine of treuth'. Those laws taught what, in
truth, constituted 'harm', and also what was 'due' to a man. According to
this view, there was no need to evaluate the equity or inequity of the local
laws of the realm according to the standards of Roman law. This was
because the old Scottish common law expressed the same sort of reliable
legal learning as Roman law. Henryson underlined this claim by applying
texts usually used to describe the authority of Roman law to describe the
authority of the local law.

Of course, Henryson would still have recognised the continuing importance of Roman law to the development of the Scottish legal system. No
lord of session could credibly have suggested anything else in the mid-
1560s. The use of the learned laws was very extensive in practice, partly
because they dealt with questions that simply had not been considered in
the old Scottish common law.[20] Henryson himself used quotations from
the texts of Roman law to discuss the authority of the local legal tradition.

---

[20] See, for example, J. D. Ford, *Law and Opinion in Scotland during the Seventeenth
Century* (Oxford and Portland: Hart, 2007), 181–246.

What he would have objected to was the idea that the old common law of the realm constituted a less authoritative guide to justice than the learned laws. For him, the Scottish legal texts taught reliable 'doctrine of treuth' concerning justice. Consequently, those texts, like the texts of the learned laws, were trustworthy guides in the attempt to discern legal truth that possessed the binding force of law.

How would Henryson have justified this position? This question will be considered shortly. It is not easy to answer, because Henryson did not provide a detailed argument in support of his claim. Yet some of his contemporaries advanced similar claims, and in the process they provided some justification for their views. Perhaps then Henryson's arguments may be rendered intelligible in light of their broader context.

C. CONTEXTUALISING HENRYSON'S CLAIMS

(1) Leslie, the Laws of King Kenneth MacAlpin and the Twelve Tables

Some of Henryson's contemporaries made it very clear that they thought of the laws of the realm as a body of learning. Leslie, for example, explained his views in his history of Scotland. This was entitled *De Origine Moribus et Rebus gestis Scotorum* (1578); the title can be translated literally as '*Concerning the Origin, Customs and Great Deeds of the Scots*'.[21] Leslie said that one who wished to understand the origins of the laws first had to understand that 'the power of passing or annulling them' was 'placed in the freely given votes of the three estates, confirmed by the assent of the king'.[22] However, he then made it very clear that what the ancient parliaments had been doing in their votes was attempting to discern legal truth. He explained this with reference to what he thought were some of the earliest surviving Scots laws. In Leslie's time, these were – quite erroneously – attributed to an ancient king, Cinead son of Alpín (842–58).[23] Leslie's contemporaries knew him by his Anglicised name of Kenneth MacAlpin. The text of the laws themselves constituted

---

[21] John Leslie, *De Origine Moribus et Rebus gestis Scotorum* (Rome, 1578); the work was translated into Scots in 1596 – see E. G. Cody and W. Murison (eds), *The historie of Scotland, wrytten first in latin by … Jhone Leslie* (Edinburgh: Scottish Text Society, 1888).

[22] Leslie, *De Origine*, 71.

[23] For the historical Cinead, son of Alpín, see Alex Woolf, *From Pictland to Alba 789–1070* (Edinburgh: Edinburgh University Press, 2007), 93–102.

a strange medieval collection of religious and secular laws, including an injunction to burn all jugglers to death.

To the Scots, Leslie claimed, the laws of Kenneth MacAlpin constituted 'an image of the Twelve Tables'.[24] The Twelve Tables were the laws of archaic Rome, from which the later legal system developed.[25] By treating the ancient laws of the Scots as an 'image' of the Twelve Tables, Leslie was, like Henryson, linking the authority of Scots law with that of Roman law. He then stated that the laws of Kenneth MacAlpin contained 'the entire universal law, now divine, now human'. All the laws of the Scottish realm flowed from this 'first and most holy original of the laws' or from the original wisdom contained therein.[26] There were strong parallels here between Leslie's praise of the laws of Kenneth MacAlpin, on the one hand, and the ancient Roman orator Cicero's praise of the Twelve Tables, on the other.[27] Again, like Henryson, Leslie emphasised that the laws of the Scottish realm expressed the same sort of authoritative learning as Roman law. He indicated that this legal truth had been discerned by the Scots through 'the freely given votes of the three estates' – meaning parliament – confirmed by the 'assent of the king'.

Leslie developed this idea when he explained another way in which legal learning was augmented in the present. He saw the role of the 'Senate' of the kingdom as of central importance here. The 'Senate' was, of course, the College of Justice. Leslie then stated that 'so long as the [Scottish] polity endures, it will always flourish by the judgement of [these] prudent men'. He noted that Senators were chosen on the basis of their virtue and genius, and their learning concerning the laws of the realm. He stressed that half of them were clerics, and half members of the nobility. Leslie considered this to be a particular blessing, as it allowed religious truth to be combined with secular prudence in the development of the law.

Leslie's basic argument was that the *methods* employed by the Scots to make laws could be trusted to reveal legal truth. If anyone had any doubt of this, they could compare some of those laws with standards of legal learning they found elsewhere. Leslie drew particular attention to the

---

[24] Leslie, *De Origine*, 71.
[25] See, for example, H. F. Jolowicz and Barry Nicholas, *Historical Introduction to the Study of Roman Law*, 3rd edn (Cambridge: Cambridge University Press, 1972), 13–14.
[26] Leslie, *De Origine*, 71
[27] See Simpson, *Early Modern Studies of the Scottish Legal Past*, 215–17, which discusses the parallels between Leslie's comments and E. W. Sutton and H. Rackman (trans.), *Cicero De Oratore* (Cambridge, MA: Harvard University Press, 1942), 1.36.165–1.45.197.

supposed parallels between the Twelve Tables and the laws of Kenneth MacAlpin. Yet Leslie also indicated that this was unnecessary. The local tradition could, in and of itself, be trusted as a body of learning.

(2) Chalmers's *Compendium*

Chalmers, who was also one of the commissioners appointed in 1566, adopted a similar view. As will be explained, this was expressed in a book he wrote in 1566 to make it easier to find and use the old laws of the realm in practice.[28] He organised the scattered and 'confusit' texts of the laws by topic into 'commoun places'. He introduced his book with a list of those commoun places, and then organised them alphabetically.[29]

In introducing his book, Chalmers started from a proposition that he argued was 'without all contrauersie' (i.e. uncontroversial).[30] This was that Mary, Queen of Scots, and her progenitors were in the same position as 'all wther princis not recognoscand ony superiors' – that is, 'as all other princes not recognising any superiors'. That meant, in turn, that the Scottish monarchs had always possessed great 'powar and auchtoritie' to make laws. Chalmers then stated that this power was equal to that of 'ony empreor within thair empyre' – that is, 'any emperor within their empire'.[31]

By making these claims, Chalmers was in fact alluding to fairly standard interpretations of the learned laws. Many medieval jurists had interpreted the texts of Roman law to conclude that *rex in regno suo est imperator* – that is, a king is an emperor in his own kingdom. This meant that whatever the texts of Roman law said about the powers of the emperor could now be understood as referring to the powers of a monarch. That claim emerged from attempts to reconcile the texts of

[28]   British Library (BL) Additional MS 27472. This volume was labelled Chalmers's '*Dictionary of Scotch Law*' in the nineteenth century. However, a less anachronistic title would be Chalmers's *Compendium of the Laws of Scotland*. The modern editors of the text (Julian Goodare, Winifred Coutts and Andrew Simpson) plan to publish the work under that title.

[29]   BL Additional MS 27472 f.1^v–2^r.

[30]   The argument advanced here concerning Chalmers's works is discussed in more detail in Simpson, 'Legislation and authority', and also in Andrew R. C. Simpson, 'Power, reason and equity: two juristic accounts of royal authority in sixteenth-century Scotland', in Jørn Ø. Sunde (ed.), *Constitutionalism before 1789: Constitutional Arrangements from the High Middle Ages to the French Revolution* (Oslo: Pax Forlag, 2014), 128–46.

[31]   BL Additional MS 27472 f.1^r.

Roman law with medieval political reality. To explain, it will be recalled that fourteenth-century Italian jurists in particular, like Bartolus and Baldus, treated the texts of Roman law as repositories of legal truth. Those texts declared that the Roman emperor was 'lord of the world'. By the fourteenth century it was commonplace to argue that the heirs of the ancient emperors of Rome were the Holy Roman Emperors – whose powerbase was largely confined to modern-day Germany.

And therein lay the problem. The emperor was not, in fact, lord of the world, however much the texts of Roman law declared this to be so. Much of medieval Europe was controlled by independent monarchs. Bartolus, Baldus and others developed various arguments to reconcile the texts with the political reality. One solution that was commonly adopted was to say that those monarchs who had refused to recognise the superiority of the Roman emperors for a very long period of time had acquired the imperial rights to govern their peoples. Furthermore, it was argued that their acquisition of such powers was sanctioned by the Roman legal doctrine of prescription. According to that doctrine, long possession of a thing could, in certain circumstances, result in the possessor acquiring ownership thereof.[32]

Chalmers clearly alluded to this learned discourse when he said that *because* the Scottish monarchs had never recognised any superiors, it *followed* that they possessed the powers of the emperor within their kingdom. As a result, he argued that it was contrary to the 'equitie and reasoun' of the learned laws to ignore the laws promulgated by the Scottish monarchs in practice. Chalmers expressly linked this claim with criticism of those who relied excessively on Roman law and the laws of other 'forregn princes'. He said there was no need whatsoever to make reference to such laws where a matter could be decided by Scottish statute or 'commoun practik'.[33] The reference to 'commoun practik' was to the idea that a steady and consistent line of decisions of the College of Justice constituted evidence of the emergence of new law. Such a claim was encountered in Chapter 6 in relation to the case of *Weymss v Forbes* (1543). There one of the arguments that the lords had authority to

---

[32] See, for example, Joseph Canning, *The Political Thought of Baldus de Ubaldis* (Cambridge: Cambridge University Press, 1987), 64–70, 93–131, 209–21. On the maxim in Scotland, see Roger Mason, 'This realm of Scotland is an empire? Imperial ideas and iconography in early Renaissance Scotland', in Barbara E. Crawford (ed.), *Church, Chronicle and Learning in Medieval and Early Renaissance Scotland* (Edinburgh: Mercat Press, 1999), 73–91. See also the detailed reconstruction of Chalmers's argument in Simpson, 'Power, reason and equity', 132–3.

[33] BL Additional MS 27472 f.1^r–1^v.

reduce infeftments rested on the fact that there was a steady line of decisions or 'practicks' to that effect.[34] Note that this idea of the authority of court decisions is rather different to that encountered in Scotland today. In the sixteenth century, the authority of a single decision was not very great, even if it represented the views of the whole College of Justice in a particular case.

Cleverly, what Chalmers had done was to suggest that the learning of Roman law itself prohibited excessive reliance on that same learning in a Scottish context. To reiterate the point, he argued that the equity and reason inherent in the learning of Roman law underpinned the authority of laws promulgated by the Scottish monarchs. Consequently, it was inconsistent with Roman law to use *Roman* learning in practice *in preference* to the laws of the Scottish monarchs. By emphasising that *no* reference should be made to Roman law where the Scots laws could resolve the matter at hand, Chalmers made his stance even clearer. He distanced himself from those lords who had argued in the 1540s that the local law should be interpreted narrowly where inconsistent with the learning of Roman law. Instead, he argued that the law of the realm should simply be followed, in so far as it was clear and dealt with the problem at hand.

In advancing this argument, Chalmers showed that he was prepared to attribute the binding force of law to that which was consistent with equity, reason and legal truth. After all, Chalmers had explicitly argued that one could discern that Scottish laws possessed binding force *through* reliance on Roman learning concerning equity and reason. So, at this fundamental level, he associated the binding force of law with the recognition of legal truth. Given that that is the case, and given that he promoted reliance on the Scottish legal tradition to develop contemporary law, it seems likely that he also thought of that tradition as a body of learning concerning justice. He never explicitly said that to be so in 1566, but it seems to be the most plausible explanation of his approach at that stage. The rest of his introduction to his book indicates that he saw parallels between the historical development of Roman law, on the one hand, and Scots law, on the other. Furthermore, in a separate work he published in 1579, he does seem to have treated the laws of the realm as a body of learning concerning truth. At that point in time he also justified the claim. Put very briefly, he argued that the laws of the realm had been open to trial, testing and refinement over many centuries through

---

[34] A very helpful discussion of the authority of practicks can be found in Ford, *Law and Opinion*, 305–12.

the law-making process. As a result, they now expressed the learning of very long experience.[35]

D. EXPLAINING THE AIMS OF THE COMMISSION OF 1566

Both Leslie and Chalmers justified their claims that the laws of the realm expressed learning in similar ways. They did so by making reference to the ways in which the laws had been made. They argued that the laws had been open to trial, testing and refinement in light of the experience of Scottish political elites over many generations. In addition to this argument, Leslie and Chalmers both emphasised the parallels between the ways in which Roman law and Scots law had developed historically. They evidently believed that the Scottish legal tradition expressed the same sort of authoritative learning as Roman law. In this regard, at least, their position was very similar to that of Henryson – although Henryson's justification for adopting his particular stance remains unclear.

What caused Henryson, Leslie and Chalmers to reconceptualise the authority of Scots law? The phenomenon can be explained in various ways. First, it seems that at least one of the lords of session had been deeply troubled by the prospect of foreign legal innovations in the late 1550s. Such concerns may, in turn, have led men like him to try to articulate defences of the authority of the Scottish legal tradition. The lord of session in question was Sir Richard Maitland. He was also one of the commissioners appointed to print the laws in 1566. He had written on the theme of legal innovation in a poem dated to the late 1550s. He exhorted his countrymen that they should '[p]ut our awin lawis to execu-tioun', and that they should punish transgressors. He continued that they should act 'In dreid sum strainge new institutioun / Cum and our custome put away'.[36] In other words, they should take action from fear that some strange new laws might supersede the old. As Maitland made clear elsewhere, he saw the laws of the realm as an essential part of the

---

[35] See David Chalmers, *La Recerche des singularitez plus remarquables, concernant l'estat d'Escosse* (Paris: Jean Feurier, 1579), sig. A3ᵛ–A4ʳ, as discussed in Simpson, *Early Modern Studies of the Scottish Legal Past*, 148–9; Simpson, 'Power, reason and equity', 134–6; and Simpson, 'Counsel and the Crown', 10–22.

[36] See Joanna M. Martin (ed.), *The Maitland Quarto. A New Edition of Cambridge, Magdalene College, Pepys Library MS 1408* (Woodbridge: Boydell Press, 2015) (hereafter MQ), 53–6 at 55 (MQ 55).

traditional order and structure of society.[37] For one thing, they underpinned the system of landholding. This was of central importance for
the maintenance of the aristocracy, to which Maitland himself belonged.
In other poems, Maitland continued to express deep mistrust for legal
innovation that departed from the old Scottish common law.[38] While his
reasons for this were quite complex, his thinking was probably informed
by the troubles of the late 1550s.

Thus some may have reconceptualised the authority of the old laws
to defend them at a time when they seemed to be under threat. Second,
it must be remembered that in 1566 Henryson, Chalmers and Leslie
were responding to a royal commission to publish in print the laws of the
realm. Arguably, one aim of the project seems to have been to present
the queen as the defender of those laws. As a result of the arguments
Henryson and his colleagues presented, the queen could now be associated with the claim that her laws expressed learning concerning truth.
Consequently, they demanded her subjects' attention.

Third, the reconceptualisation of the laws as a body of learning may have
been influenced by a more fundamental problem. This was the general
crisis of authority that had engulfed the realm during the Reformation
and the associated political rebellions. It was no longer straightforward
to identify unquestionable authority around which the whole fractured
realm would unite in obedience. Perhaps this was why Henryson and
Chalmers both emphasised that the authority of royal laws promulgated
on the advice of parliament was uncontroversial. Here they started from
a claim that virtually all members of the realm would have recognised as
true. Even the radical Protestants accepted the authority of acts of parliament. After all, the Reformation had been established through the statutory recognition of the scriptural truth they preached.[39] In fact, the only
Scots who might have limited the authority of statute were those who
held that it should be construed narrowly in light of justice and truth
of the learned laws. Henryson and Chalmers insisted that was neither
acceptable nor necessary. This was in part because the laws of Scotland
were themselves reliable guides to legal truth and justice.

Yet even this may not fully explain why these lords of session reconceptualised the authority of the laws of the realm. Their approach may have
been influenced by contemporary intellectual movements on continental

[37] Consider, for example, MQ 14, MQ 30, MQ 58.
[38] See, to name two examples, MQ 4 and MQ 50.
[39] See Julian Goodare, *The Government of Scotland 1560–1625* (Oxford: Oxford
University Press, 2004), 75.

Europe. For example, they may have been influenced by 'legal humanism'. 'Humanism' is a relatively modern term. It is used to describe a
broad set of trends in the study of the humanities during the fifteenth and
sixteenth centuries. The humanities were a range of academic subjects
of study, including literature, the classics, history, moral philosophy and
law. During the fifteenth and sixteenth centuries, it was often argued that
the true meaning of the literature of the humanities had been distorted.
The distortions had resulted from the misinterpretation of the texts in the
medieval traditions of learning. The humanists sought to recover what the
texts had meant within their original historical contexts. Some humanists
– labelled the 'legal humanists' – turned their attention to the legal texts
of ancient Rome. They denounced many of the interpretations of the texts
advanced by the followers of Bartolus as historically anachronistic and
inaccurate. Andrea Alciato (1492–1550) promoted the study of classical
Roman law in this way. From 1529 he made Bourges in France a great
international centre for the study of the ancient legal texts.[40]

Some legal humanists at Bourges applied this new historical method
of enquiry to the study of the legal traditions of their own countries. One
such jurist was Eguinaire Baron. His research led him to the conclusion
that Roman law and French law had developed along very similar historical lines. He argued that the late Roman emperors and the French monarchs promulgated laws using very similar methods. Both the Roman and
the French rulers had, apparently, been open to the counsel of the nobility in developing their laws. This indicated that the laws of both systems
had been open to trial and testing and refinement.[41]

---

[40] On humanism, see, for example, Paul O. Kristeller, 'Humanism', in Charles B.
Schmitt, Quentin Skinner and Eckhard Kessler (eds), *The Cambridge History of
Renaissance Philosophy* (Cambridge: Cambridge University Press, 1988), 113–37.
On legal humanism, see, for example, Peter G. Stein, 'Legal humanism and legal
science', *Tijdschrift voor Rechtsgeschiedenis* 54 (1986), 297–306; Randall Lesaffer,
European Legal History (Cambridge: Cambridge University Press, 2009), 338–59.
On humanism in Scotland, see the essays in John MacQueen (ed.), *Humanism in
Renaissance Scotland* (Edinburgh: Edinburgh University Press, 1990). On legal
humanism in Scotland, see John W. Cairns, T. David Fergus and Hector L.
MacQueen, 'Legal humanism and the history of Scots law: John Skene and Thomas
Craig', in John MacQueen (ed.), *Humanism in Renaissance Scotland* (Edinburgh:
Edinburgh University Press, 1990), 48–74. Note that some arguments advanced in
the last piece have been challenged forcefully in Ford, *Law and Opinion*, 222 33.
Nonetheless, the article by Cairns, Fergus and MacQueen remains very useful.
[41] See Donald R. Kelley, 'Gaius Noster: substructures of western social thought', *The
American Historical Review* 84 (1979), 619–48; see also the discussion of Baron in
Simpson, 'Legislation and authority', 112–15.

Certainly this resembled the arguments of Leslie and Chalmers to the effect that the history of the *Scottish* legal tradition somehow paralleled that of Rome. For them, the implication seems to have been that both traditions expressed the same sorts of learning. Perhaps they were influenced by the humanist thinking of men like Baron. If they were, the most obvious source of such influence would have been Henryson. Henryson had been taught by Baron, and had subsequently served as a professor at Bourges. Yet Henryson himself did not justify the claim that Scots law expressed learning on the grounds that the Scottish kings followed the same sorts of methods as the Roman emperors. Nor did he make a great deal of any idea that the historical development of Scots law paralleled that of Roman law. His comments were not inconsistent with such arguments, and perhaps he would have agreed with them. Nonetheless, his position may have been more complex. This will be considered in the conclusion of the next chapter.

E. CONCLUSION

Enough has been said for now concerning why these Scottish lords of session chose to reconceptualise the authority of their laws as a body of learning. They may have acted out of fear that the old common law might be undermined by foreign innovations. They probably acted to underline the role of the queen as the defender of the laws and liberties of the realm. They almost certainly acted to engage with the crisis of authority associated with the Reformation. In addition, they were probably influenced by contemporary continental movements such as humanism.

Nonetheless, various questions remain to be considered concerning these developments. In an important article, Green has recently argued that one group of Scottish judges – the commissaries of Edinburgh – may have been more concerned with the assertion of their power to decide disputes (their jurisdiction) than with 'abstract conceptions of the authority of law'. His argument is partly based on the fact that such 'abstract conceptions' seem to have had little impact on the legal practice of the commissaries in developing post-Reformation Scottish consistorial law.[42] Of course, it has been argued here that contemporary Scottish judges *were* concerned with articulating abstract accounts of legal authority. There seems to be abundant evidence for that point. Yet further

---

[42] Green, 'The sources of early Scots consistorial law', particularly at 128–9 and 138–9.

research does need to be carried out to explore the extent to which their theoretical views of legal authority actually influenced legal practice in the mid-sixteenth century.

What is clear is that the lords of session considered here abandoned the first assumption of their predecessors of the 1540s that was mentioned at the beginning of this chapter. They no longer maintained that the learning of Roman law and canon law constituted a more reliable guide to justice and legal 'truth' than the local laws of the Scottish realm. However, they still believed that what the experts in the College of Justice collectively recognised to be consistent with legal truth and justice could possess the binding force of law. As will be explained in the next chapter, this assumption began to run into difficulties during the early 1570s.

F. SELECTED BIBLIOGRAPHY AND FURTHER READING

(1) Books

The Actis and Constitutiounis of the Realme of Scotland ... Anno. Do. 1566 (Edinburgh: Robert Lekprevik, 1566).

Cairns, John. W., Law, Lawyers and Humanism. Selected Essays on the History of Scots Law, Volume 1 (Edinburgh: Edinburgh University Press, 2015).

Chalmers, David, La Recerche des singularitez plus remarquables, concernant l'estat d'Escosse (Paris: Jean Feurier, 1579).

Dawson, Jane E. A., Scotland Re-formed 1488–1587 (Edinburgh: Edinburgh University Press, 2007).

Ford, J. D., Law and Opinion in Scotland during the Seventeenth Century (Oxford and Portland: Hart, 2007).

Goodare, Julian, The Government of Scotland 1560–1625 (Oxford: Oxford University Press, 2004).

Green, Thomas M. (ed.), The Consistorial Decisions of the Commissaries of Edinburgh, 1564 to 1576/7 (Edinburgh: Stair Society, 2014).

[Hannay, R. K.], MacQueen, Hector L. (ed.), The College of Justice. Essays by R. K. Hannay (Edinburgh: Stair Society, 1990).

Laing, David (ed.), The Works of John Knox (Edinburgh: Wodrow Society, 1846–64).

Leslie, John, De Origine Moribus et Rebus gestis Scotorum (Rome, 1578).

Luig, Klaus, The Acts and Constitutions of the Realm of Scotland Edinburgh 1566: 'Black Acts' (Glashütten/Taunus: Auvermann, 1971).

Martin, Joanna M. (ed.), *The Maitland Quarto. A New Edition of Cambridge, Magdalene College, Pepys Library MS 1408* (Woodbridge: Boydell Press, 2015).

Skinner, Quentin, *The Foundations of Modern Political Thought* (Cambridge: Cambridge University Press, 1978).

(2) Chapters in Books

Cairns, John W., T. David Fergus and Hector L. MacQueen, 'Legal humanism and the history of Scots law: John Skene and Thomas Craig', in John MacQueen (ed.), *Humanism in Renaissance Scotland* (Edinburgh: Edinburgh University Press, 1990), 48–74.

Ford, J. D., 'Four models of union', in Hector L. MacQueen (ed.), *Stair Society Miscellany Seven* (Edinburgh: Stair Society, 2015), 179–215.

Green, Thomas, 'The sources of early Scots consistorial law: reflections on law, authority and jurisdiction during the Scottish Reformation', in Mark Godfrey, *Law and Authority in British Legal History, 1200–1900* (Cambridge: Cambridge University Press, 2016), 120–39.

Mason, Roger, 'This realm of Scotland is an empire? Imperial ideas and iconography in early Renaissance Scotland', in Barbara E. Crawford (ed.), *Church, Chronicle and Learning in Medieval and Early Renaissance Scotland* (Edinburgh: Mercat Press, 1999), 73–91.

McNeill, Peter G. B., 'Introduction', in Peter G. B. McNeill (ed.), *The Practicks of Sir James Balfour of Pittendreich* (Edinburgh: Stair Society, 1962–3).

Simpson, Andrew R. C., 'Power, reason and equity: two juristic accounts of royal authority in sixteenth-century Scotland', in Jørn Ø. Sunde (ed.), *Constitutionalism before 1789: Constitutional Arrangements from the High Middle Ages to the French Revolution* (Oslo: Pax Forlag, 2014), 128–46.

Simpson, Andrew R. C., 'Legislation and authority in early-modern Scotland', in Mark Godfrey (ed.), *Law and Authority in British Legal History, 1200–1900* (Cambridge: Cambridge University Press, 2016), 85–119.

Stein, Peter G., 'Legal humanism and legal science', *Tijdschrift voor Rechtsgeschiedenis* 54 (1986), 297–306.

(3) Articles in Journals

Simpson, Andrew R. C., 'Counsel and the Crown', *Journal of Legal History* 36 (2015), 3–42.

(4) Unpublished PhD Theses

Simpson, Andrew R. C., 'Early Modern Studies of the Scottish Legal Past: Tradition and Authority in Sixteenth Century Scots Law' (University of Cambridge, 2010).

(5) Electronic Resources

Goodare, Julian, 'Chalmers [Chambers], David, of Ormond (c. 1533–1592)', *Oxford Dictionary of National Biography* (Oxford: Oxford University Press, 2004), http://www.oxforddnb.com/view/article/5069.

Marshall, Rosalind K., 'Lesley [Leslie], John (1527–1596)', *Oxford Dictionary of National Biography* (Oxford: Oxford University Press, 2004); online edn May 2007, http://www.oxforddnb.com/view/article/16492.

McNeill, Peter G. B., 'Balfour, Sir James, of Pittendreich (c. 1525–1583)', *Oxford Dictionary of National Biography* (Oxford: Oxford University Press, 2004), http://www.oxforddnb.com/view/article/1188.

Murray, Athol L., 'Sinclair, John (c. 1510–1566)', *Oxford Dictionary of National Biography* (Oxford: Oxford University Press, 2004), http://www.oxforddnb.com/view/article/25624.

Spiller, Michael R. G., 'Maitland, Sir Richard of Lethington (1496–1586)', *Oxford Dictionary of National Biography* (Oxford: Oxford University Press, 2004), http://www.oxforddnb.com/view/article/17831.

Tucker, Marie-Claude, 'Henryson, Edward [Henry Éduoard] (1522–c. 1590)', *Oxford Dictionary of National Biography* (Oxford: Oxford University Press, 2004), http://www.oxforddnb.com/view/article/12982.

CHAPTER 10

Legal Learning and the Power of Parliament

A. INTRODUCTION

The last chapter explored how some lords of session reconceptualised the laws of the realm as a body of learning concerning legal truth. This can be seen from the way in which they handled a commission they received in 1566 to publish the laws in print. In the process, they departed from one assumption held by their predecessors in the 1540s. This was that the local laws of Scotland constituted less reliable repositories of learning than Roman law and canon law. By contrast, the laws of the realm were *now* thought of as a trustworthy guide to justice and truth. They also merited detailed study in their own right.

Nonetheless, the lords who promoted the study of the local laws maintained another assumption held by their predecessors. That which expert lawyers in the College of Justice collectively recognised to be just and consistent with legal truth could possess the binding force of law. As was stated at the end of the last chapter, this assumption began to run into difficulties in the early 1570s. In particular, some seem to have relied upon it to ask whether the learning of legal experts could be used to constrain the exercise of parliamentary powers. In more abstract terms, did the learning of legal experts reveal real and enforceable rules concerning what parliament could and could not do? Such questions emerged in the turbulent political context of the late 1560s and early 1570s. At this time Scotland endured what modern lawyers might term a 'constitutional' crisis – a dispute of such proportions that it manifested itself primarily in civil war.

This chapter will begin by outlining this political context. It will also explain why some explored the possibility that legal learning might reveal the limits of parliamentary competence. In so doing, reference will be made to the views expressed by one lord of session. Next, the chapter will examine a debate in which a straightforward solution was proposed to resolve the problem. Put simply, it was argued that the will of a parliament in political matters simply had to be obeyed. This applied regardless of whether or not that parliament had been established by force and violence, in a manner inconsistent with any standards of justice or reason. This proposal came from the radical Protestant clergy, and not from contemporary lawyers. Subsequently, the chapter will explore other ways in which perceptions of parliament's role as a law-maker developed during the 1570s. It may be the case that a new way of thinking about the authority of law was just beginning to take shape. And yet, as will be discussed in the conclusion of this chapter, contemporary lawyers continued to think of law fundamentally 'as a body of learning fashioned through expert debate'.[1] By and large, they did not abandon the idea that that which they collectively recognised to be legally true and just could possess the binding force of law.

B. LEGAL LEARNING, LEGAL AUTHORITY AND THE POWER OF PARLIAMENT

(1) The Political Context: Revolution and a Rebel Parliament

To understand why questions came to be asked concerning the limits of parliamentary power in the early 1570s, it is first necessary to consider the turbulent political context of the time. It was mentioned above that Queen Mary had faced acts of rebellion in 1565 and 1566. Her authority survived these attacks. Yet over the next year her government ran into considerable difficulties. Mary was increasingly estranged from her husband, Henry Stewart, Lord Darnley. Darnley had many enemies, and was politically extremely dangerous. By December 1566 many of Mary's leading noblemen and officers of state had agreed to dispose of him. They may well have signed a murder bond – literally, an agreement to kill him. On 9 February 1567 he was staying in the house of Kirk o' Field in Edinburgh, a site now occupied by Old College and the University of Edinburgh School of Law. At about 2 a.m. on the 10 February, the house exploded. Darnley somehow managed to escape into the garden, but he was strangled to death.

Exactly what happened remains unclear. What is certain is that many leading members of the nobility were directly involved. Among them

---

[1] J. D. Ford, *Law and Opinion in Scotland during the Seventeenth Century* (Oxford and Portland: Hart, 2007), 5.

was James Douglas, fourth Earl of Morton. Morton was one of Riccio's murderers, and he had never forgiven Darnley for betraying him to the queen at that point in time. The mastermind of the plot against Darnley may well have been Sir James Balfour, one of the lords of session. Also involved was James Hepburn, Earl of Bothwell. Mary had increasingly placed great reliance on Bothwell in governing the realm, and Bothwell hoped to take Darnley's place as her husband.[2]

Public accusations of complicity in the murder were widely levelled against Bothwell and Balfour in particular. Mary opened herself to the possibility of being implicated in the murder when she married Bothwell some months later. It is possible that Bothwell raped the queen, and forcibly compelled her to marry him. Regardless, her fortunes were, for now, aligned with his. As Bothwell's position became more precarious his supporters gradually deserted him, and by June 1567 he and Mary faced a challenge from a coalition of rebel lords, including Morton. The lords succeeded in seizing Mary, in part with the treacherous help of Balfour. He had broken his promise to hold Edinburgh Castle on her behalf in exchange for a promise of his life and a pardon for involvement in Darnley's death. The rebel lords imprisoned Mary at Lochleven Castle in Fife. There, amidst threats to her life, Mary abdicated the crown on 24 June. Her one-year-old son was proclaimed as the new king, James VI. His government would be formed by a coalition of Protestant lords, led by Mary's half-brother, the Earl of Moray. Moray summoned a parliament in December 1567. This ratified Mary's abdication, the transfer of the power to Mary's son and Moray's regency.[3] As regent, Moray also used the parliament to ratify the legislation of 1560 that had established the Protestant Reformation – something Mary had always refused to do.[4] At about the same time, in a remarkable move, Balfour used his favour with Moray to secure the office of lord president of

---

[2]   For these points, see Gordon Donaldson, *Scotland. James V – James VII*, revised edn (Edinburgh: Oliver and Boyd, 1971), 121–8; Gordon Donaldson, *The First Trial of Mary Queen of Scots* (London: B. T. Batsford Ltd, 1969), 29–73; Jenny Wormald, *Mary Queen of Scots: A Study in Failure* (London: George Philip, 1988), 159–62; John Guy, *My Heart is My Own: The Life of Mary Queen of Scots* (London: Fourth Estate, 2004), 297–313; Jane E. A. Dawson, *Scotland Re-formed 1488–1587* (Edinburgh: Edinburgh University Press, 2007), 259–60. A very useful account of Mary's career is found in Julian Goodare, 'Mary [Mary Stewart] (1542–1587)', *Oxford Dictionary of National Biography* (Oxford: Oxford University Press, 2004); online edn May 2007, http://www.oxforddnb.com/view/article/18248.

[3]   *RPS* 1567/12/105.

[4]   *RPS* A1567/12/1–5.

the session. Briefly it looked like the new regime might be threatened in May 1568 when Mary escaped from Lochleven. However, after she was defeated in battle she fled to England. There she became Queen Elizabeth's captive.[5]

Questions were raised from the outset about the legality of both Mary's abdication and also parliament's attempt to ratify it. After all, the abdication had arguably been forced under severe duress. Surely it followed that no parliament could ratify an act that in itself had no legal effect. Furthermore, some claimed that the parliament that met in December 1567 had no authority. If the queen was still the monarch, then it followed that Moray was not regent, and he had had no authority to summon a parliament. In addition, it had been convened following a forcible, armed rebellion and many leading lords had been absent from its sessions.

(2) Challenging the Statutes of December 1567: The Views of Bishop Leslie

Those loyal to the queen developed arguments to show that the actions of the rebels had been unlawful. In so doing, they drew upon the basic assumption that learning concerning legal truth could possess the binding force of law. They used such learning to probe even the limits of parliamentary authority. This ultimately provoked a remarkable and revealing backlash from those who wished to uphold the validity of the legislation of December 1567. However, before considering this, it will first be helpful to examine the ways in which one of the queen's supporters used his legal learning to defend her position.

Bishop John Leslie remained loyal to the queen following her downfall, and he followed her into exile in England.[6] There he wrote a *Defence* of Mary. In brief, his argument was that the rebels had failed to adhere to certain procedural standards recognised in the learning of Roman law and canon law when acting against their monarch. He argued that such

---

[5] For this political context, see Donaldson, *James V – James VII*, 128–31, 157–62; Peter G. B. McNeill, 'Introduction', in Peter G. B. McNeill (ed.), *The Practicks of Sir James Balfour of Pittendreich* (Edinburgh: Stair Society, 1962–63) I, xxi–xxii; Wormald, *Mary Queen of Scots*, 162–78; Dawson, *Scotland Re-formed*, 261–70.

[6] The following section of the current chapter draws heavily on Andrew R. C. Simpson, 'Power, reason and equity: two juristic accounts of royal authority in sixteenth-century Scotland', in Jørn Ø. Sunde (ed.), *Constitutionalism before 1789: Constitutional Arrangements from the High Middle Ages to the French Revolution* (Oslo: Pax Forlag, 2014), 137–42.

standards had to be observed even in the case of the 'porest and simpliest wretched creature in all Scotlande'.[7] As a result, the rebels' proceedings could have no legal force or validity.

Leslie began by examining the evidence used to accuse the queen of complicity in Darnley's murder, including various letters she had allegedly written to Bothwell. He noted that a passage in the *Codex* of Roman law required proof to be 'clearer than the mid-day light'.[8] He then commented that the rebels' use of the letters as evidence without corroboration fell foul of this requirement. This was because it was a rule of law that witnesses were to be given more credence than written testimonies. Letters were at best partial proofs, but the rebels had relied upon them much more extensively than that. Consequently, the rebels' use of the evidence of the queen's letters against her was 'contrarie to reason and lawe'.[9]

Leslie also attacked the validity of the abdication on the grounds that it was 'done by violence and forced withe feare of life'.[10] Consequently, 'whatsoeuer was builded vppon this fowndation, beinge of suche weaknes ... coulde neuer be firmelie and suerlie established and corroborated'.[11] While Leslie did not cite Roman law here, again the learned laws were on his side. This was discussed above in relation to the case of *James Douglas, third Earl of Morton v Queen's Advocate* (1543). The law provided that acts done from duress that was sufficient to overcome the will of a steadfast man would have no legal effect.

Subsequently Leslie argued that the rebels' attempts to investigate Mary's guilt were also invalid. He pointed out that the 'lawes of all well ordered common wealthes, especiallie the ciuill lawe, the principall and maistris of all other ciuill pollicies and ordinances' required a particular form of process in criminal accusations. In all judgements given against an accused, three 'seuerall and distinct' persons had to be involved. They were 'the iudges, the accuser, and the witnesses'. That was certainly

---

[7] John Leslie, *A defence of the honour of the right highe, mightye and noble Princesse Marie Quene of Scotland* ... (London, 1569), f.10ᵛ–11ʳ.

[8] Leslie, *Defence* (1569), f.11ʳ; cf. *Code*, 4.19.25 (available at http://droitromain.upmf-grenoble.fr/); Gratian, *Decretum*, C.2. q.8 c.2 (within the *Corpus Iuris Canonici*; available at http://digital.library.ucla.edu/canonlaw/).

[9] Leslie, *Defence* (1569), f.12ʳ–12ᵛ; cf. *The Digest of Justinian*, ed. Alan Watson (Philadelphia: University of Pennsylvania Press, 1985), 22.3.3; James A. Brundage, 'Proof in canonical criminal law', *Continuity and Change* 11 (1996), 329–39 at 331, 335.

[10] Leslie, *Defence* (1569), f.27ʳ; see also f.22ʳ–22ᵛ, 26ᵛ.

[11] Leslie, *Defence* (1569), f.27ʳ.

required in the old accusatorial procedure of canon law. However, the rebel lords had acted as 'accusers ... witnesse[s] [and] Iudges'. The result was 'a disordered chaos against iustice and nature'.[12]

Leslie then went on to explain 'Whie the confirmation of the rebelles doings made by an acte of parliament ys nothinge worthe'.[13] He chose to attack the validity of the parliamentary proceedings on two grounds. First, the queen's abdication had been invalid, and therefore it followed that Moray had had no authority as regent to summon a parliament.[14] Secondly, Leslie suggested that if the king, James VI, had been of age, he would have recognised that the parliamentary ratification of the abdication was 'not allowable or to be approued'. This was because 'the demission of the crowne' was extorted 'by violence and forced'.[15] It has already been suggested that that argument may have rested on learned argumentation. Was Leslie relying upon such learning concerning 'iustice' to claim that parliament could *not* have approved as valid an act that would have been treated as null by the legal truth expressed in Roman law? Was he, in fact, saying that even an undoubtedly lawful parliament could not have acted in this way? That would have implied that legal learning concerning truth could directly limit the law-making power of parliament.

That is one way in which one might read Leslie's comments. Nonetheless, it must be admitted that his comments in this regard were highly ambiguous and vague. What is undeniable is that Leslie used his learning to show that the rebels' proceedings *as a whole* were inconsistent with justice and legal truth. Of course, those proceedings included the statutes of the arguably invalid parliament of December 1567. Leslie concluded that because the rebels' acts were inconsistent with the procedural standards of the learned laws, it followed they were of 'no validitie or force'.[16] Consequently, the queen remained 'in her full auctoritie, by good reason and lawe'.[17] Mary had been wrongfully dispossessed of her crown, and consequently was entitled to restitution. Again, Leslie cited a canonist maxim to support his argument.[18]

In this way, Leslie used his legal learning to argue that the rebels' proceedings against the queen were null and void. In so doing, he touched

---

[12] See Leslie, *Defence* (1569), f.31ʳ–32ʳ. See also Brundage, 'Proof', 331.

[13] Leslie, *Defence* (1569), f.26ᵛ.

[14] Leslie, *Defence* (1569), f.26ᵛ–27ᵛ, as discussed in Simpson, 'Power, reason and equity', 140.

[15] Leslie, *Defence* (1569), f.26ᵛ–27ʳ.

[16] Leslie, *Defence* (1569), f.31ʳ.

[17] Leslie, *Defence* (1569), f.31ʳ.

[18] Leslie, *Defence* (1569), f.33ʳ–34ʳ.

on questions concerning the scope and possible limits of parliamentary power. Perhaps the learning of expert lawyers concerning legal truth revealed certain basic procedural standards to which even lawful parliaments were expected to adhere when formulating their judgements. If such arguments were taking shape in the minds of men like Leslie, they were about to be met with a remarkable response. Perhaps surprisingly, it came from the radical Protestant clergy.

(3) The Power of an Established Parliament

To explain this last point, it is first necessary to say a little more about what happened in Scotland following Mary's flight to England. Queen Elizabeth I eventually gave support to Moray's Protestant regime, and kept Mary as her prisoner. However, matters changed again in January 1570 when Moray was assassinated. A civil war broke out between supporters of Mary's restoration – known as the 'queen's men' – and those who wished to preserve the status quo under the infant James VI – known as the 'king's men'. Prominent among the queen's men was William Maitland, her secretary and the son of the elderly lord of session Sir Richard Maitland.[19] One of William's allies was James Balfour, who still had the title of lord president of the College of Justice. Balfour had probably joined the queen's men in part because the new leader of the king's men was Darnley's father, the Earl of Lennox. Lennox was unlikely to forgive Balfour's involvement in his son's death. Under cover of night, in January 1571 Balfour entered Edinburgh Castle, which was held by Mary's supporters.[20]

In May 1571, the king's men attempted to hold a parliament in the Canongate, in Edinburgh's Royal Mile. As they met, the queen's men in Edinburgh Castle opened fire on them. As one historian put it, the king's men 'had to assume undignified postures to avoid fire from the castle'. It is therefore remembered as the 'creeping parliament'. Nonetheless, it was well-attended, and this did not bode well for the queen's men.[21]

At this time, a group of Protestant ministers decided to intervene. They were king's men, but they hoped to arrange a truce between the

---

[19] On William Maitland, see Mark Loughlin, 'Maitland, William, of Lethington (1525×1530–1573)', *Oxford Dictionary of National Biography* (Oxford: Oxford University Press, 2004); online edn January 2008, http://www.oxforddnb.com/view/article/17838.

[20] See Donaldson, *James V – James VII*, 160–5; McNeill, 'Introduction', xxii–xxiv; Dawson, *Scotland Re-formed*, 267–77.

[21] Donaldson, *James V – James VII*, 164–5.

two factions. They made their way up the High Street towards the castle, passing St Giles' (where the lords of session met) and the recently rebuilt Tolbooth. They would have passed through the tenements of the Lawnmarket, which would undoubtedly have suffered damage from the cannon fire, and on up towards the great medieval tower that guarded the entrance to the fortress. The ministers were admitted through the gates and led up into the great hall of the castle, which still stands today. There they were joined by Balfour and other noblemen. They all then entered the hall itself, with its great hammer-beam roof supported by corbels displaying the symbols of Stewart monarchy. There they saw the ailing William Maitland. He had become increasingly ill as the war had gone on, and was facing some form of gradual paralysis. He was sitting down by his bed, with a small dog on his lap.[22]

All were seated, and the ministers began by saying that they had come to try to bring an end to the conflict. They asked for terms that they might use as a basis for negotiation with their fellow king's men. Maitland replied that he was not prepared to treat with those meeting in the Canongate. The 'principallis' of the Scottish nobility were members of the queen's party. Consequently, if the king's party wished to preserve their lives and lands, it was for them to offer terms to Maitland and his associates, and not the other way around. While this seemed like a point of impasse, one of the ministers, Mr John Craig, then turned to another matter. He commented that there was 'ane lauchfull authoritie establishit in the persone of the King and Regent throughout this realme' (i.e. there was 'a lawful authority established in the person of the king and regent throughout this realm'). Craig stated that this ought to be obeyed by all Scottish subjects, and he admonished the queen's men to do so.[23]

Maitland's response began with his understanding of the actions of those who had rebelled against Mary in 1567. It is worth noting that Maitland himself had been amongst them. He claimed that their aims had simply been to detach the queen from Bothwell, and to avenge Darnley's murder. However, they came to the view that this would be impossible without creating a wholly new government, at least temporarily. Consequently they agreed to make James VI monarch in her place, and to establish Moray as regent. Maitland insisted that this had all been a necessary piece of a trickery to re-establish order. Yet he confessed

---

[22] These details, and the debate summarised below, are taken from Richard Bannatyne, *Memorials of Transactions in Scotland A.D. MDLXIX – A.D. MDLXXIII* (Edinburgh: Bannatyne Club, 1836), 125–32.

[23] Bannatyne, *Memorials*, 125–6.

that he and the other lords 'did verie euill and vngodly in the vpsetting the kingis authoritie' (i.e. they 'did a truly evil and ungodly thing in establishing the king's authority'). This was because James could 'neuer justlie be king' while Mary was still alive. Maitland asked Balfour, his fellow queen's man, if this was what the rebels had had in mind all along; and the lord president replied that it was.[24]

One of the (anonymous) ministers then replied. Whatever Maitland and Balfour had thought they were doing when they established the king's authority was not particularly relevant. Most people in the realm believed they had genuinely meant to depose Mary and replace her permanently with her son.[25] Another minister subsequently commented that

> the authoritie anes established be order, with consent of the thrie estates of the realme, aucht and sould be obeyit, ay and while the same be set doun againe be the lyke power and order ...[26]

This can be rendered in modern English as follows:

> the authority once established by order, with consent of the three estates of the realm, ought and should be obeyed, until the same be put down again by the equivalent power and order ...

This clearly astonished Maitland. He suggested that the minister's claim was pure hypocrisy. After all, the Protestant ministers had in the past been very willing to challenge Catholicism without waiting for the established authority of the realm to accept their point of view. They had been content to cast down that part of the establishment in a very disorderly manner. Maitland commented that now the same could be done with the king's authority.[27]

The minister answered by drawing a distinction between matters of 'religione' and mattes of 'polycie' (broadly speaking, politics). In religious matters, as soon as a form of worship or doctrine was recognised to be wicked and false then it was to be rejected immediately. If an established authority commanded adherence to the false teaching, then it could in all good conscience be disobeyed. This was because no dishonour to God was to be suffered, not even for an hour. Yet it was different

[24] Bannatyne, *Memorials*, 126–7.
[25] Bannatyne, *Memorials*, 127–8.
[26] Bannatyne, *Memorials*, 128.
[27] Bannatyne, *Memorials*, 128.

in matters of 'polycie'. There, even if authority had been established by 'violence and tyranny', it was necessary to obey it. The minister then pointed out that St Paul in his letter to the Romans had told the early Christians to obey the Roman emperors, even though they had acquired authority by 'violence and tyranny'. In contrast, St Paul would never have commanded 'obedience to ane wicked religion'.[28]

This intriguing argument defending authority established by violence and force silenced the disputants for some time. Balfour then chose to probe the minister's claims a bit further. The lord president asked him how he knew that the king's authority was actually established. The minister replied that he knew it was so on two grounds. First, it had been established 'be the thrie estatis publictlie in parliament' (i.e. 'by the three estates publicly in parliament'). Second, it had 'resauet vniversall obedience within this realme, without erecting ony vther face of authoritie in the contrair' (i.e. 'received universal obedience within this realm, without the erection of any other semblance of authority in opposition to it'). In other words, even if an authority had been established by force and violence, once it had been ratified publicly by the three estates and universally obeyed, then it was valid. Thereafter, it had to be obeyed by all.[29] Balfour insisted on his earlier question again; how did the minister *know* the king's authority had been established? The minister – evidently becoming exasperated – responded that he was present in parliament when the matter was decided. He then commented that just as he was sure there was a little dog on Maitland's lap, so the king's authority had indeed been established.[30]

The reference to the parliament brought a quite remarkable response from Balfour. Balfour commented that the parliament was 'no lawfull parliament'. Indeed, it was 'null in the self'. In other words, both it and also its proceedings were simply void.[31] In making this claim, Balfour was almost certainly drawing on the idea that certain transactions were treated as *void* in Roman law, canon law and indeed the laws of the Scottish realm. For example, in the *Institutes* of the Emperor Justinian a stipulation – a form of legally enforceable promise – to do something impossible was treated as void. The example Justinian gave was of a stipulation to deliver a hippocentaur.[32] Likewise a purported marriage

[28] Bannatyne, *Memorials*, 128–9.
[29] Bannatyne, *Memorials*, 129.
[30] Bannatyne, *Memorials*, 129–30.
[31] Bannatyne, *Memorials*, 130.
[32] See J. B. Moyle (trans.), *The Institutes of Justinian*, 4th edn (Oxford: Clarendon Press, 1906), III.XIX.

between those without capacity to consent, such as the insane, or between underage children, would be treated as null from the outset.[33] As they had no legal validity, such transactions could not be enforced in court. Put another way, parties to such transactions could continue to act as if they had never happened, without fear of their being enforced in the courts. These agreements were simply void.

In response, the minister insisted that the parliamentary acts were valid until they were reduced by some formal process of nullity. In making this argument, he seems to have been conscious that Balfour was relying on legal learning to make his case. The minister chose to meet Balfour on his own ground. He drew on the same learning to undermine the lord president's position. The minister quoted a learned rule ultimately derived from the *Digest* of Roman law, which was '*sententia facit jus inter partes donec retractetur*'.[34] This meant that a judicial sentence constituted law between the parties until such times as it was revised. To the minister, it seemed to follow that the decision of parliament regarding Mary's abdication of the crown was valid until put aside, presumably by another parliament.[35]

On one level, the minister's response failed to engage with Balfour's basic point. Balfour was not just saying that a *decision* of the parliament of December 1567 was invalid. He was saying that the parliament *itself* was null. On that basis, it seemed to follow that its statutes were also void. Obviously that was a deeply troubling argument for the minister, as he acknowledged. If the parliament of December 1567 had been simply 'null', then the same could be said of the statues it had passed confirming the Reformation settlement.[36]

For present purposes, what matters is that both participants in the debate had articulated quite different approaches to what constituted

---

33 See William W. Buckland, *A Text-Book of Roman Law from Justinian to Augustus*, 3rd edn, revised by Peter Stein (Cambridge: Cambridge University Press, 1963), 113–14; *Digest*, 23.2.16.2; *Code*, 5.4.24.

34 See, for example, *Digest*, 1.1.11; *Digest*, 1.5.25; *Digest*, 50.17.207; for the development of the rule in Scottish practick, see, for example, Athol L. Murray and Gero Dolezalek (eds), *Sinclair's Practicks*, http://home.uni-leipzig.de/jurarom/scotland/dat/sinclair.html, cn. 214. The civilian discourse around the point was much more sophisticated than the comments given here might be thought to indicate; see, for example, the gloss to *Digest*, 50.17.207 found at [*Corpus Iuris Civilis*] ... *commentaries Accursii, scholiis Contii, paratitlis Cuiacii* ... *novae accesserunt ad ipsum Accursium Dionysii Gothofredi, I. C. notae* (Lyons, 1604), http://nrs.harvard.edu/urn-3:HLS.Libr:3491083.

35 Bannatyne, *Memorials*, 130.

36 Bannatyne, *Memorials*, 130.

valid *authority*. Balfour evidently felt that he could use his legal learning to develop his claim that the parliament and statutes of December 1567 were invalid. It seems that he used that learning to identify and articulate the possibility that the parliament was simply 'null in the self'. In other words, his legal learning helped him to articulate that the parliament in question could establish no valid authority. In this regard, there was little difference between the assumptions underpinning the approaches of Leslie and Balfour.

The most consistent way of reading the minister's comments indicates that he had a different view. He did respond to Balfour's arguments through the use of further learned argumentation. Yet it seems likely that he was only using such learned argumentation to expose flaws in Balfour's own position. That did not mean he thought that such learning was sufficient to decide the debate. Indeed, he probably thought that Balfour's legal learning was irrelevant to the question of whether or not the king's authority had been established. Such a position would have been consistent with the claim the minister had advanced earlier. This was that only two conditions had to be met in order for authority to be constituted validly. First, the three estates had to gather and establish some form of authority. It did not matter whether this happened lawfully or by force and violence. Second, all inhabitants of the realm then had to give obedience to that authority. If those two conditions were satisfied, the authority was valid. Thereafter, *it had to be obeyed*. Any laws it made were fully enforceable. As far as the minister was concerned, his position was not primarily grounded in legal learning. Rather, it was rooted in his interpretation of St Paul's letter to the Romans in the Bible.

This is probably the preferable reading of the minister's argument, assuming that he was consistent in his thought throughout the debate. For him, legal learning was not particularly relevant to the question of whether or not a particular institution or individual had the authority to make laws. If the institution or individual had been invested with authority by the three estates and then universally obeyed, then he, she or it had the power to make laws with binding force. It did not matter if this had all come about unlawfully, or by force and violence. Nor, presumably, did it matter if the laws promulgated were in some sense unjust or inconsistent with legal truth. The laws of such an authority simply had to be obeyed. The only exception arose where the laws ordered something that would dishonour God. Such commands had to be disobeyed, and indeed resisted.

This line of argument did not sit easily with the assumption that contemporary expert lawyers held concerning the authority of law. This was that the binding force of law could be attributed to that which they collectively recognised to be consistent with legal truth. By contrast, the minister approached the binding force of law quite differently. He did not locate the authority to make law in the recognition of truth as such. Rather, for him the will of the three estates in parliament *could* establish an authority with the power to make law. This would follow if – and only if – the people of the realm subsequently obeyed the authority in question.

(4) Conclusion

The political turmoil of the late 1560s and early 1570s had caused Scots to ask searching questions about the nature of legal authority itself. In the process, some challenged the validity of the parliament of December 1567 and its statutes. Those who did so sometimes used learned argumentation to articulate differences between void and valid parliaments. They were met with objections from those who wished to defend the validity of the parliament and its acts. Among them were Protestant ministers who wished to protect the legislation promulgated to confirm the settlement of the Reformation. To do this, they developed an account of what gave the law its binding force. Drawing on their understanding of St Paul's instructions in the book of Romans, they argued that the will of a meeting of the three estates, as confirmed by popular obedience, could establish authority with the power to make binding laws.

This sort of thinking featured elsewhere in contemporary Europe. On some levels, a similar claim was advanced by the French political thinker Jean Bodin. In his *Six Livres de la République* (1576), he claimed that all law-making depended on an exercise of sovereign will. In other words, once a supreme or sovereign authority had been established, *only* that authority could make binding laws. Within this scheme of things, legal learning concerning what the lawyers called 'justice' was nothing more than learning. Consequently, the consensus of learned lawyers concerning the nature of legal truth had no formal status as a source of law. Put another way, it could not be said to be able to *establish* law with binding force.[37] Of course, the minister who debated the nature of authority with Balfour in Edinburgh Castle did not go as far as to claim that. He did not say that expert consensus amongst lawyers could *never*

---

[37] On Bodin, see, for example, Quentin Skinner, *The Foundations of Modern Political Thought* (Cambridge: Cambridge University Press, 1978) II, 284–301.

constitute law; he left that question open. What he made clear was that all Scots were obliged to observe law made by an authority established by parliament and obeyed by the people. Yet there are some curious parallels between his thinking, on the one hand, and that of Bodin, on the other.[38] This will be discussed again briefly in the conclusion of this chapter.

The arguments considered here direct attention to two further matters. First, theoretical accounts of the role of parliament in the law-making process were accompanied by wide-ranging developments in parliamentary activity. Most obviously, the amount of legislation promulgated increased markedly during the late sixteenth century.[39] Yet there were other changes too. Parliament began to develop rather more ambitious projects for the reform of the common law. These developments, and the question of what may have caused them, will be examined next.[40] Second, a related question must be considered here. The assumption that the binding force of law could be attributed to that which lawyers collectively recognised to be legally 'true' evidently ran into problems at this time. Did Scottish lawyers react to the challenge? Or did they maintain their older assumption and simply continue to develop the law in light of it? Before considering all of these questions, it will be necessary to say a little more about the political context of the time.

---

[38] Note that there were also radical differences between the approaches of Bodin and the minister, particularly as regards the role of the consent of subjects in establishing the law; see Skinner, *Foundations*, II, 289.

[39] The point is made forcefully in Julian Goodare, *The Government of Scotland 1560–1625* (Oxford: Oxford University Press, 2004), 73: 'No parliament before 1579 passed as many as fifty acts; but after that date, only a small number enacted fewer, and many exceeded a hundred'.

[40] For these projects, see the highly insightful discussion in Goodare, *Government of Scotland*, 70–86. See also Arthur H. Williamson, *Scottish National Consciousness in the Age of James VI* (Edinburgh: John Donald, 1979), 64–85; John W. Cairns, T. David Fergus and Hector L. MacQueen, 'Legal humanism and the history of Scots law: John Skene and Thomas Craig', in John MacQueen (ed.), *Humanism in Renaissance Scotland* (Edinburgh: Edinburgh University Press, 1990); Ford, *Law and Opinion*, 38–9, 40, 43–4.

C. LEGISLATION AND THE 'BODY' OF THE COMMON LAW

(1) The End of the Civil War

The debate in the Great Hall of Edinburgh Castle did nothing to resolve the civil war. By the summer of 1571, the coalition of the queen's men was gradually unravelling, for a variety of reasons that need not be considered here. In August 1571 the Earl of Lennox was killed in a skirmish, and was succeeded as regent and head of the king's men by the Earl of Mar. The civil war dragged on throughout 1572. After Mar's death in October that year, the Earl of Morton in turn became regent. Balfour met with Morton to negotiate on behalf of the queen's party. Having decided to change sides again, Balfour agreed to betray the plans of Maitland and his associates to the king's party. He saw that the cause of the queen's party was increasingly hopeless. Indeed, he helped to seal its fate by convincing most of the queen's men outside Edinburgh to make peace with the king's men. He was pardoned and restored to his lands. Ultimately Edinburgh Castle itself could only be taken with the help of English artillery – most of the heavy Scottish cannons were inside the fortress. After the fortress fell, Maitland died awaiting trial. Morton was bent on revenge, and considered placing the corpse on trial in parliament for treason, as had sometimes happened in such cases in the past. Only the direct intervention of Queen Elizabeth I of England prevented that particular outcome.[41]

(2) The Commission of 1575

Morton did prove an effective regent, and he restored order to the realm. During his regency, he expressed interest in the use of parliament to develop the law, and to promote legal certainty. In 1575, he presided over the promulgation of an act that noted 'the harme quhilk this commoune weill sustenis throw want of a perfyte writtin law, quhairupoun all jugeis may knaw how to proceid and decerne'.[42] In modern English, the act was making reference to 'the harm which this polity sustains through the lack of a perfect written law, whereupon all judges may know how to proceed and decide disputes'. Consequently, it was resolved to appoint

---

[41] For these points, see McNeill, 'Introduction', I, xxv–xxxii; Dawson, *Scotland Re-formed*, 279–81.

[42] *RPS* A1575/3/7.

a commission to examine the books of law, acts of parliament and the decisions before the lords of session. The commissioners would then 'draw the forme of the body of oure lawis'. They were to include both those things that were already enacted by statute and those things that they felt *ought* to be enacted. The result of their labours would then be presented to parliament. In so far as parliament found their conclusions good and acceptable, then they would be 'ratifiit and establissit' (i.e. 'ratified and established'). The result would be the establishment of 'ane certain writtin law' to be used by all judges in reaching their decisions.

This proposal represented something of an innovation. Previous parliamentary commissions had been established to produce authoritative versions of the confused texts of the common law, such as *Regiam Majestatem* and *Quoniam Attachiamenta*. The commission of 1566 was such a project.[43] Yet the scope of the commission of 1575 was to be much broader. For example, it was supposed to incorporate the decisions of the lords of session in the 'body' of the laws. Given that the conciliar session had been operating for about a century by that point in time, this was no mean task. This last fact points to another aspect of the commission that made it much more ambitious than its predecessors. Ostensibly, it was supposed to produce a comprehensive statement of the Scottish common law. Furthermore, the requirement that the commissioners were to 'draw the forme of the body' of the law may indicate that they were expected to treat the law in a structured fashion. As early as December 1567, the lords of the articles had expressed the hope that such a task would be undertaken.[44] Another difference between the 1575 commission and most of its predecessors was the emphasis it placed on the role of the commissioners in proposing changes to the laws. The 1575 commission was clearly expected to start from the existing laws of the realm to produce a revised body of laws. It was hoped that this would subsequently be debated by parliament. To the extent the whole work was found good, it would then be 'ratifiit' and 'establissit' by the authority of parliament – however that authority was understood.

It is difficult to avoid the impression that Morton and his contemporaries were contemplating the reconstitution of the old common law so that it could be placed on a more authoritative footing. Importantly too, the reduction of the law to writing and its ratification by parliament would result in the establishment of greater legal certainty. In so doing,

---

[43] For parliamentary interest in such a project prior to 1575, see, for example, *RPS* 1426/13 and *RPS* 1469/34.

[44] *RPS* 1567/12/54.

Morton and his associates may have drawn inspiration from contemporary French efforts to reduce the customary laws of the kingdom to writing.[45] In addition, they may have been influenced by the thinking of the great Scottish humanist George Buchanan. Buchanan is best remembered today for his radical work concerning the right of the people to resist a tyrannical monarch. In his *De Iure Regni Apud Scotos Dialogus*, he insisted that even an individual citizen could lawfully take it upon himself to attack and kill a tyrant.[46] Yet Buchanan was also highly critical of the state of the legal system, the content of which was largely determined through the decisions of the lords of session. As he put it:

> in Scotland, as there are almost no laws except acts of parliament, and these in general not fixed but temporary, and as the judges as much as they can hinder the passing of statutes, all the property of the subject is entrusted to the will of fifteen men who evidently possess a perpetual tyranny, because their will alone is law ...[47]

Reducing the vast corpus of Scots law to writing, under parliamentary supervision, would of course remedy these perceived problems. It would mean that there would be a reasonably certain law according to which property rights could be determined.

Of course, Buchanan's claim that the lords' decisions were based simply on their will constituted a gross over-simplification. As has been explained, they relied extensively on what they perceived to be legal truth in making their judgements. Nonetheless, his view is at least intelligible. Given that the lords could draw on the vast learning of Roman and canon law when making decisions, it might sometimes be difficult to predict what they would recognise to be consistent with truth and

---

45   See, for example, Williamson, *Scottish National Consciousness*, 64–5; Cairns, Fergus and MacQueen, 'Legal humanism and the history of Scots law', 52; Ford, *Law and Opinion*, 54–5.

46   The best modern edition and translation of the *De Iure Regni* is Roger A. Mason and Martin S. Smith (eds), *A Dialogue on the Law of Kingship among the Scots. A Critical Edition and Translation of George Buchanan's* De Iure Regni Apud Scotos Dialogus (Aldershot: Ashgate, 2004). For the discussion of tyrannicide, see ibid. 150–9. On political thought in Scotland at this time, see James H. Burns, *The True Law of Kingship: Concepts of Monarchy in Early-Modern Scotland* (Oxford: Clarendon Press, 1996); Roger Mason, *Kingship and the Commonweal: Political Thought in Renaissance and Reformation Scotland* (East Linton: Tuckwell Press, 1998).

47   This translation is found in Ford, *Law and Opinion*, 42; it is taken from James Aikman (trans.), *The History of Scotland Translated from the Latin of George Buchanan* (Glasgow, 1827) II, 306.

justice. Thus Buchanan's views were comprehensible.[48] They were also influential. Buchanan had served as the moderator of the General Assembly (the highest court of the Protestant Church in Scotland). He retained enormous respect amongst the Reformed clergy. Furthermore, he had been a leading – and vicious – opponent of Mary, Queen of Scots. This was undoubtedly influenced by his family's traditional loyalty to Darnley's noble house, the Lennox Stewarts. He had also been given charge of the education of the young king, James VI. Admittedly, Buchanan and Morton were increasingly at loggerheads as the 1570s wore on. Nonetheless, it remains quite plausible to suggest Buchanan's influence shaped the commission of 1575.[49]

(3) Balfour's *Practicks*

It seems quite likely that the commission of 1575 actually achieved something. Historians believe that it resulted in, or at least catalysed, the production of a compendium of the laws of the realm. This is now known as Balfour's *Practicks*.[50] The man who directed the project, and who probably did quite a lot of the work, was, of course, the former lord president James Balfour. He was a member of the commission established in 1575, and he spent much of the rest of his life reducing the old laws to order. The commission had been instructed to draw the 'forme' of the body of the law, drawing from the old books of the law, statutes and the decisions of the session. As the statutes promulgated since 1424 could largely be found in Henryson's edition of 1566, it would seem that Balfour focused on the old books of the law and the decisions of the session.

Initially, the old laws were reorganised into a scheme that drew some inspiration from Justinian. The first book was entitled '*De Iure Personarum*' – that is, 'Concerning the Law of Persons'. It explored a range of laws connected with personal status and its consequences. These included rules governing the feudal relationship between superior and vassal, marriage, dowry, the care of minors by appointed tutors and guardians, and the privileges of burgesses. A great deal of the law of property appeared in this book because the feudal relationship was

---

[48]   For a much more thorough study of Buchanan's criticism of the contemporary lords of session, see J. D. Ford, 'Conciliar authority and equitable jurisdiction in early-modern Scotland', in Mark Godfrey (ed.), *Law and Authority in British Legal History* (Cambridge: Cambridge University Press, 2016), 140–69.

[49]   Concerning Buchanan's career, see Mason and Smith, *Dialogue*, xvii–xlv.

[50]   See McNeill (ed.), *Balfour's Practicks*.

seen as part of the law of persons. The second book, '*De Contractibus*'
– 'Concerning Contracts' – considered pacts and several particular contracts, including loan, certain types of security, sale, hire, gift and charters. The third book, '*De Ultimis Voluntatibus*' – 'Concerning Wills'
– explored a range of aspects of the law of succession. Rules about testaments (i.e. wills) and the inheritance of land were examined. The fourth
book, '*De Preparatoriis Iudiciorum*' – loosely translated as 'Concerning
Procedure' – dealt with rules about coming to court and making pleas.
The fifth book, '*De Actionibus Civilibus*' dealt with civil actions, and
the sixth book, '*De Actionibus Criminalibus*' dealt with criminal causes.
Finally, a seventh book, '*De Re Militari*' dealt with a range of 'military
matters', including the laws that applied on the border between Scotland
and England (the 'March Laws').[51]

This work constituted a remarkable achievement. The old medieval
laws had been completely reorganised. They could now be studied and
used in a broadly systematic manner. However, and perhaps unfortunately, the systematic clarity of this work was obscured by what happened next. Into the carefully laid-out structure of the book were
inserted hundreds of decisions of the session and a series of references to
the post-1424 statutes printed in Henryson's edition of 1566.[52] It seems
that whoever did this sometimes obscured the overall structure of the
original book. Indeed, the seven-book structure was soon abandoned
completely.[53]

The resulting compilation is today known as Balfour's *Practicks*. It
was largely finished by 1583, when Balfour died. The seven-book work
on which it was based proudly proclaimed that it had been produced at
the command of the Earl of Morton, underlining the link with the commission of 1575.[54] The final product was to be of great importance in the
subsequent development of the Scottish legal tradition. Various other
lawyers probably worked on the project, and they went on to produce
a wide range of Scottish legal literature. Most notably, Sir John Skene
of Curriehill edited and published in print Latin and Scots editions of

---

51 See National Library of Scotland (NLS) Advocates MS 25.4.11 and BL Additional
    MS 48050. A description is found in Professor Gero Dolezalek's indispensable and
    scholarly heuristic work, *Scotland Under Jus Commune* (Edinburgh: Stair Society,
    2010) II, 304–10.
52 On Balfour's work on the decisions of the session, see, for example, William
    M. Gordon, 'Balfour's *Registrum*', in Hector L. MacQueen (ed.), *Stair Society
    Miscellany Four* (Edinburgh: Stair Society, 2002), 127–37.
53 This can be seen from McNeill (ed.), *Balfour's Practicks*.
54 See National Registers of Scotland (NRS) GD 112/71/3 f.5ʳ.

Regiam Majestatem and the old books of the law.[55] These appeared in 1609.[56] In 1597, Skene also published a work explaining a range of terms in the older texts, entitled *De Verborum Significatione*.[57] This title may be translated into English as '*Concerning the Meaning of Words*'. The eccentric Habbakuk Bisset also seems to have worked for Balfour on the old laws. Later he wrote an extensive work that was largely concerned with legal procedure, known as his *Rolment of Courtis*.[58]

Nonetheless, while Balfour's project was influential, his *Practicks* did not result in the old common law being placed on a new statutory footing. While Morton himself might have sought to achieve this goal, his own time as regent was coming to an end. Following a power struggle between 1578 and 1580, he lost control of the realm. He was subsequently arrested and executed for his role in the murder of Darnley. From 1578 onwards, James VI increasingly took control of government himself.[59]

(4) Parliament as a Supreme Law-giver

The 1570s witnessed growing interest in the role of parliament as the supreme law-giver within the Scottish realm. It was hoped that its authority might be used to place a revised version of the old common law on a statutory footing. Evidently this would assist in promoting legal certainty. Contemporary French attempts to codify their customary laws probably helped to inspire this approach. Furthermore, the declaration of the whole of Scots law in statute would have responded to some of Buchanan's criticism of the contemporary legal system. No longer would so much of the content of the law be discerned and determined through the decisions of the lords of session.

While the project to draw the form of the body of the laws ultimately failed, parliament's role as the supreme law-giver within the realm was acquiring new dimensions. In the 1580s and 1590s in particular, there was a marked increase in the number of statutes promulgated. As

---

55 On Skene's probable involvement, see Athol L. Murray, 'Skene, Sir John, of Curriehill (c. 1540–1617)', *Oxford Dictionary of National Biography* (Oxford: Oxford University Press, 2004), http://www.oxforddnb.com/view/article/25669.

56 J. Skene (ed.), *Regiam Majestatem* (Latin) (Edinburgh: Thomas Finlason, 1609); J. Skene (ed.), *Regiam Majestatem* (Scots) (Edinburgh: Thomas Finlason, 1609).

57 J. Skene, *De Verborum Significatione* (Edinburgh: Robert Waldegrave, 1597).

58 Philip J. Hamilton-Grierson, *Habakkuk Bisset's Rolment of Courtis* (Edinburgh and London: Scottish Text Society, 1919–26). On his work for Balfour, see ibid II, 275.

59 See Donaldson, *James V – James VII*, 167–73; Dawson, *Scotland Re-formed*, 296–302.

Goodare has observed, even though the Scottish common law was not codified, it was being gradually transformed by wide-ranging legislation. Legislation had already shown itself capable of effecting radical reforms to the polity, in matters of religion and the authority of the crown. Other courts within the realm – such as baron courts and regality courts – could make their own statutes; yet all were subject to parliamentary authority.[60] Furthermore, writers were beginning to theorise parliament's role as a law-maker, particularly in response to the crises of the late 1560s and early 1570s. In 1586, the governing body of the Protestant kirk, the General Assembly, recognised the potential consequences of this development. It seems to have expressed real concern that parliament could validly legislate in a manner inconsistent with its interpretation of the Bible.[61] The supremacy of parliament was being articulated in new and intriguing ways.[62]

D. CONCLUSION

This chapter began by reiterating one basic assumption of sixteenth-century Scottish legal experts. When they reached consensus that a proposition was consistent with legal truth and justice, that proposition received the binding force of law. The chapter then explored how that assumption began to run into difficulties in the 1570s. It did not sit easily with the account of legal authority articulated by the anonymous minister in the debate at Edinburgh Castle in 1571. He argued that the will of parliament, coupled with the obedience of the people to that will, were the essential elements of the authority that underpinned law. A somewhat similar approach informed Bodin's more radical claim, to the effect that all law-making depended on an exercise of sovereign will. Of course, Bodin's approach also excluded the idea that expert recognition of truth could, in and of itself, possess the binding force of law.

There is evidence to show that Scottish legal experts in the College of Justice were influenced by Bodin's thinking. Yet they did not endorse the idea that only the sovereign will of a legislator could make law. Ford has argued convincingly that the jurist Thomas Craig of Riccarton (c. 1538–

---

[60] Goodare, *Government of Scotland*, 70–86, particularly at 81, 86.
[61] Goodare, *Government of Scotland*, 86.
[62] See also Julian Goodare, *State and Society in Early Modern Scotland* (Oxford: Oxford University Press, 1999), 11–37.

1608) believed that expert consensus in the session concerning legal truth possessed binding force.[63] In his *Ius Feudale* (c. 1600), Craig outlined his views. When discussing Roman law, for example, he commented that the Scots were 'bound by the laws of the Romans to the extent that they are in agreement with the laws of nature and right reason'.[64] 'Nature' and 'right reason' in this context can be broadly equated with what has been described above as legal truth and justice. In other words, to the extent that Scottish legal experts in the session *did* recognise Roman law to be consistent with such standards, it was binding.

Ford has also shown that Craig wished to promote the continued transfer of such learning into Scots law. This seems to have been influenced by the old literary motif of the *translatio studii* (i.e. 'transfer of learning'). As Scottish legal experts in the session discerned reason and justice in the established learning of Roman law, canon law and feudal law, they would incorporate it into their own emergent tradition of learning concerning legal truth. In so doing, they would create a distinctively Scottish contribution to legal learning.[65]

It seems likely that Craig's approach was indebted to the achievements of sixteenth-century Scots lawyers. In all probability, it was from them that he inherited the idea that the Scottish legal tradition already expressed some learning concerning legal truth. Presumably he was also inspired by their idea that the tradition merited detailed study in its own right. Indeed, he may have inherited more from them. It is possible that some of Craig's predecessors had already drawn upon the motif of the *translatio studii* when thinking about the authority of the laws of the realm. When Henryson said in his *Preface* to the statutes printed in 1566 that the Scottish legal system already expressed the three principles of justice found in Roman law, he may have been suggesting that it had already absorbed Roman learning. Indeed, he had appropriated such learning directly in order to expound and develop his account of the authority of Scots law. Nonetheless, it is by no means certain that Henryson anticipated Craig in this regard. Like Chalmers and Leslie, Henryson may simply have thought that the law expressed learning as a result of the methods used to create it.

Regardless, the motif of the *translatio studii* was to perform a significant role in shaping seventeenth-century Scots law. Scottish legal

---

[63] See Ford, *Law and Opinion*, 215–40.
[64] Ford, *Law and Opinion*, 225.
[65] Ford, *Law and Opinion*, 239–40, drawing on the general argument at 215–40 and earlier comments made at 181–215.

experts would continue to transfer Roman, canonist and feudal learning concerning truth into their own legal system, augmenting its authority. In the process, the substance of the old common law was transformed through the decisions of the College of Justice.

E. SELECTED BIBLIOGRAPHY AND FURTHER READING

(1) Records of the Parliaments of Scotland (*RPS*)

Act ratifying Queen Mary's abdication: *RPS* 1567/12/105.
Act ratifying the Protestant Reformation: *RPS* A1567/12/1–5.
Proposed act concerning a commission to revise and organise the laws: *RPS* 1567/12/54.
Act appointing a commission to revise and organise the laws: *RPS* A1575/3/7.

(2) Books

Bannatyne, Richard, *Memorials of Transactions in Scotland A.D. MDLXIX – A.D. MDLXXIII* (Edinburgh: Bannatyne Club, 1836).

Burns, James H., *The True Law of kingship: Concepts of Monarchy in Early-Modern Scotland* (Oxford: Clarendon Press, 1996).

Cairns, John W., *Law, Lawyers and Humanism. Selected Essays on the History of Scots Law, Volume 1* (Edinburgh: Edinburgh University Press, 2015).

Dawson, Jane E. A., *Scotland Re-formed 1488–1587* (Edinburgh: Edinburgh University Press, 2007).

Donaldson, Gordon, *The First Trial of Mary Queen of Scots* (London: B. T. Batsford Ltd, 1969).

Dolezalek, Gero, *Scotland Under* Jus Commune (Edinburgh: Stair Society, 2010).

Ford, J. D., *Law and Opinion in Scotland during the Seventeenth Century* (Oxford and Portland: Hart, 2007).

Goodare, Julian, *State and Society in Early Modern Scotland* (Oxford: Oxford University Press, 1999).

Goodare, Julian, *The Government of Scotland 1560–1625* (Oxford: Oxford University Press, 2004).

Leslie, John, *A defence of the honour of the right highe, mightye and noble Princesse Marie Quene of Scotland ...* (London, 1569).

Mason, Roger, *Kingship and the Commonweal: Political Thought in Renaissance and Reformation Scotland* (East Linton: Tuckwell Press, 1998).

Mason, Roger A., and Martin S. Smith (eds), *A Dialogue on the Law of Kingship among the Scots. A Critical Edition and Translation of George Buchanan's* De Iure Regni Apud Scotos Dialogus (Aldershot: Ashgate, 2004).

Skinner, Quentin, *The Foundations of Modern Political Thought* (Cambridge: Cambridge University Press, 1978).

Skene, John, *De Verborum Significatione* (Edinburgh: Robert Walde-grave, 1597).

Skene, John (ed.), *Regiam Majestatem* (Latin) (Edinburgh: Thomas Finlason, 1609)

Skene, John (ed.), *Regiam Majestatem* (Scots), (Edinburgh: Thomas Finlason, 1609).

Williamson, Arthur H., *Scottish National Consciousness in the age of James VI* (Edinburgh: John Donald, 1979).

(3) Chapters in Books

Cairns, John W., T. David Fergus and Hector L. MacQueen, 'Legal humanism and the history of Scots law: John Skene and Thomas Craig', in John MacQueen (ed.), *Humanism in Renaissance Scotland* (Edinburgh: Edinburgh University Press, 1990), 48–74.

Ford, J. D., 'Conciliar authority and equitable jurisdiction in early-modern Scotland', in Mark Godfrey (ed.), *Law and Authority in British Legal History* (Cambridge: Cambridge University Press, 2016), 140–69.

Gordon, William M., 'Balfour's *Registrum*', in Hector L. MacQueen (ed.), *Stair Society Miscellany Four* (Edinburgh: Stair Society, 2002), 127–37.

McNeill, Peter G. B., 'Introduction', in Peter G. B. McNeill (ed.), *The Practicks of Sir James Balfour of Pittendreich* (Edinburgh: Stair Society, 1962–3).

Simpson, Andrew R. C., 'Power, reason and equity: two juristic accounts of royal authority in sixteenth-century Scotland', in Jørn Ø. Sunde (ed.), *Constitutionalism Before 1789: Constitutional Arrangements from the High Middle Ages to the French Revolution* (Oslo: Pax Forlag, 2014), 128–46.

Simpson, Andrew R. C., 'Legislation and authority in early-modern Scotland', in Mark Godfrey (ed.), *Law and Authority in British Legal*

History, 1200–1900 (Cambridge: Cambridge University Press, 2016), 85–119.

(4) Articles in Journals

Brundage, James A., 'Proof in canonical criminal law', *Continuity and Change* 11 (1996), 329–39.

(5) Unpublished PhD Theses

Simpson, Andrew R. C., 'Early Modern Studies of the Scottish Legal Past: Tradition and Authority in Sixteenth Century Scots Law' (University of Cambridge, 2010).

(6) Electronic Resources

Goodare, Julian, 'Mary [Mary Stewart] (1542–1587)', *Oxford Dictionary of National Biography* (Oxford: Oxford University Press, 2004); online edn May 2007, http://www.oxforddnb.com/view/article/18248.

Louglin, Mark, 'Maitland, William, of Lethington (1525×1530–1573)', *Oxford Dictionary of National Biography* (Oxford: Oxford University Press, 2004); online edn January 2008, http://www.oxforddnb.com/view/article/17838.

Marshall, Rosalind K., 'Lesley [Leslie], John (1527–1596)', *Oxford Dictionary of National Biography* (Oxford: Oxford University Press, 2004); online edn May 2007, http://www.oxforddnb.com/view/article/16492.

McNeill, Peter G. B., 'Balfour, Sir James, of Pittendreich (c. 1525–1583)', *Oxford Dictionary of National Biography* (Oxford: Oxford University Press, 2004), http://www.oxforddnb.com/view/article/1188.

Murray, Athol L., 'Skene, Sir John, of Curriehill (c. 1540–1617)', *Oxford Dictionary of National Biography* (Oxford: Oxford University Press, 2004), http://www.oxforddnb.com/view/article/25669.

PART FOUR

Regal Union with England, c. 1580–1707

The previous chapters have examined the period during which the Scottish common law was transformed. They discussed the impact of the establishment of the College of Justice (or Court of Session). They showed that views were changing on the authority of the learned laws and on Scots law itself. They examined the impact of the understanding of law on debates during the Reformation and revolution. These themes of institutional reform, changing understanding of royal and legal authority, the nature of Scots law, and the role of the so-called learned laws are also important during the seventeenth century. However, the circumstances under which these conversations took place were very different.

The political structure of Scotland in the seventeenth century was unique in its history. At the beginning of the century, Scotland was joined with England in a union of the crowns. This meant that both countries were ruled by the same king, which had important legal and political significance. The impact on the understanding of royal and state authority during this period will be discussed in Chapters 11 and 12. However, in the mid-seventeenth century, the British Civil Wars culminated in a short-lived republic, which can be said to have started in Scotland in August 1651. Chapter 13 will examine the legal reforms attempted during the period of the republic. The Stewart monarchy was restored in 1660, but there was another revolution in 1689 and the reigning king was deposed. The rights of the crown were renegotiated with his successors. In the early years of the next century, in 1707, Scotland and England joined in a parliamentary union. The impact of the events in 1689 and the parliamentary union will be discussed in Chapter 19.

This new and turbulent political landscape created a context in which the law, legal institutions and understanding of the law and authority were debated and changed. Chapter 14 will examine some of the legal literature written during this period. Chapters 15 and 16 will discuss the understanding of the authority of learned and Scottish sources set down in those works. Chapter 17 will discuss the rise of the legal profession during the late sixteenth and seventeenth centuries. Chapter 18 will examine the impact of the professionalisation of one area of practice: the prosecution of witchcraft.

CHAPTER II

Authority and Government in the Scottish Reign of James VI

A. INTRODUCTION

This chapter will explore the changing perceptions of royal and state authority during the first part of the reign of James VI. It will do so with reference to the relationship between the king, the privy council, parliament and the courts. Chapter 9 examined some of the debates concerning royal authority which were had during the downfall of Queen Mary in 1567. Parliament was instrumental in constraining royal authority twice during her reign: once during the Reformation and once again when she was deposed. However, the reign of her son witnessed a reassertion of royal authority. James VI's view of kingship and the confidence with which he asserted that view had a significant impact on Scotland at the end of the sixteenth century.[1]

This chapter will examine James's reassertion of royal authority in the first forty years of his reign as King of Scotland. First, it will take account of his earliest expressions of his royal authority as a minor. Secondly, it will examine royal and state authority and governmental reform during the 1580s and 1590s after James became an adult. Thirdly, it will examine James's own view of his royal authority and responsibilities, as set down in the two works he wrote on kingship at the end of the sixteenth century. His relationship with parliament and the College of Justice or Court of Session can to some extent be seen in the context of that viewpoint.

---

[1] On views of sovereignty in sixteenth and early seventeenth century Scotland more generally, see Julian Goodare, *State and Society in Early Modern Scotland* (Oxford: Oxford University Press, 1999), ch. 1.

B. ROYAL AUTHORITY DURING JAMES'S MINORITY

The end of Mary's reign in Scotland led to civil war between the king's party and the queen's party. Various men from the noble classes fulfilled the role of head of state; those claiming to do so in the king's stead were called 'regents' and those who claimed to do so on behalf of Mary were called 'lieutenants'.

One of the debates being had at that time concerned the extent of royal authority and of the position of the monarch within the state. A vocal group of Scottish intellectuals believed in popular authority and a restricted monarchy. This group included Andrew Melville, an educational reformer who will be discussed further in Chapter 17.[2] Meanwhile, the great Scottish thinker George Buchanan regarded there to be a contract between a king and his subjects.[3] This contract could be broken by the king, he said, which would give the people the right to resist and even to lawfully kill their king.[4] The nature of royal authority thus remained a subject of great debate during the latter decades of the 1500s. These debates are important for understanding James's view of royal authority because he was as a child under the tutelage of George Buchanan. This radical thinker ensured that the prince received a thorough humanist education, which was a point of pride in James's later life. However Buchanan also treated him so cruelly that it gave him nightmares in later life.[5]

The current regent, the Earl of Morton, was deposed in 1578 when James was almost twelve. James claimed that he was now old enough to rule without a regent. At eleven, he had not yet reached legal majority. However, 'The age at which monarchs became adult and the age when they were considered able to rule in person were evidently moving

---

[2] On Melville, see also James Kirk, 'Melville, Andrew (1545–1622)', *Oxford Dictionary of National Biography* (Oxford: Oxford University Press, 2004), http://www.oxforddnb.com/view/article/18543.

[3] On Buchanan's life, see D. M. Abbott, 'Buchanan, George (1506–1582)', *Oxford Dictionary of National Biography* (Oxford: Oxford University Press, 2004); revised online edn May 2006, http://www.oxforddnb.com/view/article/3837.

[4] Roger A. Mason and Martin S. Smith (eds), *A Dialogue on the Law of Kingship among the Scots: A Critical Edition and Translation of George Buchanan's* De Iure Regni Apud Scotos Dialogus (Aldershot: Ashgate, 2004), 150–9.

[5] Jenny Wormald, 'James VI and I (1566–1625)', *Oxford Dictionary of National Biography* (Oxford: Oxford University Press, 2004); revised online edn September 2014, http://www.oxforddnb.com/view/article/14592.

targets, and the two were not always synonymous.'[6] The parliament accordingly passed in the following year an act of revocation confirming James's earlier 'acceptance of the government in his own person'.[7] However, in reality 'a series of regimes succeeded each other before James VI finally took power into his own hands in 1584.'[8]

James met challenges to his royal authority during this period. These came from warring factions of nobles, the kirk, parliament and Elizabeth I of England. These various challenges created a hostile environment in which to be a young king. As Wormald has noted, 'all these had posed serious and novel threats to the prestige and authority of the Scottish crown.'[9] For example, in 1582 he was kidnapped in a plot led by the Earl of Gowrie, a lord of session. James was imprisoned and escaped only after ten months. He responded with swift but not unrestrained force.[10] But importantly he recognised the peril of factions among the nobles, and declared himself 'universal king' and thus king to all his nobles.[11]

C. GOVERNMENTAL REFORM AND AUTHORITY DURING JAMES'S PERSONAL RULE IN THE 1580s–90s

(1) Reform in 1584 and 1587

The first two decades of James's majority witnessed a centralisation of governmental power and a rise of state authority. When James reached majority there were various institutions of government. Four of these will be examined here: the crown, parliament, the privy council and the

---

[6] Amy Blakeway, *Regency in Sixteenth-Century Scotland* (Woodbridge: Boydell Press, 2015), 74.

[7] *RPS* 1579/10/47.

[8] Blakeway, *Regency*, 4.

[9] Wormald, 'James VI and I'.

[10] James initially pardoned the Earl of Gowrie. However, a convention of the estates thereafter required Gowrie to go into exile. As he prepared to leave Scotland he conspired with other nobles to attack Stirling castle. He was arrested, denied mercy a second time, and executed. On Gowrie's life, see Sharon Adams, 'Ruthven, William, fourth Lord Ruthven and first Earl of Gowrie (c. 1543–1584)', *Oxford Dictionary of National Biography* (Oxford: Oxford University Press, 2004); revised online edn October 2006, http://www.oxforddnb.com/view/article/24375; George Brunton and David Haig, *An Historical Account of the Senators of the College of Justice, from its Institution in MDXXXII* (Edinburgh: Thomas Clark, 1832), 170–3.

[11] Wormald, 'James VI and I'.

Court of Session. The parliament was a forum in which the three estates (clerics, nobles and burgesses) debated issues and recorded their collective will in legislation.[12] The Court of Session was the highest civil court at the time. The privy council exercised executive control, making policy decisions and ensuring that these were carried out by a network of clients working in administrative offices or positions. All operated symbolically in 'the name of the crown – which was not necessarily the personal command of the king'.[13] The crown (and the monarch) was but one part of a wider government.[14]

In the 1580s and 1590s the king was to become the centre and apex of government in his realm, at least notionally. Governmental power became an aspect of the personal authority of the king.[15] During his reign, James expanded the scope of the royal prerogative and issued many proclamations.[16] Parliament became more truly a legislature which reformed the law rather than a forum for debate. James likely believed that he had the right to command parliament, although in practice he normally legislated with its advice.[17] As Goodare has said, 'The legislation of two parliaments in particular – those of 1584 and 1587 – can be seen as an absolutist manifesto.'[18]

Indeed a significant declaration of royal authority was made by parliament in 1584. Parliament was at this time still a small gathering. In 1584 it comprised twenty-one clerics, twenty-six nobles and twenty-two burgesses.[19] These men confirmed 'the royal power and authority over all states, both spiritual as temporal, within this realm'. They also declared 'that his highness, his said heirs and successors, by themselves and their councils, are and in time to come shall be judges competent to

---

[12] This legislative power was central to the authority of parliament; on which, see Julian Goodare, 'The Scottish parliament and its early modern "rivals"', *Parliaments, Estates and Representation* 24 (2004), 147–72.

[13] Goodare, *State and Society*, 17.

[14] Julian Goodare, *The Government of Scotland 1560–1625* (Oxford: Oxford University Press, 2004), 87–97. This book is an excellent introduction to government and its institutions during the period.

[15] Goodare, *Government of Scotland*, 98–9.

[16] Goodare, *Government of Scotland*, 97–102.

[17] Goodare, *Government of Scotland*, 103–6. The authors are grateful to Julian Goodare for his advice on this point.

[18] Goodare, *State and Society*, 73.

[19] Keith M. Brown, 'The second estate: parliament and the nobility', in Keith M. Brown and Alan R. MacDonald (eds), *The History of the Scottish Parliament, III: Parliament in Context, 1235–1707* (Edinburgh: Edinburgh University Press, 2010), 67–94 at 80.

all persons ... in all matters'.[20] Parliament was here recognising James's royal authority over all institutions of government and his role in the administration of justice. However, as will be shown, this does not mean that they expected him to wield power and authority in all matters of state. It was also required that 'those that possess the said two volumes [of George Buchanan] in their hands bring in and deliver the same ... [so they] may be perused and purged of the offensive and extraordinary matters'.[21]

This legislation was also controversial. The legislation had been drafted with the assistance of John Maitland of Thirlestane, a lord of session and James's secretary of state. Thirlestane's political astuteness was instrumental to the passing of the act as well as other unpopular legislation passed in the same year.[22] Church ministers, for example, were no longer permitted to 'accept, use or administer any place of judicature in whatsoever civil or criminal causes' after 1584.[23] Thirlestane would continue to be essential to the strengthening of royal and state authority over the next two decades.

A significant quantity of legislation and reform followed in 1587. One of the principal changes at that time was the admission of shire commissioners into parliament. These men were representatives of those who were not part of the peerage. This was a fourth estate comprised of lesser landowners or lairds. It seems likely that this was at least in part a fiscal measure.[24] However, it was a radical change:

> Parliament thereafter could never be quite the same. It had derived
> its authority from ancient tradition ... Tampering with parlia-
> ment's immemorial three estates to add a fourth could hardly fail
> to shake conservative beliefs about the wellsprings of parliamentary
> authority ...[25]

---

[20] *RPS* 1584/5/8. See also Goodare, *State and Society*, 74; John W. Cairns, 'Historical introduction', in Kenneth Reid and Reinhard Zimmermann (eds), *A History of Private Law in Scotland* (Oxford: Oxford University Press, 2000) I, 14–184 at 77.

[21] *RPS* 1584/5/14.

[22] Maurice Lee Jr, 'Maitland, John, first Lord Maitland of Thirlestane (1543–1595)', *Oxford Dictionary of National Biography* (Oxford: Oxford University Press, 2004), http://www.oxforddnb.com/view/article/17826.

[23] *RPS* 1584/5/12.

[24] Keith M. Brown, *Noble Power in Scotland from the Reformation to the Revolution* (Edinburgh: Edinburgh University Press, 2011), 158; Cairns, 'Historical introduction', 77.

[25] Goodare, *Government of Scotland*, 58. See also Brown, 'The second estate', 84.

The passing of this legislative package was seen as a significant accomplishment. Thirlestane was rewarded by promotion to chancellor of Scotland, the highest position in government below the king.[26]

(2) Men in Government

The nobility had formed one of the traditional power bases in Scotland.[27] The rise of state authority had an impact on the role of the nobles in governance.[28] Those who held the highest offices in government were often noble men who had proved themselves capable.[29] Participation in government gave such men the opportunity to find wealth and favour with the king. Many nobles thus sought offices of state, seeing that those who did not were often marginalised.[30]

Landed men who were not peerage nobles also participated in government. It was men like these who were added to parliament in 1587 and they had a critical role in government under Thirlestane's leadership. These men also sought wealth and favour, and hoped that their work would ensure their social advancement. Lawyers as a group had a critical role to play in the administration of the state. This is seen in the suggestion in 1587 that judges should also be admitted into parliament by virtue of their appointment, although this was not approved.[31] However, most of those lawyers who rose high in the profession to become king's advocates or lords of session were from landed families.[32]

What was thus a somewhat unusual judicial career is found in the life of John Preston of Fentonbarns. He was the son of a baker, also called John. The elder John had risen through his profession to become both a

---

[26] Lee Jr, 'Maitland, John'.

[27] On the power of the nobility before the 1580s, see Goodare, *State and Society*, ch. 2.

[28] Goodare, *State and Society*, 74–8.

[29] Goodare, *State and Society*, ch. 3.

[30] Goodare, *State and Society*, ch. 3.

[31] Goodare, *Government of Scotland*, 56.

[32] It has previously been suggested that there may have been in Scotland a *noblesse de robe*: Jenny Wormald, *Lords and Men in Scotland: Bonds of Manrent, 1442–1603* (Edinburgh: John Donald, 1985), 162. However, this suggestion has been widely criticised. For an insight into this criticism and the role of lawyers in the state more generally, see Goodare, *Government of Scotland*, 56; John Finlay, *Men of Law in Pre-Reformation Scotland* (East Linton: Tuckwell Press, 2000); Keith M. Brown, 'The Stewart realm: changing the landscape', in Steve Boardman and Julian Goodare (eds), *Kings, Lords and Men in Scotland and Britain, 1300–1625, Essays in Honour of Jenny Wormald* (Edinburgh: Edinburgh University Press, 2014), 19–33 at 29; Brown, *Noble Power*, 166–79.

burgess and dean of guild in Edinburgh. As such he had the power and resources to ensure his son received a university education. This allowed John the younger to attain sufficient learning to pass as an advocate before 1575.[33] He shortly thereafter became an assessor (legal adviser) to the town of Edinburgh and a judge in the Edinburgh commissary court. The wealth which he acquired through his professional practice allowed him to buy estates in East Lothian. He thus became a member of the landed classes. He was one of three men nominated by the king for a seat as a lord of session in 1595, and was the one elected to office by the incumbent lords. He became a member of the privy council in the same year and became one of the hardest working members of that group. In 1607 and 1609 his capability was again recognised by the king and his peers when he was elected as the acting and then the permanent lord president of the Session.[34] This example shows the extent to which social advancement was possible through participation in wider governmental activity.

Ultimately the aim of such landed men was advancement to the peerage. Admission to the peerage could be granted by the king. Goodare has shown that there was a significant increase in the number of peerages created after James's majority. In the twenty years prior, only six new peerages had been created. However, there were fourteen created between 1580 and 1599. There were thirty-six created in the decade following.[35] Goodare has suggested that 'these men were his foremost servants' and that 'a marriage between local landed power and obedience to central authority' was ensured through this 'reconstructed nobility'.[36]

Nobles and landed men also had a further role in ensuring the effective running of the state. Chapter 1 mentioned the importance of kinship networks in early Scotland. Another important network was that established through patronage. This was a system whereby a powerful man used his influence and connections to further the careers of other men (called 'clients'). The clients in turn owed loyalty to him. Goodare has shown that the nobles and advisers to the king were able to ensure that their kin and clients were appointed to governmental offices. This ensured that the patron had power and influence through a network of well-positioned, loyal men. Clients who excelled in their offices brought glory

[33] On legal education and the process of admission as an advocate, see Chapter 17.
[34] Brunton and Haig, *An Historical Account*, 234–6; Athol Murray, 'Preston, John, of Penicuik, Lord Fentonbarns (d. 1616)', *Oxford Dictionary of National Biography* (Oxford: Oxford University Press, 2004), http://www.oxforddnb.com/view/article/22726.
[35] Goodare, *State and Society*, 78 n. 46.
[36] Goodare, *State and Society*, 78.

not only to themselves but also to their patrons.[37] For example, four of the nine lords of session appointed during the period when Thirlestane was chancellor (1587–92) were related to him.[38] Nobles who held offices of state would also require the assistance of a team of deputes and clerks to undertake the work of their office. Indeed sometimes positions (such as sheriff) were largely ceremonial, with the work of the office being undertaken by these lesser men. Lawyers received many of these lesser offices and brought 'a newly professional approach to the business of government'.[39]

(3) James's View of Royal Authority and Good Kingship

(a) The Trew Law of Free Monarchies and Basilikon Doron

The determined expansion of royal and state authority was not just an attempt to improve governance. It was also a reflection of James's understanding of the nature of kingship. His view of kingship is made clear in the two books which he wrote on the subject in the 1590s. The *Basilikon Doron* (Greek for 'royal gift') was written by him for his oldest son and heir, Henry, as a manual for effective kingship. *The Trew Law of Free Monarchies* was a more theoretical text, an academic defence of his view of royal authority.

James had come to believe strongly in a theory known as the divine right of kings. This was the idea that the king's power derives from God's making him king. James therefore believed that a king had a 'double obligation' to God: 'first, for that he made you a man; and next, for that he made you a little GOD to sit on his Throne, and rule ouer other men.'[40] As such the king's right to rule (and so his royal authority) was beyond the challenge of his subjects or other foreign rulers. To challenge the king's royal authority was not just seen as treason against the king and the state: it was a blasphemy against the will of God.

James also regarded there to be an additional basis for his royal authority as king.

---

[37] Goodare, *State and Society*, 84.
[38] Goodare, *State and Society*, 82.
[39] Goodare, *Government of Scotland*, 161.
[40] [James VI], *The Workes of the Most High and Mightie Prince, James, By the Grace of God King of Great Britaine France and Ireland, Defender of the Faith, published by James, Bishop of Winton & Deane of his Majesties Chappel Royall* (London: Robert Barker & John Bill, 1616), 148.

The kings therefore in *Scotland* were before any estates or rankes of men within the same, before any Parliaments were holden, or lawes made: and by them was the land distributed (which at the first was whole theirs) states erected and decerned, and formes of gouernement deuised and established: And so it followes of necessitie, that the kings were the authors and makers of the Lawes, and not the Lawes of the kings.[41]

What James meant here was that the office of king pre-dated social order, all other offices of government and all laws. The king was the creator and origin of all aspects of the state. As such, it was from his overarching authority that all other men held their own, more limited, spheres of authority.

This view of kings as being the 'authors and makers of the Lawes' was to have an important consequence. 'A good king will frame all his actions to be according to the Law; yet is hee not bound thereto but of his good will'.[42] This meant that James did not regard himself to be bound by the law. He obeyed the law only out of 'good will'.

James recognised that there was such a thing as a bad king. However, he believed that bad kings should not be deposed because of the social upheaval which would follow and the risk of invoking God's displeasure. He thus utterly rejected the teachings of his early master, George Buchanan, as well as those of the followers of Andrew Melville. Indeed, Wormald has suggested that 'the struggle with Andrew Melville and his supporters was ... *the main inspiration*, even more than the contractual theorizing of Buchanan, for James's own theory about kingship'.[43] Indeed he saw Buchanan's writings as 'such infamous inuectiues' and recommended to Prince Henry that 'if any of these infamous libels remaine vntill your dayes, vse the Law vpon the keepers thereof'.[44]

James defended his view of divine right by drawing on the Bible as well as various humanist sources. He produced a forcefully argued, learned defence of his royal authority. He contextualised his 'mature reflections on his Scottish kingship within a European context'.[45] This meant that '*Trew Law* was more than a claim to divine right; it was

---

[41] [James VI], *The Workes*, 201.
[42] [James VI], *The Workes*, 203.
[43] Wormald, 'James VI and I', emphasis added.
[44] [James VI], *The Workes*, 176.
[45] Wormald, 'James VI and I'. See also Jenny Wormald, '"And so it follows ... that the Kinges were the authors & makers of the lawes, and not the lawes of the Kings" [James VI, *Trew Lawe of Free Monarchies*]. Did he mean it?', presented to

a restatement of imperial kingship'.[46] The statement of Scottish king-ship as imperial kingship was a reformulation and increasing of royal authority. However, James also addressed the English context. He would have been mindful of the possibility of his inheriting the English throne when he wrote. His succession to the English throne will be discussed further in the following chapter. However it is important that *Trew Law* 'illuminate[d] the intellectual common ground between James and the Henrician [i.e. Tudor English] claims to *imperium*.'[47]

However James did not aspire to be merely a powerful king. He also aspired to be a good king. His understanding of what that meant was set down in the *Basilikon Doron*. James explained what it was to be a good king:

> discharging your Office … in the points of Iustice and Equitie: which in two sundrie waies ye must doe: the one, in establishing and executing, (which is the life of the Law) good Lawes among your people: the other, by your behauiour in your owne person[.][48]

This can be translated as:

> discharging your office … in the points of justice and equity, which in two sundry ways you must do. The one, in establishing and exe-cuting (which is the life of the law) good laws among your people. The other, by your behaviour in your own person.

James saw this as an inherent part of the office of king and his duty to God. A king must recognise that he has 'receiued from God a burthen of gouernment' (i.e. 'received from God a burden of government').[49] What James meant by this is that when God made him king He also burdened him with the obligation to govern his people as a good king, rather than as a bad king or a tyrant. As such, the king must 'emploieth all his studie and paines, to procure and maintaine, by the making and execution of good Lawes' (i.e. 'employ all his study and pains to procure

---

the Scottish Legal History Group, 3 October 2015, summarised in 'Scottish Legal History Group report 2015', *Journal of Legal History* 37:1 (2016), 72–4 at 73.

[46] John Cramsie, 'The philosophy of imperial kingship and the interpretation of James VI and I', in Ralph Houlbrooke (ed.), *James VI and I: Ideas, Authority and Government* (Aldershot: Ashgate, 2006), 43–60 at 48.

[47] Cramsie, 'The philosophy of imperial kingship', 46.

[48] [James VI], *The Workes*, 155.

[49] [James VI], *The Workes*, 155.

and maintain, by the making and execution of good laws').[50] This sentence indicates that James did not see the king's role in making good laws to be one of passive reliance on his parliament and advisors. Rather the king was to dedicate himself actively to the maintenance of good laws. James's pursuit of this ideal behaviour of good governance is seen in his relationships with parliament and with the College of Justice or Court of Session.

(b) Royal authority and 'establishing ... good Lawes'

James recognised the role of parliament within 'establishing ... good Lawes'. However, he urged to his son a degree of caution with respect to parliament:

> wee haue alreadie moe good Lawes then are well execute ... And therefore hold no Parliaments, but for necessitie of new Lawes, which would be but seldome, for few Lawes and well put in execution, are best in a well ruled common-weale.[51]

This can be translated as:

> We have already more good laws than are well executed. ... And therefore hold no parliaments but for necessity of new laws. Which would be but seldom, for few laws and well put in execution are best in a well ruled commonwealth.

What this means is that good laws must be executed and applied. If there is too much law then it becomes impossible to apply it all properly. Therefore a king should ensure that only necessary laws are passed. This in turn ensures that there are not too many to apply. Parliament is the body which makes the law, so should only be called by the king when it is needed. To call it more often than this could result in the passing of acts which are malicious or do harm. The reforms of 1584 and 1587 mentioned above can be seen in the context of this understanding, as well as in the wider context of the rise of state authority.

James attended every meeting of parliament and convention of estates after 1578 until his departure from Scotland in 1603.[52] Parliament's role

---

[50] [James VI], *The Workes*, 155.
[51] [James VI], *The Workes*, 156.
[52] Keith M. Brown, Alastair J. Mann and Roland J. Tanner, *The Scottish Parliament:*

in the process of governance was also changing: after 1579 it passed more new legislation than previous parliaments had done.[53] However, James's understanding of the establishment of good laws did also include the consideration of older laws. This was in keeping with his contemporaries: the older laws had been a concern of contemporaries since the reign of his mother.[54] James's reign thus saw several commissions to make the law available to his subjects. He was too young to have had more than a symbolic role in the 1575 commission, which might have resulted in Balfour's practicks.[55] In 1592 there was another commission to collect, consider and print 'the laws and acts made in this present parliament and all other municipal laws and acts of parliament bygone'.[56] A collection of statutes from the reigns of James I and his successors was printed in 1597. Bound with it was Sir John Skene of Curriehill's exposition of legal words, called *De verborum significatione*. Skene was further responsible for the printing of the older medieval laws and the earlier statutes in 1609, in both Latin and Scots, under the overall title *Regiam Majestatem*.[57] More will be said about these works in Chapter 14.

(c) Royal authority and the practice of law

The second aspect of good governance was to ensure the proper application of those 'good Lawes'. James's advice to Henry was to 'studie well your owne Lawes' and to 'haunt your Session, and spie carefully their proceedings'.[58] The purpose of this was to ensure that the judgements of the court were just. James did indeed attend the court regularly, perhaps around twenty-five days each year.[59]

His attendance at the Session would have shown him that there were problems. Again this was a wider concern. Already by 1584 parliament

An Historical Introduction, Part 6, http://rps.ac.uk/static/historicalintro6.html. On conventions, see Goodare, *Government of Scotland*, ch. 2, especially 47–9.

53   Goodare, *Government of Scotland*, 72–3.
54   On the 1566 legislative project, see Chapter 9.
55   On which, see Chapter 10.
56   *RPS* 1592/4/67.
57   On Skene and the commissions, see Cairns, 'Historical introduction', 96–7; below, Chapters 14–16. For James's understanding about law, see for example Louis A. Knafla, 'Britain's Solomon: King James and the law', in Daniel Fischlin and Mark Fortier (eds), *Royal Subjects: Essays on the Writings of James VI and I* (Detroit: Wayne State University Press, 2002), 235–64.
58   [James VI], *The Workes*, 176.
59   T. B. Smith, 'British justice: a Jacobean phantasma', *Scots Law Times* News (1982), 157–64 at 157.

recognised 'the complaints and lamentations of sundry his good subjects, of such enormities, corruption and delays used in the session and college of justice'.[60] Not all the judges had expertise in the law, and the process of cases was sometimes slow.[61] This is not to say that the Session would have been regarded to be deeply flawed by contemporaries. Indeed, Goodare has remarked that 'Everybody, in fact, seems to have loved the court of session, one of the sixteenth century's great success stories.'[62] However, there were attempts to reform and improve the court during this period, both in terms of the men who sat as judges and the procedure of the court.

In 1579 an act of parliament said that the lord president was to be selected by his colleagues on the bench from either the spiritual or the temporal estate. Previously only judges from the spiritual estate had been eligible. The act also stressed that any appointee to the bench should be:

> a man that fears God, of good literature, understanding of the laws, of good fame, having sufficient living of his own and who can make good expedition and dispatch of matters concerning the lieges of this realm[.][63]

In 1584 a commission of men was to be appointed to reform the court. One of their duties was to identify any of the lords of session who should be replaced. They were also to recommend new men to replace them. In the end the commission never took place.[64] In 1592 the parliament reconfirmed the requirements for men to be appointed to the bench.[65] James's personal interest in the identity of the judges has also already been seen in his later involvement in Fentonbarns's election first as a lord of session and then as the lord president.

Other reforms tried to ensure what might today be called due process. The intended commission of 1584 was meant to identify the causes of the delays which were the subject of complaint. They were then to 'prescribe and appoint such good rules and constitutions as they shall think most requisite for reformation'.[66] An act in 1585 expanded the court's

---

[60] *RPS* 1584/5/33.
[61] Cairns, 'Historical introduction', 82.
[62] Goodare, *Government of Scotland*, 57. On the court generally at this time, see ibid. 160–3.
[63] *RPS* 1579/10/55
[64] J. D. Ford, 'Control of the procedure of the College of Justice in Scotland', presented to the University of Bergen Legal Culture Research Group, April 2016.
[65] *RPS* 1592/4/72. On these acts, see Cairns, 'Historical introduction', 86.
[66] *RPS* 1584/5/33.

jurisdiction to include cases relating to interferences with land holding.[67] This jurisdiction had previously been held by inferior, local courts and the impact of this change would have been 'profound'.[68] In 1590 the convention of estates considered whether new procedural reforms were necessary but 'left the reformation of the Sessions to th'examynatione and order of them selves' (i.e. 'left the reform of the Session to the examination and order of itself').[69] In 1594 an act was passed that prevented a lord of session from hearing a case in which a close family member was a litigant. Another act passed in the same year prohibited a lord of session from buying land which was being disputed in a case.[70] In 1596 an act of sederunt by the lords ordained that no man should approach them outwith court about a case, but should restrict himself to his written pleadings and court appearances.[71] Attempts were also made to curb unruly behaviour by those who attended court hearings.[72] Such reforms reflect a concern to ensure due process and efficiency of court business.

James's view of his royal authority as exercisable within the Session did on one occasion differ from that of the bench in dramatic fashion. This was the case of *Bruce v Hamilton* (1599), for which the only known evidence is a letter to the English secretary of state, Sir Robert Cecil.[73] James had been attending the court, listening to the proceedings. Once the arguments had been presented by the advocates, James ordered the judges to find for Hamilton. He noted his royal authority over them as his subjects and that 'in that matter of law and conscience, being sworn to justice, they would do as their consciences led them unless He [i.e. the king] commanded them to the contrary'.[74] The judges voted against

---

67 *RPS* 1587/7/33.

68 Cairns, 'Historical introduction', 82–3.

69 William K. Boyd and Henry W. Meikle (eds), *Calendar of State Papers relating to Scotland and Mary Queen of Scots 1547–1603* (Edinburgh: HM General Register House, 1936) X, item 430. The authors are grateful to John Ford for this reference.

70 *RPS* 1594/4/33, *RPS* 1594/4/37.

71 *An Abridgement of the Acts of Sederunt of the Lords of Council and Session, from January 1553, to February 1794* (Edinburgh: [on behalf of the Court of Session], 1794), 11–12.

72 *An Abridgement of the Acts of Sederunt*, 33–4. On these developments, see Cairns, 'Historical introduction', 85–6.

73 Markham John Thorpe, *Calendar of the State Papers Relating to Scotland* (London: Longman *et al.*, 1858) II, 767. The following account is taken from Thomas Mackay Cooper, Lord Cooper of Culross, 'The King *versus* the Court of Session', in Lord Cooper of Culross (ed.), *Selected Papers, 1922–1954* (Edinburgh: Oliver and Boyd, 1957), 116–23.

74 Cooper, 'King *versus* the Court of Session', 117.

his wishes, and found instead for Bruce. James was furious and said that he would reverse the court's decision. The lord president, Alexander Seton, warned that if the king attempted to do so then he would send letters to all the judges in Christendom asking for their support. James decided not to pursue the matter further.[75] This remarkable case shows the limits of royal authority: the judges heard cases on behalf of the king, but were not bound to his will in deciding them. However this case is exceptional and should not be regarded as evidence of a more general disconnect between royal and state authority.

James was not just interested in the Session with respect to applying good laws. He was also interested in the inferior courts. He was concerned that the nobility and their vassals should be made 'answerable to the lawes'.[76] However 'these heritable Shirefdomes and Regalities, which being in the hands of the great men, do wracke the whole countrie' (i.e. 'these heritable sheriffdoms and regalities, which being in the hands of the great men, do wreck the whole country').[77] Cairns has shown that complaints about heritable jurisdictions had also been made during the reign of James's mother.[78] In 1587 James tried to address these problems. Acts were passed to address these lairds,

> delighting in all mischiefs and most unnaturally and cruelly wasting, slaying, harrying and destroying their own neighbours and native country people, … [and] renew[ing] their most barbarous cruelties and godless oppressions[.][79]

Special hearings of the privy council would be convened to hear complaints. Lairds were required to compile a census of their tenants. They became liable for their tenants' behaviour and had to pay security against harm done by them. Similar other measures also attempted to bring these areas under central control. However, these were not all successful and further measures to extend royal and state authority to these areas continued throughout James's reign.[80]

Another challenge to the application of 'good laws' was the islands of Orkney and Shetland. These had been received in pledge from Denmark

---

[75] Cooper, 'King *versus* the Court of Session'.
[76] [James VI], *The Workes*, 162.
[77] [James VI], *The Workes*, 163.
[78] Cairns, 'Historical introduction', 91.
[79] *RPS* 1587/7/70.
[80] Cairns, 'Historical introduction', 91–3.

in 1468–9 as security for a debt which had never been paid. Law in these islands had traditionally been Norse law, but significant quantities of Scots law and feudal practice had been received by the end of the sixteenth century. This meant that the law in these isles was mixed and unique. This mixed nature of the law led to some cases of injustice, some of which were exacerbated by the earl.[81] Robert Stewart, illegitimate son of James V, had been created Earl in the Isles.[82] That grant had given him comprehensive heritable jurisdiction: he was justice, sheriff and baillie in Orkney and held the traditional legal office of *foud* in Shetland. In 1568, the earl also acquired the bishopric and the jurisdictional powers associated with it. This gave the earl extraordinary power locally: he was the highest authority with respect to political power, land holding and control of the courts.[83] In 1575 thirty-three complaints were made to the privy council against the earl. One of those complaints was that he was applying old Norse law in preference to Scots law where it gave him advantage against his vassals, tenants and other people living in the isles.[84] These charges as well as a later attempt to strip Robert Stewart of the earldom came to little effect. This was in part because he was a favourite uncle of James. However, after Robert's death in 1593, his son Patrick continued to rule the isles as a tyrant until James ordered his arrest in 1611.[85] Parliament passed an act ordering that subjects in Orkney and Shetland were to be obedient to the king's laws.[86] Patrick Stewart was executed in 1615.

D. CONCLUSION

James was one of the most important kings in Scottish history. During his reign, reform of the state constitution meant that the institutions of

---

[81] On the causes of this and the impact on the law, see Katherine E. Anderson, 'The influence of Scots and Norse law on law and governance in Orkney and Shetland, 1450–1650' (unpublished PhD thesis, University of Aberdeen, 2015).

[82] On whom, see Peter D. Anderson, 'Stewart, Robert, first Earl of Orkney (1533–1593)', *Oxford Dictionary of National Biography* (Oxford: Oxford University Press, 2004), http://www.oxforddnb.com/view/article/26504.

[83] Anderson, 'The influence of Scots and Norse law', 24.

[84] Anderson, 'The influence of Scots and Norse law', 25.

[85] On whom, see Peter D. Anderson, 'Stewart, Patrick, second Earl of Orkney (c. 1566/7–1615)', *Oxford Dictionary of National Biography* (Oxford: Oxford University Press, 2004), http://www.oxforddnb.com/view/article/26500.

[86] On which, see Goodare, 'The Scottish parliament', 161; Anderson, 'The influence of Scots and Norse law', 25–7; Cairns, 'Historical introduction', 93–4.

government were forever changed, particularly parliament. As will be shown in the next chapter, he also united Scotland and England together under one king successfully for the first time.

This chapter has shown that in the 1580s and 1590s there was an increase in royal and state authority. James's government during this period of time was effective. The institutions of government were operated by men who were loyal to the king. These men would normally participate in the setting of government policy and ensure that these policies would be effective and were implemented. This meant that there was a significant increase in royal and state authority during this period of time.

This chapter has also examined James's own view of his royal authority. His view of kingship was one of divine right. He was God's anointed king and that meant his royal authority was supreme. James's view of kingship was one informed by the wider politics of his time as well as from threats to his personal authority. He believed strongly in the divine right of monarchy, and the authority which followed from it. James saw this divine right as including a duty to rule as a good and godly king as well as a powerful one. One of the significant aspects of that was to ensure that the country was run by good laws. That included the making of good laws in the first place. During the 1580s and 1590s he reasserted royal authority in parliament, which at the time was undergoing reform in its role and increasing its efficiency. Provision of good laws also included making them widely known, so the collection and printing of old laws continued during his reign. Once a body of good laws was established, it needed to be properly applied. James thus attended the sittings of the Court of Session and legislation was passed to ensure its efficiency and good application of the laws. But the judiciary was able to resist James's direct interference with its judgements.

His desire to be a good king meant that James's relationship with parliament, the courts, the nobles and the Protestant kirk were (in general) constructive and effective. His period of Scottish rule showed him to be a strong but also a skilful and learned king. However, both his understanding of royal authority and his control over the institutions of government in Scotland were to be tested at the very beginning of the seventeenth century. The next chapter will discuss royal and state authority in the second part of James's reign.

E. SELECTED BIBLIOGRAPHY AND FURTHER READING

(1) Records of the Parliament of Scotland [*RPS*]

Act of revocation of fees and pensions which observes James's acceptance of government: *RPS* 1579/10/47.

Act setting out requirements to be eligible as a judge: *RPS* 1579/10/55.

Act declaring royal authority: *RPS* 1584/5/8.

Act preventing church ministers from acting as judges: *RPS* 1584/5/12.

Act setting out a commission for reform of the Court of Session: *RPS* 1584/5/33.

Act expanding the jurisdiction of the Court of Session: *RPS* 1587/7/33.

Act establishing a commission to collect, consider and print the laws: *RPS* 1592/4/67.

Act confirming requirements to be eligible as a judge: *RPS* 1592/4/72.

Acts regulating behaviour of judges: *RPS* 1594/4/33, 1594/4/37.

(2) Books

Blakeway, Amy, *Regency in Sixteenth-Century Scotland* (Woodbridge: Boydell Press, 2015).

Brown, Keith M., *Noble Power in Scotland from the Reformation to the Revolution* (Edinburgh: Edinburgh University Press, 2011).

Brunton, George, and David Haig, *An Historical Account of the Senators of the College of Justice, from its Institution in MDXXXII* (Edinburgh: Thomas Clark, 1832).

Finlay, John, *Men of Law in Pre-Reformation Scotland* (East Linton: Tuckwell Press, 2000).

Goodare, Julian, *State and Society in Early Modern Scotland* (Oxford: Oxford University Press, 1999).

Goodare, Julian, *The Government of Scotland 1560–1625* (Oxford: Oxford University Press, 2004).

[James VI], *The Workes of the Most High and Mightie Prince, James, By the Grace of God King of Great Britaine France and Ireland, Defender of ye Faith, published by James, Bishop of Winton and Deane of his Majesties Chappel Royall* (London: Robert Barker & John Bill, 1616).

(3) Chapters in Books

Brown, Keith M., 'The second estate: parliament and the nobility', in Keith M. Brown and Alan R. MacDonald (eds), *The History of the Scottish Parliament, III: Parliament in Context, 1235–1707* (Edinburgh: Edinburgh University Press, 2010), 67–94.

Brown, Keith M., 'The Stewart realm: changing the landscape', in Steve Boardman and Julian Goodare (eds), *Kings, Lords and Men in Scotland and Britain, 1300–1625, Essays in Honour of Jenny Wormald* (Edinburgh: Edinburgh University Press, 2014), 19–33.

Cairns, John W., 'Historical introduction', in Kenneth Reid and Reinhard Zimmermann (eds), *A History of Private Law in Scotland* (Oxford: Oxford University Press, 2000) I, 14–184.

Cooper, Thomas Mackay, Lord Cooper of Culross, 'The King *versus* the Court of Session', in Lord Cooper of Culross (ed.), *Selected Papers, 1922–1954* (Edinburgh: Oliver and Boyd, 1957), 116–23.

Cramsie, John, 'The philosophy of imperial kingship and the interpretation of James VI and I', in Ralph Houlbrooke (ed.), *James VI and I: Ideas, Authority and Government* (Aldershot: Ashgate, 2006), 43–60.

Knafla, Louis A., 'Britain's Solomon: King James and the law', in Daniel Fischlin and Mark Fortier (eds), *Royal Subjects: Essays on the Writings of James VI and I* (Detroit: Wayne State University Press, 2002), 235–64.

(4) Articles in Journals

Goodare, Julian, 'The Scottish parliament and its early modern "rivals"', *Parliaments, Estates and Representation* 24 (2004), 147–72.

Smith, T. B., 'British justice: a Jacobean phantasma', *Scots Law Times News* (1982), 157–64.

(5) Digital Sources

Brown, Keith M., Alastair J. Mann and Roland J. Tanner, *The Scottish Parliament: An Historical Introduction, Part 6*, http://rps.ac.uk/static/historicalintro6.html.

Lee Jr, Maurice, 'Maitland, John, first Lord Maitland of Thirlestane (1543–1595)', *Oxford Dictionary of National Biography* (Oxford: Oxford University Press, 2004), http://www.oxforddnb.com/view/article/17826.

Murray, Athol, 'Preston, John, of Penicuik, Lord Fentonbarns (d. 1616)',

Oxford Dictionary of National Biography (Oxford: Oxford University Press, 2004), http://www.oxforddnb.com/view/article/22726.

Wormald, Jenny, 'James VI and I (1566–1625)', *Oxford Dictionary of National Biography* (Oxford: Oxford University Press, 2004); revised online edn September 2014, http://www.oxforddnb.com/view/article/14592.

CHAPTER 12

Authority and Government after 1603

A. INTRODUCTION

The previous chapter discussed royal authority during the first part of the reign of James VI. It showed that both royal and state authority increased during the 1580s and 1590s. However, James would need to reconsider his royal authority shortly thereafter.

Elizabeth I of England had remained unmarried. She therefore had no children to succeed her on the throne. In her older years she refused to identify her successor to the throne. England had previously experienced periods of strife when the succession had been unclear. The issue of the succession had thus been 'a central – maybe even *the* central – political issue of the early and mid-Elizabethan period'.[1] A dozen people were mentioned at one time or another as a possible successor to the English throne. James ultimately inherited the throne after Elizabeth's death in 1603, uniting successfully for the first time the two nations under one monarch. However, his accession was not without resistance. James relocated to London after receiving the crown. Once he did so he met with three challenges. The first was that he had to continue effective government in Scotland during his absence. The second was that he had to learn how to rule in England, which had a very different expectation as to the role of the king in government. The third was that he might need to rule both kingdoms in a co-ordinated and coherent manner.

This chapter will look at this later part of James's reign. First, it will examine his succession to the English throne. Insight into the wider understanding of the authority of the king can be had from examining some of the pamphlets written at the time. It is clear from these

---

[1] Susan Doran, 'James VI and the English succession', in Ralph Houlbrooke (ed.), *James VI and I: Ideas, Authority and Government* (Aldershot: Ashgate, 2006), 25–42 at 25.

pamphlets that James, his Scottish subjects and his English subjects did not share a common view on his right to succeed Elizabeth. Secondly, it will look at different challenges which James, the Scots and the English faced after his accession to the English crown and relocation to London. Finally, in the conclusion, this chapter will examine the reign of James's son and heir to both thrones, Charles I.

B. THE ENGLISH SUCCESSION

(1) Competing Claims to the Throne of Elizabeth I

James's claim on the English succession was a strong one. The accepted manner of determining the succession was by primogeniture. This system of inheritance favoured the first born son. Failing a son, the throne would fall to a daughter. If the deceased monarch had no legitimate children, as in the case of Elizabeth I, then the heir would be identified by looking to the wider family. James VI was the great-grandson of Henry VIII's sister. Primogeniture supported his claim as Elizabeth's nearest living relative.

However, there was at times significant resistance to James's accession amongst certain groups of Englishmen. Some hoped, for example, for a Catholic monarch to once more reign in England. Pamphlets expressed the different views of the various groups lobbying on behalf of their preferred claimants. The Scots had a significant interest in these discussions and were active participants in these debates.

(2) *A Conference Abovt the Next Svccession to the Crowne of Ingland* (1594)

Perhaps one of the most notable arguments against James's succession came from a pamphlet called *A Conference Abovt the Next Svccession to the Crowne of Ingland* (1594). It was published in the name of 'Doleman' but was probably written by an English Jesuit called Robert Persons.[2] The *Conference* purported to be an account of two speeches by a civil and a temporal lawyer, complete with their answers to questions put to them by a rapt audience.

The civil lawyer argued in that pamphlet that primogeniture was a man-made right and so was not absolute. As such, it should not alone

---

[2] Doran, 'James VI', 29–32.

determine succession to the throne. Rather the civil lawyer encouraged the listener to consider 'what were the true causes and principal points, which ought to be chiefly regarded ... in this great action of furthering or hindering any Prince towards a crowne'?[3] By asking this question of his audience he made it clear that it was the choice of the people of England, not the bloodline, which should determine the succession. Their most important consideration should be 'the seruice of God, and religion'.[4] Therefore,

> for any man to giue his helpe, consent or assistance towards the making of a king, whom he iudgeth or beleueth to be faultie in religion, & consequently would aduance either no religion, or the wrong, if he were in authority, is a most greuous and damnable sinne.[5]

This reasoning would have excluded James from the succession. Should any listener or reader have failed to note this point, the next speech would make it abundantly clear.

The temporal lawyer examined the competing claims to the throne. He examined James's claim first. He suggested that the Scottish claim is only supported by 'common opinion of vulgar men'[6] but that he 'confesse that I haue not founde very many in Ingland' who support it.[7] He dismissed James's right by primogeniture on the basis of the civil lawyer's speech. He suggested that James descended only from the House of York and not the House of Lancaster. These were the two competing houses during the Wars of the Roses. There is here an implicit threat of renewed civil war. The temporal lawyer then suggested that English law prohibited foreign-born aliens from inheriting the throne. An act made by Henry VIII favoured the succession of other Tudor descendants, those of the House of Suffolk. Mary, Queen of Scots's conspiring against Elizabeth I polluted her bloodline in respect to the succession, so James could not inherit through her.[8] The lawyer then raised more general concerns about uniting with Scotland: her impoverishment, rebelliousness, unsavoury allies, internal resistance, and the possible

---

[3] *A Conference Abovt the Next Svccession to the Crowne of Ingland, Divided into Two Partes ... Published by R. Doleman* ([s.n.]: N., 1594), 200.
[4] *A Conference Abovt the Next Svccession,* 207.
[5] *A Conference Abovt the Next Svccession,* 216.
[6] *A Conference Abovt the Next Svccession,* 108.
[7] *A Conference Abovt the Next Svccession,* 109.
[8] *A Conference Abovt the Next Svccession,* 107–18.

usurpation of 'chiefe place[s] of credit' in James's English royal court by the Scots.[9] However, 'the woorst and most dangerous pointe of al other, [is that] considering what the state of religion is in Scotland at this day, and how different or rather opposite to that forme which in Ingland is mainteyned'.[10] The temporal lawyer's overall message was clear: James had no good legal claim on the English succession, his succession would be socially disruptive, and it would pose an unacceptable threat to the Church and established religion.

(3) The Scottish Response to the *Conference*

There has been much discussion about how James saw the question of his succession, and the extent to which this view had an impact on how he dealt with domestic issues.[11] Doran, for example, has suggested that this pamphlet greatly unnerved James, and that as a result of this discomfit he sent ambassadors to both Protestant and Catholic monarchs to campaign for their support, imported arms to prepare for war, and treated with Pope Clement VIII.[12] Additionally he encouraged there to be a swift and strong response: 'The flow of tracts from Scotland demonstrated that James meant business'.[13] Perhaps James's own *Trew Law* was in part written as a response to the *Conference*'s arguments.[14] Whether or not this is correct, it is true that the pamphlet received attention in Scotland. The Scottish advocate, Thomas Craig of Riccarton, wrote a response to the claims made in the *Conference*.

Craig's response to the *Conference* is reasoned and learned. He was an accomplished lawyer and his power of rhetorical objection and legal analysis is brought to bear in his response. His tone is often one of outrage and he repeatedly expresses his disdain for the so-called Doleman: 'I knew this man to be a Hypocrite and a subtile Knave before, but now I have him in plainly for Forgery.'[15]

---

[9] *A Conference Abovt the Next Svccession*, 120.

[10] *A Conference Abovt the Next Svccession*, 123.

[11] See, for example, Pauline Croft, *King James* (Basingstoke: Palgrave Macmillan, 2003), 32–6 (who believes that it probably did), and Jenny Wormald, 'James VI and I (1566–1625)', *Oxford Dictionary of National Biography* (Oxford: Oxford University Press, 2004); revised online edn September 2014, http://www.oxforddnb.com/view/article/14592 (who believes it did not).

[12] Doran, 'James VI', 32–3.

[13] Doran, 'James VI', 41.

[14] Doran, 'James VI', 34.

[15] Thomas Craig of Riccartoun, *The Right of Succession to the Kingdom of England, in*

Craig divided his work into two books, to answer the two speeches in turn. In the first book he responds to the civil lawyer. He proves that monarchy is a part of the law of nature, that succession by inheritance was preferable to that by election under that law, and that even Elizabeth herself cannot disavow a rightful heir by primogeniture.

He then turns to the temporal lawyer's speech. He addresses each point in turn. The law of England itself supports primogeniture. The temporal lawyer misinterpreted the statutes about foreign-born aliens, which do not apply to princes. The Scots are nonetheless not considered foreign-born aliens under English law. Foreign-born princes have inherited previously in England as well as in most other nations. James could nonetheless be considered English as much as he could Scottish. The claims made about the House of Lancaster are wrong. Craig also dismantles the miscellaneous objections which were raised about the Scots generally. One of his conclusions addresses the first point made by his adversary:

in the first place *Doleman* says, that he knows few in *England*, who favour the King of *Scots* cause. The most serene King looks for no other Friends or Favourers of his cause, but such as Love and are Friends of Truth and Justice, *England* abounds with such as much as any Country whatsoever, neither does he doubt, but the minds of the rest will be so overcome with the Justice of his Cause, and excited by the Judgments of God, who is the most severe *avenger of all unjustice and unrighteousness of men*[.][16]

Craig here presented his readers with three choices. Support James because his claim is true and just. Support James because God favours him. Fail to support him and thereby incur the wrath of God.

(4) Conclusion

By 1603 James was Elizabeth's obvious successor. He had the political support of notable Englishmen, including Elizabeth's secretary and spymaster, Robert Cecil.[17] It is possible that James was also recognised by Elizabeth as her desired successor by a wave of her hand in her final

Two Books: Against the Sophisms of Parsons the Jesuite, who Assum'd the Counterfeit Name of Doleman (London: M. Bennet, 1703), 343.

[16] Craig, *The Right of Succession*, 347.

[17] Doran, 'James VI', 40–2.

moments. Whatever the truth of the matter, the English privy council invited James to take the throne. James accepted and in doing so achieved what English kings had attempted since Edward I. However the union was not to be an instant accomplishment. James would have to renegotiate his royal authority in both kingdoms.

C. JAMES'S ROYAL AUTHORITY AFTER THE UNION

(1) Identifying the Extent of Union

In 1604 James addressed the English parliament for the first time. In that speech he set out his intention for his two kingdoms: 'I hope … no man will be so vnreasonable as to thinke that I that am a Christian King vnder the Gospel, should be a Polygamist and husband to two wiues'.[18] The 'wives' mentioned were metaphorical. James was indicating here his early intention for Scotland and England to become fully united into one kingdom.

There were several aspects to that desire. He referred to the union as bringing the two nations together 'under one Imperiall Crowne', that of 'King of Great Britain'.[19] Neither the Scots nor the English accepted the idea that they had become a single kingdom. Rather they were two separate kingdoms who happened to share a single king. Neither recognised the title of 'King of Great Britain'.[20] James nonetheless claimed the title by proclamation in 1604.[21] He also introduced a new coin (the 'unite') for circulation across the kingdom.[22] And he introduced a new flag for British ships, now known as the Union Flag or Union Jack.[23] But one of his most ambitious plans was for unification of the two legal systems.

---

[18] Charles Howard McIlwain, *The Political Works of James I* (Cambridge MA: Harvard University Press, 1918) I, 272.

[19] James F. Larkin and Paul L. Hughes (eds), *Stuart Royal Proclamations* (Oxford: Oxford University Press, 1973–83) I, 95.

[20] See Bruce Galloway, *The Union of England and Scotland, 1603–1608* (Edinburgh: John Donald, 1986), 28–9, 35–8.

[21] Larkin and Hughes (eds), *Stuart Royal Proclamations* I, 94–8. On which, see Galloway, *The Union*, 60–1; Julian Goodare, *The Government of Scotland 1560–1625* (Oxford: Oxford University Press, 2004), 106–7.

[22] On which, see Galloway, *The Union*, 59–60.

[23] Wormald, 'James VI and I'; Goodare, *Government of Scotland*, 107.

(2) Harmonising the Law

A 'perfect union' between Scotland and England would mean one parliament for both kingdoms and one legal system. James regarded this as
a necessity but it was a controversial position.[24] There was much doubt
and controversy. For example, it was unclear whether such a legal union
could extend only to public law or be more comprehensive.[25] The resistance to union meant that James soon understood that unification could
only be a gradual process.[26] Indeed those who wrote favourably about a
union of laws tended to describe the process of perfect unification as a
gradual one.[27] The most thorough examination of the question of union
on the Scottish side was by Thomas Craig of Riccarton. 'Throughout
Craig's analysis, a fundamental distinction must ... be made between the
long-term project of the union and the short-term considerations of legal
policy.'[28] Craig provided a detailed comparison of both legal systems
to show that their historical similarities meant that they were already
closely related. Indeed, Craig argued that English common law was more
substantially influenced by its feudal roots and the civilian tradition than
was normally understood. His thesis seems to have been that unification
of the laws was not necessary or even desirable at that time but a long-
term convergence was inevitable. Such a convergence could be eased by
educating lawyers to appreciate both systems and by considering their
feudal background and the reason of the civilian tradition.[29]

[24] Alain Wijffels, 'A British ius commune? A debate on the union of the laws of
     Scotland and England during the first years of James VI/I's English reign',
     Edinburgh Law Review 6:3 (2002), 315–55 at 323–4.
[25] On the union of public law: Brian P. Levack, *The Formation of the British State:
     England, Scotland, and the Union 1603–1707* (Oxford: Clarendon Press, 1987),
     69–76; Brian P. Levack, 'English law, Scots law and the union, 1603–1707', in Alan
     Harding (ed.), *Law-Making and Law-Makers in British History: Papers Presented
     to the Edinburgh Legal History Conference, 1977* (London: Royal Historical Society,
     1980), 105–19 at 105–6; Wijffels, 'A British ius commune?', 343–8.
[26] Galloway, *The Union, passim.*
[27] Wijffels, 'A British ius commune?', 321, 324.
[28] Wijffels, 'A British ius commune?', 333.
[29] Thomas Craig, *De Unione Regnorum Britanniae Tractatus, with a Translation and
     Notes by C. Sanford Terry* (Edinburgh: Scottish History Society, 1909). On which,
     see J. D. Ford, 'Four models of union', *Juridical Review* (2011), 45–76 at 60–1; Brian
     P. Levack, 'The proposed union of English law and Scots law in the seventeenth
     century', *Juridical Review* (1975), 97–115 at 105–7; Levack, *Formation of the
     British State*, 77–81; Levack, 'English law, Scots law and the union', 108–10; John
     W. Cairns, 'Historical introduction', in Kenneth Reid and Reinhard Zimmermann
     (eds), *A History of Private Law in Scotland* (Oxford: Oxford University Press,

Such an extensive union does not appear to have been on the agenda of business for the first commission for union in 1604.[30] The only laws considered at that time were those hostile to the other nation and those relating to the border regions.[31] Perfect union was, however, raised in the English parliament in 1606–7. It was discussed within wider debates about Scottish naturalisation and access to English privileges. The tone of that discussion, as well as the reaction from the king and Scottish parliament, meant it became clear that a perfect union would not follow.[32] The matter might have been discussed again in 1609 between the king and his Scottish chancellor, Alexander Seton, Earl of Dunfermline.[33] However, any hope of legal union was ultimately frustrated.

So what were the reasons given for the resistance to a union of the laws? The English parliament and common lawyers were keen to preserve the excellence of English common law from interference. They were also concerned by the civilian element of Scots law, by a fear of the differences in the royal prerogative, and also by the misconception that legislation of the Scottish parliament did not require royal assent.[34] James's reassurances did little to ameliorate these concerns.[35] Some English pamphleteers argued that a union of crowns was merely a personal union in the body of the king and in no way necessitated a union of laws.[36] They also considered the impact on English foreign policy.[37]

Meanwhile the Scots were less vocal in their opposition but were

2000) I, 14–184 at 78; Wijffels, 'A British ius commune?', 332–7. For comparable arguments made by Scottish contemporaries, see Wijffels, 'A British ius commune?', 326.

30 Galloway, *The Union*, 62.

31 Galloway, *The Union*, 65–8, 96–8; Wijffels, 'A British ius commune?', 350–1.

32 Galloway, *The Union*, 115–19, 127–30.

33 Galloway, *The Union*, 145–7; Levack, 'The proposed union', especially 108.

34 Keith M. Brown, Alastair J. Mann and Roland J. Tanner, *The Scottish Parliament: An Historical Introduction, Part 7*, http://rps.ac.uk/static/historicalintro7.html; Levack, 'The proposed union', 99–101; Levack, *Formation of the British State*, 88–90; Galloway, *The Union*, 38–9; Wijffels, 'A British ius commune?', 337–9. See, on the recognition of similarities, Wijffels, 'A British ius commune?', 328–9. On the support from the civil lawyers in England, see Levack, 'The proposed union', 103–5; Levack, *Formation of the British State*, 81–5; Levack, 'English law, Scots law and the union', 112–15; Wijffels, 'A British ius commune?', 330.

35 J. D. Ford, 'The legal provisions in the acts of union', *Cambridge Law Journal* 66 (2007), 106–41 at 114; Levack, 'The proposed union', 101; Levack, *Formation of the British State*, 90–1.

36 On the pamphlets more generally (not necessarily about law), see Galloway, *The Union*, 48–53.

37 Wijffels, 'A British ius commune?', 348–9.

also concerned. The Scots saw 'no need to change the law of a nation which met its people's needs'.[38] In 1604 they had already feared that any introduction of a new 'British law' would effectively mean that Scots law would be replaced by English law. This concern was made more real by the English parliament's insistence that Scotland simply be incorporated into it, and by James's announcement in the English parliament that this might be the solution to the English commissioners' concerns.[39] They also saw this view expressed by English lawyers and pamphleteers. The English lawyer George Saltern, for example, identified the commonality between *Glanville* and *Regiam Majestatem* with the implied suggestion that Scotland should align more closely with that ancient common law.[40]

Wijffels has observed that overall the dialogue was hampered by 'a marked lack of consensus in their understanding of each other's legal systems, and hence of the very basis of any comparison.'[41] Within only a few years of the union of the crowns, it was clear that the union of the two political and legal systems would not proceed. The matter was dropped for the next forty years.[42]

(3) Challenges in England

The difference in James's European-informed, Scottish view of kingship and the rather different understanding in England initially caused him problems. He was unfamiliar with the mechanics of the rigid English civil bureaucracy, and fell short of its procedural expectations and became frustrated in the process. Further frustrations were evident in the early years of his English reign. The Scots and English nobility were frustrated at having to compete for positions of power and trust in James's household and governments. James was frustrated that he was removed from the parliament in Scotland and that he could not enjoy the

---

[38] Wijffels, 'A British ius commune?', 332.

[39] Ford, 'The legal provisions', 113; T. B. Smith, 'British justice: a Jacobean phantasma', *Scots Law Times* News (1982), 157–64 at 159, 161; Levack, *Formation of the British State*, 85–7; Levack, 'English law, Scots law and the union', 110–11; Galloway, *The Union*, 39–40.

[40] Galloway, *The Union*, 40; Wijffels, 'A British ius commune?', 330–1. For other examples, see Wijffels, 'A British ius commune?', 325.

[41] Wijffels, 'A British ius commune?', 328. See also Levack, 'English law, Scots law and the union', 115–16. On the impediment of the differences between the two systems, see Levack, *Formation of the British State*, 91–7.

[42] Levack, 'The proposed union', 109–15; Smith, 'British justice: a Jacobean phantasma'; Cairns, 'Historical introduction', 78.

same role in the English parliament because of its different nature and two chambers. His interpretation of his prerogative powers in relation to financial levies on trade led to tensions with parliament. That he drew on European traditions in defence of these rights drew outrage from English common lawyers. Their complaint was responded to forcefully by the king in 1606. James then chose to follow his earlier advice to his son. After 1610 he called parliament again only in 1614. That parliament lasted two months before James dissolved it. That meeting of parliament achieved very little. No English parliament met again until 1621. In Scotland, James had learned to run a country effectively through administrative bureaucracy and the support of those aspirants to whom he granted office. He proceeded on that basis in England.[43]

(4) Royal Authority in Scotland after the Union

Scotland meanwhile was ruled by a king who was not physically present. Although this presented certain challenges, James remained closely connected to his Scottish affairs.[44] He had already established an effective government run by the privy council. The council and other institutions of government were able to administer Scotland for James as an independent state. Goodare has noted that 'there were hardly any attempts to govern Scotland as an appendage of England'.[45]

A new office, the king's commissioner, was instituted to represent the king in parliament. He was to make speeches on James's behalf, further the royal agenda, and hear the comments and complaints of parliament. The first appointment to this position was in 1604, to John Graham, third Earl of Montrose. He had sat at various times as a lord of session, treasurer of Scotland, and president of the privy council. At the time of his appointment as commissioner, he also held the position of chancellor, which he demitted to Alexander Seton, Earl of Dunfermline.

Seton is a good example of a coincidence of fate which made remote

---

43 Wormald, 'James VI and I'. On James VI and I in England, see, for example, Croft, *King James*, ch. 3–4; Glenn Burgess, *Absolute Monarchy and the Stuart Constitution* (New Haven: Yale University Press, 1996). On James and the law in England, see Louis A. Knafla, 'Britain's Solomon: King James and the law', in Daniel Fischlin and Mark Fortier (eds), *Royal Subjects: Essays on the Writings of James VI and I* (Detroit: Wayne State University Press, 2002), 235–64 at 243–56. A useful introductory text on English legal history is John H. Baker, *An Introduction to English Legal History*, 4th edn (Oxford: Oxford University Press, 2002).

44 Goodare, *Government of Scotland*, 109–10.

45 Goodare, *Government of Scotland*, 64.

rule in Scotland easier: 'those with whom [James] had worked in the 1590s lived on until the 1620s, so that personal knowledge and shared political experience were maintained'.[46] In 1604 Seton received the office of chancellor and was a principal Scottish negotiator in the attempt at union with England. Prior to this appointment, he had been a lord of session for almost thirty years and had been the lord president of the Session for more than ten. His career had at times been troubled. He had been accused in 1596 by the kirk of being a Catholic sympathiser after allowing the return from exile of the Catholic Earl of Huntly. He had come into confrontation with James himself when as lord president he had presided over the controversial case *Bruce v Hamilton* in 1599. However, he was by that time in favour with both the kirk and the king. The reputation that he had established before James's departure allowed the conferral upon him of significant offices of governmental authority thereafter.

Small changes to the shape of parliament which had taken place in the sixteenth century also had a profound effect:

> Having almost disappeared as a meaningful estate, the restored episcopate of thirteen archbishops and bishops ... was entirely dependent on the crown. The rapid expansion of the noble estate meant that there were some new peers who were at least temporarily grateful to the king ... [E]ven cautious intervention helped to shape a chamber more predisposed towards the king's interests. Further support for the king was provided by the more formal recognition of the role in parliament of the seven or eight officers of state and from among the larger body of over thirty privy councillors.[47]

James remained actively involved in parliamentary affairs. He was thus able to drive his political agenda tactfully but effectively. Indeed his political strength in Scotland actually increased in his physical absence.[48] But this strengthening was not absolute and was a gradual process. This is seen in the passing of the controversial Five Articles of Perth. These

---

[46] Wormald, 'James VI and I'.

[47] Brown *et al.*, *The Scottish Parliament, Part 7*.

[48] Gillian H. MacIntosh and Roland J. Tanner, 'Balancing acts: the crown and parliament', in Keith M. Brown and Alan R. MacDonald (eds), *The History of the Scottish Parliament, III: Parliament in Context, 1235–1707* (Edinburgh: Edinburgh University Press, 2010), 1–30 at 18.

legislative measures brought the Scottish kirk into line with certain religious practices in England. During James's only visit to Scotland after 1603 (in 1617) he put these measures to the General Assembly of the kirk. They were not passed at first instance, but forced through at a subsequent meeting in 1618. They were ratified by parliament in 1621 but were again controversial.

However, the overall position was one of a useful working relationship:

> James VI's astute management gave him the political initiative over the estates, and while there was a legacy of frustration and irritation over aspects of royal policy, it would be unhelpful to overlook the extent to which king and parliament co-operated in pursuing a broad legislative agenda.[49]

D. CONCLUSION

The doubt over the English succession resulted in much debate about the nature of monarchy and the right of primogeniture. Lawyers in England challenged James's right to the succession on the basis of legal as well as religious arguments. These were answered in turn by those Scots keen to secure the succession for their king. Whatever part their responses played, if any, James did succeed to the English throne in 1603. Part of his vision for uniting the two countries was to harmonise the laws. Despite his attempts to do so, resistance from the commissioners appointed as well as among the wider political classes meant that his aim was frustrated. James also had to renegotiate his royal authority in England, which had a different understanding of the rights and roles of a monarch. In Scotland, James's reforms during the earlier part of his reign had increased his royal authority and control over parliament. He was thus able to work effectively and collaboratively with his Scottish institutions of government, despite his lack of physical presence in the country. His reign's success is attributable in part to his understanding of royal authority, the law and his skill as a politician.

James was widely mourned in both kingdoms on his death. That his death was of natural causes while he still sat on the throne makes him unusual for a Stewart monarch.[50] Mary had been deposed and was later executed by Elizabeth I. James V had died of a mysterious illness in the

---

[49] Brown *et al.*, *The Scottish Parliament, Part 7.*
[50] Wormald, 'James VI and I'.

wake of the loss at the battle of Solway Moss. James IV died in battle at Flodden. James III died in battle (or flight) at Sauchieburn. James II was blown up by his own cannon. And James I had been murdered by rebels. One might have hoped that James VI's successors would also have had long and peaceful reigns. However, their inability to imitate his intelligent kingship meant this constructive relationship between the king and the institutions of government was not to last long after James's death. The Stewart dynasty would end shortly thereafter.

Charles I succeeded his father as king in 1625. He did not have James's political astuteness. Charles's first visit to Scotland after his accession was in 1633. He was greeted when he arrived with cheering in the streets, but when he left he was significantly less popular. During his visit, he called a meeting of parliament in which he presented legislation for approval. This included the confirmation and extension of unpopular new tax measures as well as religious reform, which were interpreted as attacks on both the nobility and the kirk. His legislation also included an act of revocation.[51] The normal purpose of an act of revocation was to ratify or repeal acts done during the monarch's minority. However, Charles had received the crown as an adult. The members of the Scottish parliament were also much aggrieved by the conduct of that parliamentary meeting. Charles took note of the name of any man who spoke against him.[52] His measures passed, but the damage he did to his relationship with Scotland's political elite was significant.[53]

Within five years of that first visit, Charles imposed an English liturgy upon the Scottish kirk. This led to rioting in Edinburgh. The National Covenant was drawn up by notable lawyers as a document of protest from the Scottish nation. A series of political events which followed led to revolution: first, the two successive Bishops' Wars and then the Wars of the Three Kingdoms or British Civil Wars.[54] Charles lost the Civil Wars and was put on trial by the English parliament for treason against the people of England. The issues that were debated in that trial went to

---

[51] *RPS* 1633/6/24.

[52] John R. Young, 'Charles I and the 1633 parliament', in Keith M. Brown and Alistair J. Mann (eds), *The History of the Scottish Parliament, II: Parliament and Politics in Scotland, 1567–1707* (Edinburgh: Edinburgh University Press, 2005), 101–37 at 126–8.

[53] See, for example, the supplication written by William Haig, discussed in Young, 'Charles I', 128–37.

[54] These are sometimes referred to as the English Civil Wars. On the Court of Session's role and the competition for control over the court during this period, see David Stevenson, 'The Covenanters and the Court of Session, 1637–1650', *Juridical Review* (1972), 227–47.

the crux of the constitutional framework in England. The king argued that he could only be tried by a properly constituted court. However, the court in which he was tried was established by an act of parliament which had not been passed by the House of Lords or received the ratification of the king, so was not legislation legitimately passed. He also claimed that no king could be tried by his subjects because kings held their office directly from God. The prosecution argued, however, that subjects must have the right to hold their king to account and to prevent a bad king from acting tyrannically and needlessly spilling the blood of his people. Charles was convicted by the court and was executed. England entered a period as a republic.[55]

There was precedent in Scotland that a single bad monarch could be removed, as had also happened with James III and Queen Mary. Scotland invited Charles I's son, Charles II, to be king. Negotiations between Charles II (then in exile in the Netherlands) and the Scots led finally to the young king returning to Scotland to be crowned.[56] Meanwhile, however, the relationship between Scotland and England had soured. By the time Charles II was crowned on 1 January 1651, the English army was already in Scotland under the command of the successful parliamentarian and military leader, Oliver Cromwell. By the end of 1651, Charles II had fled back into exile and Scotland was under the military rule of the new English Commonwealth.[57]

E. SELECTED BIBLIOGRAPHY AND FURTHER READING

(1) Legislative Measures

Larkin, James F., and Paul L. Hughes (eds), *Stuart Royal Proclamations* (Oxford: Clarendon Press, 1973–83).

---

[55] For a short introduction, see Cairns, 'Historical introduction', 79–81.

[56] On which, see Sharon Adams, 'In search of the Scottish republic', in Sharon Adams and Julian Goodare (eds), *Scotland in the Age of Two Revolutions* (Woodbridge: Boydell Press, 2014), 97–114 at 104–14.

[57] See Cairns, 'Historical introduction', 81–2.

(2) Books

Burgess, Glenn, *Absolute Monarchy and the Stuart Constitution* (New Haven: Yale University Press, 1996).

Craig of Riccarton, Thomas, *The Right of Succession to the Kingdom of England, in Two Books: Against the Sophisms of Parsons the Jesuite, who Assum'd the Counterfeit Name of Doleman* (London: M. Bennet, 1703).

Craig [of Riccarton], Thomas, *De Unione Regnorum Britanniae Tractatus, with a Translation and Notes by C. Sanford Terry* (Edinburgh: Scottish History Society, 1909).

Croft, Pauline, *King James* (Basingstoke: Palgrave Macmillan, 2003).

[Doleman], *A Conference Abovt the Next Svccession to the Crowne of Ingland, Divided into Two Partes ... Published by R. Doleman* ([s.n.]: N., 1594).

Galloway, Bruce, *The Union of England and Scotland, 1603–1608* (Edinburgh: John Donald, 1986).

Goodare, Julian, *The Government of Scotland 1560–1625* (Oxford: Oxford University Press, 2004).

Levack, Brian P., *The Formation of the British State: England, Scotland, and the Union 1603–1707* (Oxford: Clarendon Press, 1987).

(3) Chapters in Books

Adams, Sharon, 'In search of the Scottish republic', in Sharon Adams and Julian Goodare (eds), *Scotland in the Age of Two Revolutions* (Woodbridge: Boydell Press, 2014), 97–114.

Doran, Susan, 'James VI and the English succession', in Ralph Houlbrooke (ed.), *James VI and I: Ideas, Authority and Government* (Aldershot: Ashgate, 2006), 25–42.

Cairns, John W., 'Historical introduction', in Kenneth Reid and Reinhard Zimmermann (eds), *A History of Private Law in Scotland* (Oxford: Oxford University Press, 2000) I, 14–184.

Knafla, Louis A., 'Britain's Solomon: King James and the law', in Daniel Fischlin and Mark Fortier (eds), *Royal Subjects: Essays on the Writings of James VI and I* (Detroit: Wayne State University Press, 2002), 235–64.

Levack, Brian P., 'English law, Scots law and the union, 1603–1707', in Alan Harding (ed.), *Law Making and Law-Makers in British History: Papers Presented to the Edinburgh Legal History Conference, 1977* (London: Royal Historical Society, 1980), 105–19.

Young, John R., 'Charles I and the 1633 parliament', in Keith M. Brown and Alistair J. Mann (eds), *The History of the Scottish Parliament, II: Parliament and Politics in Scotland, 1567–1707* (Edinburgh: Edinburgh University Press, 2005), 101–37.

(4) Articles in Journals

Ford, J. D., 'The legal provisions in the acts of union', *Cambridge Law Journal* 66 (2007), 106–41.

Ford, J. D., 'Four models of union', *Juridical Review* (2011), 45–76.

Levack, Brian P., 'The proposed union of English law and Scots law in the seventeenth century', *Juridical Review* (1975), 97–115.

Stevenson, David, 'The Covenanters and the Court of Session, 1637–1650', *Juridical Review* (1972), 227–47.

Wijffels, Alain, 'A British ius commune? A debate on the union of the laws of Scotland and England during the first years of James VI/I's English reign', *Edinburgh Law Review* 6 (2002), 315–55.

(5) Digital Sources

Brown, Keith M., Alastair J. Mann and Roland J. Tanner, *The Scottish Parliament: An Historical Introduction, Part 7*, http://rps.ac.uk/static/historicalintro7.html.

Wormald, Jenny, 'James VI and I (1566–1625)', *Oxford Dictionary of National Biography* (Oxford: Oxford University Press, 2004); revised online edn September 2014, http://www.oxforddnb.com/view/article/14592.

CHAPTER 13

Interregnum or Republic in the 1650s

A. INTRODUCTION

The previous two chapters examined the strengthening of royal and state authority during the reign of James VI. However, the king himself (and with him his royal authority) was eliminated within a quarter of a century of James's death.

Charles I's mismanagement of state affairs led first to civil war and ultimately to the fall of the monarchy in England. In place of royal authority, parliamentary authority became supreme. In Scotland, Charles's son was briefly installed as Charles II. But the Scots were already at war with England before the young king was crowned. A year of fighting began in September 1650. In August 1651 the English army captured the committee of estates. After this there was no credible government in Scotland independent of the occupying English forces; this is a useful point to date the beginning of the period of the interregnum or republic in Scotland.[1] In the following month the Scottish army was defeated by the English army under the command of Oliver Cromwell.

What was the position of Scotland to be within this new state? England had entered a new constitutional period as a republic, initially called the 'Commonwealth'. Scotland was incorporated into this Commonwealth and was managed by the Commonwealth parliament through a number of commissioners. They asserted their authority to legislate for and reform Scotland's infrastructure and in essence abolished Scotland's institutions of government. Probably the most powerful of these commissioners was George Monck, head of the occupying army. Scotland had entered a period of rule by military occupation.

This chapter will examine Scotland's new constitutional position during this period. It will then consider the reforms of Scots private

---

[1] The authors are grateful to Julian Goodare for his advice on this point.

law which were attempted. Finally it will examine the changes made to the administration of justice through the reform of the courts. These changes were to have a significant impact on legal practice in Scotland during this period. This can be seen in the case of Janet Johnstone, which will be revisited throughout this chapter.

B. JANET JOHNSTONE, LADY WAMPHRAY V EARL OF ANNANDALE (1658)

In 1656 John Johnstone of Wamphray died. He left behind him only a young daughter by the name of Janet. Traditionally, lands inherited by a child would be held 'in ward'. This meant that they were administered by another man (often the feudal superior) during the child's minority. In this case, that would have been the Earl of Annandale. Janet was served as heir with a retour of the lands by an inquest in November 1657.[2] Her new estates were said to be 'all within the stewartrie of Annandaill' (i.e. 'all within the stewartry [i.e. jurisdiction] of [the Earl of] Annandale').[3] She then received documents from the Chancery which would allow her to administer the lands without Annandale's approval. Annandale challenged these documents and the matter was eventually heard by Scotland's highest civil court in July 1658.

Two aspects of the situation were debated by the parties in court. The first was evidentiary and is not relevant here. The second related to the right which parliament had to amend Scottish customary law. Annandale argued that because Janet was a minor, the lands were held of him in ward as per Scottish custom. Janet's advocate answered by saying that this was contrary to 'the act of union, ratified in parliament, whereby wards are taken away'. Annandale's response was that the feudal rights which he claimed 'being a private right of the people, and so ancient ... it cannot be taken away'. What he meant by this was that parliament did not have the right to amend ancient customary rights. The young lady's counsel responded that she 'is not obliged to dispute the reason and power of parliament'. Her advocate also argued that 'the act being made in England', it had brought Scots law into line with a more traditional, restricted and

---

[2] For a discussion of retours, see Chapter 3.
[3] *Inquisitionum ad Capellam Domini Regis Retornatarum* ([London]: Printed at the command of George III, 1811–16) I, Dumfries item 234.

equitable interpretation of feudal obligation to the superior. The entry for the case concludes that 'the Commissioners' found for the young lady.[4]

This case raises various questions. What is the 'act of union' being cited here by Janet's advocate? Why would such an act of union regulate such things as wards? Who are 'the Commissioners' who heard this case? This chapter will address these questions.

C. THE CONSTITUTIONAL POSITION OF SCOTLAND

After Scotland became part of the Commonwealth, the parliament in England issued *A Declaration of the Parliament of the Commonwealth of England, Concerning the Settlement of Scotland*. This was to form the basis of the negotiations for union. It declared 'that *Scotland* shall, and may be incorporated into, and become one Common-wealth with this of *England*'.[5] It also to some extent set out the English vision of the previous two years' events. It recognised:

> That many of the people of *Scotland* who were Vassals, or Tenants to, and had dependency upon the Noble-men and Gentry (the chief Actors in these invasions and wars against *England*) were by their influence drawn into, and have been involved with them in the same Evils[.][6]

This was the Commonwealth parliament's explicit vision of the conquest wars. The nobility who had fought against Cromwell's army were to be duly punished by confiscation of their property. However, common men had also fought on the battlefield. The Scottish commoners had been compelled to fight against Cromwell only because of the feudal duties owed to their noble superiors. In recognition of this perceived inequity, the act promised that these common men would 'not only be pardoned for all Acts past, but be set free from their former dependencies and bondage-services'.[7] So these common men were not to be punished for

---

[4] *The Decisions of the English Judges, During the Usurpation, From the Year 1655, to His Majesty's Restoration* (Edinburgh: G. Hamilton and J. Balfour, 1762), 204–5. On this work, see Adelyn L. M. Wilson, 'Practicks in Scotland's interregnum', *Juridical Review* (2012), 319–52 at 327–47.

[5] *A Declaration of the Parliament of the Commonwealth of England, Concerning the Settlement of Scotland* (London: Robert Ibbitson, 1652), 6.

[6] *A Declaration ... Concerning the Settlement of Scotland*, 8.

[7] *A Declaration ... Concerning the Settlement of Scotland*, 8.

their part in resisting Cromwell's army. There was a promise too that they would be set free from their feudal servitude by the Commonwealth parliament.

This promise to free the common men of Scotland from their feudal servitude was somewhat reminiscent of the English approach to Ireland. Ireland had been conquered by Cromwell prior to the conquest of Scotland. There the local laws were suppressed in favour of the introduction of English law. This had been used to destabilise the original, Irish nobility. Lands were seized both after the first invasion of Ireland and after a reconquest in 1641. This land was granted to loyal Englishmen and the prominence of the traditional Irish nobility decreased.[8]

The Commonwealth government's declaration was thus in keeping with its previous practice in Ireland. There seems to have been concern in Scotland that similar legal reforms would follow. Therefore, the Scots representatives to the Commonwealth government requested in 1652 that the Scots be allowed 'the enjoyment of theire owne lawes in the freedomes of theire persons and in the right and p[ro]pertie of theire estates and goodes'.[9]

In 1654 the Commonwealth parliament passed a new 'Ordinance for Uniting Scotland into one Commonwealth with England'. This ordinance did not just confirm that Scotland was part of the Commonwealth but also made further regulations. Thirty Scots were to serve in the Commonwealth parliament. Goods prohibited in England were also now prohibited in Scotland. Taxes were to be imposed equally in both countries. And, true to the parliament's earlier promise, various feudal duties were abolished. This included 'all Fealty, Homage, Vassallage and Servitude', including feudal jurisdictions of the lords' courts,[10] military services, attendance, wardships, the right of the superior to choose his vassal's wife, and payments owed on the entry of an heir.[11] Hence Janet

---

[8] J. D. Ford, *Law and Opinion in Scotland during the Seventeenth Century* (Oxford: Hart Publishing, 2007), 135.

[9] C. Sanford Terry (ed.), *The Cromwellian Union: Papers Relating to the Negotiations for an Incorporating Union between England and Scotland 1651–1652* (Edinburgh: Scottish History Society, 1902), 42; Ford, *Law and Opinion*, 135.

[10] Elsewhere the ordinance said that the Scots were to be 'hereafter freed and discharged of, and from all suits, and appearing at or in any their Lords or Superiors Courts of Justitiary, Regality, Stuartry, Barony, Bayliary, Heritable Sheriffship, Heritable Admiralty, all which ... are hereby abolished and taken away'.

[11] 'April 1654: An Ordinance for Uniting Scotland into One Commonwealth with England', in C. H. Firth and R. S. Rait (eds), *Acts and Ordinances of the Interregnum, 1642–1660* (3 vols, London: H. M. Stationery Office, 1911), 871,

Johnstone, Lady Wamphray could claim that her feudal superior (the Earl of Annandale) no longer had any wardship rights in her lands. As is seen in her case, the ordinance made important changes to landholding rights in Scotland.

The policy of breaking the Scottish nobility through feudal reform and confiscation of lands was effective. The prominent Scottish churchman (and later principal of Glasgow University), Robert Baillie, said of the nobility in 1654 'weell near all are wracked' and their estates 'sequestrate or forfault'. He lamented the nation's being 'lulled up in a lethargick fear and despaire'.[12] However, this policy also caused political dislocation because the nobility had been essential to the previous governance of the country. In 1653–5 it led to rebellion and the Commonwealth government acknowledged that a new approach was required.

After 1655 'an honest attempt was being made to introduce settled government and purity in the administration of justice for the benefit of the general population, and in consequence in this period the administration was joined by many of the most patriotic Scotsmen.'[13] By this time Oliver Cromwell had risen to become the Lord Protector of the Commonwealth. This new position gave him power and authority not unlike a contemporary king or emperor. In 1655 he instructed that a new Council of State should be installed in Scotland. It was to have a remit 'for executing such instructions, as they shall receive from him and his council'.[14] This council was a civilian executive with devolved authority, although military men did serve on it (including Monck). Importantly, two Scots were included as council members. These men were Colonel William Lockhart and Sir John Swinton of Swinton, about whom more will be said later. The council was answerable directly to Cromwell and the Commonwealth parliament. It ensured a period of increased political stability during the remainder of the interregnum or republic.

accessed via British History Online, http://www.british-history.ac.uk/no-series/acts-ordinances-interregnum/pp871-875.

[12] *The Letters and Journals of Robert Baillie, Principal of the University of Glasgow* (Edinburgh: Bannatyne Club, 1841–2) III, 249–50. On Baillie's life, see David Stevenson, 'Baillie, Robert (1602–1662)', *Oxford Dictionary of National Biography* (Oxford: Oxford University Press, 2004); revised online edn May 2008, http://www.oxforddnb.com/view/article/1067.

[13] A. R. G. Macmillan, 'The judicial system of the Commonwealth in Scotland', *Juridical Review* (1937), 232–55 at 254.

[14] Thomas Birch (ed.), *A Collection of the State Papers of John Thurloe, III: December 1654–August 1655* (London: Fletcher Gyles, 1742), 711.

D. ATTEMPTED ASSIMILATION OF THE LAWS

The rhetoric in the declaration and ordinance indicated that to some extent a union was desired. However, in reality Scotland was a conquered country. This had implications for its circumstance in English eyes. One of the great English common lawyers had been a man named Sir Edward Coke. He had advocated a theory of law which can be called conquest theory. This was essentially that the conqueror of a Christian kingdom 'may at his Pleasure alter and change the Laws of that Kingdom, but until he doth make an Alteration of those Laws, the ancient Laws of that Kingdom remain'.[15] What that means is that a conquered country's laws might be changed by its victor. To put this another way, the Commonwealth parliament now had the right to reform Scots law.

The parliament called twenty-one Scots to London as representatives to negotiate on their country's behalf.[16] These men were not equal partners in the endeavour of union but were in effect only advisers.[17] They were invited to only some of the meetings of the union committee. They complained that they were denied copies of the proposed Bill of Union and were not consulted on its terms. In April 1653, the committee recognised the Scots' desire to be governed by Scots law until a joint legal system could be constructed.[18] However, in October, a new bill was proposed for uniting Scotland and England. The Scottish contingent tried to get a clause inserted which read 'the lawes, practiques and customes of Scotland shall be the only rule by which justice shall be administrat in all cases to the people of Scotland' except 'by a new law, now or heerafter to be made by common consent in Parliament'.[19] This clause would have been in keeping with conquest theory: Scots law would continue as it had been where unchanged by the Commonwealth parliament. This clause was not, however, present in the final version of the ordinance for uniting Scotland into one Commonwealth with England when passed the following April.

Over the next few years it became clear that the Commonwealth government instead planned to simply extend English law to Scotland.

---

[15] Calvin's case (1608) 7 Co. Rep. 2a, 17b; Ford, *Law and Opinion*, 103.

[16] A. Mark Godfrey, 'Parliament and the law', in Keith M. Brown and Alan R. MacDonald (eds), *The History of the Scottish Parliament, III: Parliament in Context, 1235–1707* (Edinburgh: Edinburgh University Press, 2010), 157–85 at 183. These are not to be confused with the thirty men who were meant to sit in parliament.

[17] Ford, *Law and Opinion*, 97.

[18] Ford, *Law and Opinion*, 97.

[19] Ford, *Law and Opinion*, 98.

In 1655 instructions were issued to Scotland to 'carry on justice there according to the laws of England'.[20] However, the judges in Scotland had reported that the Scots 'pleade hard to keepe the judges to the knowne statute law', by which they meant the law of Scotland.[21] In 1656 the Commonwealth parliament considered the ordinance of union and there was much debate about whether an incorporating union could be effective without the Scots receiving English law.[22] Finally, in June 1658 instructions were received that 'all proceedings in Courts of Justice are according to the Laws of England, in order that the peaceful union of England and Scotland may be preserved'.[23] This was one of the last orders in relation to judicial administration in Scotland made before Cromwell's death in September 1658.

However, these attempts at legal assimilation seem to have little practical impact.[24] This is seen in two collections of notes on cases heard during the interregnum or republic.[25] One of these collections included cases heard between 1655 and 1659 and was probably written by an advocate recently admitted to the profession.[26] Another collection of decisions was recorded between 1657 and 1658, probably by an expectant to the bar.[27] These men recorded the authorities pleaded before the court in around eight or nine per cent of their entries.[28] These men noted that several cases made reference to acts of the pre-interregnum parliament and of Roman law. This means that the Commission was applying Scots law. This continued even after the 1658 order was received. Notes on twenty-nine cases heard during the winter session of November 1658 to

[20] Ford, *Law and Opinion*, 109.
[21] Birch (ed.), *State Papers*, IV, 106; Ford, *Law and Opinion*, 110.
[22] Ford, *Law and Opinion*, 112.
[23] Ford, *Law and Opinion*, 114. Cf. Macmillan, 'The judicial system', 241–2; Godfrey, 'Parliament and the law', 182.
[24] See also, John W. Cairns, 'Historical introduction', in Kenneth Reid and Reinhard Zimmermann (eds), *A History of Private Law in Scotland* (Oxford: Oxford University Press, 2000) I, 14–184 at 105; Brian P. Levack, 'English law, Scots law and the union, 1603–1707', in Alan Harding (ed.), *Law-Making and Law-Makers in British History: Papers Presented to the Edinburgh Legal History Conference, 1977* (London: Royal Historical Society, 1980), 105–19 at 111; Godfrey, 'Parliament and the law', 183; Thomas Mackay Cooper, Lord Cooper of Culross, 'Cromwell's judges and their influence on Scots law', in Lord Cooper of Culross (ed.), *Selected Papers, 1922–1954* (Edinburgh: Oliver and Boyd, 1957), 111–15.
[25] Wilson, 'Practicks', 327–47.
[26] Wilson, 'Practicks', 339, 343.
[27] Wilson, 'Practicks', 334.
[28] Wilson, 'Practicks', 339, 345.

February 1659 survive. Four explicitly cite acts of the pre-interregnum Scottish parliaments.[29] One cites the books of Roman law.[30] Another is framed around Roman law arguments but does not refer to any particular text.[31] Earlier Scots or Roman law would not have been appropriate sources had the Commission been applying English common law as commanded. Rather the Commission continued to apply Scots law (and refer to sources of the civilian tradition) as it had done previously, except where acts of the Commonwealth parliament explicitly departed from this.

The attempt to extend English law to Scotland failed, in part, because of the constitution of the highest civil court at the time. This was not the Court of Session but a new Commission.

E. COMMISSION FOR THE ADMINISTRATION OF JUSTICE

The Court of Session had been closed since 1650 as a result of the war. The new government did not reopen the Session but rather replaced it with a new Commission to administer justice.[32] It was these commissioners who were referred to in the report of Janet Johnstone's case.[33]

The early days of the foundation of the new court would have been both a visual and commanding display of the authority of the new government. On 3 May 1652 at the market cross in Edinburgh the establishment of a new court to administer justice was announced and published. When the new commissioners heard cases they would sit in parliament house 'gairdit every day with a number of sodgeris' (i.e. 'guarded every day with a number of soldiers').[34] This would have provided a clear visual signal of the military might of the government on behalf of which the judges were hearing cases.

One of the commissioners' first tasks was to hear the swearing of oaths of loyalty to the new Commonwealth government by those men who

---

29   *Hope v Clackmanan, Scot v tenants, Buchart v Halyburton*, and *Earl of Dunfermline v tenants of Beltie*, in *Decisions of the English Judges*, 223–4, 224, 229, 232 respectively.

30   *Wilson v Graham* cites D.12.6.1, in *Decisions of the English Judges*, 231.

31   *Lord Dudhope v Lord Argyle*, in *Decisions of the English Judges*, 228–9.

32   On the Commonwealth government's view of the earlier Court of Session, see Macmillan, 'The judicial system', 235–7.

33   On changes to the inferior courts, see Cairns, 'Historical introduction', 102–3.

34   John Nicoll, *A Diary of Public Transactions and Other Occurrences, Chiefly in Scotland, From January 1650 to June 1667* (Edinburgh: Bannatyne Club, 1836), 96.

wished to hold office. Perhaps the first group of men called to swear the oath was the writers to the signet. They were summoned before the new bench 'craveand thair oathes and declaratiounes ... the refuiseris they sould be deposed, and utheris put in thair places' (i.e. 'craving their oaths and declarations ... the refusers they should be deposed and others put in their places').[35] The oath that each man had to swear included his rec-ognition of Scotland's incorporation into the Commonwealth, that there was no longer a king, that the Commonwealth parliament now ruled Scotland, and that the swearer would be loyal to the new commonwealth government.

> I *A. B.* being chosen and deputed by _____ do declare my willing
> Consent unto the Tender of the Parliament of the Commonwealth
> of England, That Scotland be Incorporated into, and made One
> Commonwealth with England, whereby the same Government that
> is established in England without King or House of Lords, may
> be derived to the People of Scotland; and that I will be True and
> Faithful unto the said Government, and live peaceably under, and
> yield obedience unto the Authority thereof exercised in Scotland.[36]

The advocates were also required to swear this oath. A newsletter of 5 June 1652 declared that 'The Advocats all (except 3 or 4) have refused to subscribe to the Tender of the union, whereby they stand incapable to plead'.[37] This was not accurate. Ford has found in the records of the first session of the new Commission that nineteen advocates were practising during this period. That they were still allowed to practise indicates that they had signed. Five of these nineteen had not practised previously. They were admitted to practice by the new Commission. Nine of the advocates had around ten years or less experience. Perhaps those new to the profession were more cautious of abandoning their position. Of those five who were already experienced advocates, four appeared only once.[38]

Seven commissioners were appointed to comprise the new bench. Only three of these were Scots or Scots trained; the other four were Englishmen.[39] Sir John Hope of Craighall was part of a famous legal

---

[35] Nicoll, *A Diary of Public Transactions*, 94. On the swearing of the writers, see Ford, *Law and Opinion*, 96.

[36] Terry (ed.), *Cromwellian Union*, 143–4.

[37] Terry (ed.), *Cromwellian Union*, 181.

[38] Ford, *Law and Opinion*, 96.

[39] Macmillan has stressed that this should not be viewed as 'a sinister attempt by the

dynasty. His father was the former king's advocate and collector of practicks, Sir Thomas Hope, who will be discussed at length in Chapters
14–16. Sir John had been a lord of session since 1632. He had supported
the surrender of Scotland to Cromwell during the wars of conquest.[40]
Sir William Lockhart was a soldier who supported Cromwell's government (because he had been offended by Charles I). He was later to marry
Cromwell's niece and become one of his favourites.[41] John Swinton of
Swinton was a trained lawyer and had supported Cromwell in advance of
the conquest. This had seen him excommunicated by the Scottish kirk.
He was recognised by his contemporaries as 'the man of all *Scotland* that
had been the most trusted and employed by *Cromwell*'.[42] Meanwhile,
three of the four Englishmen (John March, George Smith and Edward
Moseley) were experienced advocates of the English courts. The fourth
(Andrew Owen) was just completing his studies as a doctor of laws.[43]

However, this bench was not to serve for long. Lockhart and Swinton,
two of the three Scottish judges, were appointed to the commission to
unify the laws within only a few months and were thus unable to act.[44]
In 1653, Owen and March, two of the English judges, lost their position on the bench. Owen was dismissed for preaching in Edinburgh; the
cause of March's dismissal is not recorded, but he was allowed to stay
in Edinburgh and practise as an advocate. Hope was to retire from the
bench and died in 1654. Additional appointments were made. As time
passed, the appointments were less political and more in keeping with
maintaining an effective court. The men who were appointed were two
English lawyers with twenty years of experience in practice between
them, and one Scot with thirty years at the bar and two on the bench in

authors of the Union to pack the Scottish bench with English judges': Macmillan,
'The judicial system', 237.

[40] George Brunton and David Haig, *An Historical Account of the Senators of the College
of Justice, from its Institution in MDXXXII* (Edinburgh: Thomas Clark, 1832),
289–90; Vaughan T. Wells, 'Hope, Sir John, Lord Craighall (1603x5–1654)', *Oxford
Dictionary of National Biography* (Oxford: Oxford University Press, 2004), http://
www.oxforddnb.com/view/article/13728.

[41] Timothy Venning, 'Lockhart, William (1621?–1675)', *Oxford Dictionary of National
Biography* (Oxford: Oxford University Press, 2004); revised online edn May 2006,
http://www.oxforddnb.com/view/article/16907.

[42] *Bishop Burnet's History of His Own Time* I (London: for Thomas Ward, 1724),
128; John Coffey, 'Swinton, John (c. 1620–1679)', *Oxford Dictionary of National
Biography* (Oxford: Oxford University Press, 2004), http://www.oxforddnb.com/
view/article/26851.

[43] Ford, *Law and Opinion*, 97–8; Brunton and Haig, *An Historical Account*, 346.

[44] Macmillan, 'The judicial system', 240.

the Session. Even with these appointments there were only five commissioners for the administration of justice, only one of whom had any previous experience in Scots law.[45]

This was insufficient and the Commission ceased to operate. A backlog of around 50,000 cases had arisen, which is extraordinary given the size of the population at the time.[46] The advocates began lobbying for the Commission to reopen and additional appointments were made.[47] Two new judges were appointed to deal with the judicial business which had previously been undertaken in the Outer House. The Outer House was mentioned already in Chapter 8.[48] Only competent and knowledgeable judges would have been able to undertake its work effectively.[49] It is thus unsurprising that the two new judges appointed were both experienced Scots lawyers.[50] However, it was the next three appointments which are particularly revealing of the new focus on appointing the best men, and all three were Scots. These three men next appointed were not obvious supporters of the new government. Indeed all three were said to have resisted their appointment. Sir Archibald Johnstone of Warriston (the grandson of Thomas Craig of Riccarton) and Alexander Brodie of Brodie had both served as lords of session. The third man, Sir James Dalrymple of Stair, had not served on the bench previously but was a particularly competent advocate and would later become probably the most important lawyer in Scottish legal history. In 1657–9, there were therefore eight judges who regularly sat, four Englishmen and four Scots.[51]

The Scottish appointments to the bench hampered the attempt to extend English law to Scotland. Ford has noted that the constitution of the bench in the court in 1655–6 would have meant that a Scottish judge would have sat in the Outer House. This is where the majority

---

[45] On these appointments, resignations and dismissals, see Ford, *Law and Opinion*, 98–100.

[46] Cairns, 'Historical introduction', 104. Macmillan seems to place blame for this backlog on the Session rather than the Commission: Macmillan, 'The judicial system', 236.

[47] Ford, *Law and Opinion*, 108.

[48] On the composition of the court, see Macmillan, 'The judicial system', 243–6.

[49] Ford, *Law and Opinion*, 109; Macmillan, 'The judicial system', 239. The restoration of an effective Outer House is suggested as one reason why 'There was to be an enormous increase in the volume of business handled by the court after 1655': Ford, *Law and Opinion*, 111.

[50] Ford, *Law and Opinion*, 109; Macmillan, 'The judicial system', 239.

[51] Although the balance shifted for the final session of the court, with the death of one of the English judges, George Smith: Ford, *Law and Opinion*, 114–15. Cf. Macmillan, 'The judicial system', 240.

of business was undertaken. The judges in the Inner House would thus normally have comprised four English judges and two Scots. However, the Scots judges would likely have had a leading role in the discussion of those cases.[52] Ultimately Ford has suggested that 'The assimilation of the substantive laws had apparently been impeded by the failure to send enough English judges into Scotland, and the Scots had been able to press home their advantage by securing a majority on the bench' in 1657.[53]

F. CONCLUSION

This chapter has shown that Scotland was part of the Commonwealth with England during the 1650s. This new constitutional position meant that Scotland was ruled by the Commonwealth parliament through parliamentary commissioners. In the latter half of the decade the Scottish Council of State acted as a devolved, civilian executive authority. Part of the ideological campaign of the Commonwealth government was the breaking of the old Scottish feudal structures. This goal was set out clearly in the documents of union. These can also be seen in the context of the wider goal to extend English law to Scotland. This latter aim was ultimately frustrated, partly by the practicalities of legal practice in Scotland at the time. The Court of Session had been replaced. The new bench was initially dominated by English lawyers, whereas the Scots were not all legally trained and were at least in part political appointments. However, over time the balance changed and there were a number of Scots appointments made. The Scottish judges undertook a significant proportion of the judicial business of the court. This might explain why instructions to the court to apply English law were not successfully implemented.

The changes made by Cromwell and the parliamentarians did not last after the fall of their government. After Cromwell's death in September 1658, his son was incapable of sustaining the Commonwealth. In May 1659, the Protectorate and Commonwealth fell. Scotland and England separated again into two distinct states. The Commonwealth parliament invited Charles to be King of England. He was crowned in London in May 1660. He was also restored in Scotland, but was not re-crowned

---

[52] Ford, *Law and Opinion*, 111.
[53] Ford, *Law and Opinion*, 117.

separately.[54] Royal authority was reasserted. It was exercised in Scotland through Charles's secretary of state, the Earl of Lauderdale. The Court of Session, applying Scots law, reopened in 1661. The Scottish parliament also reopened and formally declared its recognition of Charles II's royal authority.[55] New oaths to the king required to be sworn.[56] The acts passed during the interregnum or republic were rescinded.[57] Sir James Dalrymple of Stair removed all the references to practice during the period from his recently written *Institutions of the Law of Scotland* so that none would appear in the printed edition of the text.[58]

The initial return of widespread recognition of royal authority did not last long. Indicators of dissent against Lauderdale have been identified as early as 1669. In the 1670s this resistance formed into a new political association known as the 'country party'. Its aim was to limit royal authority and this became increasingly linked to Presbyterian religious thinking when Charles II's Catholic brother inherited the throne as James VII. Widespread country party thinking was to have a significant role in the deposition of James in 1688 and the installation of his daughter, Mary, and her husband, William of Orange, as the new king and queen. Scotland took the opportunity to negotiate terms with the new royal couple, the terms of which were enshrined in a new constitutional document called the Claim of Right of 1689. More will be said about this document in Chapter 19.

It was, for the rest of their lives, a source of criticism levied against those that had benefited from the interregnum regime. Sir James Dalrymple of Stair, for example, was criticised in 1689 for, amongst other things, having taken advantage of the Cromwellian occupation. He defended his acceptance:

> I was made a Judge, supposing I would be as acceptable to the nation as any, yet I did not embrace it without the approbation of the most eminent of our ministers that were then alive, who did wisely and justly distinguish, between the commissions granted by

[54] The authors are grateful to Julian Goodare for his observations on these events.
[55] *RPS* 1661/1/17.
[56] For example, *RPS* 1661/1/88. On the restoration, see Cairns, 'Historical introduction', 105–8.
[57] *RPS* 1661/1/158. On this period, see Cairns, 'Historical introduction', 105–8.
[58] Adelyn L. M. Wilson, *The sources and method of the* Institutions of the Law of Scotland *by Sir James Dalrymple, 1st Viscount Stair, with specific reference to the law of obligations* (PhD thesis, University of Edinburgh, 2011), 15–19; Ford, *Law and Opinion*, 121–2.

usurpers, which did relate only to the people, and which were no less necessary than if they had prohibit baking or brewing but by their warrand, and between these which relate to councils for establishing the usurped power, or burdening the people[.][59]

He was still being attacked for and defending his advancement during that regime thirty years after the fall of the Cromwellian regime, and despite a long and successful career during that time.

The events of the period were to leave another lasting impression on Scotland's legal history. The interregnum reforms were not sustained beyond the Restoration. However, that they had ever been attempted contributed to the creation of a lasting feeling of protectiveness over the Scottish legal system. This was to be reflected in future discussions about union with England in 1707, which will be examined in Chapter 19 and in the second volume.

G. SELECTED BIBLIOGRAPHY AND FURTHER READING

(1) Records of the Parliament of Scotland (*RPS*) and other Legislative Measures

Act recognising the royal authority of Charles II: *RPS* 1661/1/17.
Act requiring oaths of loyalty to the king: *RPS* 1661/1/88.
Act rescinding interregnum legislation: *RPS* 1661/1/158.
A Declaration of the Parliament of the Commonwealth of England, Concerning the Settlement of Scotland (London: Robert Ibbitson, 1652).
Firth, C. H., and R. S. Rait (eds), *Acts and Ordinances of the Interregnum, 1642–1660* (3 vols, London: H. M. Stationery Office, 1911), published with a table and introduction at www.british-history.ac.uk/no-series/acts-ordinances-interregnum.

(2) Books

Birch, Thomas (ed.), *A Collection of the State Papers of John Thurloe* (7 vols, London: Fletcher Gyles, 1742).

---

[59] Sir James Dalrymple, Viscount Stair, *An Apology for Sir James Dalrymple of Stair, President of the Session, By Himself* (Edinburgh: J. Ballantyne & Co, 1825), 8–9.

The Decisions of the English Judges, During the Usurpation, From the Year 1655, to His Majesty's Restoration (Edinburgh: G. Hamilton and J. Balfour, 1762).

Ford, J. D., *Law and Opinion in Scotland during the Seventeenth Century* (Oxford: Hart Publishing, 2007).

Nicoll, John, *A Diary of Public Transactions and Other Occurrences, Chiefly in Scotland, From January 1650 to June 1667* (Edinburgh: Bannatyne Club, 1836).

Terry, C. Sanford (ed.), *The Cromwellian Union: Papers Relating to the Negotiations for an Incorporating Union between England and Scotland 1651–1652* (Edinburgh: Scottish History Society, 1902).

(3) Chapters in Books

Cairns, John W., 'Historical introduction', in Kenneth Reid and Reinhard Zimmermann (eds), *A History of Private Law in Scotland* (Oxford: Oxford University Press, 2000) I, 14–184.

Cooper, Thomas Mackay, Lord Cooper of Culross, 'Cromwell's judges and their influence on Scots law', in Lord Cooper of Culross (ed.), *Selected Papers, 1922–1954* (Edinburgh: Oliver and Boyd, 1957), 111–15.

Godfrey, A. Mark, 'Parliament and the law', in Keith M. Brown and Alan R. MacDonald (eds), *The History of the Scottish Parliament, III: Parliament in Context, 1235–1707* (Edinburgh: Edinburgh University Press, 2010), 157–85.

Levack, Brian P., 'English law, Scots law and the union, 1603–1707', in Alan Harding (ed.), *Law-Making and Law-Makers in British History: Papers Presented to the Edinburgh Legal History Conference, 1977* (London: Royal Historical Society, 1980), 105–19.

(4) Articles in Journals

Macmillan, A. R. G., 'The judicial system of the Commonwealth in Scotland', *Juridical Review* (1937), 232–55.

Wilson, Adelyn L. M., 'Practicks in Scotland's interregnum', *Juridical Review* (2012), 319–52.

(5) Digital Sources

Coffey, John, 'Swinton, John (c. 1620–1679)', *Oxford Dictionary of National Biography* (Oxford: Oxford University Press, 2004), http://www.oxforddnb.com/view/article/26851.

Venning, Timothy, 'Lockhart, William (1621?–1675)', *Oxford Dictionary of National Biography* (Oxford: Oxford University Press, 2004); revised online edn May 2006, http://www.oxforddnb.com/view/article/16907.

Wells, Vaughan T., 'Hope, Sir John, Lord Craighall (1603x5–1654)', *Oxford Dictionary of National Biography* (Oxford: Oxford University Press, 2004), http://www.oxforddnb.com/view/article/13728.

CHAPTER 14

Legal Literature

A. INTRODUCTION

Scotland has a particular set of books which have been used to reveal the law. Previous chapters have made reference to different types of legal literature which were produced in medieval or early modern Scotland. This has included *Regiam Majestatem* and the medieval law books, printed editions of statutes produced by commissions, collections of decisions reflecting the 'practick' of the court, and digests which drew together various sources under subject headings. These types of legal literature continued to be produced in the seventeenth century. However, these works were produced in greater volume and took on a new character during this period. This was in part because several became printed whereas previously they had been available in manuscript only. In the late sixteenth and early seventeenth century there was also the rise of two new genres of legal literature, which can be identified as building on these earlier types of legal writing. Treatises on discrete topics of law and institutional writing on the whole of private law were an important development for Scottish legal literature during this period and remained as such thereafter.

The availability of Scottish legal literature during this period was important for several reasons. It allowed lawyers to identify with greater ease what a plausible reading of Scots law might be in a particular case. This was perhaps of particular assistance to aspiring lawyers. It will be shown in Chapter 17 that previous study of Scots law was not required for those seeking admission as an advocate in the Court of Session. This meant that a newly admitted practitioner might have had little understanding of Scots law and would have had to learn this in the early years of his practice. A lack of literature on Scots law made this task very challenging. How would one learn a legal system which was available only in disparate collections of case notes and printed collections of statutes?

The difficulty of the task can be seen in the nostalgic reflections of one of the king's advocates in the seventeenth century, Sir Lewis Stuart of Kirkhill. He had confessed to friends and colleagues 'that he had almost despaired of making the transition ... into forensic practice in Edinburgh' as a young advocate when he joined the profession in 1613.[1] Stuart was, to some extent, at an advantage over some other new advocates. He had studied Roman law in France and his father was a writer (a member of a lesser branch of the legal profession). However, it was his discovery of one particular treatise on the law, *Jus feudale* by Thomas Craig, which allowed him to learn local practice. Other practitioners also encountered this difficulty and recognised the importance of Craig's work for aspiring lawyers.[2] This was explicitly mentioned by the man who edited *Jus feudale* for print in the mid-seventeenth century.[3] In recognition of this widespread difficulty, several of the works on Scots law produced in the seventeenth century had an explicit aim of improving the education of aspiring lawyers and, sometimes, of the wider laity.

This chapter will examine five types of legal literature being produced in the seventeenth century. First, it will examine the continued practice of instituting commissions to reprint the laws. Second, it will examine the collections of decisions which reflected the practick of the court. Third, it will discuss the digests which continued (to a greater or lesser extent) in the manner of Balfour's practicks. Fourth, it will examine the earliest treatises on discrete parts of the law. Finally, it will discuss institutional writing, which can be seen as a development of the latter part of the century. Before examining these types of literature, however, it is necessary to mention briefly the method of circulation of texts during this period.

---

[1] J. D. Ford, *Law and Opinion in Scotland during the Seventeenth Century* (Oxford: Hart Publishing, 2007), 46; Francis J. Grant (ed.), *The Faculty of Advocates in Scotland 1532–1943, with Genealogical Notes* (Edinburgh: Scottish Record Society, 1944), 201.

[2] On Craig, see John W. Cairns, 'Craig, Thomas (1538?–1608)', *Oxford Dictionary of National Biography* (Oxford: Oxford University Press, 2004), http://www.oxforddnb.com/view/article/6580.

[3] Ford, *Law and Opinion*, 46.

B. MANUSCRIPT AND PRINTING IN EARLY MODERN SCOTLAND

It should be remembered that the principal method of transmission of texts during this period of time was by handwritten manuscript. This method of transmission could give rise to several problems with a text. Copies were made by writing a model text out by hand. A person who wanted a copy of a text and intended to undertake the copying himself might make deliberate changes as he wrote. He might, for example, omit sections of text which did not seem relevant to him; conversely, he might add to the text his own observations or other additional material. He might also delegate the task of copying to another person or to several different people. Professional scribes were likely to produce more accurate texts than lay scribes. However, no matter how skilled the copyist, errors and changes to the text would occur. Different manuscript copies of a text therefore varied in accuracy, legibility and content. New copies would also be made from earlier copies as texts began to circulate. This meant that the errors and changes to the text could become compounded in descendant copies. Manuscripts might also be unbound or loose, so pages could be lost or inserted out of order.[4] The organic nature of manuscript texts is shown in the example of collections of decisions below. It should also be kept in mind when consulting manuscript texts.

Printing was introduced into Scotland in 1508. The task of printing a text was normally undertaken by a professional printing house. The process was complex. A manuscript copy of the text to be printed would be provided to the house. The printer would read a short piece of the text and then reconstruct it by inserting reliefs of letters in mirror image into a frame. Letter by letter, word by word he would work to create the text which would appear on a single page. He would then cover this in printer dust and press the paper down onto it. His aim was to produce a page which was well presented. As such it was the printer who would decide on the text's spelling, abbreviations and punctuation. If he struggled to read the manuscript text provided to him, he may have to rely on his best guess as to what the author intended to say. The printed version of a text would therefore reflect (but not necessarily be identical to) what was written by the author.[5]

---

[4] Adelyn L. M. Wilson, 'The textual tradition of Stair's *Institutions*, with reference to the title "Of Liberty and Servitude"', in Hector L. MacQueen (ed.), *Miscellany Seven* (Edinburgh: Stair Society, 2016), 1–124 at 32–45.

[5] Wilson, 'The textual tradition', 65–7.

This complex process meant that printing was expensive, and was also heavily restricted. Therefore, very few law books were printed during the early modern period. Those which were printed in the sixteenth century tended to be official publications, such as the edition of the laws in 1566. In the seventeenth century, other law books (those which were likely to sell well) also began to be printed. But even these were normally circulated in manuscript for decades beforehand. Most of the legal literature mentioned in this chapter was not printed at all during the early modern period. Only in the eighteenth century did printing of law books become common.

C. EDITIONS OF THE LAWS

Chapter 9 mentioned the sixteenth-century commissions to make Scotland's laws accessible. These resulted in the reprinting of the acts of parliament after 1424 as well as the manuscript digests by Sir James Balfour of Pittendreich and David Chalmers of Ormond. There were also later such commissions. An important figure in relation to later projects to make the law accessible was the clerk register and lord of session, Sir John Skene of Curriehill.[6] He was from the north east of Scotland, and was unusual in that he was Gaelic-speaking. It is possible that he amused himself by including Gaelic puns in his legal writing.[7]

In 1597 Skene received a privilege from the king, James VI, to edit and reprint the acts of parliament from James I (1424) to the present day.[8] This privilege (which is reproduced in the book) made no mention of the edition produced during the reign of James's mother, Mary.[9] However, Skene's project can be viewed as an attempt to provide a more recent edition of the acts and thus largely address the same need – perhaps more

---

[6] On the commissions, see Ford, *Law and Opinion*, 38–9, 48–9, 53. On Skene's life, see Athol Murray, 'Skene, Sir John, of Curriehill (c. 1540–1617)', *Oxford Dictionary of National Biography* (Oxford: Oxford University Press, 2004), http://www. oxforddnb.com/view/article/25669.

[7] A. D. M. Forte, '"An marcach": a Gaelic sexual metaphor in the legal works of Sir John Skene of Curriehill?', *Scottish Gaelic Studies* 28 (2011), 49–54; A. D. M. Forte, '"Ane horss turd"? Sir John Skene of Curriehill – a Gaelic-speaking lawyer in the courts of James VI?', *Scottish Gaelic Studies* 23 (2009), 21–51.

[8] Sir John Skene of Curriehill (ed.), *The Lawes and Actes of Parliament, made be King James the First, and his Svccessovrs Kinges of Scotland* (Edinburgh: Robert Waldegrave, 1597).

[9] On which, see Chapter 9.

successfully.[10] Skene's printed edition of the acts also included various other materials. One of these was a tract by Skene called *De verborum significatione*, subtitled as an 'exposition of the termes and difficill words, conteined in the foure buikes of Regiam Majestatem, and uthers' (i.e. 'exposition of the terms and difficult words contained in the four books of Regiam Majestatem and others'). Skene explains various legal terms or concepts with reference to diverse sources. He cites Scots law, Roman law, English law and a number of humanist sources. The result might be considered to be an expanded dictionary of legal terms, and it was the first of its kind in Scotland.

Another of Skene's works was printed in 1609. Skene had produced a new edition of the oldest laws in Scotland. This new edition was printed under the overall title *Regiam Majestatem*, which was also the name of the important medieval lawbook.[11] In fact, Skene produced two new editions: one in Latin and one in Scots.[12] These new editions provided an accessible, coherent text of the medieval lawbook *Regiam Majestatem*.[13] Skene also produced edited texts of other early law books, including *Quoniam attachiamenta* (a book on practice in the feudal courts), a collection of statutes of the trade guilds, a work on the laws of the forests, a book on the laws of the Scottish burghs, and works on the courts of the barons, the burghs and the ayres. He also reprinted in that same volume the statutes of the earliest Scottish kings, from William the Lion (r. 1165–1214) to Robert III (r. 1390–1406). Skene further included in the Scots edition a short manual on procedure in the Court of Session, which highlighted the extent to which Scots procedural law had been influenced by civil law.[14]

Skene's edition of the medieval lawbooks was criticised by some because it reprinted them without taking account of which laws might be in desuetude.[15] Laws in desuetude were deemed to have lapsed through a lack of use over a long period of time. However, this does not really detract

---

[10] See Burnet's comments, reproduced in Ford, *Law and Opinion*, 40.

[11] Ford, *Law and Opinion*, 38–9, 48, 53.

[12] Sir John Skene of Curriehill (ed.), *Regiam Majestatem: The Auld Lawes and Constitutions of Scotland* (Edinburgh: Thomas Finlason, 1609); Sir John Skene of Curriehill (ed.), *Regiam Maiestatem Scotiae, veteres leges et constitutiones* (Edinburgh: Thomas Finlason, 1609).

[13] On Skene's critical, humanist treatment of his textual sources, see John W. Cairns *et al.*, 'Legal humanism in renaissance Scotland', *Journal of Legal History* 11: 1 (1990), 40–69 at 45–8.

[14] Ford, *Law and Opinion*, 507–8.

[15] Ford, *Law and Opinion*, 37–8, 40.

from Skene's achievement, which was to make the laws of Scotland available in an edited text to which lawyers could easily refer. The new edition meant that the problem which James Balfour of Pittendreich had encountered when writing his practicks (that there were many different manuscript versions of a work like *Regiam*) no longer applied.[16] Skene's intention may also have been to make these texts available to the wider laity.[17] Ford has suggested that the Latin edition might have been 'intended ... to be used by professional readers' whereas the Scots edition was explicitly for 'all Our Soveraigne Lords Leiges ... and to the universall commoditie of the common well of this Realme'.[18] There is evidence that the production of the Scots edition may have helped make the volume useful to those who perhaps did not meet the rigorous educational standards of the Court of Session's bar.[19]

It was only in the eighteenth century that the accuracy of Skene's edition of the laws was questioned.[20] Ford has suggested that Skene's liberal editing of the material might be viewed in the light of possibly conflicting desires to provide an accurate, humanist edition and to satisfy the need for a contemporary restatement of the law. Or perhaps it should be viewed in the context of the tension between promoting knowledge of Scots law and lessening the need to refer to continental learning.[21] Whatever the case,

> By arguing that the corpus of written law in Scotland should be taken to include the old books and acts, and by urging Scots lawyers to devote more time and attention to learning the local law, Skene had promoted a conception of a statutory and known [municipal law] that left limited scope for recourse to the common law, however that was understood.[22]

---

[16] Walter Goodal (ed.), *Practicks: or, A System of the More Ancient Law of Scotland. Compiled by Sir James Balfour of Pettindreich* (Edinburgh: Thomas and Walter Ruddimans, 1754), ix.

[17] Ford, *Law and Opinion*, 398.

[18] Ford, *Law and Opinion*, 398; Sir John Skene of Curriehill (ed.), *Regiam Majestatem. The Auld Lawes*, Epistle to the Reader.

[19] For examples of such groups, see Adelyn L. M. Wilson, 'The "authentick practique bookes" of Alexander Spalding', in Andrew R. C. Simpson *et al.* (eds), *Continuity, Change and Pragmatism in the Law: Essays in Memory of Professor Angelo Forte* (Aberdeen: Aberdeen University Press, 2016), 175–236 at 194, 195–200, 233.

[20] Ford, *Law and Opinion*, 56–7.

[21] Ford, *Law and Opinion*, 57.

[22] Ford, *Law and Opinion*, 130.

Skene's was not the last attempt to reprint the acts of parliament. Later editions by Thomas Murray of Glendook were produced in 1681 and 1682,[23] but were heavily based on Skene's edition.[24]

The availability of the printed acts allowed other types of literature to be based upon them. The king's advocate, Sir George Mackenzie of Rosehaugh, provided an extensive commentary on the acts of parliament.[25] He did not reproduce the statutes in that volume, but instead referred readers to both Skene's and Glendook's editions.[26] His purpose was to show how the acts printed in those other volumes should be interpreted. In doing so he made reference to the civilian tradition as well as other Scottish legal authorities and practick. Mackenzie, in his note to the reader at the beginning of his volume, mentioned the educational aim of his work: 'even after I was a Lawyer, I found that I understood not our Statutes ... and I wisht often then such an Interpreter, as now I hope this Book will be.'[27] What this means is that one of Mackenzie's explicit aims in producing his commentary was to aid in the education and understanding of lawyers, and perhaps also the wider laity as well. One can certainly imagine a lawyer at work at his desk with either Skene's or Glendook's editions of the statutes as well as Mackenzie's *Observations on the Acts of Parliament* in front of him.

D. COLLECTIONS OF DECISIONS

Collections of decisions continued to be maintained by advocates and judges. This does not appear to be the result of an official policy of record-keeping, but rather the result of many practitioners recording

---

23 Thomas Murray of Glendook (ed.), *The Laws and Acts of Parliament made by King James the First, Second, Third, Fourth, Fifth, Queen Mary, King James the Sixth, King Charles the First, King Charles the Second who now presently reigns, Kings and Queen of Scotland* (Edinburgh: David Lindsay, 1681); Thomas Murray of Glendook (ed.), *Laws and Acts of Parliament made by King James the First and his Royal Successors* (Edinburgh: for David Lindsay, 1682).

24 C. Innes, 'The Preface', in *The Act of the Parliaments of Scotland*, I ([sn]: at the command of the Queen, 1844), 1 at 29.

25 Sir George Mackenzie of Rosehaugh, *Observations on the Acts of Parliament* (Edinburgh: the Heir of Andrew Anderson, 1686). On Mackenzie's life, see Clare Jackson, 'Mackenzie, Sir George, of Rosehaugh (1636/1638–1691)', *Oxford Dictionary of National Biography* (Oxford: Oxford University Press, 2004); revised online edn January 2007, http://www.oxforddnb.com/view/article/17579.

26 Mackenzie, *Observations on the Acts of Parliament*, A4; Ford, *Law and Opinion*, 402.

27 Mackenzie, *Observations on the Acts of Parliament*, A4.

private notes on their practice. This was a habit of law men from all levels
of the profession, from those who were novices observing court proceedings through to the king's advocate and lord president of the Court of
Session. The level of detail and the aspects of the cases which were noted
was a matter of personal preference.

Other lawyers sought copies of these collections to help inform their
understanding of the reasoning of the court in earlier cases. The popularity of a collection might depend on a number of factors, such as the reputation of the recorder, the clarity with which he recorded the case and
the information which he chose to preserve. Some of these collections
have remained in manuscript. Others were printed by their recorder or
by the advocates after the recorder's death. Extracts from most of the
collections of decisions are now available in print in a nineteenth-century
compendium called Morison's *Dictionary*.[28] This compendium arranged
notes on decisions from many collections under subject headings. These
headings were drawn from the earlier compendium of Henry Home,
Lord Kames.[29] Morison's *Dictionary* provides a useful (although not
infallible) tool for accessing the decisions of the early modern period.[30]

The decisions of Sir James Dalrymple, Viscount Stair and Sir
Alexander Gibson of Durie were printed towards the end of the seventeenth century.[31] However, most collections circulated in the early

---

[28]   William Maxwell Morison (ed.), *The Decisions of the Court of Session from its
Institution to the Present Time, Digested under Proper Heads, in the Form of a
Dictionary* (Edinburgh: Bell and Bradfute, 1801–7); William Maxwell Morison (ed.),
*The Decisions of the Court of Session from its Institution until the Separation of the Court
into Two Divisions in the Year 1808, Digested under Proper Heads, in the Form of a
Dictionary* (Edinburgh: Archibald Constable and Company, 1811).

[29]   Adelyn L. M. Wilson, 'The method of William Maxwell Morison's Dictionary, with
reference to the decisions of Sir Richard Maitland of Lethington' (forthcoming).

[30]   Wilson, 'William Maxwell Morison's Dictionary'; *Index to the Decisions of the Court
of Session, Contained in all the Original Collections, and in Mr Morison's Dictionary of
Decisions* (Edinburgh: for W. and C. Tait, 1823), 499–532.

[31]   Sir James Dalrymple, Viscount Stair, *The Decisions of the Lords of Council and Session
in the most important Cases Debate before Them [1661–1681]* (2 vols, Edinburgh: Heir
of Andrew Anderson, 1683–7); Sir Alexander Gibson of Durie, *The Decisions of the
Lords of Council and Session in Most Cases of Importance, Debated, and brought before
Them; From July 1621, to July 1642* (Edinburgh: Heir of Andrew Anderson, 1690).
On these men, see J. D. Ford, 'Dalrymple, James, first Viscount Stair (1619–1695)',
Oxford Dictionary of National Biography (Oxford: Oxford University Press, 2004);
revised online edn October 2009, http://www.oxforddnb.com/view/article/7050;
Vaughan T. Wells, 'Gibson, Alexander, Lord Durie (d. 1644)', *Oxford Dictionary
of National Biography* (Oxford: Oxford University Press, 2004); revised online edn
May 2006, http://www.oxforddnb.com/view/article/10609.

modern period in manuscript only. This meant that if a lawyer wanted a copy of one of these texts then he had to find an existing copy and transcribe it himself or pay another to do so on his behalf. This practice meant that the collections of decisions were quite fluid. New cases and details were added whereas others were omitted or attributed to a different collector. A good example of this is seen in the seventeenth-century copies of a sixteenth-century collection by Sir Richard Maitland of Lethington. Maitland collected notes on cases between 1550 and 1577.[32] He included very few references to either Roman or canon law in his notes. This was an authorial choice. Other sources show that it was typical for advocates to base their arguments on learned authority.[33] Maitland simply did not record this detail in the notes which he made. However, in the seventeenth century there was concern to reflect the traditional learning in legal literature.[34] So one particular lawyer systematically supplemented his copy of Maitland's decisions with lots of references to Roman law as well as some references to the continental literature thereupon. This brought his copy of the text into line with the contemporary understanding of intellectual rigour. Other lawyers seeking a copy of Maitland's practicks therefore preferred to write out their copies from this updated version rather than one which perhaps reflected the original more closely. Therefore, most copies of Maitland's decisions which survive today present the text as a much more learned collection than it was originally.[35]

Meanwhile not all copyists were concerned to identify the original compiler of a collection of decisions. This meant that they did not always distinguish between those cases recorded by different lawyers as they copied cases into their own manuscript collections. This was the case with that same learned version of Maitland's decisions. That copy was included in a larger manuscript collection, between a copy of Sinclair's decisions and those of another sixteenth-century recorder, Sir Alexander Colville of Culross.[36] This can also be seen in collections

---

[32] A loose transcription of a reasonably reliable (although late) manuscript copy of Maitland's decisions has been printed as Robert Sutherland (ed.), *The Practiques of Sir Richard Maitland of Lethington, from December 1550 to October 1577: A Transcription of John Orr's MS, Glasgow University Library MS Gen 1333* (Edinburgh: Scottish Record Society, 2007).

[33] Gero Dolezalek, 'Alexander Colville', presented at the conference *Legal Literature in Sixteenth Century Scotland, Aberdeen, 2–3 June 2016*.

[34] See Ford, *Law and Opinion*, for example, 45–52.

[35] Adelyn L. M. Wilson, 'The transmission and use of the collected legal decisions of Sir Richard Maitland of Lethington in sixteenth and seventeenth century Scotland' (forthcoming, *The Library*, 2018).

[36] Wilson, 'The transmission and use of … Maitland'.

of seventeenth-century decisions. For example, a manuscript associated with Sir John Lauder of Fountainhall (a lord of session in the later seventeenth century) included decisions noted by several earlier recorders.[37] Two separate collections of decisions heard during the interregnum were drawn together into a single collection.[38]

There is a tendency in modern legal-historical scholarship to attempt to separate these collections back out into their constituent parts. This is extremely useful for identifying how the original text versions changed as they were circulated. It is also necessary to see how they were compiled. However, it is necessary to remember the fluidity which was characteristic of this genre of legal literature as it was perceived by contemporaries.

E. DIGESTS, DIGEST PRACTICKS OR PANDECTS

Chapter 10 examined Balfour's digest, which presented a discussion of the law arranged under subject headings. This manner of legal writing continued into the first half of the seventeenth century. Two of the most important examples took very different approaches in terms of their structure and the way in which the material was presented.

The king's advocate, Sir Thomas Hope of Craighall, compiled a digest which became known as his *Major practicks*.[39] This work was circulating by at least 1643.[40] Hope attempted to provide some kind of coherent or logical structure. He did this by arranging his subject titles by theme. The twentieth-century editor of the *Major practicks* has suggested that the titles relate to law and government, personal rights, real rights, inheritance, courts, actions, procedure, and crimes in that order.[41] Within each title Hope normally presented quotations or summaries from sources in the same order. The first sources quoted were *Regiam Majestatem*, other medieval law books, Balfour, Craig and (occasionally) Roman or canon law. An additional layer of references

[37] Adelyn L. M. Wilson, 'Practicks in Scotland's interregnum', *Juridical Review* (2012), 319–52 at 330–2.

[38] Wilson, 'Practicks', 327–8.

[39] James Avon Clyde (ed.), *Hope's Major Practicks 1608–1633* (Edinburgh: Stair Society, 1937–8). On whom, see David Stevenson, 'Hope, Sir Thomas, of Craighall, first baronet (1573–1646)', *Oxford Dictionary of National Biography* (Oxford: Oxford University Press, 2004); revised online edn May 2009, http://www.oxforddnb.com/view/article/13736.

[40] Ford, *Law and Opinion*, 44–5.

[41] Clyde (ed.), *Hope's Major Practicks*, I, xiii.

to the learned law and continental jurists might have been added by Hope's son, Lord Kerse.[42] Second, Hope included quotations from acts of parliament. He started with those acts which were printed and then gave those which remained unprinted. Third, he added any relevant acts from the privy council or acts of sederunt of the lords of session. Finally, he included his own notes on cases heard in the Court of Session between 1608 and 1633. Ford has therefore observed that the text of Hope's *Major practicks* presented 'a new trichotomy of sources, beginning with the common law found in the various books lawyers read, continuing with the statutory law contained in the records of parliament, council and session, and ending with practical observations on the decisions of the courts.'[43] The twentieth-century editor of the digest remarked that 'It consists of a collection of notes or jottings such as a busy practitioner might be expected to make as memoranda for his own professional use.'[44]

The second digest of significant importance was that by Sir Robert Spottiswoode of Pentland.[45] This was arranged under subject titles, which were presented alphabetically.[46] He thus took a different approach to Hope in terms of arrangement: alphabetical rather than systematic. Spottiswoode presented in his digest excerpts or summaries of various Scottish legal sources. Craig's *Jus feudale* was the most extensively quoted source.[47] Spottiswoode also drew on Balfour, sixteenth-century collections of decisions and a record of his own practice from 1623–36. However, there are relatively few citations or much reference to acts of parliament or the medieval law books.[48] He included significant quantities of Roman law and quotations from works by continental jurists. However, unlike Hope, these were not always presented in the same, defined order.

There are therefore some important differences between the digests of Hope and Spottiswoode. However, there are also significant similarities. Both works are essentially excerpts or summaries of legal sources, which

---

[42] Ford, *Law and Opinion*, 255.

[43] Ford, *Law and Opinion*, 441.

[44] Clyde (ed.), *Hope's Major Practicks*, I, xiii.

[45] Sir Robert Spottiswoode of Pentland, *Practicks of the Laws of Scotland* (Edinburgh: James Watson, 1706). On whom, see David Stevenson, 'Spottiswood, Sir Robert, Lord Dunipace (1596–1646)', *Oxford Dictionary of National Biography* (Oxford: Oxford University Press, 2004), http://www.oxforddnb.com/view/article/26169.

[46] Some of the manuscripts were arranged differently; see Ford, *Law and Opinion*, 201.

[47] Ford, *Law and Opinion*, 207.

[48] Ford, *Law and Opinion*, 207.

are arranged under subject headings. Both lawyers maintained notes on cases heard during their years in the profession and integrated these into their larger digests. Both also engaged (although to a differing extent) with the civilian tradition of learning.[49]

A note of caution should be exercised when considering decisions and digests. Both are often referred to as types of 'practicks'. Current understanding of this classification still rests on a division of practicks into 'decision practicks' and 'digest practicks'. This classification was put forward by McKechnie in 1936, since which time the discipline of Scottish legal history has advanced significantly.[50] The division is widely regarded as somewhat unsatisfactory. One example of why that division is unsatisfactory is found in the works of an Aberdeen advocate in the seventeenth century. Alexander Spalding worked principally in the Commissary courts in the north east of Scotland. He produced a collection of notes on cases heard during that time. He interspersed this record with notes on cases from Maitland and Balfour as well as general observations on the law and copies of other legal authorities. He also produced a separate work more along the lines of a digest, in which the titles were arranged systematically. The content was based on Balfour's practicks and Sir John Skene of Curriehill's tract on procedure but also drew heavily on Spalding's own decisions.[51] Neither Spalding's decisions nor his digest conforms particularly closely with McKechnie's definitions. The interaction of the two works might reflect something of how contemporaries understood the nature and usefulness of practicks.[52] Unfortunately, a serious advance on how to conceptualise decisions and digests has yet to be made.

F. MANUALS FOR PRACTICE

Sir Thomas Hope of Craighall was also the author of another important treatise from the first half of the seventeenth century.[53] Hope was not untypical for the period in that he hoped to use his elevated position

---

[49] Ford, *Law and Opinion*, 45.
[50] Hector McKechnie, 'Practicks, 1469–1700', in *An Introductory Survey of the Sources and Literature of Scots Law* (Edinburgh: Stair Society, 1936), 25–41 at 25–8.
[51] Wilson, 'The "authentick practique bookes"'.
[52] Wilson, 'The "authentick practique bookes"'.
[53] Sir Thomas Hope of Craighall, *Minor Practicks, or, A Treatise of the Scottish Law* (Edinburgh: Thomas Ruddiman, 1726).

within his profession to aid his sons in their own careers in law.[54] One of the ways in which he did this, so family legend held, was that he would recall various aspects of legal practice to his sons as he got dressed in the morning.[55] These concise descriptions of legal practice were written down by his sons by dictation.[56] One can picture Hope recalling detailed aspects of the law of inheritance as he pulled on his shirt before this rapt audience. These notes were eventually compiled together into a treatise called the *Minor practicks*.[57] This was a manual for practice as a lawyer from one advocate to his sons who would one day become advocates themselves. The *Minor practicks* became a popular tract among lawyers, and perhaps allowed some contemporaries to identify Hope as the successor to Craig as one of Scotland's great jurists.[58] Such comments might be true in two respects. First, both engaged to some extent with the civil and canon law.[59] Second, both were used as manuals for education by aspiring lawyers.[60] It was not, however, the only manual for practice. Sir John Skene's tract on procedure has already been mentioned, and others were produced for other courts.[61]

G. TREATISES AND INSTITUTIONAL WRITING

Treatises on individual topics of the law continued to be written and new editions of them produced. For example, at the end of the sixteenth century and the beginning of the seventeenth century four men wrote legal works on the law of the sea. Probably the best known of these

---

[54] For more on this pattern of behaviour, see Chapter 17.

[55] Hope, *Minor Practicks*, vii; Ford, *Law and Opinion*, 45. This legend is doubted by the twentieth-century editor of the *Major practicks*: Clyde (ed.), *Hope's Major Practicks*, I, xii.

[56] On the early transmission of this text, see Ford, *Law and Opinion*, 45.

[57] Another legal history legend (which is entirely apocryphal) relates to the clothing of Sir Thomas Hope of Craighall. Sir Walter Scott suggested that the practice of the Lord Advocate wearing a hat in court was attributable to Hope. However, this has shown to have been 'a late rationalisation to explain an obscure practice': John W. Cairns, 'Advocates' hats, Roman law and admission to the Scots bar, 1580–1812', *Journal of Legal History* 20 (1999), 24–61 at 26.

[58] Ford, *Law and Opinion*, 46.

[59] Ford, *Law and Opinion*, 275, 285.

[60] Ford, *Law and Opinion*, 285.

[61] On a manual for practice in the Admiralty court, probably by the admiral depute James Roberton of Bedlay, see J. D. Ford, 'A guide to the procedure of the Admiralty court', *Scottish Archives* 18 (2012), 95–107.

was by William Welwood, Master of law at St Andrews.[62] Probably the most reliable for an examination of Scottish maritime practice was by Alexander King, a depute judge in the Admiralty court.[63]

The best known treatise from the dawn of the seventeenth century was Thomas Craig's great work on the feudal law, *Jus feudale*, written probably between the 1590s and 1606.[64] This was a very large work which contextualised Scottish feudal law within the wider European tradition. It was written in Latin and was highly learned, drawing much from the continental tradition as well as Scottish legal sources. Craig also drew on his own experience of practice: he had been an advocate for around twenty years before he probably began to write.[65] Craig's work was very important and copies were sought by many lawyers during the seventeenth century.[66] Many manuscript copies of Craig's *Jus feudale* survive. Some of these are complete manuscript copies whereas others are only partial copies or summaries, in Latin or Scots, which were probably used by young lawyers as a study aid.[67] The demand for copies allowed the text to be printed in 1655.[68]

The mid-seventeenth century witnessed the birth of a new form of legal literature which became known as institutional writing.[69] The first lawyer to write a work which can be identified as 'institutional' in this sense was Sir James Dalrymple, Viscount Stair. His *Institutions of the Law of Scotland* is probably the most important Scottish law book.[70] It was initially conceived of as a collection of practicks, a digest similar to those collections of descriptions or quotations of legal authorities arranged

---

[62]   On which, see J. D. Ford, 'William Welwod's treatises on maritime law', *Journal of Legal History* 34:2 (2013), 172–210. On Welwood at St Andrews, see Chapter 17.

[63]   Ford's edition of King's treatise (Edinburgh: Stair Society, forthcoming).

[64]   John W. Cairns, 'The *Breve testatum* and Craig's *Jus feudale*', *Tijdschrift voor Rechtsgeschiedenis* 56:3 (1998), 311–32 at 317.

[65]   Cairns, 'The *Breve testatum*', 311. On Craig's career prior to writing, and the context in which he wrote, see ibid. 314–19.

[66]   Cairns, 'The *Breve testatum*', 312

[67]   On the epitomes, see Ford, *Law and Opinion*, 74–6, 80–2, 122, 247, 404; Cairns, 'The *Breve testatum*', 331–2.

[68]   Thomas Craig of Riccarton, *Jus feudale* (London: Stationery Society, 1655).

[69]   On institutional writing, see John W. Cairns, 'Institutional writings in Scotland reconsidered', *Journal of Legal History* 4:3 (1984), 76–117.

[70]   Sir James Dalrymple, Viscount Stair, *The Institutions of the Law of Scotland, Deduced from its Originals, and Collated with the Civil, Canon and Feudal Laws, and with the Customs of Neighbouring Nations* (Edinburgh: Heir of Andrew Anderson, 1st edn 1681, 2nd edn 1693).

under subject headings.[71] However, Stair's work exceeded the aim and scope of those other works. He was concerned to provide an intellectually rigorous structure to his work, with a view to reflecting a systematic approach to the law.[72] He thus did not rely on an alphabetical arrangement like Spottiswoode, or on *Regiam* as Balfour had. Rather he adapted the structure of the *Institutes*, the Roman emperor Justinian's textbook on Roman law. Stair wrote a treatise which considered first matters of jurisprudence and then the whole of Scots private law. Nor did Stair simply assemble Scottish authorities under his headings. Rather he drew discussions about various legal authorities into an overall narrative on the law. His was a critical examination of the development and current state of Scots law which extended to around 400,000 words in the first printed edition.

He made reference to Scottish authorities but also a wide range of other authorities, including Roman and canon law as well as early modern legal writers from several jurisdictions. Stair's understanding of the authority of these laws – and of the source of legal authority – was to have significant impact on contemporary understanding, as will be discussed in the following two chapters.

Stair's *Institutions* (as with Craig's *Jus feudale*) remained in manuscript for around twenty years after it was written in 1659–62. It was first printed in 1681, and a second edition followed in 1693. That second edition was significantly larger and the titles were divided differently. The original material on Scots private law was divided into three 'books'. A fourth book was added on the law of actions or procedure. This was partially derived from an earlier work by Stair on procedure called the *Modus litigandi* ('Method of litigation'). Stair's second printed edition was also significantly more learned than the first. For example, the number of references to Roman law more than doubled between editions.[73] It is this second expanded edition which was used as the basis for the four posthumous editions by later editors.[74]

Some later jurists adopted the institutional style which was arguably first used in Scotland by Stair. The king's advocate, Sir George Mackenzie also wrote an institutional work, which was first printed in

---

[71] Ford, *Law and Opinion*, 85–6.
[72] Neil MacCormick, 'The rational discipline of law', *Juridical Review* (1981), 146–60.
[73] Adelyn L. M. Wilson, *The sources and method of the* Institutions of the Law of Scotland *by Sir James Dalrymple, 1st Viscount Stair, with specific reference to the law of obligations* (PhD thesis, University of Edinburgh, 2011), especially 3.1.1.
[74] Wilson, 'The textual tradition', 65–73.

1684.[75] This was a much shorter and less complex exposition on the law. Like Justinian's *Institutes*, it was written as a student textbook. It thus provided an introduction for those who wanted to learn Scots law. This was useful because Scots law was often self-taught during this period, as will be discussed in Chapter 17. Mackenzie approached Scots law from a different viewpoint than Stair. They both also had different understandings of the authority of certain legal sources.[76] This means that Stair and Mackenzie did not always agree on their understanding of particular legal rules.[77] Both sources should therefore be consulted when trying to understand what the law might have been during the later seventeenth century.

Institutional writing continued into the eighteenth and nineteenth centuries. This will be examined in the second volume. However, it is useful to note here that the other two most important institutional writers were John Erskine and George Joseph Bell. Erskine's *Institute of Scots Law* (1773) and Bell's *Commentaries on the Law of Scotland* (1826) are, with Stair, the most important institutional works on Scots law.

H. CONCLUSION

This chapter has examined some (but certainly not all) of the most important contributions to Scottish legal literature in the seventeenth century. It has shown that Skene produced around the turn of the century an edition of the medieval laws as well as the acts of the Scottish parliament from the earliest time to the (then) present day. This continued the aim of the 1566 project mentioned in previous chapters, to aid lawyers and subjects by making the written law more accessible. However, it was not always clear how a statute should be applied. Hence Mackenzie's *Observations on the Acts of Parliament* showed how that legislation might be interpreted with reference to the learned law, other statutes and Scottish practick.

Collections of decisions of the court continued to be produced by individual lawyers. They conformed to a basic structure of recounting the

---

[75] Sir George Mackenzie of Rosehaugh, *The Institutions of the Law of Scotland* (Edinburgh: John Reid, 1684).

[76] Hector L. MacQueen, 'Mackenzie's Institutions in Scottish legal history', *Journal of the Law Society of Scotland* (1984), 498–501.

[77] See, for example, Adelyn L. M. Wilson, 'Stair, Mackenzie and risk in sale in seventeenth century Scotland', *Fundamina* 15:1 (2009), 168–90 at 170–3.

facts of the case, the arguments of the advocates, and the decision of the judges. Focus was on the debate at the bar rather than the decision of the bench. Collections would also, however, reflect the personal interests of their recorders, so the details which were recorded in the notes would vary between collections. Some were widely sought by lawyers, so many manuscript copies were produced. The transmission of the text in this way meant that the texts of these collections were highly fluid and changeable.

Digests of the law were also produced. However, one has to be cautious when considering works such as those digests by Spottiswoode and Hope (as well as earlier similar projects by Balfour and Chalmers) as being one discrete genre of legal literature. Whereas Spottiswoode emphasised the learned law, explicit reference to this was rare in Hope and perhaps entirely lacking from Balfour and Chalmers. The arrangement of titles was alphabetical in Chalmers and Spottiswoode but thematic in Balfour and Hope.

Manuals for practice such as Hope's *Minor practicks* were also made available during this period. This became an influential text because of its usefulness during a period in which there was little formal education for lawyers. This will be discussed further in Chapter 17.

Treatises such as Craig's *Jus feudale* and then later in the seventeenth century Stair's *Institutions* were to have a significant impact on contemporary understanding of the law and the nature of legal authority. New works of Scottish legal literature in the seventeenth century were later to surpass or replace earlier works. Skene's edition of *Regiam Majestatem* meant that reference to the earlier, unedited text was rendered unnecessary. Reference to the decisions recorded by Sinclair and even to Balfour's practicks became less common, with more recent collections being preferred.[78]

The study of this literature allows significant insight into contemporary perceptions of the authority of learned law and Scottish legal sources. This will be discussed in the following two chapters. However, it is worth noting at this stage that some of the literature produced during the seventeenth century also later came to be regarded as having inherent legal authority itself. In the nineteenth century certain legal works were seen to be so authoritative that they became binding on legal practice.[79] The term used to denote these works in modern Scottish legal practice is 'institutional writing'. This term is used in recognition

---

[78] Ford, *Law and Opinion*, 84.

[79] J. W. G. Blackie, 'Stair's later reputation as a jurist', in David M. Walker (ed.), *Stair Tercentenary Studies* (Edinburgh: Stair Society, 1981), 207–27.

of the fact that some of the works regarded as authoritative sources of law were printed under the title of 'Institutions of the Law of Scotland'. This was, for example, the name given by Stair to his great treatise. Indeed Stair's *Institutions* is recognised as the greatest of these institutional works. Mackenzie's *Institutions*, in contrast, has somewhat more doubtful authority in this regard.[80]

I. SELECTED BIBLIOGRAPHY AND FURTHER READING

(1) Books

Clyde, James Avon (ed.), *Hope's Major Practicks 1608–1633* (Edinburgh: Stair Society, 1937–8).

Craig, Thomas of Riccarton, *Jus feudale* (London: Stationery Society, 1655).

Dalrymple, Sir James, Viscount Stair, *The Institutions of the Law of Scotland, Deduced from its Originals, and Collated with the Civil, Canon and Feudal Laws, and with the Customs of Neighbouring Nations* (Edinburgh: Heir of Andrew Anderson, 1st edn 1681, 2nd edn 1693).

Dalrymple, Sir James, Viscount Stair, *The Decisions of the Lords of Council and Session in the most Important Cases Debate before Them [1661–1681]* (2 vols, Edinburgh: Heir of Andrew Anderson, 1683–7).

Ford, J. D., *Law and Opinion in Scotland during the Seventeenth Century* (Oxford: Hart Publishing, 2007).

Gibson, Sir Alexander of Durie, *The Decisions of the Lords of Council and Session in Most Cases of Importance, Debated, and brought before Them; From July 1621, to July 1642* (Edinburgh: Heir of Andrew Anderson, 1690).

Hope, Sir Thomas of Craighall, *Minor Practicks, or, A Treatise of the Scottish Law* (Edinburgh: Thomas Ruddiman, 1726).

Mackenzie, Sir George of Rosehaugh, *The Institutions of the Law of Scotland* (Edinburgh: John Reid, 1684).

Mackenzie, Sir George of Rosehaugh, *Observations on the Acts of Parliament* (Edinburgh: Heir of Andrew Anderson, 1686).

Morison, William Maxwell (ed.), *The Decisions of the Court of Session from its Institution until the Separation of the Court into Two Divisions in*

---

[80] Cairns, 'Institutional writings'.

the Year 1808, Digested under Proper Heads, in the Form of a Dictionary (Edinburgh: Archibald Constable and Company, 1811).

Skene, Sir John of Curriehill (ed.), *The Lawes and Actes of Parliament, made be King James the First, and his Svccessovrs Kinges of Scotland* (Edinburgh: Robert Waldegrave, 1597).

Skene, Sir John of Curriehill (ed.), *Regiam Majestatem: The Auld Lawes and Constitutions of Scotland* (Edinburgh: Thomas Finlason, 1609).

Spottiswoode, Sir Robert of Pentland, *Practicks of the Laws of Scotland* (Edinburgh: James Watson, 1706).

Sutherland, Robert (ed.), *The Practiques of Sir Richard Maitland of Lethington, from December 1550 to October 1577: A Transcription of John Orr's MS, Glasgow University Library MS Gen 1333* (Edinburgh: Scottish Record Society, 2007).

(2) Chapters in Books

Blackie, J. W. G., 'Stair's later reputation as a jurist', in David M. Walker (ed.), *Stair Tercentenary Studies* (Edinburgh: Stair Society, 1981), 207–27.

McKechnie, Hector, 'Practicks, 1469–1700', in *An Introductory Survey of the Sources and Literature of Scots Law* (Edinburgh: Stair Society, 1936), 25–41.

Wilson, Adelyn L. M., 'The textual tradition of Stair's *Institutions*, with reference to the title "Of Liberty and Servitude"', in Hector L. MacQueen (ed.), *Miscellany Seven* (Edinburgh: Stair Society, 2016), 1–124.

Wilson, Adelyn L. M., 'The "authentick practique bookes" of Alexander Spalding', in Andrew R. C. Simpson *et al.* (eds), *Continuity, Change and Pragmatism in the Law: Essays in Memory of Professor Angelo Forte* (Aberdeen: Aberdeen University Press, 2016), 175–236.

(3) Articles in Journals

Cairns, John W., 'Institutional writings in Scotland reconsidered', *Journal of Legal History* 4:3 (1984), 76–117.

Cairns, John W., 'The *Breve testatum* and Craig's *Jus feudale*', *Tijdschrift voor Rechtsgeschiedenis* 56:3 (1998), 311–32.

Cairns, John W., *et al.*, 'Legal humanism in renaissance Scotland', *Journal of Legal History* 11: 1 (1990), 40–69.

Ford, J. D., 'William Welwod's treatises on maritime law', *Journal of Legal History* 34:2 (2013), 172–210.

MacCormick, Neil, 'The rational discipline of law', *Juridical Review* (1981), 146–60.

MacQueen, Hector L., 'Mackenzie's Institutions in Scottish legal history', *Journal of the Law Society of Scotland* (1984), 498–501.

Wilson, Adelyn L. M., 'Stair, Mackenzie and risk in sale in seventeenth century Scotland', *Fundamina* 15:1 (2009), 168–90.

Wilson, Adelyn L. M., 'Practicks in Scotland's interregnum', *Juridical Review* (2012), 319–52.

(4) Digital Sources

Cairns, John W., 'Craig, Thomas (1538?–1608)', *Oxford Dictionary of National Biography* (Oxford: Oxford University Press, 2004), http://www.oxforddnb.com/view/article/6580.

Ford, J. D., 'Dalrymple, James, first Viscount Stair (1619–1695)', *Oxford Dictionary of National Biography* (Oxford: Oxford University Press, 2004); revised online edn October 2009, http://www.oxforddnb.com/view/article/7050.

Jackson, Clare, 'Mackenzie, Sir George, of Rosehaugh (1636/1638–1691)', *Oxford Dictionary of National Biography* (Oxford: Oxford University Press, 2004); revised online edn January 2007, http://www.oxforddnb.com/view/article/17579.

Murray, Athol, 'Skene, Sir John, of Curriehill (c. 1540–1617)', *Oxford Dictionary of National Biography* (Oxford: Oxford University Press, 2004), http://www.oxforddnb.com/view/article/25669.

Stevenson, David, 'Hope, Sir Thomas, of Craighall, first baronet (1573–1646)', *Oxford Dictionary of National Biography* (Oxford: Oxford University Press, 2004); revised online edn May 2009, http://www.oxforddnb.com/view/article/13736.

Wells, Vaughan T., 'Gibson, Alexander, Lord Durie (d. 1644)', *Oxford Dictionary of National Biography* (Oxford: Oxford University Press, 2004); revised online edn May 2006, http://www.oxforddnb.com/view/article/10609.

(5) Research Theses

Wilson, Adelyn L. M., *The sources and method of the* Institutions of the Law of Scotland *by Sir James Dalrymple, 1st Viscount Stair, with specific reference to the law of obligations* (PhD thesis, University of Edinburgh, 2011).

CHAPTER 15

Legal Authority and the Learned Laws

A. INTRODUCTION

It has been seen in previous chapters that Roman law was integral to the practice of the College of Justice or Court of Session during the sixteenth century. Chapter 7 showed that the collection of decisions by John Sinclair reveals a practice of framing Scots law according to the learned laws, or interpreting it narrowly where it was inconsistent with the learned laws, during the earliest period of the court. The decisions collected by the sixteenth-century lord of session Alexander Colville of Culross also show that the court attempted to 'bring the local practice into line with the learned laws'.[1] There is probably sufficient evidence to suggest that this was the typical approach of the court for much of the sixteenth century. It might reflect a view that the learned laws were a reliable guide to legal truth.

Advocates continued to draw on learned sources in their pleadings in the seventeenth century. However, the way in which they understood and conceptualised that learning was changing. This can be seen in practice in the case of John Waldrop and John Colquhoun, which was heard in the court in 1628. This chapter will briefly examine this case and then show further how understanding was changing with reference to three sets of contemporaries. Sir John Skene of Curriehill and Thomas Craig of Riccarton wrote early in the century. Sir Thomas Hope of Craighall and Sir Robert Spottiswoode of Pentland wrote in the 1620s–30s. And finally Sir James Dalrymple, Viscount Stair and Sir George Mackenzie of Rosehaugh wrote in the last half of the century. This area of legal-historical scholarship is still being developed and the perception which contemporary lawyers had of various legal authorities is still much

---

[1] J. D. Ford, *Law and Opinion in Scotland during the Seventeenth Century* (Oxford: Hart Publishing, 2007), 202–3.

debated. The following two chapters represent one interpretation of this evidence.

B. *JOHN WALDROP V JOHN COLQUHOUN* (1628)

Thomas Waldrop [or Wardrop] was mentally handicapped to the extent that he was not competent to manage his own affairs. According to the law he therefore required a tutor or guardian. This person would provide a financial security called a 'caution' and give oaths for his faithful administration of his office. Normally a tutor or guardian would be the nearest male relative on the paternal side of the family. This could include a brother, father, paternal uncle, and so forth. The relatives on this side of the family were called 'agnates'. Thomas's closest agnate was his younger brother, John. He either did not come forward as a tutor or he failed to provide the caution within the normal period of time. Therefore a more distantly related agnate called John Colquhoun received a grant from the king to become Thomas's tutor. John Waldrop raised a form of action to be named the tutor instead of Colquhoun.[2]

The case was heard in the Court of Session in 1628. Waldrop cited an act of parliament from 1585 in his favour. That act had related to a private matter. One of the previous earls of Arran had also required a tutor. That tutor had been his nearest male relative on his father's side, his nearest agnate. The tutor had then been exiled for crimes against the state. Parliament had passed the 1585 act to identify Arran's next nearest agnate as his new tutor. John Waldrop argued that the act showed that he as the nearest agnate was the rightful tutor by law.

Colquhoun responded by observing that the 1585 act had said that the agnates should be 'received and preferred according to the disposition of the common law'.[3] This reference to 'common law' he interpreted as Roman law. He found two texts of Roman law (both in Justinian's *Codex*, a compilation of imperial legislation) which required that the tutor be appointed in a timely manner. Essentially Colquhoun was arguing that parliament had intended that the statute be read in the wider context of the tradition of civilian learning, and that this learning meant that the

---

[2] Sir Robert Spottiswoode of Pentland, *Practicks of the Laws of Scotland* (Edinburgh: James Watson, 1704), 163; Sir Alexander Gibson of Durie, *The Decisions of the Lords of Council and Session in Most Cases of Importance, Debated, and brought before Them; From July 1621, to July 1642* (Edinburgh: Heir of Andrew Anderson, 1690), 349.

[3] *RPS* 1585/12/40.

statute was supplemented by additional caveats.[4] One of those caveats was that appointment had to be made promptly, as per Justinian's *Codex*. Colquhoun then observed that Waldrop had not put himself forward as tutor for more than a year. He argued that, by this inaction, Waldrop had failed to discharge the office of tutor faithfully. Therefore, he could not base his legal argument on the act.

The counter-arguments put forward by Waldrop (if there were any) were not preserved in either of the existing reports of this case. Nor is the reasoning of the judges explained. However, the lords of section favoured John Waldrop, so the argument put forward by Colquhoun was not successful.

This case is one of many examples which show that arguments based on Roman law continued to be pleaded in the Court of Session in the seventeenth century. But the court here was not persuaded by the argument that the Scottish statute should be interpreted in light of the wider Roman legal tradition. This was despite there being reference to the tradition of Roman law within the statute itself. This is contrary to the approach seen in Sinclair's practicks, discussed in Chapter 7, by which certain statutes were interpreted in light of the learning and truth of Roman law. So why did the court reject Colquhoun's argument? Does this represent a change in the understanding of the relationship between Scots and Roman law since the time of Sinclair?

C. THE AUTHORITY OF THE LEARNED LAWS IN WRITING AT THE BEGINNING OF THE SEVENTEENTH CENTURY

(1) Sir John Skene of Curriehill, c. 1540–1617

Chapter 14 showed that Skene's principal works were the editions of the medieval lawbooks and acts of parliament as well as his examination of legal terms, *De verborum significatione*. Cairns, Fergus and MacQueen have suggested that in these and Skene's other works:

> Skene is critical of what he perceives as a growing preference for Roman over Scots law in contemporary legal circles. He claims that lawyers tend to devote all their energies to acquiring a knowledge of Roman law and thereby neglect the law of Scotland, which ought

---

[4] On the difference between civil law and Roman law, see William M. Gordon, 'The civil law in Scotland', *Edinburgh Law Review* 5 (2001), 130–44 at 132–9.

to be their first and proper concern, a point elegantly driven home with a quotation from the Digest. Primacy of place is to be given to *lex scripta*, followed by [native] custom and, finally, 'the customs of foreign peoples', among which he includes Roman law.[5]

What this means is that Skene continued to consider the civilian tradition to be relevant to the practice of law in Scotland. Indeed his work made frequent reference to that traditional body of learning. He cited Roman law, continental jurists, canon law, Norman and English law in his *De verborum significatione* and in his tract on procedure. In doing so, 'he undoubtedly favoured the Civil law over the Canon in citations of the *utrumque ius*'.[6] The relationship which Skene envisaged between Scots law and the civil law is not yet fully understood.[7] However, it is possible that the view implicit in the work of the 1566 project (that Scots law was a body of learning and truth) was now being more widely understood. Skene's work might suggest that he saw Scots law as being learned in its own right. Perhaps he believed that the principles of Scots law could be applied without the need to bring them into line with the traditional *ius commune*. Rather, Skene's view may have been that one should make a legal case principally with reference to Scottish sources. Only if these were unable to resolve the issue should a lawyer seek an answer in the civil law or by analogy. The learning of the *ius commune* was useful to him in his writing: he used it to draw out comparisons and to show the learning of Scots law. But it was not to be preferred to Scots law.

(2) Thomas Craig of Riccarton, c. 1538–1608

Thomas Craig meanwhile began his *Jus feudale* with a discussion of the earliest laws of mankind. He explained that a system called natural law was something resorted to by early man. This is '*in animus hominum insito*

---

[5] John W. Cairns *et al.*, 'Legal humanism in renaissance Scotland', *Journal of Legal History* 11: 1 (1990), 40–69 at 53, quoting from Sir John Skene of Curriehill (ed.), *Regiam Majestatem, Scotiae veteres leges et constitutiones* (Edinburgh: Thomas Finlason, 1609), Dedication to the King.

[6] John W. Cairns, '*Ius civile* in Scotland, ca. 1600', *Roman Legal Tradition* 2 (2004), 136–70 at 159. For a note of the sources cited, see Gero R. Dolezalek, 'French legal literature quoted by Scottish lawyers, 1550–1650', in Bernard d'Alteroche *et al.* (eds), *Mélanges en l'honneur d'Anne Lefebvre-Teillard* (Paris: Éditions Panthéon-Assas, 2009), 375–91 at 386–7.

[7] Cairns, '*Ius civile*', 159.

naturae instinctu' (i.e. 'the intuitive appreciation of right which is native in human character').[8] Early man resorted to this sense of justice in judgements. From this arose a common understanding of conduct (which can be called the law of nations). Later again arose substantive national law.[9] Craig saw Roman law as such a system of substantive national law. He praised it in the strongest terms for its truth and influence.[10] However, he observed that recourse to Roman law had by that time been restricted in several nations.[11] He then stated: '*Nos tamen in hoc qualicunque regno Romanorum legibus ita obligamur quatenus legibus naturae & rectae rationi congruunt.*'[12] This can be translated as: 'In our own realm of Scotland we are bound by Roman Law so far as it appears to us to be consonant with natural equity and reason.'[13]

Craig then acknowledged that recourse to Roman law was sometimes necessary because of a lack of Scottish sources available during that period. Some areas of the law and some forms of action were particularly close to Roman law.[14] Indeed he recognised that:

> *Et ut verè dicam in rebus omnibus nostris & circa omnes res, hoc jus Civile ita diffunditur, ut nulla ferè quaestio, nulla facti species occurrat, in quo ejus vis & usus singularis non appareat manifestè;*[15]

This can be translated as:

> [A]nd to say truly, this Civil law so permeates all our law suits and about all business that scarcely no issue or no type of case arises in which its force and particular practice is not plainly obvious[.][16]

---

8   Thomas Craig of Riccarton, *Jus feudale* (London: Stationers Society, 1655), 2; James Avon Clyde (trans.), *The Jus Feudale by Sir Thomas Craig of Riccarton* (Edinburgh: William Hodge & Co., 1934), 1.1.5.
9   Ford, *Law and Opinion*, 222; John W. Cairns, 'The civil law tradition in Scottish legal thought', in David L. Carey Miller and Reinhard Zimmermann (eds), *The Civilian Tradition and Scots Law: Aberdeen Quincentenary Essays* (Berlin: Duncker and Humblot, 1997), 191–223 at 200.
10 Clyde (trans.), *Jus feudale*, 1.2.12.
11 Clyde (trans.), *Jus feudale*, 1.2.13.
12 Craig, *Jus feudale*, 11.
13 Clyde (trans.), *Jus feudale*, 1.2.14 (amended).
14 Clyde (trans.), *Jus feudale*, 1.2.14.
15 Craig, *Jus feudale*, 11.
16 Cairns, '*Ius civile*', 157 (amended). For a looser translation, see Clyde (trans.), *Jus feudale*, 1.2.14.

This might seem to be a complete endorsement of the authority and use-fulness of Roman law. However, Craig's position was significantly more subtle. His understanding is apparent only several titles later into the *Jus feudale* where he discussed the sources of reference for Scots law. Here Craig set out a hierarchy of laws. Natural law (*ius naturale*) was justice in its truest sense, which was discernible through reason and equity.[17] The second category of law was the *ius gentium*. This comprised those laws consistently followed across many nations which could to some extent be viewed as human civilisation's interpretation of natural law. Craig confirmed that the *ius gentium* or 'law of nations' should be applied when dealing with foreigners. However, he believed that it could be departed from by statute for cases between citizens of the same nation.[18] The third category was national law, and in Craig's case that was Scots law.[19] Should a case between citizens be heard which could not be decided with reference to a Scottish source of law, then a lawyer should look to the feudal law, then canon law, then the civil law.[20]

There is at first glance a contradiction here in Craig's discussions of the relationships between natural law, Roman law and Scots law. The first point to consider is that Craig seemingly saw substantive national law (including Scots law) as the ultimate achievement of the development of natural law and the law of nations. This is apparent when Craig's hierarchy in the context of what he said in the first title is taken into account. That natural law and the law of nations were men-tioned in title eight before the sources of Scots law shows that Craig saw these as being earlier sources of law. It does not imply that they are to be regarded as more authoritative than Scottish sources when resolving contemporary legal difficulties. Indeed Ford is clear that Craig expected lawyers to begin their analysis with Scottish sources:[21] 'The progression recommended here was clearly from *ius proprium* [i.e. Scots law] to *ius commune*'.[22] It is possible that Craig believed that where *ius proprium* fails to give an answer, then the lawyer should resort to those earlier types of law, natural law and the law of nations. These were embodied in the learned laws. Craig understood that the civilian

[17] Clyde (trans.), *Jus feudale*, 1.8.6–7.
[18] Clyde (trans.), *Jus feudale*, 1.8.8. See also John W. Cairns, 'Historical introduction', in Kenneth Reid and Reinhard Zimmermann (eds), *A History of Private Law in Scotland* (Oxford: Oxford University Press, 2000) I, 14–184 at 99–100.
[19] Clyde (trans.), *Jus feudale*, 1.8.9.
[20] Cairns, '*Ius civile*', 154–5.
[21] Ford, *Law and Opinion*, 228.
[22] Ford, *Law and Opinion*, 229.

tradition was reflecting (or perhaps superseding) the *ius gentium* and *ius naturale*.[23]

Craig's suggestion that reference should be made to the canon law before the civil law contradicts Skene. However, Craig limited the application of canon law to areas of the law such as the procedure of the Commissary court and legal issues within its jurisdiction.[24] Therefore, Craig saw canon law's authority as heavily restricted in terms of its scope. 'Craig nonetheless had several discussions of and allusions to Canon law and did cite its sources, though relatively infrequently.'[25] Cairns has suggested that overall Craig's view might have been 'that Canon law now had little continuing impact on the development of Scots law'.[26] Instead Craig drew heavily on the civil law. He often cited texts of Roman law, sixteenth-century jurists from the French schools and the famous Italian commentators Bartolus and Baldus. However, he did not often cite other jurists from the medieval period.[27]

(3) Conclusions on Skene and Craig

What can be concluded about the use of civil law and canon law by these two writers? It has been observed that:

> Skene and Craig united in their relegation of Roman law to a place below that of native Scottish sources ... Craig, however, appears readier [than Skene] to recognise that Roman law has been used by Scots lawyers and will continue to be used in cases of difficulty; but, agreeing with Skene, only where there is no written or customary Scottish source[.][28]

This means that both recognised that there was a continuing role for Roman law in Scottish practice. Both recognised a continuing but more muted role for canon law.[29] But their understanding of the importance

---

[23] Cairns, '*Ius civile*', 158; Ford, *Law and Opinion*, 229. See also Peter Stein, 'The influence of Roman law on the law of Scotland', *Juridical Review* (1963), 205–45 at 218–19.

[24] Cairns, '*Ius civile*', 156.

[25] Cairns, '*Ius civile*', 152.

[26] Cairns, '*Ius civile*', 153.

[27] Cairns, '*Ius civile*', 151.

[28] Cairns *et al.*, 'Legal humanism in renaissance Scotland', 53; Cairns, 'The civil law tradition', 203.

[29] See also Cairns, 'Historical introduction', 99–101.

of the learned laws respective to that of Scottish sources was materially different to that of Sinclair and Colville in the sixteenth century. This can be seen in Craig's *Jus feudale* where he discussed the 1585 act which was debated in the case between Waldrop and Colquhoun. Craig noted the traditional rules of the feudal law with respect to those deemed in need of guardianship:

> *Si furiosus, proximo agnato permittitur; donec in Comitiis publicis Lythcoae habitis anno 1585 utriusque par ratio facta sit, & personae fatui & furiosi, & bonorum administratio proximo adjudicata; Quod tamen sine ratione factum puto, cum tutela feudi semper in vassallo inhabili ad dominum redire solet.*[30]

This can be translated as:

> Both the care of the person and the administration of the property used to belong to the superior in the case of an idiot, and to the nearest agnate in the case of a lunatic, until the parliament held at Linlithow in 1585 placed the idiot and the lunatic in the same position, and gave the care of both person and property to the nearest agnate. There was however little reason for this in my opinion, since the custody of feudal estate ought in all cases in which the vassal is [incapable] to return to the superior.[31]

Craig here expressed the view that he disagreed with the position taken by the 1585 act of parliament. However, he accepts this as the position in Scots law. He does not attempt to undermine that rule or to interpret it in light of the contrary view found in the feudal law.

D. THE AUTHORITY OF THE LEARNED LAWS IN WRITING c. 1630

(1) Sir Thomas Hope of Craighall, 1573–1646

Hope's *Major practicks* was his digest of legal authorities under subject headings. He was in that work explicit about his view of the authority of

---

[30] Craig, *Jus feudale*, 273. See also the same view expressed later in the text: Clyde (trans.), *Jus feudale*, 2.20.5.

[31] Clyde (trans.), *Jus feudale*, 2.18.29 (amended).

the learned laws. A particularly interesting comment is found in his first title: 'the act of parliament 1493 c.51 allowes directlie the constitutions of the civil and cannon law in this realme' (i.e. 'the act of parliament 1493 allows directly the constitutions of the civil and canon law in this realm').[32] What this means is that parliament had confirmed that the learned laws could be cited in Scotland. Ford has suggested that Hope's reasoning here might be complex:

> his purpose may have been to defend the view that [the learned laws] formed a residual common law ... enjoying no greater authority than the writings of philosophers, poets and historians. This would certainly have been more consistent with the use he made of the learned laws both in the later titles of his major practicks and in his minor practicks. ... Hope's purpose in claiming that the civil and canon laws were regarded as common law in Scotland could not have been to indicate that definitive solutions were to be drawn from them in cases left doubtful by statutes and decisions.[33]

Hope's view of the learned laws seems to have been that they could still be cited because parliament had allowed this and because reference to them might be helpful. However, the learned laws were not binding on Scottish practice. This understanding is seen later in this same title of Hope's practicks, where he paraphrases sections of Craig's *Jus feudale*:

> *Nos in hoc regno Romanorum legibus ita obligamur quatenus legibus naturae et rectae rationis congruunt. ... Et quoties quid arduum occurrit in foro vel judiciis, ejus solutio inde est petenda.*[34]
>
> *Ubi denique novus aliquis casus supervenit qui neque jure scripto neque consuetudine comprehenditur, ad jus civile recurrendum est. ... Quod ubi in aliquibus per jus cannonicum est innovatum, in iis jus pontificium prefertur.*[35]

This can be translated as:

---

32 James Avon Clyde (ed.), *Hope's Major Practicks 1608–1633* (Edinburgh: Stair Society, 1937–8) I, 1.14 [3].

33 Ford, *Law and Opinion*, 275.

34 Clyde (ed.), *Hope's Major Practicks*, I, 1.1.2 [1]; Clyde (trans.), *Jus feudale*, 1.2.14, 1.8.17.

35 Clyde (ed.), *Hope's Major Practicks*, I, 1.1.5 [2]; Clyde (trans.), *Jus feudale*, 1.8.17.

> In our own realm of Scotland we are bound by Roman Law so far as it appears to us to be consonant with natural equity and reason.[36] In our own courts it affords the key to the solution of many a difficulty.[37]
>
> If neither a Scots act, nor the custom of Scotland as evidenced by the decisions of the courts, nor the Feudal Law, provides the answer to a legal problem, we must betake ourselves to the Civil Law. … When however it is inconsistent with the Canon Law … the Canon Law is preferred in Scotland.[38]

Hope therefore explicitly received Craig's explanation of the use of Roman law, although without its full complexity. Hope's position is rather more pragmatic. Ford is correct that this explicit position reflects Hope's treatment of Roman law both later in the *Major practicks* and in his manual for practice, the *Minor practicks*. Only rarely did Hope provide quotations or summaries of Roman or canon law in the *Major practicks*. Hope mentioned the civil law twice in the *Minor practicks* but on both occasions he distinguished it from the position taken by Scottish practick.[39]

(2) Sir Robert Spottiswoode of Pentland, 1596–1646

Spottiswoode's approach to learned authority was very different to that of Hope. This reflected a difference in his aim when writing. Hope was compiling sources for practical reference in the *Major practicks*, and was instructing aspiring lawyers on elements of Scottish practice in the *Minor practicks*. However, Spottiswoode used his digest of Scottish practice 'to transfer authority from the schools [of continental legal learning] to the courts'.[40] His digest is thus rich with material drawn from Roman and canon law as well as the various continental works thereupon.

Spottiswoode followed Skene (rather than Craig and Hope) with regard to the respective authority of Roman and canon law: 'in Spottiswoode's

---

[36] Clyde (trans.), *Jus feudale*, 1.2.14 (amended).

[37] Clyde (trans.), *Jus feudale*, 1.8.17.

[38] Clyde (trans.), *Jus feudale*, 1.8.17.

[39] Thomas Hope of Craighall, *Minor Practicks, or, a Treatise of the Scottish Law* (Edinburgh: Thomas Ruddiman, 1736), 122, 124. It has been said that the *Minor practicks*, 'contains not a single [observation of practick] from beginning to end, nor a single reference either to works of authority or to judicial decision': Clyde (ed.), *Hope's Major Practicks*, I, xiii. However, this is not correct.

[40] Ford, *Law and Opinion*, 211.

approach to the *ius commune*, Canon law had been overwhelmed by Civil law.'[41] Spottiswoode cited the books of canon law only twice and did not cite any of the great canonist writers. However, there was less obvious acknowledgement of the canon law: 'doctrines of Canon law underpinned the thinking' of sections of text where there were no explicit citations.[42]

However, Spottiswoode provided many citations of Roman law texts as well as civilian writers.[43] Several of the great French legal human-ists of the sixteenth century were cited. Indeed Cairns has noted that 'Spottiswoode cited relatively contemporary, indeed modern, Civilian works on substantive law and that, among the authors he preferred, Humanists tended to predominate.'[44] He showed that 'Spottiswoode's work largely ignored the older authors',[45] citing them infrequently and only in quotations of more recent writers. The exception to this practice was Bartolus, whom Spottiswoode cited a few times. Spottiswoode also, like Sinclair, cited collections of decisions from continental courts as well as works on procedure.[46] However, whereas he often reproduced the learned citations found in the reports of sixteenth-century practicks, Ford has noted that 'There was rather less reference to the texts, glosses and commentaries of the civil and canon laws in his own reports ... but he too recorded the express citation of the *Digest* or "the Doctors" along with clear allusions to learned sources.'[47] Ford has concluded that Spottiswoode's references to the learned laws were sometimes intended to draw comparisons between Scottish and civilian learning.[48]

(3) Conclusions on Hope and Spottiswoode

Hope and Spottiswoode both wrote around the 1630s. They both accepted that reference to Roman and canon law could still be made in Scottish practice. However, they did so in a manner which broadly reflects Craig's earlier thinking and can be contrasted with that of Sinclair, which was dis-cussed in Chapter 7. Scottish legal sources should be preferred to Roman and canon law. Spottiswoode used these sources to transfer their learning into discussion of Scots law. They were used to elucidate and explain the

---

41 Cairns, '*Ius civile*', 165.
42 Cairns, '*Ius civile*', 161.
43 On his use of continental literature, see Dolezalek, 'French legal literature', 387–8.
44 Cairns, '*Ius civile*', 163.
45 Cairns, '*Ius civile*', 164.
46 Cairns, '*Ius civile*', 164; Ford, *Law and Opinion*, 191–200.
47 Ford, *Law and Opinion*, 204.
48 Ford, *Law and Opinion*, 209–11.

Scots law, which was being read in the context of that wider learning. Hope's pattern of citation meanwhile means that his digest might at first glance be compared with Balfour rather than Spottiswoode in terms of its treatment of learned law. However, this would not be correct. Both Balfour and Hope aimed to make the written sources of Scots law available more easily. But Balfour's intention was also to promote the sources of Scots law as a repository of learning and truth, to give it the same intellectual credibility as the learned law. Hope wrote after the intellectual integrity of Scots law (and the authority of its sources) was beyond widespread doubt. Hope did not need to wish for Scots law to be viewed with the same respect as Roman law. Hope's view was that, as far as practice in the court was concerned, the authority of Scots law exceeded that of Roman law.

How do the views of Spottiswoode and Hope relate to the earlier interpretation of the statute in the case between Waldrop and Colquhoun? Although Hope did not mention the case in his record of practical observations,[49] he was likely one of the advocates who pleaded the case on behalf of Colquhoun.[50] Hope's approach in that case is consistent with what is seen in his works more broadly. The reference to Roman law was a tool for helpful interpretation because it was explicitly allowed by the statute itself. Hope recorded in his *Major practicks* that the act should be interpreted 'accordeing to the disposition of the comon law'.[51]

Spottiswoode meanwhile recorded the case in his digest in significant detail. This may suggest that he was also involved in it.[52] He was a lord of session at the time when the case was heard and may well have had a role in deciding the case.[53] Later in his digest he provided two passages of Latin text discussing the statute and comparing it with the position in England. This text seems to be a summary of Craig's *Jus feudale*.[54] However, Spottiswoode did not preserve in his digest Craig's

---

49 Clyde (ed.), *Hope's Major Practicks*, I, 4.10 [335].

50 Gibson of Durie records that one of the advocates for Waldrop was one 'Hope': Durie, *Decisions*, 349. Although he does not specify a forename, Sir Thomas Hope of Craighall would seem to have been the only Hope in practice as an advocate at that time. Francis J. Grant (ed.), *The Faculty of Advocates in Scotland 1532–1943, with Genealogical Notes* (Edinburgh: Scottish Record Society, 1944), 104–5.

51 Clyde (ed.), *Hope's Major Practicks*, I, 4.10.47 [333].

52 Spottiswoode, *Practicks*, 163.

53 David Stevenson, 'Spottiswood, Sir Robert, Lord Dunipace (1596–1646)', *Oxford Dictionary of National Biography* (Oxford: Oxford University Press, 2004), http://www.oxforddnb.com/view/article/26169.

54 Spottiswoode, *Practicks*, 344, where he summarises Craig (Clyde (trans.), *Jus feudale*, 2.20.5).

sense of dissatisfaction with the rule. But this was unnecessary: the law was certain and it was not Spottiswoode's purpose to critique the law in such a manner.

E. THE AUTHORITY OF THE LEARNED LAWS IN WRITING DURING THE LATER SEVENTEENTH CENTURY

(1) Sir James Dalrymple, Viscount Stair, 1619–1695

Sir James Dalrymple, Viscount Stair had a different view of legal authority from earlier Scottish lawyers in three ways. First, he saw natural law as a system of substantive legal rules which could be deduced through reason and from sources which reflect the history and breadth of human experience. Second, he did not understand the learned law as a repository of learning and truth in the manner of previous generations of lawyers. Third, he understood the authority of substantive law to derive from the sovereign. This next section of this chapter will examine Stair's understanding of the authority of natural and learned law. His views of sovereign authority will be discussed in the next chapter.

Stair's development of the understanding of natural law must be understood in the context of continental legal scholarship. A treatise called *De jure belli ac pacis* (*On the Law of War and Peace*) by a Dutch lawyer called Hugo Grotius was published in 1625. This was to become a very influential book and it popularised legal scholarship based on natural law. There was pressing political need at the time to establish rules for the interaction between states. Such laws would today be called international law. In the seventeenth century there were no great supra-national political institutions or multi-party treaties. But complex questions were being asked. Under what circumstances can a state declare a just war against another state? What rights do indigenous people have in the land which they occupy? Such questions could not be answered with reference to national law. Nor could such questions be answered by the learned laws. The authority of these systems did not extend to such issues. Canon law could not, for example, be justly applied to the non-Christian peoples of South America. However, an answer could be found in natural law because this system was inherent in the nature of the world and all men upon it.

Natural law was not to Grotius just an abstract concept of justice but a legal system. Men's deeds could be regarded as either in conformity with or in opposition to it. From this system of natural law arose both obligations and rights. Human reason and experience could be used to deduce these substantive legal rules. Grotius cited the Bible to understand divine law. He drew on sources from classical antiquity (including Roman law and ancient philosophers) to show the learning of human experience. He drew on legal writers from across the Christian world (Catholic and Protestant) to show the breadth of human understanding. By drawing on these sources and applying critical reason to their content and lessons, Grotius was able to construct a complex system of legal rules which could be seen to govern the actions of states as well as individual men.[55]

Grotius's *De jure belli ac pacis* was one of Stair's most important sources when he wrote the *Institutions of the Law of Scotland* in 1659–62.[56] Stair developed Craig's thinking about the three categories of law in light of Grotius's influence. For Stair (as for Grotius) natural law was a discernible system of legal rules which captured the ideal of justice. However, man was not entirely bound by natural law: 'humane Laws are added, not to take away the Law of Nature, and of Reason, but some of the effects thereof, which are in our power.'[57] What this means is that nature gave men certain rights, but men could then surrender some of those rights. For example, Stair explained that men are born free by the law of nature. However, a man could limit his liberty by giving authority to another to govern a wider society of men. He could engage in contracts which would compel him to do something or refrain from doing something. He could be taken into or give himself into slavery.[58]

---

[55]   Much has been written on Grotius. However for a useful introduction to Grotius's natural law theory, see Richard Tuck, 'Introduction', in Richard Tuck (trans.), *The Rights of War and Peace by Hugo Grotius* (3 vols, Indianapolis: Liberty Fund, 2005). This book also offers a useful translation of Grotius's treatise.

[56]   On Stair's use of Grotius, see Adelyn L. M. Wilson, *The sources and method of the* Institutions of the Law of Scotland *by Sir James Dalrymple, 1st Viscount Stair, with specific reference to the law of obligations* (PhD thesis, University of Edinburgh, 2011), ch. 4.

[57]   Sir James Dalrymple, Viscount Stair, *The Institutions of the Law of Scotland, Deduced from its Originals, and Collated with the Civil, Canon and Feudal Laws, and with the Customs of Neighbouring Nations* (Edinburgh: Heir of Andrew Anderson, 1st edn 1681, 2nd edn 1693), 1.14/1.1.15.

[58]   Stair, *Institutions*, title 2. On Stair's understanding of liberty and the importance of this discussion in understanding the purpose of the *Institutions*, see J. D. Ford, 'Stair's title "Of Liberty and Servitude"', in A. D. E. Lewis and D. J. Ibbetson (eds), *The Roman Law Tradition* (Cambridge: Cambridge University Press, 1994),

This view of legal authority greatly affected how Stair structured his discussions throughout the *Institutions*. The *Institutions* was (from a certain perspective) an exposition of a framework of rights provided by natural law as interpreted by human law. Stair began each discussion of a point of law by setting out the natural law rule first. Natural law could be discerned with reference to the Bible representing divine law and the law of nations representing the breadth and history of human experience. To identify that human experience and reason, Stair cited Roman law, canon law, feudal law, continental and English legal literature, and writers of classical antiquity. Of course these sources did not always agree, so human reason had to be used. Natural law could only be identified by a critical reading of the sources. For example, Stair believed that natural law gave a husband certain rights over his wife's property. To prove this he cited passages from a book of the Bible, Genesis, which showed Adam's superiority over Eve. He also cited jurists who agreed with his opinion from Burgundy, France, Germany, Spain and the Netherlands. However, Roman law did not award such rights to a husband. Stair therefore explained that in this case 'The *Roman Law* hath exceedingly varied in this matter from the Natural Law'[59] and as such should not be followed.

Stair's understanding of the authority of Roman and canon law was thus very different to that of earlier writers. The authority of the learned laws was no longer quite that they were repositories of truth and learning, nor that they were a common law to be used instrumentally where Scots law was lacking. Rather Stair said Roman law was 'followed for its equity'.[60] What this means is that Stair believed that Roman law was generally a system which was close to natural law so could be used as a tool to identify and interpret the system of natural law. He recognised the historical importance of Roman, canon and feudal law meaning 'these (especially the Civil Law) have great weight with us, namely in cases where a Custom is not yet formed; but none of these have with us the Authority of Law'.[61] This was important. The old learned laws were

---

135–58; Neil MacCormick, 'The rational discipline of law', *Juridical Review* (1981), 146–60 at 152–8.

[59] Stair, *Institutions*, 4.3/1.4.11.

[60] Stair, *Institutions*, 1.11/1.1.12.

[61] Stair, *Institutions*, 1.15/1.1.16. On the understanding of Stair's use of Roman law and canon law, see Wilson, 'The sources and method', especially 8.2.1–2; W. M. Gordon, 'Stair's use of Roman law', in A. Harding (ed.), *Law-Making and Law-Makers in British History: Papers Presented to the Edinburgh Legal History Conference, 1977* (London: Royal Historical Society, 1980), 120–6; W. M. Gordon, 'Roman law

a source to which lawyers might often resort. However, they were not binding, even where there was no Scottish authority.

After Stair explained the natural law position he would then show how this had been interpreted in Scotland with reference to cases and acts of parliament. Stair took this approach to highlight throughout the *Institutions* the importance of natural law and its close relationship to Scots law. Indeed Stair saw Scots law's 'nearness to Equity' as being its core strength. It meant Scots law 'may be well paralleled with the best Law in *Christendom*'.[62]

Of course sometimes no Scottish sources might exist on a particular issue. Stair suggested that 'Where our antint [i.e. ancient] Law, Statutes, and our recent Customs and Practiques are defective [i.e. lacking], recourse is had to Equity, as the first and universal Law, and to expediency'.[63] Stair therefore attempted to discern the natural law position and then provided guidance to the reader on how this should be interpreted locally. Stair was clear, for example, that the Roman rule that the owner of a document should be the person who owned the paper rather than the person who wrote upon it was 'every where in Desuetude'. To show this he cited Grotius as well as the German lawyer Mynsinger and turned to basic logic: 'it were very unreasonable to think, that the Evidents and Securities of Lands, or any Manuscript, should be accessory to the Paper ... which were only designed to bear and preserve the Writ'.[64] Therefore, by implication, natural law recognised that the writer was the owner of the document, and in turn that this rule should be followed in Scotland.[65]

This was not Stair bringing Scots law into line with continental learning as had been done in the sixteenth century. Nor was he importing that learning into Scots law as Spottiswoode had done. Rather this was Stair acknowledging that this was the position of natural law and Scots law

---

as a source', in D. M. Walker (ed.), *Stair Tercentenary Studies* (Edinburgh: Stair Society, 1981), 107–12. For alternative views on Stair's use of Roman and canon law, see G. McLeod, 'The Romanization of property law', in Kenneth Reid and Reinhard Zimmermann (eds), *A History of Private Law in Scotland* (Oxford: Oxford University Press, 2000) I, 220–44; J. J. Robertson, 'Canon law as a source', in D. M. Walker (ed.), *Stair Tercentenary Studies* (Edinburgh: Stair Society, 1981), 112–27; Cairns, 'The civil law tradition', 204–6.

[62] Stair, *Institutions*, 1.15/1.1.16.
[63] Stair, *Institutions*, 1.15/1.1.16. On this passage, see Ford, *Law and Opinion*, 427–8.
[64] Stair, *Institutions*, 12.37/2.1.39.
[65] On the citations and sources of this passage, see Wilson, 'The sources and method', 79, 127, 164, 230.

accorded to it. This close relationship with natural law was something which Stair believed should be preserved. Natural law was the most authoritative system of law, having been created by God.

(2) Sir George Mackenzie of Rosehaugh, 1636/8–1691

A less nuanced position can be found slightly later in Mackenzie's *Institutions*. He also put forward the idea that there were different categories of law, but his vision of these wider categories seems to have been more abstract and traditional than Stair's view. Natural law was equated to 'rather *innate instinct*, than *positive Law*'. The law of nations comprised obligations which arise from natural law (such as revering God) and 'these general conclusions, in which ordinarily all Nations agree'.[66] Among the examples of the latter category he mentioned '*Obligations* arising from *promises*' and 'ransoming of *Prisoners* [of war]'.[67] The authority of Roman law he saw in light of this but in a far more concrete way than Stair:

> The *Romans*, having studied with great *exactness*, the principles of *Equity*, and *Justice*. Their Emperor *Justinian*, did cause digest all their Laws into one body, which is now called ... the *Civil Law*; And as this *Civil Law* is much respected generally, so it has great influence in *Scotland*, except where Our own express Laws, or *Customes*, have receded from it.[68]

Similar statements are found in his treatise on criminal law:

> And that the civil law is our rule where our own statutes and customs are silent or deficient is clear from our own lawyers[.][69]

Mackenzie cited Craig and Skene in support of this view, which somewhat obscures the nuance of their arguments. Mackenzie's statements here reflect his wider use of authority in his works. In his *Institutions of*

---

[66] This and previous quotation from Sir George Mackenzie of Rosehaugh, *Institutions of the Law of Scotland* (Edinburgh: John Reid, 1684), 1.1, 2.

[67] Mackenzie, *Institutions*, 1.1, 3. On Mackenzie's understanding of natural law, see Cairns, 'The civil law tradition', 207–8.

[68] Mackenzie, *Institutions*, 1.1, 3–4.

[69] Olivia Robinson (ed.), *The Laws and Customs of Scotland in Matters Criminal by Sir George Mackenzie* (Edinburgh: Stair Society, 2012), 9. See also Cairns, 'The civil law tradition', 208–11.

the Law of Scotland, he cited only acts of parliament and the medieval law books as Scottish legal authorities. This was in keeping with his understanding of the importance of legislation, which will be discussed in the next chapter. Where there was no written law, Mackenzie presented Roman law rules as Scots law.[70]

(3) Stair, Mackenzie and *Mayor of Berwick v the Laird of Haining* (1661)

The practical difference between the views of Stair and Mackenzie with respect to the authority of Roman law is seen in a case between the Mayor of Berwick and the Laird of Haining over fishing rights.[71] Haining owned land on which there was a loch, which he began draining. Water from that loch ultimately flowed into the River Tweed. The mayor had fishing rights in the Tweed. He brought an action against Haining arguing that the draining of the loch was poisoning the river and driving away the fish. This case was heard by the Court of Session with Stair on the bench, while Mackenzie appeared as the advocate for Haining. Both Stair and Mackenzie wrote accounts of the case. Mackenzie kept a record of the argument which he made before the judges. Stair's account in his collection of decisions is in the typical style of a judge. He set out first the argument by the pursuers, then the argument set out by Mackenzie, and finally the judges' decision. He explains that the pursuers cited 'many Interdicts in the Civil Law' which restricted owners' actions in respect of their property.[72] Mackenzie's record of his speech shows that he, in response, cited several texts of Roman law to show that an owner's normal use of land could not be restricted by his neighbours. He also said that the only restrictions on the use of rivers related to navigation rights and not to pollution. Stair noted both of these arguments, but did not record the citations of the Roman texts. Indeed Stair did not record the arguments in terms of Roman law at all. His description of the argu-

---

[70] Baird Smith suggests that the emphasis which Mackenzie places on statutes erodes the view that he saw 'Roman law as part of the law of Scotland': David Baird Smith, 'Roman law', in *An Introductory Survey of the Sources and Literature of Scots Law* (Edinburgh: Stair Society, 1936), 171–82 at 180. However, Mackenzie's view that Roman law was common law is not mutually exclusive with his understanding of the authority of statute.

[71] Cf. Cairns, 'The civil law tradition', 211.

[72] Sir James Dalrymple, Viscount Stair, *The Decisions of the Lords of Council and Session in the most Important Cases Debate before Them [1661–1681]* (2 vols, Edinburgh: Heir of Andrew Anderson, 1683–7) I, 49.

ments put forward by Mackenzie was that they were about the natural behaviour of man and natural law. Stair's final comment before setting out the judges' decision is very interesting:

> And as for the *Roman Interdicts*, they neither meet the Case, nor are they *Laws* for us, where the Civil Law is not a Law, but an Example we follow freely when we find it Just and fit.[73]

The location of this statement in Stair's report suggests that it is the third and final argument made by Mackenzie.[74] But nowhere does Mackenzie make such a statement in his written pleading. Indeed such a comment would be contrary to his later-stated understanding of the authority of Roman law. This statement is not Mackenzie's – it is Stair's. This is one of those rare statements of judicial understanding, a judge's subjective comment on the authorities and arguments pleaded before him.

This case therefore shows the importance of the difference in Mackenzie's and Stair's views of legal authority. Mackenzie saw Roman law as the common law of Scotland, and here framed it as if it were indeed the law of Scotland. Stair extrapolated from those texts what the natural law position was, but approached the texts themselves with the scepticism of one who saw them as lacking in direct authority. Mackenzie may not have known when he won his case that day how much intellectual distance there was between him and one of the most experienced judges on the bench.

F. CONCLUSION

During the seventeenth century Roman law continued to be very important to Scottish practice. Only a few selected examples have been discussed here. This trend is seen in the cases between Waldrop and Colquhoun as well as that between the mayor of Berwick and the laird of Haining. Both of these cases proceeded at least in part on Roman law arguments. However, further study into Scottish practice is required to understand how universal this approach was.

This chapter has shown that the use of Roman law in court also has to be seen in the context of the wider intellectual understanding of the authority of the learned laws. This had changed substantially. The

---

[73] Stair, *Decisions*, I, 50.
[74] As it has been seen by, for example, Ford, *Law and Opinion*, 492–3.

collected legal decisions of Sinclair and Colville suggest that the court in the sixteenth century had interpreted Scottish legal sources in light of the reasoning of the learned laws, or had construed them narrowly where that was not practicable. However, those involved in the 1566 project had promoted the view that Scots law was also a body of truth and learning. This view may have been promoted in later endeavours to make the law more accessible, such as in Balfour's practicks.

By the beginning of the seventeenth century, lawyers were no longer questioning the intellectual integrity or authority of Scots law. Skene and Craig seem to have believed that the principles of Scots law need not have been brought into line with the sources of learned law when resolving legal problems. Both were, however, receptive to the use of Roman law and canon law as well as the literature thereupon. Skene used the learned laws for comparison and elucidation of learning. Craig accepted that these sources were still binding where Scottish sources were silent on an issue and where local practitioners recognised them to be consistent with justice.

Thirty years later, Hope explicitly drew on Craig's view but overall he gave little recognition to the learned laws in his written works. Spottiswoode differed from his contemporary in his approach. He attempted to transfer the learning of Roman law and the wider civilian tradition into Scots law through frequent quotation of its works. Twenty years later again, Stair saw the authority of Roman law and the civilian tradition in their ability to reflect in many instances the position of natural law. This he saw as an ideal system of discernible legal rules. This was very different to his contemporary Mackenzie, who regarded Roman law (as interpreted by the literature thereupon) as the common law of Scotland and resorted to it when there was no clear Scottish authority.

Understanding of the authority of the learned laws was thus becoming increasingly complex and diverse. However, these authors were largely united in their understanding that Scottish legal sources should be preferred to those of the learned laws. Their understanding of the respective importance of the various Scottish sources of law will be discussed in the following chapter.

G. SELECTED BIBLIOGRAPHY AND FURTHER READING

(1) Books

Clyde, James Avon (ed.), *Hope's Major Practicks 1608–1633* (Edinburgh: Stair Society, 1937–8).

Clyde, James Avon (trans.), *The Jus Feudale by Sir Thomas Craig of Riccarton* (Edinburgh: William Hodge & Co., 1934).

Dalrymple, Sir James, Viscount Stair, *The Institutions of the Law of Scotland, Deduced from its Originals, and Collated with the Civil, Canon and Feudal Laws, and with the Customs of Neighbouring Nations* (Edinburgh: Heir of Andrew Anderson, 1st edn 1681, 2nd edn 1693).

Dalrymple, Sir James, Viscount Stair, *The Decisions of the Lords of Council and Session in the most Important Cases Debate before Them [1661–1681]* (2 vols, Edinburgh: Heir of Andrew Anderson, 1683–7).

Ford, J. D., *Law and Opinion in Scotland during the Seventeenth Century* (Oxford: Hart Publishing, 2007).

Gibson, Sir Alexander of Durie, *The Decisions of the Lords of Council and Session in Most Cases of Importance, Debated, and brought before Them; From July 1621, to July 1642* (Edinburgh: Heir of Andrew Anderson, 1690).

Hope, Sir Thomas of Craighall, *Minor Practicks, or, A Treatise of the Scottish Law* (Edinburgh: Thomas Ruddiman, 1726).

[Mackenzie, Sir George of Rosehaugh], *Pleadings in Some Remarkable Cases before the Supreme Courts of Scotland since the Year 1661* (Edinburgh: George Swintoun, James Glen and Thomas Brown, 1673).

Mackenzie, Sir George of Rosehaugh, *The Institutions of the Law of Scotland* (Edinburgh: John Reid, 1684).

Robinson, Olivia F. (ed.), *The Laws and Customs of Scotland in Matters Criminal by Sir George Mackenzie* (Edinburgh: Stair Society, 2012).

Skene, Sir John of Curriehill (ed.), *Regiam Majestatem: The Auld Lawes and Constitutions of Scotland* (Edinburgh: Thomas Finlason, 1609).

Spottiswoode, Sir Robert of Pentland, *Practicks of the Laws of Scotland* (Edinburgh: James Watson, 1706).

Tuck, Richard (trans.), *The Rights of War and Peace by Hugo Grotius* (3 vols, Indianapolis: Liberty Fund, 2005).

(2) Chapters in Books

Baird Smith, David, 'Roman law', in *An Introductory Survey of the Sources and Literature of Scots Law* (Edinburgh: Stair Society, 1936), 171–82.

Cairns, John W., 'The civil law tradition in Scottish legal thought', in David L. Carey Miller and Reinhard Zimmermann (eds), *The Civilian Tradition and Scots Law: Aberdeen Quincentenary Essays* (Berlin: Duncker and Humblot, 1997), 191–223.

Cairns, John W., 'Historical introduction', in Kenneth Reid and Reinhard Zimmermann (eds), *A History of Private Law in Scotland* (Oxford: Oxford University Press, 2000) I, 14–184.

Dolezalek, Gero R., 'French legal literature quoted by Scottish lawyers, 1550–1650', in Bernard d'Alteroche *et al.* (eds), *Mélanges en l'honneur d'Anne Lefebvre-Teillard* (Paris: Éditions Panthéon-Assas, 2009), 375–91.

Ford, J. D., 'Stair's title "Of Liberty and Servitude"', in A. D. E. Lewis and D. J. Ibbetson (eds), *The Roman Law Tradition* (Cambridge: Cambridge University Press, 1994), 135–58.

Gordon, W. M., 'Stair's use of Roman law', in A. Harding (ed.), *Law-Making and Law-Makers in British History: Papers Presented to the Edinburgh Legal History Conference, 1977* (London: Royal Historical Society, 1980), 120–6.

Gordon, W. M., 'Roman law as a source', in D. M. Walker (ed.), *Stair Tercentenary Studies* (Edinburgh: Stair Society, 1981), 107–12.

McLeod, G., 'The Romanization of property law', in Kenneth Reid and Reinhard Zimmermann (eds), *A History of Private Law in Scotland* (Oxford: Oxford University Press, 2000) I, 220–44.

(3) Articles in Journals

Cairns, John W., '*Ius civile* in Scotland, ca. 1600', *Roman Legal Tradition* 2 (2004), 136–70.

Cairns, John W. *et al.*, 'Legal humanism in renaissance Scotland', *Journal of Legal History* 11:1 (1990), 40–69.

Gordon, William M., 'The civil law in Scotland', *Edinburgh Law Review* 5 (2001), 130–44.

MacCormick, Neil, 'The rational discipline of law', *Juridical Review* (1981), 146–60.

Robertson, J. J., 'Canon law as a source', in D. M. Walker (ed.), *Stair Tercentenary Studies* (Edinburgh: Stair Society, 1981), 112–27.

Stein, Peter, 'The influence of Roman law on the law of Scotland', *Juridical Review* (1963), 205–45.

(4) Research Theses

Wilson, Adelyn L. M., *The sources and method of the* Institutions of the Law of Scotland *by Sir James Dalrymple, 1st Viscount Stair, with specific reference to the law of obligations* (PhD thesis, University of Edinburgh, 2011).

CHAPTER 16

Legal Authority of Scottish Sources

A. INTRODUCTION

It was shown in the previous chapter that in the seventeenth century it was almost universally accepted that Scottish legal sources should be preferred to the traditional learned law. However, there was some disagreement as to the authority of the different sources of Scots law in relation to each other.

It has already been shown that Mackenzie was rigorous in his presentation of arguments based on Roman law in the case between the mayor of Berwick and the laird of Haining concerning the pollution of the River Tweed and the impact on its fishing. He gave a similarly vociferous account of the authority of acts of parliament in a case heard in 1662.

Sir David Murray of Gospertie was one of those men who achieved recognition in the court of James VI. As a privy councillor he helped to punish those who had kidnapped the king in the Ruthven raid. He had helped the king's passage of legislation as a lord of the articles in parliament. He had served as a justice in the Hebrides. And he was a central figure in securing the passage of James's controversial Five Articles of Perth. In recognition of these many services, he was given the lordship of Scone and later made Viscount Stormont.[1]

Murray was childless when he received these favours so he asked for the grant of lands to be tailzied.[2] More information about tailzies can be

---

[1] Alan R. MacDonald, 'Murray, David, first viscount of Stormont (d. 1631)', *Oxford Dictionary of National Biography* (Oxford: Oxford University Press, 2004), http://www.oxforddnb.com/view/article/19599. On the line of the Viscounts of Stormont, see *Burke's Peerage, Baronetage and Knightage*, 107th edn (London: Burke's Peerage Ltd, 2003), 2734.

[2] For the first document which did so, which was supplemented by others later, see John Maitland Thomson (ed.), *Registrum magni sigilli regum Scotorum: The Register*

found in Chapter 3. What is important here is that this tailzie gave a legal right to a list of named relatives to inherit his lands and title. To ensure that the estate was preserved, the tailzie explicitly stated that the relatives could not 'do any deed whereby the saids Lands might be evicted or apprised from them, without the consent of all the persons contained in that Tailzie'.[3] Should anyone do otherwise then that person would forfeit the lands and title. These would then be bestowed on the next individual named in the tailzie.

After the viscount's death, the lands and title passed first to his cousin, Mungo Murray, and then to John, Earl of Annandale. Unfortunately Annandale was a spendthrift and accumulated significant debts before he died. After Annandale's death, the lands and title were inherited by the fourth man named in the tailzie, Andrew Murray of Balvaird. He was concerned that Annandale's creditors would seek payment of the debts from the viscountcy estate. If that were to happen, then essentially Balvaird as the new viscount would be liable to pay the debts. So he petitioned the Court of Session to recognise that the wording of the tailzie prevented Annandale from encumbering the estate with debts. He asked the court to recognise that he had therefore received the estate free from any obligation to Annandale's creditors.

The advocate for Annandale's creditors suggested that no paction or agreement could so restrict rights in property. To prevent property being encumbered with debt would be such a significant legal rule that:

> it could in justice only be altered by a publick Law, wherein the Estates of Parliament (who are with us only Judges of what is convenient for the Nation in general) might declare, that it were fit to turn such a paction as this into a Law: and since for so many Ages, the Parliament has not thought this fit, nor have privat families ever introduced any such pactions till now, we must either judge, that these are not fit for privat families, or that those understood not their own interest.[4]

This argument related directly to legal authority. The advocate here argued that only parliament was able to create law which was binding on

---

of the Great Seal of Scotland AD 1593–1608 (Edinburgh: HM General Register House, 1890), 781–3.

[3] [Sir George Mackenzie of Rosehaugh], *Pleadings in Some Remarkable Cases before the Supreme Courts of Scotland since the Year 1661* (Edinburgh: George Swintoun, James Glen and Thomas Brown, 1673), 40.

[4] Mackenzie, *Pleadings*, 43.

the whole nation. He further argued that an absence of an act of parliament or custom to introduce this kind of paction or agreement meant that it could not be accepted as law.

Mackenzie was hired as the new viscount's advocate. He was highly dismissive of the other advocate's assessment:

> I do confess, (my Lords) that those specious pretences, especially when prest with so much zeal, and eloquence, may make impressions upon such as are not intimatly acquaint with the principles of Law; but I hope, where we have such Judges as your Lordships, there can be little hazard from such objections[.][5]

He then proceeded to show that the civil law allowed a person to dispose of his property with conditions attached.[6] He argued that pactions between private individuals are not restricted to issues which have previously been subject to legislation, but that acts of sederunt and *Regiam Majestatem* both confirm that pactions once made are binding.[7]

The lords of session found for the new viscount. Stair's report of the case reads as though it were decided only on the specific wording of the tailzie and does not reflect upon these discussions of authority.[8] However, this debate raises questions about how lawyers in the seventeenth century understood the authority of acts of parliament, *Regiam* and custom. This chapter will examine these questions. It will first discuss contemporary understanding of the authority of acts of parliament, practick and custom. It will then examine their understanding of the authority of *Regiam Majestatem*, which became a highly controversial source during this period.

---

5 Mackenzie, *Pleadings*, 45.
6 Mackenzie, *Pleadings*, 45.
7 Mackenzie, *Pleadings*, 45–6.
8 Sir James Dalrymple, Viscount Stair, *The Decisions of the Lords of Council and Session in the most Important Cases Debate before Them [1661–1681]* (2 vols, Edinburgh: Heir of Andrew Anderson, 1683–7) I, 85. See also Gilmour's note on the case (which appears to describe this hearing, although is dated as though a later action between the parties): *A Collection of Decisions of the Lords of Council and Session, in Two Parts. The First contains Decisions from July 1661, to July 1666. Observ'd by Sir John Gilmour of Craigmiller ... The Second Part contains Decisions from November 1681, to January 1686. Observ'd by Sir David Falconer of Newton* (Edinburgh: James Watson, 1701), 28–30.

B. ACTS OF PARLIAMENT, PRACTICK AND CUSTOM

Writing at the beginning of the seventeenth century, Craig saw the acts of parliament as being the most authoritative source of Scots law.[9] He declared that '*neque enim praetor ea, apud nos ullum jus scriptum certum & stabile habemus*' (i.e. 'in Scotland we have no other body of positive written law of comparable authority').[10] However, he recognised the doctrine of desuetude, the rule by which a statute lapsed through lack of use.[11] He criticised the freedom with which the judiciary had sometimes interpreted or disregarded statutes.[12] He was clear that '*Si quando vero jure proprio destituamur, tum rerum perpetuo sic judicatarum consuetudo observatur*' (i.e. 'If no assistance is to be had in that quarter [i.e. statutes], then the custom of Scotland as shown by the settled course of judicial decision ... must be followed').[13] His view was that practick was the second most authoritative source after statutes, it representing custom. However, he did not believe that practick or custom could contradict statutes.[14] Lines of cases on the same point should be acknowledged, rather than single decisions. This would prevent sharp practices or inexperience on the part of the advocates or judge in one case jeopardising wider practice.[15]

The view expressed by Craig that statutes were more authoritative than practick or custom was prevalent in the seventeenth century. Hope (writing around thirty years later) agreed with Craig's view. He quoted in his *Major practicks* Craig's explanation that the only source of national written law was parliamentary statute.[16] Hope declared in his *Major practicks* that 'No judges within this realm hes pouer to mak lawes bot the parliament allanerlie' (i.e. 'No judges within this realm have power

---

[9] Note that this should not be confused with the notion of supremacy of parliament, which is a different issue.

[10] Thomas Craig of Riccarton, *Jus feudale* (London: Stationers Society, 1655), 38; James Avon Clyde (trans.), *The Jus Feudale by Sir Thomas Craig of Riccarton* (Edinburgh: William Hodge & Co., 1934), 1.8.9. See also ibid. 1.8.12.

[11] Clyde (trans.), *Jus feudale*, 1.8.9; J. D. Ford, *Law and Opinion in Scotland during the Seventeenth Century* (Oxford: Hart Publishing, 2007), 413.

[12] Clyde (trans.), *Jus feudale*, 1.8.9.

[13] Craig, *Jus feudale*, 39; Clyde (trans.), *Jus feudale*, 1.8.13.

[14] Clyde (trans.), *Jus feudale*, 1.8.14.

[15] Clyde (trans.), *Jus feudale*, 1.8.15.

[16] Ford, *Law and Opinion*, 248.

to make laws but the parliament only').[17] Thus for Hope 'the acts of parliament took the first place in any enquiry, followed by the custom ... established in decisions.'[18] This understanding of the respective authority of statutes and cases is reflected throughout the *Major practicks*. Hope arranged his sources so that statutes always appeared before his practical observations in the subject titles.

Mackenzie, who practised during the Restoration period, also saw statutes as being the most authoritative source. Hence one of his great contributions to Scottish legal literature was a detailed examination of the correct interpretation of acts of parliament, the *Observations on the Acts of Parliament*. Indeed within that book he described statutes as 'the chief Pillars of our Law'.[19] In his earlier work on criminal law he had described them as 'our proper law'.[20] He 'wished that nothing were a crime which is not declared to be so by a statute, for this would make subjects inexcusable ... and prevent the arbitrariness of judges'.[21] What this means is that if all law (in this case criminal law) was set out in statutes then there would be no excuse for the people to not know the law and no possibility of judges making arbitrary decisions. However, he acknowledged a 'constant tract of decisions, past [passed] by the *Lords of Session*'[22] as well as ancient customs as sources of unwritten law.[23]

However, this view of the primacy of statutes was not universal. Mackenzie's contemporary, Stair, had a different understanding of the authority of Scottish sources. It has been shown in previous chapters that Scottish lawyers recognised that sources such as Roman law reflected advanced classical learning. Scottish legal material could also be seen as a repository of learning and truth. However, a new idea of legal authority was becoming popular on the continent. This began with a French jurist

---

17   James Avon Clyde (ed.), *Hope's Major Practicks 1608–1633* (Edinburgh: Stair Society, 1937–8) I, 1.1.2 [1].

18   Ford, *Law and Opinion*, 248.

19   Sir George Mackenzie of Rosehaugh, *Observations on the Acts of Parliament* (Edinburgh: Heir of Andrew Anderson, 1686), A4.

20   Olivia F. Robinson (ed.), *The Laws and Customs of Scotland in Matters Criminal by Sir George Mackenzie* (Edinburgh: Stair Society, 2012), 7; see also Sir George Mackenzie of Rosehaugh, *Institutions of the Law of Scotland* (Edinburgh: John Reid, 1684), 1.1, 5.

21   Robinson (ed.), *The Laws and Customs*, 6.

22   Mackenzie, *Institutions*, 6.

23   Mackenzie, *Institutions*, 7. On Mackenzie's view of authority, see Hector L. MacQueen, 'Mackenzie's Institutions in Scottish legal history', *Journal of the Law Society of Scotland* (1984), 498–501. On his view of legislative authority, see Ford, *Law and Opinion*, 474–81.

called Jean Bodin, who wrote in the sixteenth century. He asserted that legal authority derived from the authority of a legislative sovereign. Laws which did not have the assent of the sovereign were not binding. This was a very different vision of authority than what has been discussed in previous chapters. Bodin was suggesting that it was not the learned opinion of a body of expert lawyers which created law, but the exercise of the will of a legislative sovereign.[24]

Ford has suggested that this idea of sovereign authority was central to Stair's view of the law. Stair said that national law comprised that 'which could be understood no other, than what their Soveraign Authority should find Just and Convenient.'[25] It was from this sovereign authority which the authority of national law stemmed. In Scotland (and in most nations at this time) that sovereign authority would be the king. Ford has discussed the importance of this viewpoint. He has said that Stair 'maintained that all positive laws must derive in some way from the exercise of sovereign authority'.[26] He has also suggested that Stair believed that 'learned laws did not amount to positive laws unless approved by the sovereign ... [and] regarded the learned laws as no more than a guide to how natural equity might be implemented by the legislator.'[27]

This view of legal authority had a significant impact on Stair's understanding of the relative importance of different Scottish legal sources. He believed that the 'positive Laws of Soveraigns' which were assented to over time by many kings became recognised as custom.[28] Thus he recognised the authority of 'our ancient and immemorial *Customs*, which may be called our Common Law'.[29] These customs included points of law which had been recognised since time immemorial but which did not need to be set out in any particular statute. This might include, for example, inheritance of land by primogeniture.

Acts of parliament were made by the king in parliament, which gave them authority; however, they 'are lyable to *Desuetude*, which never

---

[24] Much has been written on Bodin's view of sovereignty. A useful starting point might be had in Julian H. Franklin (ed.), *Bodin on Sovereignty* (Cambridge: Cambridge University Press, 1992).

[25] Sir James Dalrymple, Viscount Stair, *The Institutions of the Law of Scotland, Deduced from its Originals, and Collated with the Civil, Canon and Feudal Laws, and with the Customs of Neighbouring Nations* (Edinburgh: Heir of Andrew Anderson, 1st edn 1681, 2nd edn 1693), 1.15/1.1.16.

[26] Ford, *Law and Opinion*, 539.

[27] Ford, *Law and Opinion*, 549.

[28] Stair, *Institutions*, 1.15/1.1.16.

[29] Stair, *Institutions*, 1.15/1.1.16.

incroaches on the other' (i.e. 'they are liable to desuetude, which never encroaches on the other').[30] Meanwhile judges participated in the exercise of sovereignty. The decisions and acts of sederunt of the lords of session provide 'recent Customs or Practiques' and 'being formal, are irreducible' and both interpret and (in certain circumstances) can derogate from acts of parliament.[31] Stair did not recognise precedent in the modern conceptualisation but did recognise that a line of cases on the same point were to some extent authoritative:

> there is much difference to be made betwixt a custome by frequent Decisions, and a simple Decision, which hath not like force, especially if it be invested with many Circumstances of Fact. But such are more effectual, if they be in any abstract point of Law. Yet frequent agreeing Decisions, are more effectual than Acts of Sederunt themselves, which do easily go into Desuetude.[32]

Stair's understanding of the root of legal authority therefore had an impact on his understanding of the importance of different Scottish legal materials.

C. REGIAM MAJESTATEM

There was also controversy over the authority of the medieval law book, *Regiam Majestatem*. In Chapter 14 it was mentioned that a new edition of *Regiam Majestatem* as well as the other medieval law books and statutes of the early kings was undertaken by Sir John Skene of Curriehill. The edited text was published in 1609 in Latin and Scots translation.[33] Skene's endeavour was similar in aim to the earlier 1566 project discussed in Chapter 9. The introduction to Skene's volume acknowledged that James VI had 'commanded the auld Lawes, of this his kingdom, to be sighted, corrected and collected in ane buke, and volume' because the country cannot 'indure without gude Lawes'.[34] This new edition of

---

30 Stair, *Institutions*, 1.15/1.1.16.
31 Stair, *Institutions*, 1.15/1.1.16.
32 Stair, *Institutions*, 1.15/1.1.16 'especially ... Law' omitted from 1693 edition.
33 See *RPS* 1592/4/67, 1607/3/27. On this commission, see John W. Cairns, 'Historical introduction', in Kenneth Reid and Reinhard Zimmermann (eds), *A History of Private Law in Scotland* (Oxford: Oxford University Press, 2000) I, 14–184 at 96–7.
34 Sir John Skene of Curriehill (ed.), *Regiam Majestatem. The Auld Lawes and*

Regiam made the text both certain and available. In the sixteenth century, James Balfour of Pittendreich had used several manuscript copies of *Regiam Majestatem* to consult the text.[35] Now a consultation of many copies was not necessary. Citations of the text could more readily be understood. The translation into Scots meant that the text was also now available to those who did not have Latin or whose Latin was not at the standard required to read complex legal texts. This might have been particularly useful for those lawyers who were working in courts other than the Session, where the requirements for education were less arduous.

One such lawyer seems to have been Alexander Spalding, who was briefly mentioned in Chapter 14. He was an advocate who worked principally in the Commissary court in Aberdeen. He maintained a collection of decisions of the courts in the north east of Scotland between around 1620 and 1645. He also drew these decisions into a digest which also contained much material taken from Balfour and Skene's tract on procedure. Spalding seems not to have had Latin and he relied on Skene's Scots edition of *Regiam Majestatem* and the other early laws.[36]

However, the importance of *Regiam Majestatem* was challenged in the seventeenth century. Thomas Craig in his *Jus feudale* said of *Regiam Majestatem*:

> *Nam cum omne jus perfectum & omnibus suis partibus absolutum esse debeat, nigari non potest jus hoc ex actis publicis regni purgandum & corrigendum esse viris doctis:* [37]

This can be translated as:

> The original sources of law should be perfect and without blemish in every part, and the *Regiam Majestatem* is undoubtedly a blot on the jurisprudence of our country which those learned in the law should make it their business to have expunged and removed[.][38]

Constitutions of Scotland (Edinburgh: Thomas Finlason, 1609), Epistle to the Reader ii.

[35] Walter Goodal (ed.), *Practicks: or, A System of the More Ancient Law of Scotland. Compiled by Sir James Balfour of Pettindreich* (Edinburgh: Thomas and Walter Ruddimans, 1754), ix.

[36] Adelyn L. M. Wilson, 'The "authentick practique bookes" of Alexander Spalding', in Andrew R. C. Simpson *et al.* (eds), *Continuity, Change and Pragmatism in the Law: Essays in Memory of Professor Angelo Forte* (Aberdeen: Aberdeen University Press, 2016), 175–236.

[37] Craig, *Jus feudale*, 38 citing the Digest of Roman law.

[38] Clyde (trans.), *Jus feudale*, 1.8.11.

He suggested that *Regiam Majestatem* drew so heavily on the English tract of *Glanville* that it could not be considered to be an accurate account of Scots law.[39] That is not to say that Craig never relied upon *Regiam Majestatem* when discussing the law in later titles of the *Jus feudale*.[40] But Craig's references to this source are infrequent and do not greatly contradict his explicit criticism of the source.

One of the reasons that Craig's treatise was so important was that many advocates used it as a source to teach themselves Scots law. Indeed, Craig intended this so included certain discussions to aid those '*juniores, quorum studia hoc opusculo promovere cupio*' (i.e. 'young men [advocates], whose studies I wish to advance by this little book').[41] This meant that Craig's dismissal of *Regiam Majestatem* became influential because aspiring lawyers began their practice with his doubt about this source in their minds.

Not everyone adhered to Craig's view. Sir Thomas Hope of Craighall defended the authority of *Regiam Majestatem* in his *Major practicks*. He said that 'A commissione for reformeing of Regiam Majestatem and Quoniam Attachiamenta ... proves that they have the auctority of lawes'.[42] What he meant by this is that an act parliament in 1425 had given authority to a commission to edit these two law books. Hope believe that this act gave recognition to *Regiam Majestatem* and *Quoniam attachiamenta* as authoritative legal sources and confirmed that parliament was satisfied that they might be used in legal practice. He also mentioned the old legend that *Regiam Majestatem* was commissioned by David I, which Hope believed meant it was 'maid be auctority of the prince' or at least that the commission to edit the book had the king's royal assent.[43] He suggested that *Regiam Majestatem* had since been cited in many acts of parliament.[44] Hope's use of *Regiam Majestatem* in the *Major practicks* confirms that he viewed it as a source of Scots law. He often arranged the quotations from *Regiam Majestatem* to be the first

---

[39] Craig, *Jus feudale*, 38–9. See also, Ford, *Law and Opinion*, 39–40; Cairns, 'Historical introduction', 97.

[40] Ford, *Law and Opinion*, 39.

[41] Craig, *Jus feudale*, 37. For a different translation, see Clyde (trans.), *Jus feudale*, 1.8.6. On the use of Craig's *Jus feudale* as an educational text, see John W. Cairns, 'The *Breve testatum* and Craig's *Jus feudale*', *Tijdschrift voor Rechtsgeschiedenis* 56:3 (1998), 311–32 at 331–2.

[42] Clyde (ed.), *Hope's Major Practicks*, I, 1.1.8 [2].

[43] Clyde (ed.), *Hope's Major Practicks*, I, 1.1.10 [2]. On which, see Ford, *Law and Opinion*, 249.

[44] Clyde (ed.), *Hope's Major Practicks*, I, 1.1.10 [2].

excerpts to be presented in his titles.[45] The twentieth-century editor of Hope's *Major practicks* thus said that he 'is expressing his own view of the authority to be attributed to the "Regiam Majestatem" in the Law of Scotland. He does not accept Craig's distinctly unfavourable opinion'.[46] However, Hope did not quote from *Regiam Majestatem* often in comparison to some other sources.[47]

Sir George Mackenzie of Rosehaugh also rejected Craig's argument. He did not mention Craig directly, but addressed his criticism in both his *Matters Criminal* and his *Institutions*. In *Matters Criminal*, he stated that 'The fourth branch of our criminal law are the books of *Regiam Majestatem*, which are *in criminalibus* (in criminal causes) looked upon as authentic.'[48] By 'authentic' he means that they are authentic sources of Scots law, which answers Craig's criticism. In his *Institutions* he made a similar point:

> The books of *Regiam Majestatem* ... are generally looked upon as part of *Our Law*, and they, and the *leges burgorum*, and the other tractates, joyned by *Skeen* to them, are called the *old books of Our Law*[.][49]

Mackenzie cited *Regiam Majestatem* quite heavily in his *Matters Criminal* and also cited it (although infrequently) in his *Institutions*.[50]

Others were more greatly influenced by Craig's criticism of *Regiam Majestatem*. Spottiswoode, for example, cited it only five times. Two of these citations are in quotations from Craig's *Jus feudale*.[51] This means that Spottiswoode would appear to have made little use of *Regiam Majestatem* when compiling his digest. Later collectors of decisions seem to rarely mention *Regiam Majestatem* relative to other sources.[52] This

---

[45] Clyde (ed.), *Hope's Major Practicks*, I, xvi.
[46] Clyde (ed.), *Hope's Major Practicks*, I, xvi.
[47] Julian Goodare, *The Government of Scotland 1560–1625* (Oxford: Oxford University Press), 83–4.
[48] Robinson (ed.), *The Laws and Customs*, 10.
[49] Mackenzie, *Institutions*, 6.
[50] See for example, Robinson (ed.), *The Laws and Customs*, 56, 112.
[51] John W. Cairns, '*Ius civile* in Scotland, ca. 1600', *Roman Legal Tradition* 2 (2004), 136–70 at 139.
[52] *A Collection of Decisions of the Lords of Council and Session ... Obser'd by Sir John Gilmour of Craigmiller [and] Sir David Falconer of Newton; Sir John Nisbet of Direlton, Decisions of the Lords of Council and Session ... December 1665, to June 1677* (Edinburgh: George Mosman, 1693).

could be reflective of a widespread hesitancy to rely upon a source which was of uncertain authority.

However, the first lawyer to explicitly and entirely reject the authority of *Regiam Majestatem* was Stair. He supported Craig's understanding of the problems with *Regiam Majestatem*:

> *Craig* doth very well observe, near that place, that these Books called *Regiam Majestatem,* are no part of our Law, but were compyled for the Customs of *England,* in 13. Books, by the Earl of *Chester,* and by some unknown and inconsiderat hand, stollen thence, and resarcinate into these four Books, which pass amongst us[.][53]

Stair later refreshed the reader's memory that

> the Books, called *Regiam Majestatem* ... hath been compeiled by some Stranger, who hath not fully known our Law, but by mistake, hath resolved most Cases, by the Customs of other Nations, especially of *England*.[54]

Unlike Craig, Stair in the *Institutions* never drew on *Regiam* as authority for a point of Scots law. His dismissal of it as a reliable source was total.

D. CONCLUSION

This chapter has shown that there was a degree of controversy with respect to the authority of the different sources of Scots law. Statutes became widely recognised as being the most authoritative source. This was argued particularly strongly by Mackenzie. Parliament was now an active legislature, reforming the law in easily available printed acts. Earlier legislation had been made widely available by the efforts of law commissions and, in particular, Skene. Because parliament could change the law, it was the most recent statute which was the most authoritative.[55] Somewhat apart from his contemporaries, Stair re-envisaged the root of legal authority as being in the exercise of sovereign authority.

Stair can also be distinguished from his predecessors in respect of his view of *Regiam Majestatem*. Craig had shown that *Regiam Majestatem*

---

[53] Stair, *Institutions*, 1.15/1.1.16.
[54] Stair, *Institutions*, 26.27/3.4.27. Spelling of '*Regiam*' corrected for ease of understanding.
[55] Goodare, *Government of Scotland*, 82–3.

owed so much of its content to the English tract of *Glanville* that it could not be safely regarded to reflect Scots law on any given point. In the period that followed, this view became widely acknowledged. Goodare has suggested that during this period of 1560–1625 'The old laws were now being reduced to talismans.'[56] When Stair wrote in the second half of the seventeenth century, he rejected *Regiam Majestatem* as a source of Scots law.

E. SELECTED BIBLIOGRAPHY AND FURTHER READING

(1) Books

Clyde, James Avon (trans.), *The Jus Feudale by Sir Thomas Craig of Riccarton* (2 vols, Edinburgh: William Hodge & Co., 1934).

Clyde, James Avon (ed.), *Hope's Major Practicks 1608–1633* (2 vols, Edinburgh: Stair Society, 1937–8).

Dalrymple, Sir James, Viscount Stair, *The Institutions of the Law of Scotland, Deduced from its Originals, and Collated with the Civil, Canon and Feudal Laws, and with the Customs of Neighbouring Nations* (Edinburgh: Heir of Andrew Anderson, 1st edn 1681, 2nd edn 1693).

Dalrymple, Sir James, Viscount Stair, *The Decisions of the Lords of Council and Session in the most Important Cases Debate before Them [1661–1681]* (2 vols, Edinburgh: Heir of Andrew Anderson, 1683–7).

Ford, J. D., *Law and Opinion in Scotland during the Seventeenth Century* (Oxford: Hart Publishing, 2007).

Franklin, Julian H. (ed.), *Bodin on Sovereignty* (Cambridge: Cambridge University Press, 1992).

Gibson, Sir Alexander of Durie, *The Decisions of the Lords of Council and Session in Most Cases of Importance, Debated, and brought before Them; From July 1621, to July 1642* (Edinburgh: Heir of Andrew Anderson, 1690).

Hope, Sir Thomas of Craighall, *Minor Practicks, or, A Treatise of the Scottish Law* (Edinburgh: Thomas Ruddiman, 1726).

[Mackenzie, Sir George of Rosehaugh], *Pleadings in Some Remarkable Cases before the Supreme Courts of Scotland since the Year 1661* (Edinburgh: George Swintoun, James Glen and Thomas Brown, 1673).

---

[56] Goodare, *Government of Scotland*, 81.

Mackenzie, Sir George of Rosehaugh, *The Institutions of the Law of Scotland* (Edinburgh: John Reid, 1684).

Robinson, Olivia F. (ed.), *The Laws and Customs of Scotland in Matters Criminal by Sir George Mackenzie* (Edinburgh: Stair Society, 2012).

Skene, Sir John of Curriehill (ed.), *Regiam Majestatem: The Auld Lawes and Constitutions of Scotland* (Edinburgh: Thomas Finlason, 1609).

Spottiswoode, Sir Robert of Pentland, *Practicks of the Laws of Scotland* (Edinburgh: James Watson, 1706).

(2) Chapters in Books

Cairns, John W., 'Historical introduction', in Kenneth Reid and Reinhard Zimmermann (eds), *A History of Private Law in Scotland* (Oxford: Oxford University Press, 2000) I, 14–184.

Wilson, Adelyn L. M., 'The "authentick practique bookes" of Alexander Spalding', in Andrew R. C. Simpson *et al.* (eds), *Continuity, Change and Pragmatism in the Law: Essays in Memory of Professor Angelo Forte* (Aberdeen: Aberdeen University Press, 2016), 175–236.

(3) Articles in Journals

Cairns, John W., '*Ius civile* in Scotland, ca. 1600', *Roman Legal Tradition* 2 (2004), 136–70.

MacQueen, Hector L., 'Mackenzie's Institutions in Scottish legal history', *Journal of the Law Society of Scotland* (1984), 498–501.

CHAPTER 17

Advocates in the Court of Session and Inferior Jurisdictions in Aberdeen

A. INTRODUCTION

Much has been said throughout this book about particular lawyers and their daily practice. The purpose of this chapter is to provide an overview of the history of the profession. It will principally focus on two branches of the profession. The first example taken will be the advocates working in the highest branch of the profession in the Court of Session. The second will be those men of law in Aberdeen, also called advocates, who are taken as an example of those who worked in the inferior courts.

The early history of men of law was discussed in Chapter 6.[1] As time passed there were several specialisms recognised within the legal profession. The clearest picture is of the professionals working in the Court of Session. John Finlay has noted:

> The membership of the College included both the advocates, who at least from the seventeenth century acted through their own corporate structure ... and the writers to the signet who, probably from an earlier date, had formed their own society ... It was in the sixteenth century, as advocates grew in status and specialisation, that the more mechanical oversight of processes came to be the province of the writer, or law agent, with advocates restricting themselves to work of more intellectual consequence.[2]

---

[1] See also John W. Cairns, 'A history of the faculty of advocates to 1900', in *The Laws of Scotland: The Stair Memorial Encyclopedia* (Edinburgh: Law Society of Scotland/Butterworths, 1996) XIII, 499 at para. 1240; R. K. Hannay, *The College of Justice* (Edinburgh: Stair Society Supplementary, 1990), 135; John Finlay, 'Ethics, etiquette and the early modern Scots advocate', *Juridical Review* (2006), 147–78 at 148–9, 153–4; G. Donaldson, 'The legal profession in Scottish society in the sixteenth and seventeenth centuries', *Juridical Review* (1976), 1–19 at 2–3, 5, 7–9.

[2] John Finlay, 'The lower branch of the legal profession in early modern Scotland',

These advocates had the right to plead or present cases before the lords of session, and normally also in any inferior court.[3] Only eight men of law were mentioned as having a right of audience in the foundation documents of the College of Justice in 1532.[4] Shortly thereafter, the advocates began to act in their mutual interests.[5] Several examples show this sense of a collective self. In 1538 the advocates received a collective right or 'privilege'.[6] From at least 1582 there was a dean of advocates, a recognised leader of the community.[7] Cooperation between the advocates has been seen in the petitioning of the bench to resume the administration of justice during the interregnum.[8] In 1670 the advocates withdrew from practice in the Session for two months in protest at new rules of court.[9] A further secession of advocates occurred in 1674 after some of their members were expelled from practice.[10]

There was plenty of work for those who proved themselves capable as advocates. As the centuries passed, there was an increasing quantity of work to be had for men of law. A general increase in litigiousness meant more cases were coming to the courts so more parties were seeking men of legal expertise. Periods of political turbulence caused surges in the number of cases, both in terms of criminal prosecutions and civil litigation.[11] At the same time, widespread bankruptcies during lean

---

Edinburgh Law Review 11 (2007), 31–61 at 36–7. See also Finlay, 'Ethics, etiquette', 150–1.

[3] Finlay, 'The lower branch', 52. Cf. Hannay, The College of Justice, 138. On the court at this time and the process of pleading, see Hector L. MacQueen, 'Two visitors in the Session, 1629 and 1636', in Hector L MacQueen (ed.), Miscellany Four (Edinburgh: Stair Society, 2002), 155–68.

[4] Cairns, 'A history of the faculty of advocates', para. 1241; Hannay, The College of Justice, 136–7.

[5] Finlay, 'Ethics, etiquette', 149–50, 152.

[6] Cairns, 'A history of the faculty of advocates', para. 1242; Hannay, The College of Justice, 137.

[7] John W. Cairns, 'Historical introduction', in Kenneth Reid and Reinhard Zimmermann (eds), A History of Private Law in Scotland (Oxford: Oxford University Press, 2000) I, 14–184 at 86–7; Hannay, The College of Justice, 144–5.

[8] Cairns, 'A history of the faculty of advocates', para. 1246.

[9] Cairns, 'Historical introduction', 125.

[10] Clare Jackson and Patricia Glennie, 'Restoration politics and the advocates' secession, 1674–1676', Scottish Historical Review 91:1 (2012), 76–105; Cairns, 'Historical introduction', 125–6; Cairns, 'A history of the faculty of advocates', para. 1252.

[11] N. T. Phillipson, 'Lawyers, landowners, and the civic leadership of post-union Scotland: an essay on the social role of the faculty of advocates 1661–1830 in 18th century Scottish society', Juridical Review (1976), 97–120 at 102–4.

periods required the assistance and management of lawyers. Increases in trade and commercial activities likewise meant men of law were needed. Increasing wealth meant more people could afford to pay lawyers. Such increases in the amount of work available meant that the practice of law became desirable as a profession. Legal business could be supplemented by administrative offices in the institutions of government. The practice of law thus attracted both high-born men and those of lower birth.[12]

The quantity of business which an advocate could hope to secure is witnessed in collections of decisions. One collection of 260 decisions on cases heard between 1655 and 1659 records the names of the advocates which appeared in around eighty-five per cent of the noted cases. Within this short time period some of the more successful lawyers appear a significant number of times. Two brothers, Sir Andrew Gilmour and Sir John Gilmour, are noted as appearing in 124 cases. Sir Peter Wedderburn is noted as appearing in forty-nine cases. Both John Gilmour and Wedderburn were elevated to the bench after their time at the bar.[13] However, such a promotion was not typical: only around half of the ordinary lords of session had once practised as advocates.[14] A new lawyer need not labour for years without recognition. '[A] single high-profile case could establish an advocate's reputation and secure him clients and income.'[15] Sir Thomas Hope of Craighall provides a good example of this. Within a year of his admission to the bar, he pleaded in defence of six ministers who had been accused of treason. He lost the case but the skill and learning which he demonstrated meant many took notice of the newly admitted advocate. This case allowed him to quickly establish himself within the profession.[16]

The second body of men of law mentioned by Finlay were the writers to the signet. Historically, these men were clerks but over time they became recognised as a lesser branch of the legal profession.[17] Writers

[12] Phillipson, 'Lawyers, landowners', 100–1.
[13] Adelyn L. M. Wilson, 'Practicks in Scotland's interregnum', *Juridical Review* (2012), 319–52 at 338–41.
[14] Phillipson, 'Lawyers, landowners', 104.
[15] Finlay, 'Ethics, etiquette', 163. On the wealth of advocates, see Donaldson, 'The legal profession', 13–16.
[16] James Avon Clyde (ed.), *Hope's Major Practicks 1608–1633* (Edinburgh: Stair Society, 1937–8) I, vii; David Stevenson, 'Hope, Sir Thomas, of Craighall, first baronet (1573–1646)', *Oxford Dictionary of National Biography* (Oxford: Oxford University Press, 2004); revised online edn May 2009, http://www.oxforddnb.com/view/article/13736.
[17] Finlay, 'The lower branch', 38; John Finlay, 'Pettyfoggers, regulation, and local

produced deeds and documents, ensured proper registration of these and other interests, stood as trustees, worked in arbitrating out-of-court settlements, and managed the progress of cases in the Session.[18] This group of men incorporated in 1594 to protect their common interests and to regulate admission into their profession.[19] This created a distinction between the writers to the signet, who were members of this official body, and ordinary writers, who were not. Joining the writers of the signet was a mark of professional recognition and competence. A formal rule stated that all writers to the signet had to be admitted as notaries public before admission to the society, which meant that (in theory at least) the lords of session had confirmed their capacity to produce high-quality documents.[20] The writers to the signet worked closely with the advocates, both on different aspects of cases and more generally in their common professional interests.[21] There was discussion of amalgamating the two professions, but they remained separate.[22] Some writers to the signet transferred to advocacy, although this was not common.[23]

The different spheres of work of advocates and writers in Edinburgh were not maintained in other towns. Rather, in the localities, the same men appear to have routinely undertaken both types of work. There were clusters of men of law in most of the larger population centres. However, 'Aberdeen had one of the strongest, and apparently most lucrative, local bars in the country and the advocates there enjoyed a reputation for more than ordinary skill which brought them employment from neighbouring counties.'[24] Work in the inferior courts could thus bring prosperity. The Aberdonian advocate Alexander Spalding was one such wealthy local lawyer. Despite personal scandal and twice relocating his family during this period, his record of practice suggests that he was normally involved in at least ten cases per year and some-

---

courts in early modern Scotland', *Scottish Historical Review* 87:1 (2008), 42–67 at 45; *A History of the Society of Writers to Her Majesty's Signet* (Edinburgh: for the Society, 1890), x–xx.

[18] Finlay, 'The lower branch', 52–5.

[19] *History of the Society of Writers*, xx–xxv.

[20] Finlay, 'The lower branch', 47–8. Gaps in the register of admission mean that it cannot be confirmed whether this rule was always followed in the seventeenth century; a re-iteration of the rule in 1684 after a complaint might suggest that it was not. The authors are grateful to John Finlay for this point.

[21] Finlay, 'The lower branch', 42–3.

[22] Cairns, 'Historical introduction', 88; Finlay, 'The lower branch', 42.

[23] Finlay, 'The lower branch', 43–5.

[24] Finlay, 'The lower branch', 49.

times double or treble that number. By the end of his career he had the money to afford a substantial home and had secured office within the local Commissary court.[25]

This chapter will examine three aspects of the profession. First, it will examine the process of admission as an advocate in the Court of Session. Secondly, it will discuss the provision of legal education at Scottish universities during the late sixteenth and seventeenth centuries. Thirdly, it will examine the process of admission as an advocate in Aberdeen, which was a lesser branch of the profession. Finally, it will examine the relationships between lawyers and the rise of legal dynasties.

B. ADMISSION AS AN ADVOCATE IN THE COURT OF SESSION

Advocacy was a learned, high-status profession. A man seeking admission as an advocate in the Court of Session in the sixteenth century would have had one of two types of education. First, he could prove that he had studied Roman law at a university. This study was normally undertaken at one of the great universities on the continent, for reasons which will be discussed below. Such formal learning would then have to be supplemented with a period of time spent as an expectant to the bar. This meant that he would have attended the court to watch cases and learn Scottish practick. From at least 1580, men hoping for admission on this basis had to prove their academic learning by giving a public lesson. This was a speech in the form of a disputation on a point of Roman law before the lords of session.[26] This method of entry was the more common: around two thirds of entrants to the bar between 1575 and 1608 were admitted in this way.[27] The alternative was to be admitted on the basis of a long period of previous practice in Scots law.[28] Men entering on this basis needed to provide references from practising advocates to establish that

---

[25] Adelyn L. M. Wilson, 'The "authentick practique bookes" of Alexander Spalding', in Andrew R. C. Simpson et al. (eds), *Continuity, Change and Pragmatism in the Law: Essays in Memory of Professor Angelo Forte* (Aberdeen: Aberdeen University Press, 2016), 175–236.

[26] John W. Cairns, 'Advocates' hats, Roman law and admission to the Scots bar, 1580–1812', *Journal of Legal History* 20:2 (1999), 24–61 at 35. See also Hannay, *The College of Justice*, 139–44.

[27] Cairns, 'Advocates' hats', 34; Hannay, *The College of Justice*, 145–7. On the later period, for which there is less evidence, see Hannay, *The College of Justice*, 148–52.

[28] Cairns, 'Advocates' hats', 34.

the candidate had the appropriate experience and reputation. This route of entry was called admission on a bill.[29]

This distinction between these two routes of admission became more pronounced during the seventeenth century. The testing of academic learning became more protracted. It is likely that the public lesson was meant to be a rigorous test of learning.[30] The candidate probably traditionally chose the topic. This would normally be a topic of Roman law, although Stair gave his lesson on feudal practice.[31] During the interregnum, however, candidates started to be referred to the dean of advocates for an additional trial of their knowledge. Cairns has identified this as an innovation which was coupled with a reduction in the amount of time which was spent as an expectant.[32] This additional trial survived the Restoration.[33] In 1664 an act of sederunt formalised this new process. Nine advocates should be elected as examiners for a one-year period to test entrants' learning. Those who passed their examination would have the topic of their lesson selected by the dean of advocates.[34]

Meanwhile, admission in recognition of prior practice continued into the interregnum and then the Restoration period. However, this process became controversial. The reason for this was threefold. First, advocacy in the Session was meant to be a learned profession. This is seen in Mackenzie's recorded pleadings, which 'put forward a vision of the advocate as skilled in both oratory and law' and so present the Scottish advocate as fulfilling the roles of the Roman jurist and orator.[35] However, the men admitted in recognition of their previous experience of practice were not tested on (and perhaps did not possess) academic learning. Some of these men even said explicitly that they had undertaken the requisite study abroad but did not feel able to undertake the

[29] Cairns, 'Advocates' hats', 38.
[30] Cairns, 'Advocates' hats', 36–7.
[31] Cairns, 'Advocates' hats', 37–8; J. D. Ford, *Law and Opinion in Scotland during the Seventeenth Century* (Oxford: Hart Publishing, 2007), 7–21; Adelyn L. M. Wilson, *The sources and method of the* Institutions of the Law of Scotland *by Sir James Dalrymple, 1st Viscount Stair, with specific reference to the law of obligations* (PhD thesis, University of Edinburgh, 2011), 1.2.2. A transcript of the lecture has been printed as 'Scotstarvet's "Trew Relation"', *Scottish Historical Review* 13:4 (1916), 380–92.
[32] Cairns, 'Advocates' hats', 40.
[33] Cairns, 'Advocates' hats', 40–2; Hannay, *The College of Justice*, 153.
[34] Cairns, 'Advocates' hats', 42–3; Hannay, *The College of Justice*, 153–4, 159–60.
[35] Cairns, 'Historical introduction', 126; John W. Cairns, 'The formation of the Scottish legal mind in the eighteenth century: themes of humanism and enlightenment in the admission of advocates', in Neil MacCormick and Peter Birks (eds), *The Legal Mind: Essays for Tony Honoré* (Oxford: Clarendon Press, 1986), 253–77 at 255–63.

trial.[36] Secondly, it was harder to compel these men to pay the fee for admission.[37] Thirdly, and perhaps most importantly, the advocates had less control over such admission to their ranks. The advocates were concerned to ensure that the men admitted were of suitable character and reputation.[38] They also wanted to control the number of men who would be competing for business.[39]

In 1681 the advocates lodged a complaint with the lords of session about the number of men admitted without a trial.[40] In 1688 the advocates were successful in getting an act of sederunt to confirm that the lords of session would test thoroughly any candidate for this route of admission on their knowledge of the municipal law.[41] However, there was still a degree of manipulation of the system by the lords of session in favour of their relatives and clients. During the 1680s, the sons of two lords of session, the nephew of the chancellor and a servitor of Stair were admitted by extraordinary process.[42] As a result, in 1691 the lords of session were prevented from thereafter admitting their relatives without trial. The following year they had to remit all candidates to the dean so that he could test their knowledge of practice in Scotland before their public lesson. A full private trial was introduced in 1696.[43] These reforms to extraordinary admission made it much less appealing than the ordinary route. Candidates were now rigorously tested, still had to pay double the entrance fee, and this route of entry was less prestigious.[44] This combination of factors meant that extraordinary admission stopped. From 1697 to 1706 all those 101 men admitted as advocates did so on the basis of ordinary admission and trial on the civil law.[45]

---

[36] Cairns, 'Advocates' hats', 44–5.
[37] On the fees, see Hannay, *The College of Justice*, 155–8.
[38] On the understanding of the advocate and his virtue, character and social status see Finlay, 'Ethics, etiquette', especially 154–60.
[39] John Finlay, 'Lawyers and the early modern state: regulation, exclusion, and numerus clausus', *Canadian Journal of History* 44 (2009), 383–410.
[40] Cairns, 'Advocates' hats', 43–4; see also Hannay, *The College of Justice*, 154–5.
[41] Cairns, 'Advocates' hats', 46.
[42] Cairns, 'Advocates' hats', 46–7.
[43] Cairns, 'Advocates' hats', 47; Cairns, 'A history of the faculty of advocates', para. 1256; cf. Hannay, *The College of Justice*, 155.
[44] Cairns, 'Historical introduction', 128.
[45] Cairns, 'Advocates' hats', 48. On admission as an advocate and limitation of the number of advocates admitted to practice in Europe more generally, see Finlay, 'Lawyers and the early modern state', especially 389–97, 399–400.

C. UNIVERSITY EDUCATION IN LAW

It was mentioned above that the candidates for admission to the bar who petitioned the court on the basis of their academic learning had normally attended a continental university. This was partly in recognition of the prestige that was held by some of the institutions in France, Germany and the Netherlands.[46] However, study abroad was also necessary because there was little if any teaching of law at the Scottish universities at this time.[47]

Formal provision of education in law was provided in the late sixteenth century only by King's College in Aberdeen and St Andrew's University. There would normally have been a master of canon law (the 'canonist') and a master of civil law (the 'civilist') at King's College from its foundation in 1495.[48] However, there was a new foundation of the institution in the 1570s. This re-foundation was modelled on the post-Reformation curriculum at Glasgow, at which law teaching had been abolished. That had been designed by the great educational reformer, Andrew Melville, and made no provision for the future teaching of law.[49] This meant that the King's College offices of canonist and civilist were formally defunct by the 1590s. In practice their teaching may have stopped long before this.[50]

Meanwhile, teaching of law by William Skene at St Andrews in the

---

[46] Cairns, 'Historical introduction', 128–89; Hannay, *The College of Justice*, 146–7; Peter Stein, 'The influence of Roman law on the law of Scotland', *Juridical Review* (1963), 205–45 at 215–16; David Baird Smith, 'Roman law', in *An Introductory Survey of the Sources and Literature of Scots Law* (Edinburgh: Stair Society, 1936), 171–82 at 176–9; Phillipson, 'Lawyers, landowners', 107–8, 120.

[47] On earlier instruction, see for example Donaldson, 'The legal profession', 3–7.

[48] Hector L. MacQueen, 'The foundation of law teaching at the University of Aberdeen', in David L. Carey Miller and Reinhard Zimmermann (eds), *The Civilian Tradition and Scots Law: Aberdeen Quincentenary Essays* (Berlin: Duncker & Humblot, 1997), 53–71 at 53–61; Peter John Anderson (ed.), *Officers and Graduates of University and King's College, Aberdeen MVD–MDCCCLX* (Aberdeen: New Spalding Club, 1893), 29–31.

[49] On Melville's curriculum and its impact, see Steven J. Reid, *Humanism and Calvinism: Andrew Melville and the Universities of Scotland, 1560–1625* (Farnham: Ashgate, 2011).

[50] John W. Cairns, 'The law, the advocates and the universities in late sixteenth-century Scotland', *Scottish Historical Review* 73:2 (1994), 171–90 at 179, 188; MacQueen, 'Foundation of law teaching', 61; Adelyn L. M. Wilson, 'Legal practice and legal institutions in seventeenth century Aberdeen, as witnessed in the lives of Thomas Nicolson of Cockburnspath and his associates' (forthcoming).

1570s seems to have had both a learned and a practical focus.[51] After his death in 1582 the post was held by Skene's stepson, who held it for four years but as a sinecure.[52] He in turn was succeeded by William Welwood, who was mentioned briefly in Chapter 14 as an author of tracts on maritime law.[53] Welwood was engaged in a blood feud, which interrupted his teaching and ultimately led to the collapse of law teaching at St Andrews around the turn of the century.[54] Therefore, by the end of the sixteenth century there was no reliable provision of legal education at any Scottish university.

In the seventeenth century, the teaching of law was reinvigorated at King's College in Aberdeen as a result of the intervention of Bishop Patrick Forbes of Corse in 1619. New masters of canon law and civil law were appointed. The former position lasted only temporarily. The third canonist (James Sandilands the younger) was deprived of that office because his teaching was deemed to be overly influenced by Catholic sentiments. He subsequently transferred to the position of civilist. Only one further holder of the chair of canonist is known. Robert Forbes held the post at least during the 1680s before his death in 1687. The position of canonist therefore survived only around a century after the Reformation, and about sixty years after its reintroduction by Bishop Patrick Forbes.[55]

Meanwhile, the chair of civilist was more or less continuously appointed through the seventeenth century.[56] The holders of the chair did not all actually hold classes or teach. The teaching which was provided appears to have been elementary in nature, similar to that provided by William Skene.[57] Indeed it was insufficiently learned to provide the

---

[51] Cairns, 'The law, the advocates and the universities', 176–83; John W. Cairns, 'Academic feud, bloodfeud, and William Welwood: legal education in St Andrews, 1560–1611', *Edinburgh Law Review* 2 (1998), 158–79 (part one), 255–87 (part two) at 168–70. On the earliest teaching of law at St Andrews, see MacQueen, 'Foundation of law teaching', 64–6.

[52] Cairns, 'The law, the advocates and the universities', 183–4; Cairns, 'Academic feud', 170–1.

[53] On which, see J. D. Ford, 'William Welwod's treatises on maritime law', *Journal of Legal History* 34:2 (2013), 172–210.

[54] Cairns, 'The law, the advocates and the universities', 185–6; Cairns, 'Academic feud', 173–9, 255–87.

[55] Wilson, 'Thomas Nicolson of Cockburnspath'; Anderson (ed.), *Officers and Graduates*, 30.

[56] Anderson (ed.), *Officers and Graduates*, 29–32; John W. Cairns, 'Lawyers, law professors, and localities: the Universities of Aberdeen, 1680–1750', *Northern Ireland Legal Quarterly* 46 (1995), 304–31 at 306; MacQueen, 'Foundation of law teaching', 61–3.

[57] The authors are grateful for John Ford's observations on this point.

level of education required by the advocates in the Court of Session.[58] Two examples show that difference in standard. James Sandilands the younger had never studied law on the continent but was nonetheless appointed first as canonist and then as civilist. James Scougall, who was the commissary of Aberdeen and civilist at King's College, was admitted as an advocate in the Session in 1687 extraordinarily saying he had not undertaken 'Close application to that studdy' of Roman law sufficient to pass the normal trial.[59] What he was claiming here was that his study of Roman law was insufficient to undertake the trial. Rather, the education which was provided at King's College was probably sufficient only for men who wished to enter practice in the local Commissary, Sheriff or Burgh courts.[60]

D. ADMISSION AS AN ADVOCATE IN ABERDEEN

The practitioners of law in Aberdeen were also called advocates but theirs was a lower branch of the profession which worked in the inferior courts. Aberdonian advocates also gained entry to their profession during this period either by demonstrating their formal learning or by serving as an apprentice to an experienced practitioner. However, the standard of academic learning which had to be proved was much lower. They did not need to attend classes on Roman law at one of the great institutions of continental learning. The classes in law at King's College likely provided a sufficient introduction to the law.[61]

One hundred and twenty men are recorded as having entered as an Aberdonian advocate in the sixteenth and seventeenth centuries. Forty-one had undertaken at least a Master of Arts at a university. Twenty had undertaken apprenticeships with other Aberdonian advocates. Ten had both a formal, university education and had also served an apprenticeship.[62] This means that some of the men hoping to enter the profession in Aberdeen would probably have attended the classes on law at King's College. After completing their studies (or perhaps alongside their studies) they would attend the sessions of the Commissary court. This court sat at St Machar's Cathedral in the burgh of Old Aberdeen,

---

[58] Cairns, 'Lawyers, law professors', 309–13.
[59] Cairns, 'Advocates' hats', 45; Anderson (ed.), *Officers and Graduates*, 8, 30.
[60] Cairns, 'Lawyers, law professors', 313–15.
[61] Cairns, 'Lawyers, law professors', 305.
[62] Wilson, 'The "authentick practique bookes"', 178–9.

ten minutes' walk from the university. Often one of the masters of law also held the office of Commissary judge,[63] so a young advocate would study with this man in class and then be involved in or watch cases heard by him in court.

Meanwhile, the master–apprentice relationship was central to the education of aspiring lawyers. Many of these connections built on existing relationships between the men involved: many were related, through blood or marriage. A good example of this is found in the Paip family. Alexander Paip's record of admission to practice in 1549 is the earliest found in Aberdeen. His son, Robert, followed his father into practice in 1581 on the basis of his having acquired a Master of Arts at university. Robert had seven sons, two of whom (Alexander and William) entered as advocates in Aberdeen on the basis of apprenticeships to their father as well as holding degrees in the arts.[64] Such professional networks, concurrent with broader kinship networks and patronage networks, formed an important aspect of local practice as it did in the Session.

E. RELATIONSHIPS BETWEEN LAWYERS

The process of admission into the legal professions required entrants to come from families who could either afford years of university education or arrange apprenticeships with relatives or friends. Law became in the late sixteenth century the profession of choice for those men of lesser nobility and for sons of burgesses – those whose families had the money to support their education.[65] The effect was the rise of the legal dynasty, as sons followed their fathers into the law and those fathers aided in the promotion of their sons' careers.[66] These relationships were of great importance within the legal profession in the early modern period.

These professional networks were evident among the advocates in Edinburgh. A good example of this is found in the family of Sir Thomas Hope of Craighall. He was the son of a Scot who had lived as a burgess of Dieppe in France until he left as a result of the St Bartholomew's

---

[63] Anderson (ed.), *Officers and Graduates*, 30–1; Wilson, 'Thomas Nicolson of Cockburnspath'.

[64] John Alexander Henderson (ed.), *History of the Society of Advocates in Aberdeen* (Aberdeen: for the University, 1912), 289–90.

[65] Cairns, 'A history of the faculty of advocates', para. 1243; Phillipson, 'Lawyers, landowners', 100–1. On the law and the church as the professions of choice for these men, see Donaldson, 'The legal profession', 9.

[66] See Donaldson, 'The legal profession', 10–13.

Day massacre.[67] The death of his father while he was still studying the arts in Scotland meant that Hope's early career was no longer supported financially by his immediate family so he could not undertake study of law on the continent. After graduating in the arts in 1592 he seems to have apprenticed to a cousin, John Nicolson of Lasswade, an advocate and commissary.[68] He later acknowledged Nicolson as 'my maister under whom I lernit not only my calling as a Citizen but my calling as a Christian' (i.e. 'my master under whom I learned not only my calling as a citizen but my calling as a Christian').[69] By 1600 Hope was named as the new solicitor and advocate for the kirk. This shows that he was working independently, at least on occasion. Nicolson died in January 1605 and Hope was admitted to practice a few weeks later. The sederunt books record Hope having been a servitor 'for foir or fyve yearis bygane' with 'ane desyre to attane to some measure of knawledge in the Civill and Cannon Lawes'.[70] It is not clear whether those years were during the 1590s prior to his appointment to the kirk or thereafter, but it seems likely that this was the former. He entered as an advocate only in 1605. In the following year Hope established himself as a man of great reputation and learning. Charles I appointed him as king's advocate in 1626 (initially jointly), a post which he held until his death in 1646.[71]

Three of Sir Thomas's four sons (John, Thomas and James) followed their father into the law, and all became lords of session.[72] His position as king's advocate and reputation as a man of legal learning would have been

---

67 Ann Hope, 'Sir Thomas Hope, Lord Advocate to Charles I', in Hector L. MacQueen (ed.), *Miscellany Four* (Edinburgh: Stair Society, 2002), 145. Cf. Stevenson, 'Hope, Sir Thomas, of Craighall'.

68 Cf. Stevenson, 'Hope, Sir Thomas'.

69 Hope, 'Sir Thomas Hope', 151.

70 Hope, 'Sir Thomas Hope', 147.

71 Hope, 'Sir Thomas Hope', 148.

72 George Brunton and David Haig, *An Historical Account of the Senators of the College of Justice, from its Institution in MDXXXII* (Edinburgh: Thomas Clark, 1832), 289–90, 306, 321–2; Arthur H. Williamson, 'Hope, Sir James, of Hopetoun, appointed Lord Hopetoun under the protectorate (1614–1661)', *Oxford Dictionary of National Biography* (Oxford: Oxford University Press, 2004); revised online edn May 2009, http://www.oxforddnb.com/view/article/13722; J. A. Hamilton, 'Hope, Sir Thomas, of Kerse (1606–1643)', revised by Sharon Adams, *Oxford Dictionary of National Biography* (Oxford: Oxford University Press, 2004), http://www.oxforddnb.com/view/article/13735; Vaughan T. Wells, 'Hope, Sir John, Lord Craighall (1603x5–1654)', *Oxford Dictionary of National Biography* (Oxford: Oxford University Press, 2004), http://www.oxforddnb.com/view/article/13728; Francis J. Grant (ed.), *The Faculty of Advocates in Scotland 1532–1943, with Genealogical Notes* (Edinburgh: Scottish Record Society, 1944), 104–5.

very helpful to them. The Hope family legend that the *Minor practicks* was dictated by Sir Thomas to his sons as he dressed in the morning was mentioned in Chapter 14. All three sons studied the arts at Scottish universities and at least one (James) was sent for legal education in France. John Hope sat on the bench as Lord Craighall. His own son, Archibald, sat on the bench as Lord Rankeillor. Archibald's sons, Thomas and John, also became advocates.

Sir Thomas Hope also furthered the ambitions of the son of his master and cousin. He wrote in respect to the appointment of a new king's advocate after his death that 'oblischement caryis me in the first place to my cousing Mr Thomas Nicolsoun in respect of the band of blood betuix him and me and of the memorie of his worthie father and befoir him of his thryis worthie uncle my maister' (i.e. 'obligation carries me in the first place to my cousin, Mr Thomas Nicolson, in respect of the bond of blood between him and me and of the memory of his worthy father and before him of his thrice worthy uncle, my master').[73] Sir Thomas Hope's own servitor or secretary, Alexander Burnett of Carlops, also became an advocate in 1633.[74]

This kind of legal patronage was also seen in the inferior regional courts. This is seen in the aforementioned example of the Paip family. Alexander Paip, an advocate in Aberdeen who was admitted in 1549, was followed into the law by his son Robert in 1581; his two sons, William and Alexander, were admitted in 1618 and 1615 respectively. William and the younger Alexander were apprenticed to their father, as has been mentioned. Robert, William and Alexander all married daughters of other advocates in Aberdeen. These wider familial relationships could be drawn on to find masters for would-be apprentices. They also brought business: Robert Paip did work for several individuals with whom there may have been connections through marriage.[75] Men could also be encouraged to demit offices of state to ambitious relatives. Offices within the court system could be traded or sold as commodities, so it was common for these to be passed between family members. For example, the younger Alexander Paip held the office of sheriff depute of Aberdeen in 1625–30. He received it from his brother, William, who had held the office since 1618. Meanwhile, William Anderson (Alexander's father-in-law) left his office of sheriff clerk in his will to his other son-in-law,

---

[73] Hope, 'Sir Thomas Hope', 151.
[74] Grant (ed.), *The Faculty of Advocates in Scotland*, 24.
[75] Adelyn L. M. Wilson, 'Men of law and legal networks in Aberdeen, 1600–1650' (forthcoming). Cf. Cairns, 'A history of the faculty of advocates', para. 1247.

Patrick Chalmer. Patrick received the office in 1630 and appointed his younger brother, John, as the sheriff clerk depute. He then demitted the senior office to him in 1646.[76]

F. CONCLUSION

This chapter has examined certain aspects of the professional life of men of law in early modern Scotland. It has shown that advocates working in the Court of Session were the highest branch of the profession. These men worked together for their common interest, with the dean of advocates being the leader of the group. They were particularly concerned about controlling admission to their profession. This could be achieved either by a demonstration of formal learning in Roman law or by a period of practice in the lesser branches of the profession or as a servitor to an advocate or lord of session. The latter route was controversial so became increasingly regulated until by the end of the seventeenth century it was so unappealing that no candidates for admission chose it. Those who wished to establish their academic learning had normally studied Roman or canon law on the continent. This was partly because of the prestige of these institutions but also because law teaching at Scottish universities largely failed at this time.

The reform of the curriculum after the Reformation meant that support for the teaching of law was lost first at Glasgow and thereafter at King's College in Aberdeen. Teaching of law at St Andrews meanwhile became intermittent and then failed when the master, William Welwood, became engaged in a local blood feud. Law teaching was (at least in theory) reinvigorated at King's College in 1619 but was at a level appropriate only to those who wished to enter practice locally in the inferior courts. Although therefore unfit for the advocates in the Court of Session, standards were lower for the men of law working in Aberdeen. This seems to have sufficed for the academic training for these men, who could alternatively be admitted on the basis of a period of prior practice. They would learn their trade in the Commissary court and later might seek admission to plead in the local Sheriff court.

Professional networks formed a critical part of legal practice. Networks could be established through blood, through marriage or through professional cooperation such as master–apprentice relationships. Such networks assisted those who wished to enter the profession, through the

---

[76] Wilson, 'Thomas Nicolson of Cockburnspath' (forthcoming).

provision of knowledge and understanding, by supporting a student undertaking university education, or by training apprentices and servitors. These networks could bring legal business, helping to develop the portfolio of work available to the lawyer. They could also lend support in acquiring offices by recommending a person who might be suitable, or even by providing them directly by gift, sale or inheritance.

G. SELECTED BIBLIOGRAPHY AND FURTHER READING

(1) Books

Anderson, Peter John (ed.), *Officers and Graduates of University and King's College, Aberdeen MVD–MDCCCLX* (Aberdeen: New Spalding Club, 1893).

Brunton, George and David Haig, *An Historical Account of the Senators of the College of Justice, from its Institution in MDXXXII* (Edinburgh: Thomas Clark, 1832).

Ford, J. D., *Law and Opinion in Scotland during the Seventeenth Century* (Oxford: Hart Publishing, 2007).

Grant, Francis J. (ed.), *The Faculty of Advocates in Scotland 1532–1943, with Genealogical Notes* (Edinburgh: Scottish Record Society, 1944).

Hannay, R. K., *The College of Justice* (Edinburgh: Stair Society Supplementary, 1990).

Henderson, John Alexander (ed.), *History of the Society of Advocates in Aberdeen* (Aberdeen: for the University, 1912).

A History of the Society of Writers to Her Majesty's Signet (Edinburgh: for the Society, 1890).

Reid, Steven J., *Humanism and Calvinism: Andrew Melville and the Universities of Scotland, 1560–1625* (Farnham: Ashgate, 2011).

(2) Chapters in Books

Cairns, John W., 'The formation of the Scottish legal mind in the eighteenth century: themes of humanism and enlightenment in the admission of advocates', in Neil MacCormick and Peter Birks (eds), *The Legal Mind: Essays for Tony Honoré* (Oxford: Clarendon Press, 1986), 253–77.

Cairns, John W., 'A history of the faculty of advocates to 1900', in *The*

Laws of Scotland: The Stair Memorial Encyclopedia (Edinburgh: Law Society of Scotland/Butterworths, 1996) XIII, 499–536.

Cairns, John W., 'Historical introduction', in Kenneth Reid and Reinhard Zimmermann (eds), *A History of Private Law in Scotland* (Oxford: Oxford University Press, 2000) I, 14–184.

Hope, Ann, 'Sir Thomas Hope, Lord Advocate to Charles I', in Hector L. MacQueen (ed.), *Miscellany Four* (Edinburgh: Stair Society, 2002), 145–53.

MacQueen, Hector L., 'The foundation of law teaching at the University of Aberdeen', in David L. Carey Miller and Reinhard Zimmermann (eds), *The Civilian Tradition and Scots Law: Aberdeen Quincentenary Essays* (Berlin: Duncker & Humblot, 1997), 53–71.

Wilson, Adelyn L. M., 'The "authentick practique bookes" of Alexander Spalding', in Andrew R. C. Simpson *et al.* (eds), *Continuity, Change and Pragmatism in the Law: Essays in Memory of Professor Angelo Forte* (Aberdeen: Aberdeen University Press, 2016), 175–236.

(3) Articles in Journals

Cairns, John W., 'The law, the advocates and the universities in late sixteenth-century Scotland', *Scottish Historical Review* 73:2 (1994), 171–90.

Cairns, John W., 'Lawyers, law professors, and localities: the Universities of Aberdeen, 1680–1750', *Northern Ireland Legal Quarterly* 46 (1995), 304–31.

Cairns, John W., 'Academic feud, bloodfeud, and William Welwood: legal education in St Andrews, 1560–1611', *Edinburgh Law Review* 2 (1998), 158–79 (part one), 255–87 (part two).

Cairns, John W., 'Advocates' hats, Roman law and admission to the Scots bar, 1580–1812', *Journal of Legal History* 20:2 (1999), 24–61.

Donaldson, G., 'The legal profession in Scottish society in the sixteenth and seventeenth centuries', *Juridical Review* (1976), 1–19.

Finlay, John, 'Ethics, etiquette and the early modern Scots advocate', *Juridical Review* (2006), 147–78.

Finlay, John, 'The lower branch of the legal profession in early modern Scotland', *Edinburgh Law Review* 11 (2007), 31–61.

Finlay, John, 'Pettyfoggers, regulation, and local courts in early modern Scotland', *Scottish Historical Review* 87:1 (2008), 42–67.

Finlay, John, 'Lawyers and the early modern state: regulation, exclusion, and *numerus clausus*', *Canadian Journal of History* 44 (2009), 383–410.

Jackson, Clare and Patricia Glennie, 'Restoration politics and the advocates' secession, 1674–1676', *Scottish Historical Review* 91:1 (2012), 76–105.

Phillipson, N. T., 'Lawyers, landowners, and the civic leadership of post-union Scotland: an essay on the social role of the faculty of advocates 1661–1830 in 18th century Scottish society', *Juridical Review* (1976), 97–120.

'Scotstarvet's "Trew Relation"', *Scottish Historical Review* 13:4 (1916), 380–92.

Wilson, Adelyn L. M., 'Practicks in Scotland's interregnum', *Juridical Review* (2012), 319–52.

(4) Digital Sources

Stevenson, David, 'Hope, Sir Thomas, of Craighall, first baronet (1573–1646)', *Oxford Dictionary of National Biography* (Oxford: Oxford University Press, 2004); revised online edn May 2009, http://www.oxforddnb.com/view/article/13736.

CHAPTER 18

Advocates, Witches and Judicial Torture

A. INTRODUCTION

Chapter 17 examined the rise of the professional man of law in the sixteenth and seventeenth centuries. This chapter will show the impact which the involvement of the advocates and central legal authorities had on the prosecution of the crime of witchcraft. This is important because:

> Witchcraft trials spearheaded the state's move towards public prosecution. Before the late sixteenth century, crimes had been interpersonal and had largely been pursued by and through aggrieved private prosecutors. Now the lord advocate began to act as a public prosecutor[.][1]

In the late sixteenth and seventeenth century Scotland experienced a prolific number of prosecutions of witchcraft. The crime (or the fear of it) caused panic among the Scots, who genuinely believed that witches were among them and doing the Devil's work. The Scottish campaign against witches began in earnest in 1590–1 with the prosecutions of men and women in what would come to be known as the North Berwick witch trials.

James VI was to marry a Danish Princess, known in Scotland as Anne of Denmark. Her journey to Scotland was jeopardized first by two cannons exploding during her leaving celebrations, killing several men. Then her ship encountered such storms that it was almost wrecked and had to shelter in the bay at Oslo in Norway. James set sail for Norway to collect his bride and was married in the bishop's palace there.

---

[1] Julian Goodare, 'Witch-hunting and the Scottish state', in Julian Goodare (ed.), *The Scottish Witch-Hunt in Context* (Manchester: Manchester University Press, 2002), 122–45 at 140.

Their onward voyage was also beset by storms. The King of Denmark blamed one of his state officials for the problems of Anne's voyage, thinking that her ship had not been properly readied. That official in turn blamed witchcraft. Trials were held. Women who confessed under torture to using witchcraft to jeopardise the voyage were encouraged to reveal the names of their co-conspirators. Members of the Scottish royal court were implicated. James decided to hold his own investigation in Scotland.[2]

The Scottish witches were largely identified as living in East Lothian, particularly around North Berwick, Prestonpans and Tranent. The Scottish witch hunt started with a young woman named Geillis Duncan. She was a healer who was suspected by her employer of using 'some extraordinary and unlawful means' in her work.[3] Therefore her employer 'did with the help of others torment her with the torture of the pilliwinks [thumbscrews] upon her fingers, which is a grievous torture, and binding or wrinching [tightening] her head with a cord or rope, which is a most cruel torment also'.[4] These tortures applied pressure on the fingers until they popped and on the head until the person was in agony. Even under these tortures, Geillis did not confess.[5] Therefore they looked for what was known as a 'Devil's mark'. This was a place on the body of a witch where 'the Devil doth lick them with his tongue' and where they could not feel pain.[6] This was identified by 'pricking' the witch with a long pin. Under this further torture, Geillis Duncan confessed to her own witchcraft and then began naming other witches. These other men and women were then tortured in turn and began naming further compatriots. Accordingly more than sixty people from East Lothian, Edinburgh

---

[2] On this incident and the possibility of Danish influence on Scotland, see P. G. Maxwell-Stuart, 'The fear of the king is death: James VI and the witches of East Lothian', in Brian P. Levack (ed.), *New Perspectives on Witchcraft, Magic and Demonology, III: Witchcraft in the British Isles and New England* (London: Routledge, 2001), 367–81.

[3] Lawrence Normand and Gareth Roberts (eds), *Witchcraft in Early Modern Scotland: James VI's Demonology and the North Berwick Witches* (Liverpool: Liverpool University Press, 2000), 311; *Newes from Scotland, Declaring the Damnable Life of Doctor Fian, a Notable Sorcerer, who was Burned at Edenbrough in Ianuarie last* (London: for William Wright, 1591; reprint London: Shakespeare Press, 1816), A3v. It should be remembered that 'Of all the texts generated by the North Berwick witch trials, *News from Scotland* is the most propagandistic': Normand and Roberts (eds), *Witchcraft*, 290.

[4] Normand and Roberts (eds), *Witchcraft*, 312.

[5] Normand and Roberts (eds), *Witchcraft*, 312; *Newes from Scotland*, A4r.

[6] Normand and Roberts (eds), *Witchcraft*, 313; *Newes from Scotland*, B1r.

and the port of Leith were identified as witches. Another twenty people were accused in Ross-shire and Aberdeenshire.[7]

James VI personally participated in the trials. A remarkable account survives of the questioning of Agnes Sampson by the king and his councillors. She was initially questioned by the king and the privy council at Holyrood House but refused to confess to any witchcraft. As such, 'they caused her to be conveyed away to prison, there to receive such torture'.[8] She was shaved and then pricked as a witch. Having been tortured, she was 'brought again before the king's Majesty and his council'.[9] She confessed to them that she had been one of 200 witches who had rowed up the coast to North Berwick. She said Geillis Duncan had played a song on a Jew's harp to accompany them into the town. James called for the imprisoned Geillis to be brought before the council to play the song for them, which she duly did.[10] Agnes then explained that the Devil had entered the kirk in the shape of a man, stood with his bared bottom over the pulpit and commanded each witch to 'kiss his buttocks in sign of duty to him'.[11] The Devil then explained that 'the king is the greatest enemy he hath in the world'.[12] This story was so extraordinary that James found it hard to believe and 'his Majesty said they were all extreme liars'.[13] Agnes then recounted to the king 'the very words which passed between the king's Majesty and his queen at Upslo [Oslo] in Norway the first night of their marriage'.[14] She also gave a highly detailed account of the spell which she cast to 'put him to such extraordinary pains as if he had been lying upon sharp thorns and ends of needles.'[15] Then apparently she christened a cat, 'bound to each part of that cat the chiefest parts of a dead man', then sailed it out to sea and recounted a curse.[16] This she said was 'the cause that the king's Majesty's ship, at his coming forth of Denmark, had a contrary wind'.[17]

---

[7]   Christina Larner et al., *A Source Book of Scottish Witchcraft* (Glasgow: Glasgow University Department of Sociology, 1977), 3–9.

[8]   Normand and Roberts (eds), *Witchcraft*, 313; *Newes from Scotland*, B1r.

[9]   Normand and Roberts (eds), *Witchcraft*, 314; *Newes from Scotland*, B1v.

[10]   Normand and Roberts (eds), *Witchcraft*, 315; *Newes from Scotland*, B1v.

[11]   Normand and Roberts (eds), *Witchcraft*, 315; *Newes from Scotland*, B2r. On witches and sex with the devil, see Christina Larner, *Enemies of God: The Witch-hunt in Scotland* (London: Chatto and Windus, 1981), 148–9.

[12]   Normand and Roberts (eds), *Witchcraft*, 315; *Newes from Scotland*, B2r.

[13]   Normand and Roberts (eds), *Witchcraft*, 316; *Newes from Scotland*, B2r.

[14]   Normand and Roberts (eds), *Witchcraft*, 316; *Newes from Scotland*, B2r-v.

[15]   Normand and Roberts (eds), *Witchcraft*, 316; *Newes from Scotland* B2v–3r.

[16]   Normand and Roberts (eds), *Witchcraft*, 316; *Newes from Scotland*, B3r.

[17]   Normand and Roberts (eds), *Witchcraft*, 317; *Newes from Scotland*, B3r.

After relating this extraordinary story, Agnes Sampson was tried for her crimes. Her case was pursued by the king's advocate and her fate determined by an assize of seventeen men. The assize convicted her of fifty-three criminal charges.[18] A record of her trial noted that she

> was ordained by the justice pronounced by the mouth of James Shiel, dempster, to be taken to the castle of Edinburgh and there bound to a stake and worried [strangled] while she was dead, and thereafter her body to be burned in ashes and all her moveable goods to be escheat and inbrought [forfeited] to our sovereign lord's use[.][19]

This episode in Scotland's history raises several questions about legal practice during this period.[20] This chapter will examine the reasons behind the belief in witchcraft and its early prosecution in Scotland. It will then examine the procedure by which those accused of witchcraft, such as Agnes Sampson, were prosecuted at this time. One of the very important aspects of the history of witchcraft is the centralisation of its prosecution and the increasing participation of advocates in trials of witchcraft. This can be seen to have had a significant impact on the rate of acquittal and eventually the restriction in the prosecution of witch-craft and the use of judicial torture. This chapter will examine the rise of judicial scepticism after 1662 and again after 1689.

B. THE CRIME OF WITCHCRAFT AND ITS PROSECUTION BEFORE 1590

The trials of the North Berwick witches were not the first in Scotland. Prior to the 1560 Reformation, responsibility for arranging the prosecution

[18] Normand and Roberts (eds), *Witchcraft*, 231–6; Robert Pitcairn, *Criminal Trials in Scotland, from AD MCCCCLXXXVIII [1488] to AD MDCXXIV [1624]* (3 vols, Edinburgh: William Tait, 1833) I, pt 1, 230–41.

[19] Normand and Roberts (eds), *Witchcraft*, 246; Pitcairn, *Criminal Trials* I, pt 1, 241. The case is described only briefly in Hugo Arnott, *A Collection and Abridgement of Celebrated Criminal Trials in Scotland, from AD 1536, to 1784* (Edinburgh: William Smellie, 1785), 349. For an account of the records, see William Roughead, 'Scottish witch trials: the witches of North Berwick', *Juridical Review* (1913), 161–84.

[20] It has also been the focus of extensive discussion in the academic literature. For a summary of this debate, see Julian Goodare, 'Witchcraft in Scotland', in Brian P. Levack (ed.), *The Oxford Handbook of Witchcraft in Early Modern Europe and Colonial America* (Oxford: Oxford University Press, 2013), 300–17 at 304.

of witches lay with the church courts.[21] Witchcraft was an omnipresent threat in the minds of early modern Europeans. Witches are mentioned in several places in the Bible, the most famous of which passages reads in the contemporary version: 'Thou shalt not suffre a witche to liue'.[22] Instructions on how to identify and punish witches could be found in a fifteenth-century book called the *Malleus Maleficarum* (1486; 'The Hammer of Witches'). It gained popularity across the continent, although there is not significant evidence of its use in early modern Scotland.[23]

After the Reformation, a number of acts of parliament were passed on crimes and other matters which had religious connotations, one of which was that of witchcraft. In 1563 the Scottish parliament passed an act which ordained that no person could thereafter

> use any manner of witchcraft, sorcery or necromancy, nor give themselves out to have any such craft or knowledge thereof, thereby abusing the people, or that any person seek any help, response or consultation from any such users or abusers foresaid of witchcraft, sorcery or necromancy under the pain of death, which is to be executed against the user and abuser as well as the seeker of the response or consultation; and this is to be put to execution by the justice, sheriffs, stewarts, bailies, lords of regalities and royalties, their deputies and other judges ordinary competent within this realm with all rigour, having the power to execute the same.[24]

This act thus allowed local legal officers to investigate crimes of witchcraft and to put to death those convicted of the same. The first 'large-scale local hunt' may have been in the east of Scotland in 1568–9, although it was not particularly successful.[25] Local prosecution of witches continued in the years thereafter. For example, Christine Douglas and Jonet Fultoun were accused of witchcraft resulting in human illness and with conversing with the Devil in the Edinburgh burgh court in 1579. They were convicted by that court and executed by strangulation and burning.[26] However, witchcraft trials were not common before 1590. Perhaps

---

[21] Goodare, 'Witch-hunting and the Scottish state', 124–5.

[22] Geneva Bible (1560 edition), Exodus 22.18.

[23] The authors are grateful for the advice of Julian Goodare on this point.

[24] *RPS* A1563/6/9. On earlier cases, see Larner, *Enemies of God*, 65–6.

[25] Michael Wasser, 'Scotland's first witch-hunt: the eastern witch-hunt of 1568–1569', in Julian Goodare (ed.), *Scottish Witches and Witch-Hunters* (Basingstoke: Palgrave Macmillan, 2013), 17–33, quoted text at 17; Larner *et al.*, *A Source Book*, 172.

[26] Edinburgh City Archives, Canongate Burgh Court Book 1577–80, SL150/1/3,

only around forty people were accused between 1563 and 1589, and only around twenty-five trials appear to have taken place.[27]

C. THE TRIAL OF AGNES SAMPSON AND ITS AFTERMATH

Agnes's trial was founded on an initial complaint by another person, in this case another woman accused of witchcraft. Prosecutions of witchcraft were unusual in their nature because sometimes a spate of prosecutions would happen all at once. Part of the cause of that was that one accused witch would be compelled to name fellow witches under torture. A community which felt that it was under imminent threat of witchcraft also became more concerned to identify witches in its midst. Hence what happened with Geillis Duncan, Agnes Sampson and the other witches in 1590–1. Indeed, most Scots who were accused of witchcraft were named by a fellow witch rather than a neighbour or enemy.[28] A person who had been convicted of the crime could be tortured for those names.[29]

Geillis Duncan's accusation began criminal proceedings against Agnes. The first stage of the proceedings was the process before the king. This was effectively a pre-trial stage of proceedings to gather evidence against possible witches. Witchcraft trials would normally have had such a stage. However, it would not typically have been before the king:

> The pre-trial investigation was usually organized by a local church court, either the kirk session, the parish committee of post-Reformation Scotland, or its superior court, the presbytery. These courts were powerful bodies, keen to enforce godly discipline. They could not execute anyone, but they could summon suspects and witnesses, interrogate them, and compile dossiers of evidence.[30]

370–3. See for other examples Julian Goodare et al., *The Survey of Scottish Witchcraft*, http://www.shca.ed.ac.uk/Research/witches/; Larner et al., *A Source Book*, 172–3. For a discussion of witchcraft between 1563 and 1590, see Larner, *Enemies of God*, 67–8.

[27] Larner et al., *A Source Book*, 238–9.

[28] Goodare, 'Witchcraft in Scotland', 303. On reputation as a factor in naming, see Larner, *Enemies of God*, 103–5.

[29] Olivia F. Robinson (ed.), *The Laws and Customs of Scotland in Matters Criminal by Sir George Mackenzie* (Edinburgh: Stair Society, 2012), 392.

[30] Goodare, 'Witchcraft in Scotland', 303.

During this pre-trial stage, the king and his councillors ordered Agnes's torture. Judicial torture in seventeenth-century Scotland was not used as a method of punishment. Rather it was a device used by prosecuting authorities as a method of evidence collection prior to trial. One of the aspects of Scots criminal law was that more than one piece of evidence was required to indicate someone's guilt before that person could be tried of a crime.[31] There were many ways in which this requirement might be satisfied. Normally this would be through witness testimony as well as the confession of the accused. The difficulty was that few people were eager to confess to crimes when the punishment was agonising death. Therefore, the prosecuting persons could seek a warrant from the privy council to use torture to elicit a confession.[32]

This mechanism for evidence gathering was not limited to cases of witchcraft. Thirty-nine torture warrants were issued between 1590 and 1690 and only two of these were issued against those accused of witchcraft.[33] One of these was for the North Berwick witch trials and another in respect of six men accused of witchcraft and murder in 1610.[34] This should not be seen to suggest, however, that there was little torture of witches. Rather it is clear that most witchcraft prosecutions did not secure a warrant.[35] Levack has suggested that accordingly 'local magistrates were using torture illegally'.[36] However, whether the local authorities would have considered themselves to have been proceeding illegally if using torture without a warrant is unclear.[37]

There were many methods of torture used in Scotland, some of which have already been mentioned.[38] That a confession was extorted through

---

[31]   On the influence of civil law on this requirement, see Brian P. Levack, 'Judicial torture in Scotland during the age of Mackenzie', in Hector L. MacQueen (ed.), *Miscellany Four* (Edinburgh: Stair Society, 2002), 185–98 at 189ff.

[32]   The requirement for a warrant was introduced by the privy council in 1662. See Robinson (ed.), *The Laws and Customs*, 391; Brian P. Levack, 'State building and witch hunting in early modern Europe', in Jonathan Barry *et al.* (eds), *Witchcraft in Early Modern Europe: Studies in Culture and Belief* (Cambridge: Cambridge University Press, 1996), 96–115 at 105.

[33]   Brian P. Levack, 'The decline and end of Scottish witch-hunting', in Julian Goodare (ed.), *The Scottish Witch-Hunt in Context* (Manchester: Manchester University Press, 2002), 166–81 at 174; Levack, 'Judicial torture', 196.

[34]   Levack, 'State building and witch hunting', 105–6.

[35]   Levack, 'The decline and end of Scottish witch-hunting', 174.

[36]   Levack, 'State building and witch hunting', 106.

[37]   Cf. Goodare, 'Witchcraft in Scotland', 306–7. The authors are grateful to Julian Goodare for his advice on this point.

[38]   For others, see R. D. Melville, 'The use and forms of judicial torture in England and Scotland', *Scottish Historical Review* 2 (1905), 225; Larner, *Enemies of God*, 107–12.

judicially sanctioned torture was not regarded to compromise the credibility of that confession in the early seventeenth century. Indeed there was a minority view that torture was actually required for a confession to be credible or truthful. This did begin to change from the middle of the century.[39] Mackenzie noted in his *Matters Criminal* the concern that 'some obstinate persons do oft-times deny truth, whilst others who are frail and timorous confess for fear what is not true'.[40] Withstanding torture and still refusing to confess did not in Scotland grant freedom from prosecution. Mackenzie notes that this was contrary to civilian thinking but acknowledges three cases heard in the seventeenth century where withstanding torture was not deemed to be evidence of innocence.[41] Mackenzie's role in the prosecution of witches will be discussed later in this chapter.

Agnes did confess after torture, telling a remarkable tale of her witchly crimes.[42] This provided sufficient evidence to proceed to trial. The 1563 act had allowed even inferior judges to try witches. Therefore a trial could be held either centrally in the justiciary court or in a local court by virtue of a 'commission of justiciary' (a warrant authorising prosecution). The justiciary court was a criminal court located in Edinburgh. This had by the 1520s in effect replaced the justiciar and justice ayres mentioned in previous chapters.[43]

The extent to which there was serious oversight of local proceedings has been the subject of much debate. Goodare has summarised this debate:

> I showed that the [privy] council expected prospective commissioners to produce a detailed written case against the suspect, and refused to grant a commission if this was inadequate. ... Levack accepted much of this but continued to emphasize that authorizing local elites to hold trials represented a lower degree of central control than holding trials in courts directly organized from the centre – a point that I would, in turn, accept.[44]

[39] Larner, *Enemies of God*, 109.
[40] Robinson (ed.), *The Laws and Customs*, 391.
[41] Robinson (ed.), *The Laws and Customs*, 391–2.
[42] The bizarre nature of this tale was not unusual. See the accounts set down in the rest of the *Newes from Scotland*. See for a later period, Larner, *Enemies of God*, 151–6.
[43] John W. Cairns, 'Historical introduction', in Kenneth Reid and Reinhard Zimmermann (eds), *A History of Private Law in Scotland* (Oxford: Oxford University Press, 2000) I, 14–184 at 53.
[44] Goodare, 'Witchcraft in Scotland', 306. See also on the act, prosecutorial jurisdiction and commissions, Goodare, 'Witch-hunting and the Scottish state', 125–30.

This is an important point because 'Such ad hoc local courts tried about nine-tenths of the witches, with most of the remainder being sent to the central justiciary court in Edinburgh.'[45] Thus, as Goodare has commented, overall '[a]fter 1598, hardly any witches were executed except as a result of a deliberate decision by the central authorities'.[46] The issue of central oversight of proceedings should not be regarded as adversarial: 'we should recognise the harmonious co-operation between [local authorities] identifying witches and privy council authorising trials.'[47] The central oversight was normally provided by the privy council, which authorised such ad hoc local trials by granting commissions upon local request.[48] In the mid-seventeenth century, parliament and the committee of estates also granted such commissions.[49] Agnes Simpson was one of those who was prosecuted in the justiciary court.[50] The evidence gathered by the king's questioning was used as evidence against her at that trial.

Several men acted in an official capacity during Agnes's trial. The king's advocate prosecuted the case against Agnes. It was (and is still) possible for private individuals to prosecute cases, even for serious offences such as homicide.[51] However, the king's advocate appeared here because of the king's interest in the case. The trial was conducted in the justiciary court. The justice (or justice general) was the most senior judge within that court, and justice deputes could be appointed to assist him in hearing cases.[52] The assize was a collection of local men who were deemed to have knowledge of the people involved and the events so could find the truth of the matter. The assize can be compared to the modern jury, but there are some important differences. The men on the assize were selected for their knowledge of the case, not their impartiality. Partiality might be particularly acute when the assize feared that acquitting the accused person might lead to further risk to their community, such as in the case of witchcraft. Mackenzie noted 'I have observed that scarce ever any who were accused before a country assize

---

45   Goodare, 'Witchcraft in Scotland', 303. See also Larner, *Enemies of God*, 112–13.
46   Goodare, 'Witch-hunting and the Scottish state', 139.
47   Goodare, 'Witch-hunting and the Scottish state', 134.
48   Goodare, 'Witch-hunting and the Scottish state', 124–30.
49   Goodare, 'Witch-hunting and the Scottish state', 135–6.
50   Julian Goodare, 'The framework for Scottish witch-hunting in the 1590s', *Scottish Historical Review* 81:2 (2002), 240–50.
51   See also, on the earlier period, Chapter 4.
52   On this court, see Robinson (ed.), *The Laws and Customs*, 309–13; Julian Goodare, *The Government of Scotland 1560–1625* (Oxford: Oxford University Press), 163–5.

of neighbours did escape that trial.'[53] Should the assize find the accused guilty of the offence, then in the case of witchcraft this would normally mean execution.[54] A capital sentence was read out to the court not by the justice but by an official called the dempster, the doom sayer.

Although without the benefit of a defence advocate, Agnes's trial was conducted entirely legally. However, as mentioned, sometimes witches were prosecuted (and tortured) outside of the judicially sanctioned processes. Perhaps the most extreme instance of this was the case of Alison Balfour, a resident of Orkney. In 1594 she had the misfortune of being caught between the rivalry of Patrick Stewart, Earl of Orkney and his brother, John. Alison was accused of being a witch and conspiring with John to murder Patrick. She initially refused to confess. Therefore she, her husband and her two young children were all tortured so that she would confess. She was put to the 'caschielaws' or thumbscrews. Her husband was crushed by weights. Her son was subjected to the boot, wherein his legs were crushed by stakes being driven into a boot by blows from a hammer. Her daughter was put into thumbscrews.[55] All of this torture was done extra-judicially at the command of the earl. Indeed children could not be legally tortured in Scotland.[56] Alison finally confessed. John Stewart's servant, Thomas Palpla, was likewise tortured extra-judicially by the earl and confessed. Both Alison and Thomas renounced their confessions as false on all points, but both were nonetheless executed. After the executions, an assize was convened to try John formally for conspiring to murder Patrick with the assistance of a witch. It took account of the renunciations of the two confessions and acquitted John of the crime.[57] It is unclear how often similar events might have happened across Scotland.

James VI later wrote a book drawing on his experiences with the North Berwick witches. This book was called *Daemonologie* (1597) and called for the prosecution of witches throughout his realm.[58] This publication

---

[53] Robinson (ed.), *The Laws and Customs*, 71.
[54] On the execution of witches, see Laura Paterson, 'Executing Scottish witches', in Julian Goodare (ed.), *Scottish Witches and Witch-Hunters* (Basingstoke: Palgrave Macmillan, 2013), 196–214; Larner, *Enemies of God*, 113, 115.
[55] On which, see Melville, 'The use and forms of judicial torture'.
[56] Robinson (ed.), *The Laws and Customs*, 392.
[57] Pitcairn, *Criminal Trials*, I, pt 2, 373–7.
[58] For a summary of some of the literature on this work, and whether it reflects that James was already sceptical about witchcraft prosecutions, see Goodare, 'Witchcraft in Scotland', 305.

coincided with a second spate of witch hunts.[59] Around 400 people were accused of witchcraft, although not all were tried. During the hunt some detection techniques were proved fraudulent. In particular, the ability of a witch from Fife to miraculously detect other witches just by looking at them was disproved. Wasser has shown that this contributed to a degree of scepticism about the prosecution of witchcraft being expressed during the hunt. Lawyers within the privy council, Session and justiciary court reacted to the uncritical prosecution of witches.[60] This in turn led to greater regulation by the central government authorities,[61] largely through the mechanism of commissions discussed above. Wasser suggests that this was the cause of a comparative lull in witchcraft prosecutions between 1596 and 1628. Probably less than 200 people were prosecuted in that thirty-year period.[62]

Later spates of witchcraft prosecutions occurred in the late 1620s and 1640s.[63] These perhaps occurred in part because a portion of the more sceptical lawyers within the privy council were not present, following the recently re-established circuit courts at the time. There were also wider initiatives to punish religious crimes at these times.[64] The interregnum government and court system in the 1650s took a dim view of the prosecution of witchcraft and the use of judicially sanctioned torture

---

[59] On the 1597 witchcraft hunt (and reflections on *Daemonologie*) see Julian Goodare, 'The Scottish witchcraft panic of 1597', in Julian Goodare (ed.), *The Scottish Witch-Hunt in Context* (Manchester: Manchester University Press, 2002), 51–72; Larner, *Enemies of God*, 70–2. Note, however, that although James VI is clearly connected to both sets of prosecutions, Levack has been clear that 'These commissions ... represented responses to local pressures for prosecution, not initiatives taken by the king or privy council': Levack, 'State building and witch hunting', 101. For a summary of the debates of this and related points, see Goodare, 'Witchcraft in Scotland', 305–7. The authors are grateful to Julian Goodare for his advice on this point.

[60] Michael Wasser, 'The privy council and the witches: the curtailment of witchcraft prosecutions in Scotland, 1597–1628', *Scottish Historical Review* 82:1 (2003), 20–46 at 29–31, 36.

[61] Wasser, 'The privy council and the witches', 31–7.

[62] Wasser, 'The privy council and the witches', 27–8.

[63] Larner *et al.*, *A Source Book*, 238–9; Larner, *Enemies of God*, 61, 72–4. For an examination of the debates on 'witchcraft panics', see Goodare, 'Witchcraft in Scotland', 309–10.

[64] Wasser, 'The privy council and the witches', 45–6; Levack, 'The decline and end of Scottish witch-hunting', 170–1. On the latter period, see Paula Hughes, 'Witch-hunting in Scotland, 1649–1650', in Julian Goodare (ed.), *Scottish Witches and Witch-Hunters* (Basingstoke: Palgrave Macmillan, 2013), 85–102.

in those prosecutions.[65] The effect of this was that there was a flurry of prosecutions when the king was restored: more than 600 people were accused of witchcraft in 1661–2.[66] The new reality was brutal. The king's advocate, Sir George MacKenzie of Rosehaugh, complained that 'poor Innocents die in multitudes by an unworthy Martyredom, and Burning comes in fashion'.[67]

In total, research has found that more than 3,800 people were accused of witchcraft in Scotland in the early modern period. Of those 305 persons whose sentence is known, two-thirds were executed.[68] In respect to the size of its population, around five times the number of witches were executed in Scotland than the European average.[69] Probably around eighty-five per cent of these were female.[70] Indeed, '[t]he average witch was the wife or widow of a tenant farmer, probably fairly near the bottom of the social structure.'[71] Perhaps as high as forty per cent worked as healers, midwives or other such professions.[72]

D. JUDICIAL SCEPTICISM AFTER 1662

The high number of prosecutions in 1661–2 meant that opinion began to turn against the prosecution of witches. Levack has suggested that, in Europe and the colonies,

[f]our changes in particular had a bearing on the number of witch-craft trials and convictions and executions: 1) the tighter control, supervision and regulation of local witchcraft trials by central and

---

65 On witchcraft prosecution during this period, and the impact of this upon the Restoration, see Brian P. Levack, 'The great Scottish witch hunt of 1661–1662', *Journal of British Studies* 20:1 (1980), 90–108 at 91–95. Cf. Larner *et al.*, *A Source Book*, 238–9; Larner, *Enemies of God*, 74–6.

66 Levack, 'The decline and end of Scottish witch-hunting', 169; Levack, 'The great Scottish witch hunt'; Larner *et al.*, *A Source Book*, 238–9.

67 [Sir George Mackenzie of Rosehaugh], *Pleadings in Some Remarkable Cases before the Supreme Courts of Scotland since the Year 1661* (Edinburgh: George Swintoun, James Glen and Thomas Brown, 1673), 196.

68 Julian Goodare *et al.*, *The Survey of Scottish Witchcraft*. Cf. the earlier work of Larner, *A Source Book*, which lists 3069.

69 Goodare, 'Witchcraft in Scotland', 302.

70 Goodare, 'Witchcraft in Scotland', 302; Larner, *Enemies of God*, 91.

71 Larner, *Enemies of God*, 89.

72 Goodare, 'Witchcraft in Scotland', 303. This is much higher than is apparent from Larner *et al.*, *A Source Book*, 242–6. On healing, see Larner, *Enemies of God*, 138–43.

superior courts; 2) the restriction and in some cases the prohibition of torture in witchcraft cases; 3) the adherence of trial judges to more demanding standards of proof; and 4) the admission of more lawyers to represent witches at their trials.[73]

This combination of factors was present in Scotland after 1662. The following section of this chapter will examine these factors in Scotland, although not in the order mentioned by Levack.

(1) Increased Standards of Proof and the Pleading of Advocates

It was seen above that Agnes Sampson did not have the services of an advocate in her defence. However, in the seventeenth century advocates started to become involved in the defence of witches. This had the effect that the evidentiary burden on the prosecuting party increased. One example of this is found in a case pleaded by Mackenzie in defence of a woman who was referred to by him as Maevia. He employed two tactics in his defence, both of which were common in defensive pleadings against witchcraft. The first was the claim that the events could be attributed to natural causes, and the second was to ridicule the alleged facts.[74]

The evidence against Maevia was strong.[75] Mackenzie admitted that she had entered the house of another woman and whispered curses to her. Later that other woman had fallen ill of a 'distemper'. The woman recovered only after Maevia (presumably a healer) had treated her with plantain leaves and prayed over her. Two other women who had been accused of witchcraft before Maevia had also accused her of turning into a dove to fly with them to meet other witches.[76] She was thus charged with three crimes of witchcraft: bringing disease, healing by charms, and transformation.

Mackenzie undermined each of the charges in turn. In response to the first charge, he explained that only those people who were ignorant of nature would attribute natural processes to witchly charms. The whispering of a general threat fell below the legal standards of specificity. He showed this by citing continental legal literature as well as previous

---

[73] Brian P. Levack, 'The decline and end of witchcraft prosecutions', in Marijke Gijswijt-Hofstra *et al.*, *Witchcraft and Magic in Europe*, V: *The Eighteenth and Nineteenth Centuries* (London: Athlone Press, 1999), 1–93 at 13.

[74] On these defences, see Larner, *Enemies of God*, 178–84. On the case of Maevia and Mackenzie's view of witchcraft, see ibid. 186–90.

[75] Andrew Lang, *Sir George Mackenzie, King's Advocate ... 1636 (?)–1691* (Clark: Lawbook Exchange, 2005), 44.

[76] Mackenzie, *Pleadings*, 186.

Scottish practick.[77] The prosecution failed to show any means by which Maevia had made the woman sick. Indeed her illness could simply be attributed to the woman having allowed her fearful character to whip her into a distempered panic. He concluded by arguing that the law insists that the court cannot convict 'if the inferences be not demonstrative, and undenyable'.[78]

He then addressed the claim that Maevia had healed the sick woman. Mackenzie suggested that plantain may well be a natural cure. Or perhaps the woman believed it had cured her when in fact it had no effect. He also pointed out that you cannot burn a woman for simply praying for the help of Jesus.[79]

The charge that Maevia had turned into a dove received particular derision from Mackenzie:

> This Article seems to me very ridiculous; for I might debate, that the Devil cannot carry Witches bodily, as *Luther*, *Melanchton*, *Alciat*, *Vairus* and others assert, because it is not probable, that God would allow him the permission constantly to work this miracle, in carrying persons to a publick place, where they joyn in blaspheming His Name, and scorning His Church. Nor is it proper either, to the nature of heavy Bodies to flee in the air, nor to Devils who are spirits, and have no armes, nor other means of carrying their Bodies: but I may confidently assert, that he cannot transform a woman into the shape of a Dove, that being impossible; for how can the Soul of Woman inform and actuat the body of a Dove, these requiring diverse Organs, and administrations; and to believe such transmutations, is expresly declared Heresie by the Canon Law, and to deserve excommunication[.][80]

Mackenzie had worked as justice depute during the flurry of witch-craft prosecutions in 1661–2. He had therefore been involved in many witchcraft trials as a judge.[81] He used his concluding paragraph of his defence of Maevia to express his frustration with such cases:

> none now labour under any extraordinar Disease, but it is instantly said to come by Witch-craft, and then the next old deform'd or

---

[77] However, on the belief of the power of curses, see Larner, *Enemies of God*, 142–4.
[78] Mackenzie, *Pleadings*, 188.
[79] Mackenzie, *Pleadings*, 189–93.
[80] Mackenzie, *Pleadings*, 194.
[81] Lang, *Sir George Mackenzie*, 39–42, 45

envyed woman is presently charged with it; from this ariseth a confused noise of her guilt, called *diffamatio* by Lawyers, who make it
a ground for seizure, upon which she being apprehended is imprisoned, starved, kept from sleep, and oft times tortured: To free
themselves from which, they must confess; and having confest,
imagine they dare not thereafter retreat. And then Judges allow
themselves too much liberty, in condemning such as are accused
of this crime, because they conclude they cannot be severe enough
to the enemies of GOD; and Assisers are affraid to suffer such
to escape as are remitted to them, lest they let loose an enraged
Wizard in their neighbour-hood. And thus poor Innocents die in
multitudes by an unworthy Martyredom, and Burning comes in
fashion[.][82]

This case shows how the involvement of advocates for the accused
resulted in the evidence presented to the court being tested rigorously.
Claims of supernatural powers (such as those which had seen Agnes
Sampson executed) were now dismissed by advocates. This testing of
the evidence meant that acquittals increased and courts became more
sceptical of this kind of prosecution.

(2) Central Supervision of Trials

Central involvement and supervision of trials was long-standing. This
is seen (for example) in the aforementioned granting of commissions
for prosecution locally and in the work of the justiciary court. However,
in the later seventeenth century there was a shift towards curtailment
of prosecution.[83] The justices in 1662 had already become sceptical of
evidence pleaded and charges of witchcraft. This had led to a number
of acquittals and eventually the end to those judicial proceedings in
the justiciary court.[84] The privy council prohibited the arresting of a
witch without the permission of the council or a magistrate or judge
in 1662. It prohibited torture except by its warrant. And it imprisoned
two notorious witch-prickers. Levack has noted that this restricted significantly the ability to prosecute witches without official oversight after

---

[82] Mackenzie, *Pleadings*, 196.
[83] Goodare, 'Witchcraft in Scotland'. The authors are grateful to Julian Goodare for
his advice on this point.
[84] Levack, 'The great Scottish witch hunt', 103–4; Larner, *Enemies of God*, 77–8;
Larner *et al.*, *A Source Book*, 40–9.

1662.[85] There was an effort to ensure the justiciary court heard witchcraft cases.[86] The privy council ensured that those trials which were allowed to proceed locally by commission had one of the justice deputes among the list of approved commissioners.[87]

A reconstitution of criminal jurisdiction took place in the early 1670s. The circuit courts were re-established in 1671, but took time to become truly regular.[88] The operation of the circuit courts meant that a justice would periodically visit the localities. More than forty witchcraft cases were heard by these courts between 1671 and 1709. The fate of most of the accused is unknown. Only two witches are known to have been executed, two were convicted but not given capital punishments, and five were acquitted.[89]

In 1672 the justiciary court was reconstituted as the High Court of Justiciary. Five lords of session were to sit as lords commissioners of justiciary with the lord justice general and lord justice clerk. Rules were put in place to ensure that the accused's advocate was kept properly apprised of written proceedings. They were also to receive the names of witnesses and assizers. These rules would ensure that a proper defence could be mounted.[90]

(3) Restricting the Use of Torture

It was said towards the end of the seventeenth century that torture 'never was so much put in practice in *Scotland* for many Hundred years, as it was during the Mild Government of King *Charles* II.'[91] However,

---

[85] Levack, 'The great Scottish witch hunt', 105–6. See also Larner, *Enemies of God*, 76.

[86] Levack, 'The decline and end of Scottish witch-hunting', 172.

[87] Levack, 'The decline and end of Scottish witch-hunting', 173; Goodare, 'Witch-hunting and the Scottish state', 136.

[88] Levack, 'The decline and end of Scottish witch-hunting', 172–3. Cf. Cairns, 'Historical introduction', 122.

[89] Larner *et al.*, *A Source Book*, 57–60. For a detailed discussion of the trial of two alleged witches by the Circuit court in 1671, although perhaps untypical ones, see Larner, *Enemies of God*, 120–33.

[90] Cairns, 'Historical introduction', 122. For a brief summary of the procedure more generally, see John W. Cairns, 'Hamesucken and the major premiss in the libel, 1672–1770: criminal law in the age of enlightenment', in Robert F. Hunter (ed.), *Justice and Crime: Essays in Honour of the Right Honourable the Lord Emslie* (Edinburgh: T. & T. Clark, 1993), 138–79 at 142–5.

[91] Anonymous, *A Vindication of the Presbyterians in Scotland* (London: Edward Golding, 1692), 22.

restraint was beginning to be exercised in the use of torture to find evidence for criminal prosecutions. In 1662 the privy council prohibited the use of torture without its warrant.[92] In 1664 it insisted that the confession of a witch would have to be voluntary in order to form the basis of a commission of justiciary.[93] In 1665 it refused to give a warrant to torture an Englishman named Giles Thyre who was accused by the king's advocate of committing adultery and murder, despite pressure to do so from the king's advocate.[94]

However, the attempted regulation of the use of torture was not entirely successful. Torture was still used without permission in the local setting. Mackenzie dismissed those cases against witchcraft in which torture had been applied without permission when he became the king's advocate in 1677.[95] The privy council felt the need to formally restate the rule requiring its warrant the following year.[96] However, although Mackenzie abhorred the endless prosecution of witches, he was not opposed to the use of torture in crimes against the state.[97] In the 1680s, the use of torture became highly political because of its use in such crimes against the state.

At the end of the 1680s, the constitutional settlement of Scotland was renegotiated. The document produced was called the Claim of Right; more will be said about this in the following chapter. However, it is important for present purposes that one of the clauses of the Claim of Right was the limitation of torture: 'That the using of torture without evidence or in ordinary crimes is contrary to law'.[98] The wording of this protection had two important caveats. First, a person might still be tortured for a confession if there was some other evidence that he had committed the offence. Secondly, a person might still be tortured if accused of an 'extraordinary' offence. This clause did not protect those accused of witchcraft or crimes against the state, because both were defined as extraordinary crimes.

A good example of this is a case in which the estates gave permission for the use of torture very shortly before the Claim of Right was passed. They made clear in their permission that it was an extraordinary case and did not create a precedent for the use of torture in future cases. This

---

[92] Levack, 'Judicial torture', 198; Levack, 'The great Scottish witch hunt'. 105.
[93] Levack, 'Judicial torture', 186.
[94] Robinson (ed.), *The Laws and Customs*, 391.
[95] Levack, 'Judicial torture', 197.
[96] Levack, 'Judicial torture', 198.
[97] Levack, 'Judicial torture', 187.
[98] *RPS* 1689/3/108.

case involved the murder of the lord president of the Court of Session, Sir George Lockhart of Carnwath, by a disgruntled litigant. Lockhart himself was a fascinating historical character. He had been Cromwell's advocate during the interregnum. He had re-established his career in the Restoration to become the dean of advocates in 1672. He had challenged the authority of the Court of Session (which nearly led to a constitutional crisis) between 1674 and 1676, and he had secured promotion from advocate to lord president in 1686.[99] The disgruntled litigant who killed him was called Chiesley of Dalry. Lockhart had pronounced a decreet-arbitral against Chiesley which meant that he had to aliment his wife and ten children with a considerable sum of money. Chiesley was so outraged by the decision that he lay in wait near Lockhart's home and shot him in the back as the judge walked home from the Sunday church service. The estates gave permission for Chiesley to be tortured for his confession and to reveal whether he had any accomplices. The estates also appointed a panel of assessors to determine whether there was sufficient cause to torture a writer by the name of William Calderwood, an alleged accomplice to the crime.[100] Chiesley was tortured, confessed and was subsequently tried. His conviction was secured on the basis of the confession and the testimony of five witnesses. These witnesses included an advocate and a writer to the signet who had both heard him threaten to harm or kill Lockhart. Another advocate and a student of divinity saw the shot and had arrested Chiesley at the scene. The final witness was the doctor of medicine who witnessed Lockhart's dying from the wound. Chiesley was sentenced to have his right hand cut off, symbolic of his cutting off the hands of the state by murdering a state official. He was then hanged until dead while his pistol hung round his neck.[101]

E. CONCLUSION

This chapter has shown that the widespread prosecution of witchcraft in Scotland began after the Reformation. Witchcraft tended to be prosecuted in spates of cases, because those accused of witchcraft would be encouraged to provide the names of other witches. Those named

---

[99] George Brunton and David Haig, *An Historical Account of the Senators of the College of Justice, from its Institution in MDXXXII [1532]* (Edinburgh: Thomas Clark, 1832), 419–26.

[100] *RPS* 1689/3/84.

[101] Hugo Arnott, *Celebrated Criminal Trials in Scotland*, 150–4.

individuals would then be questioned in turn. One of the earliest flurries of prosecutions was that of the North Berwick witches in 1591. These people were accused of attempting to murder James VI and his bride, Anne of Denmark. The prosecution of one of these witches, Agnes Sampson, reveals much of the method of prosecution of witch-craft at the time and in later years. The charge against her was inves-tigated by an evidence-gathering process in the presence of the king. This allowed the use of judicial torture to elicit her confession. That confession was then used as evidence at a trial held by the justices. The evidence was heard by an assize of local, knowledgeable men who con-victed her of the crime. This chapter has also shown that the increasing involvement of the advocates and central supervision by the justices had the effect of increasing the rate of acquittal and eventually reduc-ing the number of cases tried. The Claim of Right in 1689 restricted the use of judicial torture to only extraordinary crimes (which included witchcraft).

This chapter has also shown the impact which was had by the increas-ing centralisation and professionalisation of the prosecution of witchcraft. The combination of legal reforms meant that prosecutions occurred less often and were more closely scrutinised by the central authorities. One example of the impact of this is seen in the case of the Paisley witches, who were accused of bewitching Christian Shaw in 1697.[102] There were two trials respecting these events. In 1697 thirty-five people were formally accused of witchcraft. However, 'the witches were reduced to seven, all of whom were convicted and executed'.[103] This represents a significant reduction in the rate of successful prosecution when compared to the North Berwick witches just over a century earlier. A subsequent trial in 1699–1700 was dismissed for lack of evidence.[104] Wasser suggests that this dismissal was, fundamentally, because of widespread scepticism. It was also because the temporary panic which had justified the executions in 1697 had by then subsided.[105] It was said by a contemporary that in these prosecutions 'neither the Prisoners nor Confessants, were distem-pered by being kept from Sleep, tortured or the like, which were too usual in former times; but all the Measures were strictly observed, that are

---

[102] On this case, see Michael Wasser, 'The western witch-hunt of 1697–1700: the last major witch-hunt in Scotland', in Julian Goodare (ed.), *The Scottish Witch-Hunt in Context* (Manchester: Manchester University Press, 2002), 146–65.

[103] Wasser, 'The western witch-hunt', 149.

[104] Wasser, 'The western witch-hunt', 155.

[105] Wasser, 'The western witch-hunt', especially 164. See also Ian Bostridge, *Witchcraft and Its Transformations, c. 1650 – c. 1750* (Oxford: Clarendon Press, 1997), 24–33.

requisite to a truly Impartial Judgment.'[106] If this is correct, it shows how attitudes had changed. In 1708 the use of torture was abolished entirely.

The 1563 act itself was finally repealed only with the Witchcraft Act 1735. The new level of scepticism about witches is evident in the wording of that act, which made it an offence to

> pretend to exercise or use any kind of witchcraft, sorcery, inchant-ment, or conjuration, or undertake to tell fortunes, or pretend, from his or her skill or knowledge in any occult or crafty science, to discover where or in what manner any goods or chattels, supposed to have been stolen or lost, may be found[.][107]

The wording of this statute did not presuppose that witches existed, which had been the widespread view in the seventeenth century. Rather its wording suggested that witchcraft was now regarded to be a pretence, a crime of fraud rather than against God.

The Witchcraft Act was passed by the new British parliament after the Union of Parliaments in 1707. As such this act extended not just to Scotland but also to England and Wales. More will be said about this important union in the second volume of this book. However, this act provides a rather curious example of the difference between the earlier Scottish parliament and the new British parliament. Legislation of the British parliament does not fall to desuetude so remains on the statute books until repealed. The Witchcraft Act was therefore, quite remark-ably, the basis for two successful prosecutions in the Old Bailey court in England in 1944, towards the end of the Second World War. The first was of Helen Duncan, a Scot at that time residing in Portsmouth in England who was convicted and imprisoned under the act when she revealed during a séance that a British warship had been sunk. The second was of a Jane Rebecca Yorke, who was convicted but merely fined on account of her advanced age.[108] One thinks back to Mackenzie's warning that people 'should not be ensnared by pursuits upon old buried laws, which scarce lawyers study or know'.[109] The act has since been repealed.

---

[106] Richard Boulton, *Compleat History of Magick, Sorcery and Witchcraft* (London: for E Curll and others, 1715–16) II, 165.

[107] c. 5, 9 Geo II.

[108] A transcript of the trial with appendices was prepared by two English barristers-at-law: *The Trial of Mrs. Duncan, edited with a foreword, by C. E. Bechhofer Roberts and a note on the Old Bailey by Helena Normanton* (London: Jarrolds, 1945).

[109] Robinson (ed.), *The Law and Customs*, 7.

F. SELECTED BIBLIOGRAPHY AND FURTHER READING

(1) Records of the Parliament of Scotland (*RPS*)

Act setting out post-Reformation prosecution of witchcraft: *RPS* A1563/6/9.
Claim of Right: *RPS* 1689/3/108.

(2) Books

Arnott, Hugo, *A Collection and Abridgement of Celebrated Criminal Trials in Scotland, from AD 1536, to 1784* (Edinburgh: William Smellie, 1785).

Bostridge, Ian, *Witchcraft and Its Transformations, c. 1650 – c. 1750* (Oxford: Clarendon Press, 1997).

Larner, Christina, *Enemies of God: The Witch-hunt in Scotland* (London: Chatto and Windus, 1981).

Larner, Christina, *et al.*, *A Source Book of Scottish Witchcraft* (Glasgow: Glasgow University Department of Sociology, 1977).

[Mackenzie, Sir George of Rosehaugh], *Pleadings in Some Remarkable Cases before the Supreme Courts of Scotland since the Year 1661* (Edinburgh: George Swintoun, James Glen and Thomas Brown, 1673).

Normand, Lawrence, and Gareth Roberts (eds), *Witchcraft in Early Modern Scotland: James VI's Demonology and the North Berwick Witches* (Liverpool: Liverpool University Press, 2000).

Pitcairn, Robert, *Criminal Trials in Scotland, from AD MCCCCLXXXVIII [1488] to AD MDCXXIV [1624]* (3 vols, Edinburgh: William Tait, 1833).

Robinson, Olivia F. (ed.), *The Laws and Customs of Scotland in Matters Criminal by Sir George Mackenzie* (Edinburgh: Stair Society, 2012).

The Trial of Mrs. Duncan, edited with a foreword, by C. E. Bechhofer Roberts and a note on the Old Bailey by Helena Normanton (London: Jarrolds, 1945).

(3) Chapters in Books

Cairns, John W., 'Historical introduction', in Kenneth Reid and Reinhard Zimmermann (eds), *A History of Private Law in Scotland* (Oxford: Oxford University Press, 2000) I, 14–184.

Goodare, Julian, 'The Scottish witchcraft panic of 1597', in Julian Goodare (ed.), *The Scottish Witch-Hunt in Context* (Manchester: Manchester University Press, 2002), 51–72.

Goodare, Julian, 'Witch-hunting and the Scottish state', in Julian Goodare (ed.), *The Scottish Witch-Hunt in Context* (Manchester: Manchester University Press, 2002) 122–45.

Goodare, Julian, 'Witchcraft in Scotland', in Brian P. Levack (ed.), *The Oxford Handbook of Witchcraft in Early Modern Europe and Colonial America* (Oxford: Oxford University Press, 2013), 300–17.

Hughes, Paula, 'Witch-hunting in Scotland, 1649–1650', in Julian Goodare (ed.), *Scottish Witches and Witch-Hunters* (Basingstoke: Palgrave Macmillan, 2013), 85–102.

Levack, Brian P., 'State building and witch hunting in early modern Europe', in Jonathan Barry *et al.* (eds), *Witchcraft in Early Modern Europe: Studies in Culture and Belief* (Cambridge: Cambridge University Press, 1996), 96–115.

Levack, Brian P., 'The decline and end of witchcraft prosecutions', in Marijke Gijswijt-Hofstra *et al.*, *Witchcraft and Magic in Europe*, V: *The Eighteenth and Nineteenth Centuries* (London: Athlone Press, 1999), 1–93.

Levack, Brian P., 'The decline and end of Scottish witch-hunting', in Julian Goodare (ed.), *The Scottish Witch-Hunt in Context* (Manchester: Manchester University Press, 2002), 166–81.

Levack, Brian P., 'Judicial torture in Scotland during the age of Mackenzie', in Hector L. MacQueen (ed.), *Miscellany Four* (Edinburgh: Stair Society, 2002), 185–98.

Maxwell-Stuart, P. G., 'The fear of the king is death: James VI and the witches of East Lothian', in Brian P. Levack (ed.), *New Perspectives on Witchcraft, Magic and Demonology, III: Witchcraft in the British Isles and New England* (London: Routledge, 2001), 367–81.

Paterson, Laura, 'Executing Scottish witches', in Julian Goodare (ed.), *Scottish Witches and Witch-Hunters* (Basingstoke: Palgrave Macmillan, 2013), 196–214.

Wasser, Michael, 'The western witch-hunt of 1697–1700: the last major witch-hunt in Scotland', in Julian Goodare (ed.), *The Scottish Witch-Hunt in Context* (Manchester: Manchester University Press, 2002), 146–65.

Wasser, Michael, 'Scotland's first witch-hunt: the eastern witch-hunt of 1568–1569', in Julian Goodare (ed.), *Scottish Witches and Witch-Hunters* (Basingstoke: Palgrave Macmillan, 2013), 17–33.

(4) Articles in Journals

Goodare, Julian, 'The framework for Scottish witch-hunting in the 1590s', *Scottish Historical Review* 81:2 (2002), 240–50.

Levack, Brian P., 'The great Scottish witch hunt of 1661–1662', *Journal of British Studies* 20:1 (1980), 90–108.

Roughead, William, 'Scottish witch trials: the witches of North Berwick', *Juridical Review* (1913), 161–84.

Wasser, Michael, 'The privy council and the witches: the curtailment of witchcraft prosecutions in Scotland, 1597–1628', *Scottish Historical Review* 82:1 (2003), 20–46.

(5) Digital Sources

Goodare, Julian, *et al.*, *The Survey of Scottish Witchcraft*, http://www.shca.ed.ac.uk/Research/witches/.

CHAPTER 19

Revolution and Union

A. INTRODUCTION

Chapter 13 examined the changes to the law and institutions of judicial administration during the interregnum. It also reflected on the fact that little of these reforms survived the Restoration of the king. The Restoration period did not last long. This chapter will examine two important renegotiations of constitutional and legal understanding which followed. The first occurred in 1689, during a period of revolution in which a new constitutional document was created called the Claim of Right. The second occurred in 1707, when a negotiated treaty of union joined Scotland with England into a single state with one British parliament. This was to be one of the most significant events in Scottish history and provides a fitting end point for this volume.

B. REVOLUTION AND THE CLAIM OF RIGHT

(1) James VII and Forfeiture of the Crown

In December 1688 the king, James VII and II, fled the British Isles after a Dutch invasion at the invitation of a revolutionary parliament in England. It passed the Bill of Rights, a constitutional statement which presented James's flight as evidence of his abdication of the throne. It invited as the new joint monarchs James's daughter, Mary, and her Dutch husband, William of Orange.[1]

---

[1] On the problems that led up to this event, see John W. Cairns, 'Historical introduction', in Kenneth Reid and Reinhard Zimmermann (eds), *A History of Private Law in Scotland* (Oxford: Oxford University Press, 2000) I, 14–184 at 108–10.

The Scots felt equally aggrieved by James's behaviour as king. A Scottish convention of estates met the following March to consider its position. It produced a parallel document, called the Claim of Right. However, the Claim cannot simply be regarded as a copy of the English Bill of Rights.[2]

First, the Claim declared that James had 'forfeited the right to the crown' because of various offences against the kirk, institutions of government and people of Scotland. These offences were 'utterly and directly contrary to the known laws, statutes and freedoms of this realm.'[3] In making this argument, the Scots rejected the English approach of creating a legal fiction to disguise the revolutionary nature of their act. The Scots were more direct. In declaring that James VII had forfeited the crown they were also returning to the theory of social contract argued against James's great-grandmother, Mary.[4] Indeed, the Scots even went so far as to describe the monarchy as 'a legal[ly] limited monarchy'.[5] James had broken that social contract so the Scots were asserting their legal and constitutional right to depose him.[6] They also declared a second reason why the deposing of James was legal and appropriate:

> King James VII, being a professed papist, did assume the regal power and acted as king without ever taking the oath required by law, whereby the king, at his access to the government, is obliged to swear to maintain the Protestant religion, and to rule the people according to the laudable laws[.][7]

James's coronation had been in England on the first day on which the Scottish parliament met after the death of Charles II. James had taken the English coronation oath. Charles II was the last monarch to be crowned in Scotland.[8]

---

2 On this points, see Cairns, 'Historical introduction', 110; Aidan O'Neill, 'The sovereignty of the (Scottish) people: 1689 and all that', *Judicial Review* (2013), 446–63 at 447–50; Tim Harris, 'The people, the law, and the constitution in Scotland and England: a comparative approach to the Glorious Revolution', *Journal of British Studies* 38 (1999), 28–58 at 47.

3 *RPS* 1689/3/108.

4 O'Neill, 'Sovereignty of the (Scottish) people', 448–9.

5 *RPS* 1689/3/108.

6 O'Neill, 'Sovereignty of the (Scottish) people', 448–9.

7 *RPS* 1689/3/108.

8 On the Claim, see for example O'Neill, 'Sovereignty of the (Scottish) people'.

(2) Renegotiating the Constitutional Settlement

After James VII was formally deposed, the Scots expressed their desire to bestow the crown on William. Mary meanwhile had immediately upon being crowned in England ceded power to her husband on the grounds that it was against natural law for her to have equal authority to her husband. However, this offer of the Scottish crown came with a number of caveats. The Scots intended to negotiate with William before he was installed as king. They therefore created a new constitutional settlement which affected the power of the king and protected what they saw as fundamental rights. Royal authority in Scotland would never again reach the heights that it had under James VI:

> The revolution ... brought to the political surface deep-rooted and conflicting ideas about the royal succession, the nature of the church and the extent to which the crown's power should be limited ... Many of the crown's prerogative powers were swept away, authority was placed firmly in the hands of a parliament freed from the lords of the articles, and bishops were abolished, replaced by a presbyterian church.[9]

The Claim included several protections related to law and process. '[T]he imprisoning of persons without expressing the reason thereof and delaying to put them to trial is contrary to law.' Men could not be prosecuted 'upon stretches of old and obsolete laws, upon frivolous and weak pretences, upon lame and defective probation'. The Claim also said that the king should not direct judges on how to decide any particular case. It gave a right against self-incrimination in capital crimes. It limited the use of torture 'without evidence or in ordinary crimes'.[10] This clause was discussed with respect to witchcraft and crimes against the state in Chapter 18.

There was one particular clause which was to have particular impact on the legal future of Scotland. Parliament had long retained some jurisdiction in a limited number of cases at first instance.[11] However, it

[9] Keith M. Brown, 'The second estate: parliament and the nobility', in Keith M. Brown and Alan R. MacDonald (eds), *The History of the Scottish Parliament, III: Parliament in Context, 1235–1707* (Edinburgh: Edinburgh University Press, 2010), 67–94 at 90.

[10] *RPS* 1689/3/108.

[11] For example, it could hear cases on high treason. In practice the hearing of cases was delegated to a sub-committee with legal expertise. This committee would then make a recommendation to parliament on how the case should be decided. This

was not an appeal court and could not hear appeals from the Court of Session.[12] This means that parliament could not re-examine the judgement of the Session to identify whether the interpretation of the law or facts was correct. 'What remained less certain was whether protestations for remeid of law might nonetheless be legitimate *as something distinct from appellations.*'[13] A protestation for remeid of law was essentially a form of complaint to parliament that the Session had failed to provide justice. Litigants could by this mechanism make allegations of partiality and inappropriate behaviour on the part of the lords of session which should render their judgement voidable by parliament. This was a claim that there had been a procedural irregularity and a request to review the sentence of the court. Litigants began to use this process after the Restoration. This process became controversial so in the 1670s was eventually declared impossible.[14] However, one of the clauses of the Claim of Right reversed this decision. It gave 'the right and privilege of the subjects to protest for remedy of law'.[15]

(3) Protestations for Remeid of Law, 1689–1707

The right set out in the Claim was tested shortly thereafter. A widow named Lady Castlehaven and her son in law, Sir James Foulis of Colinton, had been engaged in a legal dispute. The case concerned her husband's use of income from her estates and her right to income from that land after his death. The Court of Session heard the case in 1690. It found in favour of Sir James, who was a former lord of session himself. Lady Castlehaven wrote what she called an appeal to king and parliament. She did so on the grounds that the court's decision was contrary to a contract

recommendation was almost always accepted by parliament as a whole. On this, see W. B. Gray, 'The judicial proceedings of the parliaments of Scotland, 1660–1688', *Juridical Review* (1924), 135–51 at 136–9. For examples of treason cases heard, see ibid. 139–42. On the exercise of jurisdiction of the court before the Claim, see Philip J. Hamilton-Grierson, 'The appellate jurisdiction of the Scottish parliament', *Scottish Historical Review* 15 (1918), 205–22.

[12] On the background to this, see J. D. Ford, 'Protestations to parliament for remeid of law', *Scottish Historical Review* 88:1 (2009), 57–107 at 64–5.

[13] Ford, 'Protestations to parliament', 72 (emphasis added).

[14] Cairns, 'Historical introduction', 123; A. Mark Godfrey, 'Parliament and the law', in Keith M. Brown and Alan R. MacDonald (eds), *The History of the Scottish Parliament, III: Parliament in Context, 1235–1707* (Edinburgh: Edinburgh University Press, 2010), 157–85 at 176–7; A. M. Godfrey, *Civil Justice in Renaissance Scotland, The Origins of a Central Court* (Leiden: Brill, 2009), 33–6.

[15] *RPS* 1689/3/108.

which she had with her late husband and was also against law and justice. Sir James responded that no appeal to parliament was possible and had not been introduced by the Claim of Right. Much debate followed on whether the lady had intended to submit an appeal or a protestation. There was also much debate about the capacity of parliament to hear these respective requests. The facts and law of the case were also debated afresh. Parliament rescinded the sentence of the lords of session but provided no guidance on how the Claim of Right should be interpreted with respect to appeals or protestations for remeid of law.[16]

In 1693 when parliament stopped sitting it said that litigants with protestations still pending could wait for a sub-committee to hear their complaint. Alternatively these litigants could ask the lords of session to review their decision, which was the traditional mechanism for what might be called appeal. By this time a handful of protestations had been made to parliament.[17] Ford has noted that this represented 'recognition that a court of law, even when it strictly adhered to the law and in this sense behaved quite justly, might still on occasion deliver decisions that were unjust in their substance.'[18]

Sir James Dalrymple, Viscount Stair, in the same year included a comment on protestations in the second printed edition of his *Institutions*. He saw protestations for remeid of law as restricted to special circumstances. He argued that these could not be interpreted as a general form of appeal because this 'cannot be thought to have been the meaning of the *Estates*'.[19] He therefore concluded that if parties could ask the lords of session to review their own decision then they could not instead choose to lodge a protestation.[20] Rather, protestation was to be reserved for those instances 'whensoever the Session determines beyond, and without the Authority, given them by the King and Estates in Parliament; for they have but a limited Jurisdiction.'[21] Here Stair was arguing that the lords of session had a specific jurisdiction and could not hear cases which were outwith their competence. Should they do so then that was when a

---

[16] On this case, see Ford, 'Protestations to parliament', 73–9; Godfrey, *Civil Justice in Renaissance Scotland*, 67.

[17] Ford, 'Protestations to parliament', 79–82.

[18] Ford, 'Protestations to parliament', 82.

[19] Dalrymple, Sir James, Viscount Stair, *The Institutions of the Law of Scotland, Deduced from its Originals, and Collated with the Civil, Canon and Feudal Laws, and with the Customs of Neighbouring Nations* (Edinburgh: Heir of Andrew Anderson, 1st edn 1681, 2nd edn 1693), -/4.1.56.

[20] Stair, *Institutions*, -/4.1.57.

[21] Stair, *Institutions*, -/4.1.58.

protestation for remeid of law should be available.[22] However, a dissatis-fied litigant could not protest to parliament if he simply saw the judge-ment as unfair.[23]

When a committee was established by parliament in 1695 to hear protestations for remeid of law as well as other business, several lords of session were appointed to it. Six cases were lodged with the commit-tee during the short parliamentary session that summer. Only one was heard by the time parliament disbanded. It concerned a decision about the estate of Sir Thomas Nicholson of Carnock, the son of John Nicolson of Lasswade. The protestation was unsuccessful.[24] Another protestation heard the following year was about payment of debts by a failed partner-ship. It was eventually remitted back to the lords of session.[25] By 1700 a further thirteen cases were put forward for remeid of law. Another thirteen seem to have been lodged between 1700 and 1707.[26] Overall the successful hearing of a protestation was unusual:

> Of the fifty cases in which parties are known to have protested for remeid of law between 1689 and 1707 only nine were brought to a conclusion in parliament. In two the process was declared null and void, in five the decision of the session was adhered to, and in two the decision was altered.[27]

However, this clause was to prove very important in the development of jurisdiction after the union of parliaments in 1707.

C. UNION

(1) The Path to Union

Towards the end of the seventeenth century, Scotland's economy began to suffer from a decline in its national industries. A restriction on inter-national trade as a result of English legislation restricting trade with its colonies, and war between England and its continental neighbours, also

---

[22] Stair, *Institutions*, -/4.1.58.
[23] Stair, *Institutions*, -/4.1.61.
[24] Ford, 'Protestations to parliament', 85–6; *Burke's Peerage, Baronetage and Knightage* 107th edn (London: Burke's Peerage Ltd, 2003), 701.
[25] Ford, 'Protestations to parliament', 86–7.
[26] Ford, 'Protestations to parliament', 87, 91.
[27] Ford, 'Protestations to parliament', 95.

proved problematic. The Scottish parliament therefore passed an act in 1695 to found the 'Company of Scotland Trading to Africa and the Indies'.[28] The intention was to establish a new Scottish colony. Darien in Panama was later identified as appropriate. The colony would use that narrow stretch of land between North and South America as an express way for goods to save merchants having to sail all the way around the coast. The money for the venture was raised entirely within Scotland, a huge sum of around £400,000, approximately half of Scotland's total capital. Unfortunately, the venture would be a total failure by 1700. Various factors contributed to the failure of the Darien scheme. Two of these factors led to animosity between Scotland and England. The English East India Company was concerned that this rival Scottish company would harm English trade, so it prevented English investment in the scheme before the ships set sail. Secondly, the English parliament in 1699 prohibited its colonies from trading with the Scots at Darien. This meant that the Scottish settlers had no way to get supplies. The failure of the Darien scheme had a profound impact on Scotland's morale and economy. Scotland was in essence a bankrupt state in 1700.[29]

As a result, there was an outpouring of animosity towards the English. A proposal was made in parliament 'that whoever had advised his majesty's answer to the address of the parliament of England against our Indian and African Company in the year 1695 ... are enemies to this kingdom'.[30] Parliament wrote an address to the king reminding him that he had given his assent to the founding act. It claimed that what the English had done constituted 'undue intermeddling in the affairs of this kingdom and an invasion upon the sovereignty and independence of our king and parliament'. It also observed that the proclamations of the English parliament had meant that its colonies had refused to trade with the Scots in even basic supplies such as food. This was 'contrary to the very rules of common humanity ... injurious and prejudicial to the rights and liberties of the company, and ... inhumane, barbarous and contrary to the law of nations'. Ultimately the Scots' address requested compensation for the losses sustained in the venture.[31]

Relations between the two countries were further strained by an impending succession crisis. William and Mary were childless. Mary had

[28] *RPS* 1695/5/104.
[29] On the Darien scheme, see John McKendrick, *Darien: A Journey in Search of Empire* (Edinburgh: Birlinn, 2016).
[30] *RPS* 1700/10/168.
[31] *RPS* 1700/10/185.

died in 1694. Primogeniture meant that both the Scottish and English crowns would pass to Mary's sister, Anne, when eventually William died. However, Anne's only surviving son had died in 1700. Anne had no other children so there was no clear line of succession after her death. Both the Scottish and the English parliament were concerned by the implication of this. Their responses as the most powerful institutions of government in their respective countries led to a 'war' of legislation. 'An unforeseen consequence of weaker executive government faced by two strong and competing parliaments in London and Edinburgh was the enormous strain placed on Anglo-Scottish relations.'[32]

The English parliament passed the Act of Settlement in 1701 to avert a succession crisis. This act declared that the English crown would pass to the House of Hanover on the death of Anne. The Scots had not been consulted. This compounded the bad feeling in the wake of the Darien failure and the Scots took significant offence. In 1703 the Scottish parliament discussed several policy measures which were distinctly anti-English. The Act of Security, for example, declared that after Anne's death the next monarch would not be the same person who was to be king or queen in England unless various assurances were made. The act was refused royal assent by the high commissioner in 1703, but passed in 1704. The English response was the Alien Act 1705. Unless Scotland by Christmas Day agreed to full parliamentary union and accepted the Hanovarian succession then Scottish possessions in England would be forfeit and trade with England and her colonies would be prohibited.[33]

Had the threat in the Alien Act come to pass it would have been devastating for a nation still recovering from economic shock. The Scottish parliament in September 1705 formally asked the queen to appoint Scottish commissioners for union and arrange the repeal of the English act.[34] Among the thirty-one Scots were eminent lawyers: the lord chancellor, lord president of the Court of Session, the justice clerk, four lords of session and the solicitor general.[35]

---

[32] Brown, 'The second estate', 91.
[33] Cairns, 'Historical introduction', 113–15. It has been suggested that the English perspective on Anglo-Scottish union should be viewed in the context of the union between the Old and New English East India Companies, which was underway by 1702 and completed in 1706, and which provided a precedent and culture of union. Andrew Mackillop, 'A union for empire? Scotland, the English East India Company and the British union', *Scottish Historical Review* 87:2 (Supplement) (2008), 116–34.
[34] *RPS* 1705/6/93.
[35] A. J. MacLean, 'The 1707 union: Scots law and the House of Lords', *Journal of Legal History* 4 (1984), 50–75 at 52.

By July 1706 the commissioners had negotiated twenty-five draft 'articles of union' which would result in a full parliamentary union. Among the arrangements were various fiscal measures, including a payment of £400,000 to the Scots (called the 'Equivalent'). It is important to recognise that this was not compensation from England for the losses resulting from the Darien scheme. It was a payment in recognition that Scotland's taxes would increase after the union, part of which tax revenue would be used to pay English pre-union debts. However, the Scots after its receipt decided to use much of the money to compensate shareholders and re-establish Scotland's economy after the Darien venture.[36] There were three particularly important articles for the law: articles eighteen, nineteen and twenty.

(2) Article Eighteen

The new unified state would require a system of public law. This was set down in article eighteen. This new public law would need to apply not just within the borders of the two kingdoms but also in the various colonies. England's colonies already applied English law. In part that contributed to the decision that the public law of the new state would be English law. The article read:

> That the laws concerning regulation of trade, customs, and such excises, to which Scotland is, by virtue of this treaty, to be liable, be the same in Scotland, from and after the union, as in England ... that the laws which concern public right, policy and civil government may be made the same throughout the whole united Kingdom[.][37]

Cairns has noted that 'the model of Union chosen was essentially to incorporate Scotland into existing English legislative structures'.[38]

Article eighteen also identified the system of private law which would apply after the union. There was less imperative that a single private law would apply in both Scotland and England. Previous attempts at union had failed to merge the two separate legal systems, as has been discussed in Chapters 12 and 13. The Scots commissioners in 1604 had been clear that both Scots law and the courts should remain unchanged after the

---

[36] Cairns, 'Historical introduction', 115.
[37] *RPS* 1706/10/257.
[38] Cairns, 'Historical introduction', 115.

Union of the Crowns. Attempted legal union during the interregnum had failed. Scottish commissioners appointed to additional projects at closer union in 1670 and in the early reign of William and Mary had again expressed the desire that Scots law remain independent.[39] There was now recognition that a union of laws was not necessary to political union.[40] In advance of the 1707 union the same discussions were had.[41] The commissioners on that occasion did not attempt to merge the two systems. Rather, article eighteen read: 'no alteration be made in laws which concern private right, except for evident utility of the subjects within Scotland'.[42] This meant that Scots law would survive the union unchanged. However, the new parliament would be able to change it in the future.[43] Few changes were in fact made in the decades following the union.

(3) Article Nineteen

Article nineteen reflected on the court structure after the union. This article protected the Court of Session and the recently constituted High Court of Justiciary:

> as [they are] now, constituted by the laws of that kingdom, and with the same authority and privileges as before the union, subject, nevertheless, to such regulations for the better administration of justice as shall be made by the parliament of Great Britain[.][44]

What this meant was that these two courts would remain unchanged. However, the parliament could change the courts and the privileges

---

[39] J. D. Ford, 'The legal provisions in the acts of union', *Cambridge Law Journal* 66 (2007), 106–41 at 109–10. On the 1670 project, see J. D. Ford, *Law and Opinion in Scotland during the Seventeenth Century* (Oxford: Hart Publishing, 2007), 446–56; T. B. Smith, 'British justice: a Jacobean phantasma', *Scots Law Times* News (1982), 157–64 at 162.

[40] Brian P. Levack, *The Formation of the British State: England, Scotland, and the Union 1603–1707* (Oxford: Clarendon Press, 1987).

[41] Ford, 'The legal provisions', 110–13. On discussions of how this might have been achieved and the views expressed by legal union at the time and in the wider European context, see J. D. Ford, 'Four models of union', *Juridical Review* (2011), 45–76.

[42] *RPS* 1706/10/257.

[43] On article eighteen, see Cairns, 'Historical introduction', 115–16; Ford, 'The legal provisions', 107–8.

[44] *RPS* 1706/10/257.

of their members in the future. The article also *seemed* to ensure that Scottish cases would be heard in Scotland. The article stated:

> and that no causes in Scotland be cognoscible by the courts of chancery, queen's bench, common-pleas, or any other court in Westminster Hall; and that the said courts, or any other of the like nature after the union, shall have no power to judge, review or alter the acts or sentences of the judicatures within Scotland, or stop the execution of the same[.][45]

This article listed some of the most important courts in England: the Chancery, Queen's Bench and Common Pleas. However, it failed to mention the highest court in England. The House of Lords was the second chamber of the English parliament and had jurisdiction as an appeal court for English cases before the union. It would be retained as the second chamber of the new British parliament. One might assume that the mention of the parliament's building, Westminster Hall, was a reference to that court. But a loophole was created here because the House of Lords did not meet in Westminster Hall. Nor was it a court of 'the like nature'. Therefore, the House of Lords was not excluded from hearing Scottish cases. The jurisdiction of the Court of Session could not be said to have been changed if appeals did go to the House of Lords because the Claim of Right 1689 allowed protestations for the remeid of law to the Scottish parliament. The loophole was not accidental: the legal expertise of the Scots commission was probably too great for such a loophole to be created by mistake.[46] The second volume will examine this issue in greater depth, but it is worth observing here that civil appeals were established very quickly after the union. Criminal appeals followed but were eventually stopped after a capital case in 1765.[47]

The care with which the articles were negotiated and worded is reflected in the debate of this clause in the Scottish parliament. The draft of the nineteenth article was read in parliament three times in 1706: twice in October and once again in December.[48] It was finally debated in detail on 2 and 3 January 1707. The debate generated by one aspect of the

[45] *RPS* 1706/10/257.
[46] MacLean, 'The 1707 union', especially 60–72. See also on MacLean's thesis and on this part of article nineteen, O'Neill, 'Sovereignty of the (Scottish) people', 454–7; Ford, 'Protestations to parliament', 97–9; Ford, 'The legal provisions', 122–5.
[47] On which, Ford, 'Protestations to parliament', 99–107.
[48] *RPS* 1706/10/30, 1706/10/31, 1706/10/191.

article does appear to have been somewhat heated: the original article did
not specify any eligibility requirements for a man to be named as a lord
of session. Chapter 11 has shown that there was a significant amount of
regulation on this in Scotland previously. It is clear that members of the
Scottish parliament were keen to have this reflected in this new constitutional document. It was thus proposed during the debate that a further
clause be added to article nineteen specifying that anyone appointed as
a lord of session had to have been an advocate or principal clerk for five
years. After much further debate, it was agreed that an appointee could
also have been a writer to the signet for ten years. Writers were to have
to undergo an additional trial to establish their expertise in the civil law
before they could be appointed as a judge in that court. Parliament voted
that all of these requirements should in the future be amendable by the
new British parliament.[49] The amendment was accepted by the English.
Hence article nineteen acknowledged:

> that, hereafter, none shall be named by her majesty or her royal
> successors to be ordinary lords of session, but such who have served
> in the college of justice as advocates, or principal clerks of session
> for the space of five years, or as writers to the signet for the space of
> ten years, with this provision, that no writer to the signet be capable
> to be admitted a lord of the session unless he undergo a private and
> public trial on the civil law before the faculty of advocates, and be
> found by them qualified for the said office two years before he be
> named to be a lord of the session, yet so as the qualifications made
> or to be made for capacitating persons to be named ordinary lords
> of session may be altered by the parliament of Great-Britain[.][50]

(4) Article Twenty

Article twenty was brief, commanding

> [t]hat all heritable offices, superiorities, heritable jurisdictions,
> offices for life and jurisdictions for life, be reserved to the owners
> thereof as rights of property, in the same manner as they are now
> enjoyed by the laws of Scotland, notwithstanding of this treaty.[51]

---

[49] *RPS* 1706/10/195–7.
[50] *RPS* 1706/10/257. On this clause with respect to other courts, see Cairns,
      'Historical introduction', 116; MacLean, 'The 1707 union', 53–60.
[51] *RPS* 1706/10/257.

The protection of these rights should be considered in light of the removal of such rights during the interregnum.[52] This had been a political statement at the time, as was discussed in Chapter 13. However, the new British parliament abolished heritable jurisdictions and military feudal tenures in two acts passed in 1746.[53] Both of these legislative measures were a reaction to the second Jacobite rebellion, which ended in April that same year.[54]

D. CONCLUSION

In 1689 the Scottish estates deposed James VII, claiming that he had forfeited the crown through his tyranny. The Scots invited the next in the Stewart line, Mary, and her husband, William of Orange, to take the throne. In doing so they took the opportunity to renegotiate the constitutional settlement. A document called the Claim of Right was produced which limited royal authority and also provided a right to protestation for remeid of law from decisions of the Court of Session to parliament. The circumstances in which a dissatisfied litigant could exercise this right remained controversial and only a few were successful between 1689 and 1707.

Scotland and England were united in a parliamentary union in 1707. The terms of this union were set down in the so-called 'articles of union'. These set out the constitutional arrangements of the new state. The nation's trade and public law was to be English law. However, Scotland would retain a separate system of private law. Heritable jurisdictions and superiorities were to remain unchanged. While there were changes to some courts, the Session was to remain unchanged as it had existed before the union. In reality, however, a loophole existed within the relevant article which would allow future appeals to the House of Lords.

The articles were approved by parliament but they were not widely popular. One of the Scottish commissioners for union was strongly opposed to the union. George Lockhart of Carnwath was the son of the murdered lord president of the same name. He

only reluctantly accepted [a place on the commission] in order to supply his political allies with information on its deliberations. During the last session of the Scottish parliament he spoke and

---

[52] Ford, 'The legal provisions', 121–2.
[53] 1746 c.43 20 Geo II, c.50 20 Geo II.
[54] Cairns, 'Historical Introduction', 147–9.

protested frequently against the Act of Union, and by November 1706 was actively involved in conspiracies to oppose it by force.[55]

Protests against the union were widespread and protest documents submitted to parliament had received many signatures from people across the country.[56] Officials were attacked, there was rioting in the streets and copies of the articles were burned.[57] The articles had to be signed in secret for the safety of the officials involved.

The new British parliament first met on 23 October 1707. However, tensions between the Scots and the English were not immediately resolved. Controversies followed. Considerable tension was caused by the reform of the Scots law of treason, the abolition of the Scottish privy council, the establishment of an explicitly English-style Justice of the Peace, challenges to Scottish voting rights and perceived attacks on the Scottish kirk. In 1713 an unsuccessful vote was held in the House of Lords to dissolve the new British parliament and disunite the two countries. Further disgruntlement (and personal grudges) led to the first Jacobite rising in 1715. This rebellion was started by the Earl of Mar and intended to restore the line of James VII and II, which still survived in exile. The rebellion failed and the political settlement was confirmed.[58] The British parliament of the United Kingdom would last at least another 300 years.

---

[55] Daniel Szechi, 'Lockhart, George, of Carnwath (1681?–1731)', *Oxford Dictionary of National Biography* (Oxford: Oxford University Press, 2004); revised online edn May 2011, http://www.oxforddnb.com/view/article/16902. See also George Lockhart of Carnwarth, *Memoirs Concerning the Affairs of Scotland, from Queen Anne's Accession to the Throne to the Commencement of the Union of the Two Kingdoms of Scotland and England, in May, 1707*, 3rd edn (London: J. Baker, 1714). On this work, and the rivalries between the commissioners revealed therein and in other sources, see Christopher A. Whatley and Derek J. Patrick, 'Contesting interpretations of the union of 1707: the abuse and use of George Lockhart of Carnwath's *Memoirs*', *Journal of Scottish Historical Studies* 27:1 (2007), 24.

[56] Some of these are reproduced with commentary in Lockhart of Carnwarth, *Memoirs*, 232–48, 286–8.

[57] Lockhart of Carnwarth, *Memoirs*, 273–7; George Harris Healey (ed.), *The Letters of Daniel Defoe* (Oxford: Clarendon Press, 1955), 133–6.

[58] On these events, see Cairns, 'Historical introduction', 117–18.

E. SELECTED BIBLIOGRAPHY AND FURTHER READING

(1) Records of the Parliament of Scotland (*RPS*)

Claim of Right: *RPS* 1689/3/108.
Articles of Union: *RPS* 1706/10/257.

(2) Books

Ford, J. D., *Law and Opinion in Scotland during the Seventeenth Century* (Oxford: Hart Publishing, 2007).

Lockhart, George of Carnwarth, *Memoirs Concerning the Affairs of Scotland, from Queen Anne's Accession to the Throne to the Commencement of the Union of the Two Kingdoms of Scotland and England, in May, 1707*, 3rd edn (London: J. Baker, 1714).

(3) Chapters in Books

Brown, Keith M., 'The second estate: parliament and the nobility', in Keith M. Brown and Alan R. MacDonald (eds), *The History of the Scottish Parliament, III: Parliament in Context, 1235–1707* (Edinburgh: Edinburgh University Press, 2010), 67–94.

Cairns, John W., 'Historical introduction', in Kenneth Reid and Reinhard Zimmermann (eds), *A History of Private Law in Scotland* (Oxford: Oxford University Press, 2000) I, 14–184.

Godfrey, A. Mark, 'Parliament and the law', in Keith M. Brown and Alan R. MacDonald (eds), *The History of the Scottish Parliament, III: Parliament in Context, 1235–1707* (Edinburgh: Edinburgh University Press, 2010), 157–85.

(4) Articles in Journals

Ford, J. D., 'The legal provisions in the acts of union', *Cambridge Law Journal* 66 (2007), 106–41.

Ford, J. D., 'Protestations to parliament for remeid of law', *Scottish Historical Review* 88:1 (2009), 57–107.

Ford, J. D., 'Four models of union', *Juridical Review* (2011), 45–76.

Gray, W. B., 'The judicial proceedings of the parliaments of Scotland, 1660–1688', *Juridical Review* (1924), 135–51.

Hamilton-Grierson, Philip J., 'The appellate jurisdiction of the Scottish parliament', *Scottish Historical Review* (1918), 205–22.

Harris, Tim, 'The people, the law, and the constitution in Scotland and England: a comparative approach to the Glorious Revolution', *Journal of British Studies* 38 (1999), 28–58.

MacLean, A. J., 'The 1707 union: Scots law and the House of Lords', *Journal of Legal History* 4 (1984), 50–75.

O'Neill, Aidan, 'The sovereignty of the (Scottish) people: 1689 and all that', *Judicial Review* (2013), 446–63.

Smith, T. B., 'British justice: a Jacobean phantasma', *Scots Law Times News* (1982), 157–64.

Index